The Commonplace Book of
Sir John Strangways
(1645–1666)

MEDIEVAL AND RENAISSANCE

TEXTS AND STUDIES

VOLUME 275

RENAISSANCE ENGLISH TEXT SOCIETY

SEVENTH SERIES

VOLUME XXIX (FOR 2004)

Sir John Strangways, aged 78. Artist unknown. Reproduction by
Thomas Photos (Oxford). Thanks to the Warden and Fellows of
Wadham College, Oxford, for permission to reprint it here.

The Commonplace Book of Sir John Strangways (1645–1666)

edited by

Thomas G. Olsen

Arizona Center for Medieval and Renaissance Studies

in conjunction with

Renaissance English Text Society

Tempe, Arizona

2004

The editor and publisher gratefully acknowledge the
Beinecke Rare Book and Manuscript Library
for its assistance in the publication of this volume.

Library of Congress Cataloging-in-Publication Data

Strangways, John, 1585–1666.
 The commonplace book of Sir John Strangways (1645–1666) / edited by
  Thomas G. Olsen.
   p. cm. — (Medieval and Renaissance Texts and Studies ; v. 275)
 (Renaissance English Text Society ; 7th ser., v. 29)
 Includes bibliographical references and index.
 ISBN 0–86698–318–X (alk. paper)
  1. Commonplace-books. I. Olsen, Thomas G. II. Title. III. Medieval and
 Renaissance Texts and Studies (Series) ; v. 275. IV. Renaissance English
 Text Society (Series) ; v. 29.

PR 3717.S57C66 2004
821'.4–dc22

                                                              2004059459

This book is made to last.
It is set in Book Antiqua,
smythe-sewn and printed on acid-free paper
to library specifications.

Printed in the United States of America

for Marinella

TABLE OF CONTENTS

Acknowledgements   xi

Abbreviations of Frequently Cited Works   xiii

Introduction
        Sir John Strangways   1
        The Commonplace Section and Its Time and Place   16
        Verse and Versification   23
        The Text   48
        Editorial Practices   50

Section A: Commonplaces   54

Section B: Poems   127

Appendix 1 :   257
        Commendatory verses by Sir John Strangways,
        from Thomas Coryate, *Coryats Crudities hastily
        gobled up in five Moneths travells* (1611), d^v–d2

Appendix 2:   259
        Sir John Strangways to the Commons, 1 April 1647,
        BL Harl. 158. f.270

Appendix 3:   261
        A poem by Sir John Strangways, from Dorset R.O.,
        Ilchester Deposit, D124/Box 263

Textual Notes   269

Commentary   288

Title and First-line Index   322

Acknowledgements

I would like to thank, at SUNY New Paltz, Gerald Benjamin, Dean of Liberal Arts and Sciences, and William Vasse, former Vice President for Academic Affairs, for a one-semester teaching reduction and The Beinecke Library for a generous month-long Beinecke Fellowship that allowed me to be resident at Yale during a crucial phase of the project. I would like also to acknowledge Thomas Photos of Oxford for supplying the photograph of the portrait of Sir John Strangways and to thank the Warden and Fellows of Wadham College, Oxford, for permission to include it in this edition.

Like many other undertakings of this nature, this one has also been aided by the expertise, energy, and sheer kindness of many individuals. I would like to thank Stephen R. Parks, Curator of the Osborn Collection of the Beinecke Library at Yale, for first suggesting the project and for supporting it from its earliest phases. I was also supported in the early stages of my work by Clarence H. Miller, then visiting in the Yale Department of English. Maija Jansson of the Yale Center for Parliamentary History, Rowan Greer of the Yale Divinity School, Robert Babcock, and Earle Havens of the Beinecke Library all contributed very generously and significantly to my efforts by answering many questions and offering many useful suggestions. They again and again proved Yale to be not only an intellectually stimulating but also a wonderfully congenial place to work.

Several British colleagues-at-large were likewise generous with their knowledge and time. Clifford Davies supplied needed information concerning the portrait of Strangways that hangs in Wadham College, Oxford, and Simon Keynes answered several queries touching Strangways's antiquarian interests, while David Loades clarified an important matter concerning Strangways's use of Foxe, and J. P. Ferris was helpful in providing biographical details. Andy Mousley read the Introduction in draft and provided many helpful insights. David L. Smith also read the Introduction and kindly shared with me his considerable knowledge of Stuart parliamentary history as well as his draft DNB entry on Strangways.

Closer to home, John N. King made many helpful suggestions for the general shape of the project and offered welcome encouragement, while Terry Belanger helped me to understand some textual aspects of the manuscript, and my former colleague Philip Daileader helped me with Strangways's

Latin entries. Steven Florczyk and my wife Marinella Garatti, both of SUNY
New Paltz, helped me immensely in checking transcriptions. My colleagues
J. David Blankenship and Jeff Miller and my department chair, Daniel
Kempton, all generously fielded my sometimes arcane questions.

I owe a deep dept of gratitude to those closest to this project: the
Renaissance English Text Society editorial committee, organized by Arthur
F. Kinney, whose members oversaw the preparation of this edition and made
many helpful suggestions. Laetitia Yeandle aided me in the early stages of
the project, and Arthur F. Marotti offered guidance at all stages. George W.
Pigman III and Lois Potter joined the committee in its final stages and read
parts of the transcription and the Introduction, both helping to improve this
edition with their apt suggestions. Professor Potter was aided in checking my
transcriptions by Michael Clody. The committee's generosity and knowledge
improved this edition in innumerable ways, as did the thoughtful suggestions and careful reading of RETS's wonderful editor Bill Gentrup. Finally,
the committee's indefatigable chair, George Walton Williams, provided welcome support, advice, and encouragement at every turn; one could not ask
for better professional expertise and guidance, nor for a more pleasant
working relationship. I thank him in particular for the many, many ways that
he supported and encouraged my endeavors.

ABBREVIATIONS OF FREQUENTLY CITED WORKS

1 Institutes   Sir Edward Coke. *The First Part of the Institutes Of the Laws of England.* London, 1628.

2 Institutes   Sir Edward Coke. *The Second Part of the Institutes Of the Laws of England. Containing the Exposition of Many Ancient, and Other Statutes.* London, 1642.

3 Institutes   Sir Edward Coke. *The Third Part of the Institutes Of the Laws of England: Concerning High Treason, and other Pleas of the Crown, and Criminal Causes.* London, 1644.

4 Institutes   Sir Edward Coke. *The Fourth Part of the Institutes Of the Laws of England: Concerning the Jurisdiction of Courts.* London, 1644.

Bayley   A. R. Bayley. *The Great Civil War in Dorset.* Taunton: Barnicott and Pearce, 1910.

CJ   *Journals of the House of Commons.* London, 1628–.

DNB   Leslie Stephen and Sidney Lee, eds. *Dictionary of National Biography.* 63 vols. London: Smith, Elder, & Co., 1885–1901.

Foxe   John Foxe, ed. *The Ecclesiastical Historie Containing the Acts and Monuments of Martyrs.* London, 1641.

Holinshed   *Holinshed's Chronicles of England, Scotland, and Ireland.* 6 vols. London, 1807–8.

OCD   Simon Hornblower and Anthony Spawforth, eds. *The Oxford Classical Dictionary* 3rd ed. Oxford and New York: Oxford University Press, 1996.

ODCC   F. L. Cross and E. A. Livingstone, eds. *The Oxford Dictionary of the Christian Church* 3rd ed. Oxford and New York: Oxford University Press, 1997.

OED   *The Oxford English Dictionary* 2nd ed., prepared by J. A. Simpson and E. S. C. Weiner. New York: Oxford University Press and Oxford: Clarendon Press, 1989.

RP   *Rotuli Parliamentorum; ut et Petitiones, et Placita in Parliamento.* 6 vols. [London: 1767–77].

SL   Danby Pickering, ed. *The Statutes at Large from Magna Charta to the End of the Eleventh Parliament of Great Britain.* 24 vols. Cambridge, 1763–69.

SR   *The Statutes of the Realm Printed By Command of His Majesty King George the Third.* 11 vols. London, 1810–32.

Wynter   Philip Wynter, ed. *The Works of the Right Reverend Joseph Hall.* 10 vols. Oxford, 1863.

A collection of some notes for my
owne private use, gathered out of
severall authors as they have bin
read by me, Strangwayes: whereof
most in the Tower — 1645. during the
tyme of my said imprisonment theer://

Quid fugiam video: sed quid sequar non habeo.

I haue not striven against my hart to make a syde:
now hath my Conscience bin oppressed by affection://
Strangwayes
1645.

Giue me o lord hands to my worke: & giue
me worke fitt for my hands.//

Studium puerium est Maxima pars studiorum
Non semper in vno gradu; sed in vna via:
Contrariens: Robur: Contrariensium.
Animalia Gregalia non sunt nociva:
Animalia Solitaga semper nociva.
minerba quasi newbos minucas.//

The Commonplace Book of Sir John Strangways (Osborn MS b.304), page 1. By permission of the Beinecke Rare Book and Manuscript Library.

6

14: If you Imagine ther is noe other life but this, then
you condemne not only the wisest of men of folly: but
the comforts, & the graces, & the therates & the promises
& the commaunds, & directions of god, of Falshood: And yet
Atheisticall soule, that dares imagine the god of Truth to be
a Lyer, shall find that god almightie will giue him his portion
with Lyers & vnbeleeuers for euer, in the lake that burneth
with fyre & Brymstone: || . Tis a principall of immorta=
litie, & makith man to dispute, weither the soule be immor=
tall: all pietie is founded in the thought of immortality:
And it is obserued amongst all the phylosophers, that those
destroyed all Religion, that held the soule to be Mortall.

15: Vnderstanding: Will: Memory: in the Soule: 1 Know=
ledge: 2: Righteousnes= 3: Holines: is the Image
of God:

16: Germanorum bibere est Bibere: whence it is that they
abound in Brewers; hauing 777 of the Trade:
40: Bakers: one Lawyer: one physition in the towne
of Hamburge: Heylings Geogra: pag: 256 & 260.
Lucus: a non Lucendo: Mons: a non mobendo; Bellum:
quasi minime bellum. ||

17: The sun is - 160 - Tymes greater then the Earth (as Astrono=
mers resolue) though rather vpon probable conjecture, then
certayne Demonstration: The Moone is - 39 - tymes lesse then
the Earth: Some of the fixed starres (as Astronomers) affi=
rme are - 107 - tymes greater then the Earth:

18: Plynie in his Naturall History: lib: 32: Cap: ii: writes that some=
Whales are - 600 - foot long: & - 360 - foot broad. ||

The Commonplace Book of Sir John Strangways (Osborn MS b.304),
page 6. By permission of the Beinecke Rare Book and Manuscript
Library.

INTRODUCTION

Sir John Strangways

Sir John Strangways (1585–1666) left a relatively full record of his long public life, as documented in numerous parliamentary records and other accounts.[1] His political career began when James I had been on the throne of England less than a full decade, and it ended with his death about a half decade after the restoration of Charles II. During the tumultuous 1640s, however, Strangways was moved to compose the much more inwardly-directed commonplace entries and poems that make up this volume, writings which form a very different sort of life record. Though I believe that he was principally motivated to write by the catastrophic political events of the 1640s rather than by his own internal impulses, as many theorists have demonstrated in recent years, the public and private worlds cannot be easily separated.[2] Instead, these spheres of experience inform each other in sometimes overt, but usually covert, complex, and subtle ways that make a record such as the one presented here an especially interesting and important kind of document.

---

[1] Using Dorset Record Office sources, J. P. Ferris correctly gives Strangways's date of birth as 1585, *pace* Mary Freer Keeler in her *The Long Parliament, 1640–41: A Biographical Study of Its Members* (Philadelphia: The American Philosophical Society, 1954), 353. See J. P. Ferris, "Strangways, Sir John," *The House of Commons*, ed. Basil Duke Henning, 3 vols. (London: Secker & Warburg, for The History of Parliament Trust, 1983), 3:498–99.

[2] See, for example, Stephen Greenblatt's seminal *Renaissance Self-Fashioning* (Chicago: University of Chicago Press, 1980). Greenblatt's study has become something of a *locus classicus* for theorizing this intersection between public and private, generating an extensive literature on the subject of selfhood. See also Francis Barker, *The Tremulous Private Body: Essays on Subjection* (Ann Arbor, Mich.: University of Michigan Press, 1984), as well as the shorter discussions by Peter Burke, "Representations of the Self From Petrarch to Descartes," and Jonathan Sawday, "Self and Selfhood in the Seventeenth Century," both in Roy Porter, ed., *Rewriting the Self: Histories from the Renaissance to the Present* (London and New York: Routledge, 1997), 17–28, 29–48.

Strangways's commonplace book owes its existence to his imprisonment in the Tower between 29 November 1645 and 15 May 1648 on charges of high treason. The nearly 150 leaves of Strangways's manuscript, divided by him into commonplace entries (here called Section A) and poems (Section B), have a very precise historical context that can be recovered, described, and subjected to close, profitable analysis.[3] But they also have qualities that point again and again to the less easily defined intersection where public events and the private means for understanding and acting upon external circumstances meet to create a literary record.

Strangways was the younger son but eventual inheritor of the considerable fortune of his father, John Strangways of Melbury, Dorset (d. 1593).[4] The family could trace their line to the time of Richard II. From the middle of the sixteenth century they had grown very prosperous from farming and rents, and if they were typical of West-Country gentry of the period, they may also have augmented their income in the wool trade and sea transport. Sir John's great-great grandfather Giles Strangways (the elder) was granted monastery lands at Abbotsbury, Dorset, in the thirty-fifth year of Henry VIII's reign.[5] The family established themselves as prominent members of the local gentry, his father possessing at least ten properties and holding what one local historian has called "an honourable place in the Dorset army when the Armada came."[6] Not only were the family particularly prosperous among the local gentry, but they also extended their influence by marrying with the gentry of neighboring counties.[7] Strangways's mother Joan (d. 1603) was the sister of

---

[3] Throughout this Introduction, all citations to the manuscript refer to the pagination supplied by an archivist (e.g., A.12 refers to Commonplace Section page 12, and B.43 refers to Verse Section page 43). Because several scholars have already used the archival pagination in their citations, I thought it useful to conform to their practice. For ease of reference, however, in my Textual Notes and Commentary I have keyed my notes to the pagination of this edition. The archival pagination is given in square brackets in the right margins of both sections.

[4] The best short biographical essays are those by Keeler, *Long Parliament*, 353–54, and by David L. Smith in the *Dictionary of National Biography* (Oxford University Press, 2004). I am grateful to Dr. Smith for sharing with me his essay in draft form.

[5] J. J. Foster, *Wessex Worthies (Dorset)* (London: Dickinsons, 1920), 43. And see Helen Miller, "Strangways, Sir Giles I (1486–1546)" in S.T. Bindoff, *The House of Commons, 1509–1558* (London: History of Parliament Trust, 1982), 3:395–97.

[6] Rachel Lloyd, *Dorset Elizabethans at Home and Abroad* (London: Murray, 1967), 267–68.

[7] J. P. Ferris, "The Gentry of Dorset on the Eve of the Civil War," *Genealogist Magazine* 15 (1965): 106, 108.

Nicholas Wadham, the founder of Wadham College, Oxford, and in 1607 Strangways married Grace Trenchard, daughter of Sir George Trenchard, a prominent member of the Dorset gentry, and sister to John Trenchard, who later sat as MP for Wareham. By 1603 Strangways had already inherited a considerable part of the family estate (his elder brother dying of the plague), and in 1609 he succeeded to one-third of the lands in Somerset and Dorset of his uncle Nicholas Wadham.[8]

In 1601 he matriculated at Queen's College, Oxford, and in 1611 he was granted special admission to the Middle Temple. In that same year he refused a baronetcy, and it is clear that he had already been knighted before that time, by June 1608.[9] Though there is no evidence that Strangways took a degree at Oxford—leaving without a degree being a common practice among the gentry and aristocracy, who had little practical use for the credentials a degree provided—there is considerable evidence in his writings that he was quite versed in the university and legal curricula of his age. His poems and commonplace entries suggest a good knowledge of the Latin authors typically read in the late Tudor and early Stuart curricula as well as a fondness for epigrams quite characteristic of those of his age and social station.[10] Throughout both the poems and commonplace entries there also runs a deep engagement with the logic of legal principles, precedence, and political theory.

Thomas Coryate's huge comic work *Coryats Crudities: hastily gobled up in five Moneths travells* appeared in 1611, and among the dozens of humorous dedicatory verses and mock panegyrics that preface the work, including works by Ben Jonson, John Donne, and many other prominent literary figures, is a whimsical contribution by Strangways—apparently his only published literary endeavor and one quite at odds with the more serious tenor of the poems of his commonplace book (see Appendix 1). Since Coryate attended Gloucester Hall, now Worcester College, from 1596 until about 1599, it would appear that he and Strangways were never enrolled at Oxford

---

[8] See John Hutchins, *The History and Antiquities of the County of Dorset* (Westminster: William Shipp and James Whitworth Hodson, 1863), 2:662–63 for a complete genealogical survey of the family. See also Keeler, *Long Parliament*, 364, and Ferris, "Strangways, Sir John," 3:498–99.

[9] Keeler, *Long Parliament*, 353; Ferris, "Strangways," 3:498.

[10] Hoyt Hopewell Hudson, *The Epigram in the English Renaissance* (Princeton: Princeton University Press, 1947), especially chapters 3-4.

at the same time.[11] The nature of their association remains obscure, though it is likely that, as a Somerset man, Coryate knew Strangways in some context other than Oxford. It is possible that Coryate, who was known for his gregarious good humor, was welcomed back to Oxford, or known among the Inns of Court in some capacity other than as a matriculated student. Perhaps Strangways did not even know him and merely participated in a literary event, along with more than sixty others.

The following year Strangways began a public career that would last half a century, serving as sheriff of Dorset in 1612–13, as Justice of the Peace, and as a member of the lieutenancy. He then served as MP for Dorset in James I's second parliament (the "Addled Parliament" of 1614), and again in 1621. In 1618 he accompanied Lord Digby on a venture to Cadiz. In 1622, as nephew to Nicholas Wadham and co-inheritor of his large estate in Somerset and Devon, Strangways contributed £100 to the great east window in the Wadham College chapel, which bears the following inscription:

> Hæc fenestra ornata est svmptibvs
> Dñi. Johannis Stranwayes Militis
> Vnvs ex coheredibvs fvndatoris.[12]

Between 1621 and 1629, Strangways was quite active in national politics, serving by turns as MP for Dorset (1621, 1624, 1628–29), Weymouth (1625) and Melcombe Regis (1626), though it would appear that he resorted to a number of questionable strategies in order to secure such a "sustained monopoly" in local elections.[13]

The king's refusal to call a parliament during the 1630s explains Strangways's relative isolation from London politics during this period. In the Short Parliament, however, he was once again vocal in defense of what he once termed "liberty in Parliament . . . for without that we sate there in vayne," even siding in this instance with John Pym, who was soon to be

---

[11] Michael Strachan, *The Life and Adventures of Thomas Coryate* (London: Oxford, 1962), 1–5. Note, however, that Strachan incorrectly identifies Exeter College as the successor of Gloucester Hall.

[12] T. G. Jackson, *Wadham College* (Oxford: Clarendon, 1898), 163, and see also 163–67 and 170.

[13] The phrase is that of John K. Gruenfelder, in his "Dorsetshire Elections, 1604–1640" *Albion* 10 (1978): 1–13, see especially p. 1. Gruenfelder demonstrates that Strangways used a fairly typical combination of social influence as well as strategic marriages and friendships to maintain power in, and to influence the outcomes of, local elections.

Strangways's political nemesis.[14] He was likewise openly supportive of the principle that the fundamental purpose of parliaments was to represent grievances.

At this point, little in Strangways's political career would have suggested that he would ever achieve renown as a staunch defender of royal prerogative. During the period of the Personal Rule of Charles I, he contended quite vigorously with the king in various ways, particularly over finances, the redress of grievances, and significant points of religious reform. For example, in a letter signed by Charles I on 28 June 1626, he is among those named as fomenters of "the Troubles of Parliament[,] of divers things tending much to our dishonour, and to the stirring up of the disaffection of divers of the members of both Houses for the furtherance of their prisonable ends."[15] In debate in the Commons, he proclaimed that "wee will trust the Kinge if he will inable us to," slyly placing the burden of respecting parliamentary privilege on the shoulders of Charles.[16] Strangways worked vigorously for the impeachment of Buckingham in 1626, eventually becoming one of Buckingham's great enemies in Parliament. Like many others in Dorset, he opposed Ship Money and he refused the Forced Loan of 1627, an action for which he was briefly taken into custody.[17] Nor would these be the last times Strangways would contend with crown policies: in 1637 he was brought up before the Star Chamber on charges of illegal gold exportation, and in 1639 he refused, for the second time, a loan to the king.[18]

Strangways's decisions during the period of the Personal Rule probably do not signal any particular animosity toward the king but rather a deep, abiding commitment to the traditions of law and procedure that Charles I constantly sought to circumvent or suppress. David Underdown aptly characterizes Strangways's efforts in preserving "the sanctity of English law" during this critical period, quoting from Strangways himself: "We do well know that our estates, lives, and fames are preserved by the laws, and that

---

[14] Esther S. Cope and Willson H. Coates, eds., *Proceedings of the Short Parliament of 1640*, Camden Fourth Series, vol. 19 (London: Royal Historical Society, 1977), 159.

[15] BL Egerton MS 2978, f.18.

[16] Cope and Coates, *Proceedings of the Short Parliament*, 171.

[17] Wallace Notestein, *The Journal of Sir Simonds D'Ewes* (New Haven: Yale University Press, 1923), 63; David Underdown, *Fire From Heaven: Life in an English Town in the Seventeenth Century* (New Haven: Yale University Press, 1992), 183–84; Robert C. Johnson, ed., *Commons Debates, 1628* (New Haven: Yale University Press, 1977), 1:65.

[18] Keeler, *Long Parliament*, 353.

the King is bound by his laws."[19] In the opening months of the Long Parliament, before strict lines separating the king's party from the party of the parliamentarian cause were sharply drawn, Strangways's position was anti-Scots but not anti-parliamentarian.[20] He was prominent among his fellow parliamentarians, but as debate grew increasingly radical, he allied himself with the king's party, no doubt more out of an abiding respect for the rule of law and traditional privileges than any deep devotion to the sovereign himself.

As the increasingly radical course of events altered the entire political landscape in the following months, Strangways's politics, moderate but in many important ways quite opposed to the king's policies, began to shift to some of his causes. For example, in February 1641 he argued with Cromwell over the political enfranchisement of the bishops, a debate that moved a group of radical MPs to urge that he be censured and inspired Sir Simonds D'Ewes to defend him in equally vigorous terms.[21] By this time, he was one of the "emerging leaders of a powerful royalist faction" that would continue to contend with the radicals who comprised or supported the Junto.[22] In November 1641, he reported to the Commons that "hee last night was encompassed with above 200 sworded and staved [people who] told him they came to him for his vote for the putting down off the Bishops." The angry mob would soon identify him as "one off the greatest enemies wee have."[23] In March of the following year, he argued openly with Pym—another sign that he was moving in a direction opposite that of the radical Junto that would soon direct the Commons.[24]

Strangways returned to Dorset in the summer of 1642, apparently bent on what the Commons characterized as some "ill service."[25] There can be no

---

[19] David Underdown, *A Freeborn People: Politics and the Nation in Seventeenth-Century England* (Oxford: Clarendon Press, 1996), 84, quoting Strangways, A.47.

[20] Conrad Russell, *The Causes of the English Civil War* (Oxford: Clarendon, 1990), 15.

[21] Notestein, *Journal of Sir Simonds D'Ewes*, 339–40.

[22] Anthony Fletcher, *The Outbreak of the Civil War* (New York: New York University Press, 1981), 134, and see also 143.

[23] William Havelock Coates, *The Journal of Sir Simonds D'Ewes* (New Haven: Yale University Press, 1942), 213n. See also Edward Hyde, Earl of Clarendon, *The History of the Rebellion and Civil Wars in England*, ed. W. Dunn Macray, 6 vols. (Oxford: Clarendon, 1888; reprint, 1958), 1:463n–64n.

[24] Notestein, *Journal of Sir Simonds D'Ewes*, 493n.

[25] David L. Smith, *Constitutional Royalism and the Search for Settlement, c. 1640–1649* (Cambridge: Cambridge University Press, 1994), 99.

doubt that Strangways realized by this point that the collective will of the Junto no longer accorded with his own more moderate designs for political reform based upon a centrist Protestantism and respect for legal and procedural traditions. Like nearly everyone in England, he was being pulled more and more deeply into a conflict he had hoped to avoid, a war very few wanted.[26] He was one of the first Royalist MPs to be disabled, on 6 September 1642. In July of that year, he was fined £4,000 by the Committee for the Advance of Money—the first of many fines and sequestrations he and his son Giles would incur, leaving the family something like £35,000 poorer by the time of the Restoration.[27] Strangways moved to the king's party because the monarch had gone a long way towards reforming those aspects of his rule to which moderate reformers had most vociferously objected and because, to such moderates, the radical Junto now posed a greater threat to social stability and the legal ordering of political life than the king did.[28] Indeed, the whole "social hierarchy" of Strangways's world was gravely at risk, making Charles seem a far better alternative than he had ever seemed prior to this time.[29] In late 1642, just days before the Battle of Edgehill, a watershed event in terms of polarizing the rival parties, Strangways again attempted a reconciliation between ideological rivals, showing himself far more flexible and open to negotiation than the monarch he had, in effect, begun to support.[30] He would continue to lobby for negotiated peace until he took up arms in 1645, and, as this manuscript repeatedly demonstrates, during his imprisonment he would reflect extensively upon his country's failures to achieve a peaceful solution to its political differences.

During the Oxford Parliament, he worked with other MPs and several dozen peers to avoid war and instead to craft a workable solution to the country's political controversies.[31] This particular effort at peace-making in 1644, quite late in the series of events leading to the crisis of 1649, demonstrates Strangways's approach to the seemingly intractable problems

---

[26] See an excellent discussion of the widespread will for neutralism and accommodation in Derek Hirst, *Authority and Conflict: England 1603–1658* (Cambridge, Mass.: Harvard University Press, 1986), 223–30. On Strangways in particular, see Underdown, *Freeborn People*, 85–87.

[27] Hutchins, *History and Antiquities*, 2:664. And see *Journals of the House of Commons* (London, 1628–), 2:728–29, 754.

[28] Smith, *Constitutional Royalism*, 77, 80; see also 81, 86, and 91.

[29] Fletcher, *Outbreak of the Civil War*, 287. And see Underdown, *Freeborn People*, 115.

[30] Smith, *Constitutional Royalism*, 111–12.

[31] Ibid., 117–18.

between king and parliament earlier in the 1640s. Because of his participation in the Oxford Parliament, however, his name was included in a list of fifty-eight MPs who were not to be pardoned.[32]

What emerges from this record is that Strangways was committed to the two central principles espoused by the faction of moderate Royalists, as analyzed by David L. Smith in his *Constitutional Royalism and the Search for Settlement, c. 1640–1649*: the rule of law and the avoidance of extreme godly zeal.[33] Strangways brought a spirit of moderation, compromise, flexibility, and, most of all, due process to his politics; and he must have counted his failure to effect any peaceful consensus during these years as a deep personal disappointment, even before he was imprisoned and subjected to great financial losses. As a "Constitutional Royalist," Strangways supported a particular variety of limited monarchy that had many general precedents in English political history but which also emerged much more explicitly as a position in political debate during the reign of Charles I, especially during the early 1640s. More a "nexus of interlocking ideas" about the right relationship between parliamentary and royal privileges than a strictly defined group of beliefs,[34] Strangways's central guiding principles were sufficiently threatened during the radical early 1640s for him to move from the position of a rather bold critic of the king to one of Charles's more prominent supporters. In June 1626, for example, Strangways spoke in the House, urging that "All kings that are not tyrants or perjured, will keep themselves within the bounds of the laws of the[ir] kingdoms," but by November 1641, as we have seen, he had already been marked as one of the greatest enemies of the radical reformers.[35]

Yet it was the political spectrum and not Strangways that changed so dramatically in these years and eventually led to a crisis that would transform his political and personal life. As Smith demonstrates, Strangways was remarkably consistent in his commitment to a doctrinally moderate Protestantism, the supremacy of the law, and the time-honored privileges of both parliament and the monarch. His consistency cost him a great deal both

---

[32] Hutchins, *History and Antiquities*, 2:664.

[33] Smith, *Constitutional Royalism*, 3, 61, and passim. Smith's explanation of Strangways's political beliefs in relation to the larger arena in which they developed is by far the most thorough treatment available. Many of the observations that follow here are indebted to this excellent study.

[34] Ibid., 217.

[35] William B. Bidwell and Maija Jansson, eds., *Proceedings in Parliament, 1626*, 3 vols. (New Haven: Yale University Press, 1991–92), 3:370; quoted in Smith, *Constitutional Royalism*, 58.

personally and financially, and it occasioned the outpouring of common-place entries and verse that we find in these pages, which amount to an extended vindication of his moral and political commitments. Had there been no parliamentary crisis in the first years of the 1640s, there would have been for Strangways no personal crisis of belief and, I am reasonably sure, no manuscript.

Meanwhile, events in Dorset had by this time also reached a point of crisis. In September 1642, Lord Bedford's troops twice laid siege to Sherborne Castle, an important stronghold of Royalists within a county generally divided between supporters of the king and backers of the Parliamentarian cause.[36] Because it lay between the Royalist strongholds of Oxford and the southwest of England, Dorset had considerable strategic importance to the king's cause. In addition, as control of coastal towns meant potentially increased ease of communication between Royalist troops and their continental supporters, the town was also considered strategically important by the Parliamentarians.[37] Although Dorset saw no particularly significant battles, the region was constantly occupied by both parties and subjected to the side-effects of many marches to or from Devon.[38] Sherborne Castle, where Strangways would eventually take up arms, was the last truly important Royalist stronghold in Dorset and so remained throughout the first half of the 1640s an important prize to both parties.

By March 1643, Strangways had entered with other Dorset Royalists into a pact of mutual protection against any hostile forces that might enter the county.[39] Despite these preparations, however, when William Waller's forces advanced into Dorset, Strangways "and all his malignant crew" were forced to flee to Oxford, for their defensive agreements were not sufficient to protect Strangways's own estates, including the family's manor house at Abbotsbury.[40] On 29 April, Hercules Langrishe, a major in the regiment of Nathaniel Fiennes, wrote from Dorchester, reporting that

> Wee left of our musketiers 80 in the towne that the beach and towne may be the better kept, and on Wensday marched away with the rest of our foote being 200 and all our horse being 240 to Abbotsbury a

---

[36] Mrs. Edward Fripp [*sic*], "Political History" in William Page, ed., *A History of Dorset, The Victoria History of the Counties of England*, vol. 2 (London: Archibald Constable, 1907), 156.

[37] Bayley, 2.

[38] Fripp, "Political History," 159.

[39] Bayley, 63.

[40] Ibid., 65; and see Hutchins, *History and Antiquities*, 1:xvii.

house of Sir John Stranguydges that is very stronge, yet did we there find noe resistance, for all the neighbours and men servants were fled, and the Lady and women servants saied that there were noe armes.[41]

"After much seekinge," Langrishe's regiment did find a considerable cache of "ordnance, many muskets, coates of maile, brown bills, with many bullets and much powder," but neither plate nor money. While they were quartered there, the troops demanded £500 to be paid within ten days, under threat of taking "all away from the house and land." Enraged over the discovery of the weapons and by Lady Strangways's slowness in pledging the sum demanded, Langrishe claims, "they did 200[li] worth of hurt, but her Ladyship deserved no better usage for shee is of a most malignant spirit."[42]

Some months later, hostilities returned to the house at Abbotsbury. In early November 1644, Anthony Ashley Cooper, who would later become a great supporter of Charles II as the first earl of Shaftesbury, came from Dorchester to lead another, more decisive, assault on Abbotsbury. Cooper's forces prevailed this time, and nearly the entire Royalist regiment garrisoned there was captured. Despite the victory, several dozen Parliamentarian soldiers were killed when, after the taking of the house, barrels of gunpowder stored there were accidentally exploded.[43]

In late July 1645, after several years of skirmishes and campaigns in Dorset, Sir Thomas Fairfax and his army remained in the county in hopes of rooting out the remaining resistance there, principally among the Royalist-sympathizing Clubmen and a garrison of Royalists at Sherborne Castle under the command of Lewis Dyve, Strangways's son-in-law. The campaign against Sherborne Castle was evidently important enough for Fairfax to take an active role in overseeing the undermining and artillery operations and for Cromwell himself to visit the site of the siege.[44] After a council of war in late July, on 1–2 August, Cromwell and Fairfax viewed the castle and settled on a strategy for its taking.[45]

Following a determined effort using undermining, heavy artillery, and even diplomacy, the castle was finally captured on 15 August, following the

---

[41] Bayley, 70.

[42] Ibid., 70.

[43] Ibid., 227–28, and see W. D. Christie, *A Life of Anthony Ashley Cooper, First Earl of Shaftesbury 1621–1683*, 2 vols. (London and New York: Macmillan, 1871), 1:62–67.

[44] Bayley, 281–82.

[45] Fripp, "Political History," 160.

opening of "a breach that thirty men might enter abreast."[46] Fairfax noted the zeal and determination of the garrison, confessing that "This business of Sherborne has tried the skill and resolution of the soldiers more than anything that has yet fallen out."[47] Especially after the decisive Parliamentarian victory at the Battle of Naseby in June of that year, the defeat of the garrison at Sherborne "was an irreparable loss to Charles, for with it he lost many officers, gentlemen, and soldiers," as well as supplies of arms and "important papers, which, immediately published by the Parliament, did much harm to his cause."[48] The castle itself was completely demolished in October.

Some details concerning the chain of events leading to Strangways's imprisonment are not entirely clear, but he certainly escaped capture during the siege of Sherborne Castle. His son Giles was not so fortunate, for parliamentary records confirm that on 29 August

> Mr *Gyles Strangwaies* was brought to the Bar: And, kneeling there, Mr Speaker, by the Command of the House, acquainted him with the Greatness of his Crime in betraying his Trust, and in being the Occasion of shedding so much Blood; and in applying his Endeavors to the Destroying of Religion, the publick Liberty, and the *English* Nation: And for that, for all these, he was committed for High Treason, by the Judgment of the House, to the Tower.[49]

Lewis Dyve was committed at the same time, but Strangways himself was certainly still a free man until the autumn of that year, as documented in the records of the Commons of 25 October. The entries for this day acknowledge the receipt of a letter of Captain Moulton of three days before "relating the seizing upon Sir *John* Strangeways," and record the Commons' order for "the securing Sir *John* Strangeways, and sending him Prisoner to the Governor of Gloucester; and to the Governor of Gloucester, to receive him as a Prisoner, and to secure him safely as a Prisoner, until the House take farther Order."[50]

---

[46] Bayley, 285.

[47] Ibid., 288.

[48] Fripp, "Political History," 161.

[49] *CJ*, 4:257.

[50] Ibid., 4:321. Hutchins quite incorrectly reports that Sir John was captured at the siege of Sherborne (*History and Antiquities*, 2:664). I am grateful to John Ferris for pointing out this often-repeated error of fact and for aiding me in getting to the truth of the matter.

On 29 November he was, like his son before him, brought to the bar to hear his sentence. He was committed to the Tower for high treason, a fact he recorded in the commonplace book and which is corroborated by the records of the Commons:

> *Ordered,* that Sir *John Strangewaies* be forthwith sent for, and brought to the Bar by the Serjeant at Arms.
>
> *Resolved,* & c., That Sir *John* Strangewaies be forthwith committed Prisoner to the *Tower,* for committing High Treason against the Parliament and Kingdom.
>
> Sir *John Strangewaies* was brought to the Bar; and, kneeling there, Mr Speaker acquainted him with the horridness and Transcendency of his Crimes and Treasons; and that he was, by Order of this House, committed Prisoner to the *Tower* for High Treason.[51]

Strangways's manuscript gives 15 May 1648 as the date of his actual release (see below, Section B.127), though by mid-March of that year his petition of the previous year was read (see Appendix 2), and by April he had successfully sued to compound for his release and the release of his son Giles. Each was to pay £5,000, "the whole Ten Thousand Pounds to be employed for the supply of the instant Necessities of the Navy." Giles was released upon payment of the first installment in April and Sir John the following month.[52]

His time of captivity was certainly not always spent under the strictest restraint, but this was a period nonetheless marked by many forms of duress and by his ongoing negotiations for his liberty and lands. He was, for example, permitted visits even by MPs and was one of the several Royalist recipients of King Charles's gift of two fat bucks for a feast in August of 1647.[53] During his imprisonment, he shared living space and no doubt

---

[51] Ibid., 4:357–58.

[52] Ibid., 4:489, 500, 537.

[53] An important contemporary document, however, suggests that, at least some of the time, the prisoners of the Tower did in fact lack the most basic provisions and amenities: see *A True Relation of the Cruell and Unparallel'd Oppression Which Hath Been Illegally Imposed Upon the Gentlemen, Prisoners in the Tower of London* (London, 1647). For reasons that I cannot explain, Strangways's name does not appear among the persons mentioned in this petition, though his son Giles's does. See also Thomas Wright, *Political Ballads Published in England During the Commonwealth* (London: C. Richards for the Percy Society, 1841), 88; *CJ*, 4:431; and Appendix 2.

political and moral ideas with a number of other captured Royalists, as he and other sources record (see B.1). Among his fellow prisoners were, in addition to his son and son-in-law, John Paulet, Marquess of Winchester, and Thomas Coningsby, both of whom translated meditative works, and Matthew Wren, Bishop of Ely.[54]

After leaving the Tower, Strangways returned to Dorset (by the order of the Commons he was given "Liberty to go into *Dorsetshire*, or where else he please"[55]), no doubt a man quite broken in spirit—to say nothing of the fact that he was given the maximum allowable fine for delinquency, £10,000. On 22 June, the sequestration of his property was finally taken off, and in the following year he was granted an extension of the fine to which he had pledged himself in order to secure his release and the release of his son Giles.[56] A particularly touching letter of 23 October 1649 to Sir Simonds D'Ewes gives some indication of the personal suffering he endured during the events of the previous years. He alludes to a promise he made while a prisoner in London to furnish D'Ewes with a basis for a pending legal claim. But he is soon reduced to apology:

> And I kn[e]w nothing to the contrarie when I came out of the Tower, but that I should be very well able to performe my word in this particular to you. But upon my coming home, I finde the greatest part of all my evidences either burnt or plundered, and those few that are left to be soe disordered, being all throwne into one heape, and soe tumbled into a great chest, that I am not able at present to give you any satisfaction to your desires. Besides, I have had a long desperate sickness, of which I am not yett fully recovered, which hath kept me from that employment which I soe much love—I meane, to peruse old evidences: this putt together, I hope, will plead my pardon; and when upon search (if it be not destroyed) I shall meet with anye thing in this kinde which may conduce to the ende

---

[54] Paulet translated Jacques Hugues Quarré's *Devout Entertainment of a Christian Soule* (1648) and Coningsby translated Boethius's *The Consolation of Philosophy* (1664).

[55] *CJ*, 5:537. But see Appendix 3, lines 3–4, p. 261.

[56] Hutchins, *History and Antiquities*, 2:664. *CJ*, 5:610. A very detailed record of the fines and sequestrations is given in Charles Herbert Mayo, *The Minutes of the Dorset Standing Committee* (Exeter: William Pollard & Co., 1902), 9, 18, 21, 44, 76, 78, 142–43, 207, 216, 257, 326–27, and 394.

you desire, I shall not fayle faithfully to preserve itt, and carefully send it unto you.[57]

Like many other defeated Royalists, Strangways spent the 1650s removed from politics, lying low in Melbury Samford, no doubt bitter and hoping for some favorable shift in national politics. Grace, his first wife, died in 1652, and the next year he married again.[58] In what his family life consisted during this period we cannot be sure, but it is well documented that his finances were in a precarious state during his incarceration, and he frequently sought legal recourse to restore or block further depredation upon his estates.[59] What ultimately happened to his large collection of "evidences," some of them dating back to the Anglo-Saxon period, remains a mystery. We know that they were used by the antiquarian John Leland in the 1530s and also that, after he succeeded to his inheritance in 1606, Strangways allowed Sir William Pole, Thomas Gerard, and Henry Spelman to use the collection.[60] Though the events to which he alludes in the letter to D'Ewes obviously diminished the collection, a great deal must have remained, for in the early 1650s the antiquarian William Dugdale praised Strangways for sharing with him what remained of the archive.[61]

A poem of about this period, not included in the commonplace book but given in Appendix 3, suggests that Strangways lived under certain travel (and perhaps other) restrictions for at least part of the decade. In a verse survey of his estates, he writes in May of 1650 that "the State hath me denyde / Above five miles from home to ride" (3–4) and hints that this long poem must serve him in the place of an actual survey. That he could remain within five miles of Melbury and still not visit all his estates, as stipulated by "the State," is in itself an indication of his considerable wealth, reflected clearly in the lengthy description of all the properties he owned.

Strangways apparently took no part in the failed Penruddock's Rebellion of 1655, though he was nonetheless rounded up and jailed for a time, in response to which he composed a poem "Upon a Private & Retyred Life"

---

[57] James Orchard Halliwell, *The Autobiography and Correspondence of Sir Simonds D'Ewes* (London, 1845), 2:316–17.

[58] His second wife was named Judith Edwards: see Smith, *New DNB*. See also Ferris, "Strangways, Sir John," 3: 498.

[59] See Mayo, *The Minutes of the Dorset Standing Committee*, passim.

[60] Simon Keynes, "The Lost Cartulary of Abbotsbury" *Anglo-Saxon England* 18 (1989): 211–12.

[61] Ibid., 215, 221–25, 235–38.

(B.138–39).[62] Later that year he appeared before Major-General Desborough and was released only after pledging to pay the Decimation Tax, a much-contested punitive measure levied against Royalists.[63]

At the Restoration Strangways was prominent in several ways. He and his son Giles signed a declaration of the knights and gentry of Dorset on 16 April 1660 and a declaration of thanksgiving on 12 June, delivered before the king at Whitehall.[64] The document of 16 April is especially revealing, for the Royalist signatories do not claim victory so much as call for mutual forgiveness, disclaiming any association with radicals of all affiliations, whom they brand "men of those wilde Principles." It is a characteristic statement of a Constitutional Royalist like Strangways, whose name appears prominently in the document, third among the forty-one signatories. On 14 May 1660, amid a spirited celebration lasting several days, Strangways read the king's proclamation and added his own commendations to the populace for their loyalty to the monarch's cause.[65] Sometime after his imprisonment with his father, Giles had a medal struck, which described his incarceration, the face showing his portrait and the reverse an image of the White Tower and the dates of his imprisonment.[66]

Strangways, his son Giles, and his grandson Thomas all sat as MPs in the first Restoration Parliament, Sir John representing Weymouth and Melcombe Regis. Apart from his participation in the celebrations at the Restoration and in the Cavalier Parliament, his advanced age seems to have made him prefer retirement to public life. A full-length portrait of him still hangs in Wadham College. It is dated 1663, "Aetatis. Suae: 78," and depicts a portly, alert man dressed in damask coat and broad-brimmed hat. He is seated, holding a letter addressed to him, and in the upper right appears the

---

[62] See also the discussion in Underdown, *Fire*, 215; see also David Underdown, *Royalist Conspiracy in England, 1649–1660* (New Haven: Yale University Press, 1960; reprint, Hamden, Conn.: Archon Books, 1971), 127–58.

[63] On the Decimation Tax, see Smith, *Constitutional Royalism*, 278–79.

[64] *A Declaration of the Knights and Gentry in the County of Dorset* (London, 1660); and see Bayley, 387.

[65] *Mercurius Publicus* no. 21, 17–24 May 1660, 329, 331; and see David Underdown, *Revel, Riot and Rebellion: Popular Politics and Culture in England, 1603–1660* (Oxford: Oxford University Press, 1987), 271–72.

[66] John Evelyn, *Numismata: A Discourse of Medals, Antient and Modern* (London, 1697), 114–15; Edward Hawkins, "Dorsetshire Numismatics; The Ancient Mints, with Notices of Some Medals Connected with the County," *Archaelogical Journal* 23 (1866): 126–28.

Strangways coat of arms, which is divided into eighteen quarterings.[67] Whether the portrait was originally intended for or commissioned by the college has not been determined; nor has the artist's identity. Three years after the portrait was painted, he died, on 30 December 1666, aged 82, and was buried at Melbury Samford.[68]

The Commonplace Section and Its Time and Place

Sir John Strangways was not a life-long creative writer or aspirant to literary fame but a man of politics and affairs who was constrained by circumstances to become a writer. His imprisonment was the impetus for him to gather the material he collected as commonplace entries in Section A of this manuscript, and to write the verse that makes up Section B. Indeed, there is a general correspondence between the commonplace section and the verse, a characteristic that signals a certain practical, even prosaic, approach on Strangways's part to the fundamental purposes and pleasures of literary art. The commonplace section begins with a notice that explicitly frames his efforts as useful and timely:

> A Collection of some notes for my owne private
> use, gathered out of severall authors as they have
> bin read by me, JStrangways: wherof most in the
> Tower—1645. during the Tyme of my sad impry-
> sonment ther: | |.

Quid fugiam video: sed quid Sequar non habeo

I have not striven against my hart to make a syde:
nor hath my Conscience bin oppressed by affection: | |.
JStrangways
1645.

---

[67] Jackson, *Wadham College*, 183; R. Lane-Poole, *Catalogue of Portraits in the Possession of the University, Colleges, City, and County of Oxford*, 3 vols. (Oxford: Clarendon Press, for the Oxford Historical Society, 1912–26), 3:216–17. I am grateful to Cliff Davies of Wadham College, Oxford, for his help in locating information on the portrait. The portrait is reproduced on p. iv.
[68] Hutchins, *History and Antiquities*, 2:679.

Several Latin and English maxims follow, these followed in turn by "A Short prayer before our going to heare the word preached," dated 11 January 1646. I see no reason to doubt Strangways's assertion that the majority of his entries were composed in 1645 (i.e., through March 25, 1646), during the time of his "sad imprysonment."

The commonplace section consists of forty-seven leaves containing 370 numbered entries. Most of these are limited to a few lines, but they are frequently interrupted by longer groupings arranged under headings such as "Certayne Notes & Rules to Direct us & Incite us to & in the service of God" and "Of Anger" (A.33–35, 92–94) and by notes taken directly out of published sources such as Sir Richard Baker's *A Chronicle of the Kings of England* (1643 edition), Foxe's *Actes and Monuments* (probably the 1632 or 1641 edition), and Peter Heylyn's *Mikrokosmus: A Little Description of the Great World* (1627, or later, edition). Entries are generally in English, but Latin aphorisms and sentences occur throughout, often translated into English by Strangways himself. One long subsection, called "The Severall Mottoes of the Severall Emperors Ending with Ferdinand the Second," contains 121 numbered mottoes in Latin and in English translation (A.81–88).

Although the early modern practice of keeping commonplace books tended to encourage the collection of apt phrases and ideas on a wide range of subjects as a general preparation for life's various challenges and opportunities, Strangways's entries are generally quite closely tied to his immediate circumstances as a political prisoner. Two central concerns dominate this section: self-vindications of his political decisions and his general worldview and exercises in what we might term general moral philosophy. With respect to the first theme, the commonplace entries are yet another reminder that Strangways's position as a prisoner was precarious and that any arguments he could lodge in defense of his support for the monarch would, at very least, have a consolatory or spiritually therapeutic value to an incarcerated and beleagured man. Hence, he devotes a great deal of the commonplace section to collections of legal and moral knowledge in his own defense, such as the section entitled "Delinquencie is perpetratio delicti, or derelictio Legis. He is noe delinquent who obeyeth the Law" (A.40–42). With respect to the second theme, his fondness for collecting aphorisms, wise sayings, proverbs, and epigrams is a reminder of his debt to the early modern commonplace tradition as it had evolved in the schools and the society at large from the end of the fifteenth century.

This movement has been the subject of several excellent studies which bear directly upon the academic training and intellectual habits that Strangways brought with him into the Tower and out of which both his commonplace entries and some of his verse proceed.[69] The collecting of commonplaces can be traced to the dawn of Western rhetoric and logic, ultimately to Aristotle via a line that—especially for English writers—includes, among others, Cicero, Quintillian, and the author of the pseudo-Ciceronian *Ad Herennium*. The "places" (*topoi* in Greek and *loci* in Latin), sometimes conceived as imaginary mental "spaces" and sometimes rather more literally thought to occupy spatial positions within the breadth of human knowledge, were supposed to contain material for argumentation, drawn from ancient authorities and arranged and stored for future use, much as (in perhaps the most famous formulation of the process) bees selectively gathered from many sources in order to produce the purest "nectar." Originally developed to prepare their possessors for oratorical occasions, by the seventeenth century they were more specifically associated with the written tradition and provided, arguably, the very foundation of the early modern English hermeneutical system that Agricola and Ramus were influential in promulgating.[70]

By its paradoxical nature as an idea both commonly understood and yet expressed in some fresh way,[71] the commonplace developed under English humanism into one of the cornerstones of the educational system in which Strangways and countless others of his and earlier generations were schooled. Always implicitly moral even in the classical tradition, the "doctrine of the places" became under English Protestantism more explicitly a vehicle for understanding moral philosophy and for articulating ideas

---

[69] The best book-length studies are Walter J. Ong, S.J., *Ramus, Method, and the Decay of Dialogue* (Cambridge, Mass.: Harvard University Press, 1958); Sister Joan Marie Lechner, O.S.U., *Renaissance Concepts of the Commonplaces* (New York: Pageant Press, 1962; reprint, Westport, Conn.: Greenwood Press, 1974); Mary Thomas Crane, *Framing Authority: Sayings, Self and Society in Sixteenth-Century England* (Princeton: Princeton University Press, 1993); and Ann Moss, *Printed Commonplace-Books and the Structuring of Renaissance Thought* (Oxford: Clarendon Press, 1996). See also Hudson, *Epigram in the English Renaissance*, chapters 3–4, and the excellent catalogue to the 2001 exhibition at the Beinecke Library of Yale University: Earle Havens, *Commonplace Books: A History of Manuscripts and Printed Books from Antiquity to the Twentieth Century* (New Haven: The Beinecke Rare Book and Manuscript Library, 2001).

[70] Ong, *Ramus*, chapter 1; Lechner, *Renaissance Concepts of the Commonplaces*, 1–7; Crane, *Framing Authority*, chapter 1. The most extensive discussion of developments in the seventeenth century is in Moss, *Printed Commonplace-Books*, especially chapters 7–9.

[71] Crane, *Framing Authority*, 8.

concerning the ethical pursuit of the good life, just as they tended to serve culturally conservative ends—what Ann Moss aptly calls "a control on present experience."[72]

In many respects, Strangways's "Collection of some notes" conforms to these practices, for he does indeed seem to conceive of the commonplace section as a repository, an elaborate vessel, a harvest, or raw material much like cut timber awaiting a use—all metaphors commonly circulated in the early modern period to describe the process of "gathering and framing," collecting and organizing, the authority of classical antiquity and modern thought.[73] As Mary Thomas Crane argues in her study of sixteenth-century commonplacing, the results of this widely taught and practiced method became the basis not only of certain fundamental educational practices in England but also "a necessary form of cultural capital for upward mobility in the newly bureaucratized state."[74] While Strangways was not a part of the *arriviste* classes upon whom Crane's study principally focuses, through his educational experiences he was trained in the methods of gathering and framing she analyzes. His manuscript participates in an intellectual tradition that his father and probably his grandfather would have understood and one that a figure as intellectually rigorous as John Locke not only endorsed but to which he also contributed.[75]

In other ways, however, Strangways—though clearly intending to keep a commonplace book as his generation understood the method—departs from such doctrinaire characteristics of the tradition as using strict alphabetical headings and Ramistic dialectical categories. The tradition dictated that commonplaces be organized under headings or groupings, which in their most unimaginative forms could amount to little more than convenient mental pigeonholes that, according to one view, encouraged the rote recording and endless redeployment of platitudes during the entire early modern period.[76] While Strangways does indeed organize some of his material in the time-honored fashion (and is not immune from repeating platitudes), the majority of his entries are numbered sequentially throughout the manuscript, without headings and very often without any implied pattern, principle of

---

[72] Ibid., 39 and 50–51; Moss, *Printed Commonplace-Books*, vi.

[73] Crane, *Framing Authority*, 3, and see "Introduction," passim.

[74] Ibid., 6.

[75] John Locke, *A New Method of Making Common-Place Books* (London, 1706), was first published in French in 1686 as part of the *Bibliothèque Universelle*. Locke was a relative latecomer to the tradition but was very influential. See Moss, *Printed Commonplace-Books*, 278–79.

[76] Crane, *Framing Authority*, 3.

organization, or unifying theme. Instead of interrelated parts of a whole gathered under a central proposition, his numbered entries function as usually discrete propositions, statements of moral or political positions to be stored for later use. This long excerpt reveals a great deal about Strangways's organizing patterns throughout the manuscript:

15: 1 Understanding: 2 Will: 3 Memory: in the Soule: 1 Knowledge: 2: Righteousnes: 3: Holines: is the Image of God:

16: Germanorum vivere est Bibere: whence it is that they abound in Brewers; having 777 of the Trade: 40: Bakers: one Lawyer: one physition in the towne of Hamburge: Heylings Geogra: pag: 256 & 260.
Lucus: a non Lucendo: mons: a non movendo: Bellum: quasi minimè bellum. | |.

17: The sun is — 160 — Tymes greater then the Earth (as Astronomers resolve) though rather upon probable conjecture, then certayne demonstration: the Moone is — 39 — tymes lesse then the Earth: Some of the fixed starres (as Astronomers affirme) are — 107 — tymes greater then the Earth:

18: Plynie in his Naturall History: lib: 32: Cap: 11: writes that some whales are — 600 — foot long: & — 360 — foot broad. | |.

19: Sinceritie & Safetie meet always togither

20: pecora: signifyes great Cattle: pecudes: Small Cattle: Jumentum quasi juvamentum:

21: Betweene the Creation & the giving of the law in Mount Sinay weare — 2544 — yeares: & 888 — yeares from the Flood to the rayning of Manna: & the flood was sent upon the world in the yeare of the age of the world 1656: | |.

22: God Speaketh of himselfe plurally by the word |US| fowre tymes in Scripture: Gen: 1:16: Gen: 3:22: Gen: 11:7 & Esay: 6:8:

23: Note the Impartiallitie of Scripture Storie, which concealeth not the fowlest faults of those it prayseth most: as we may observe in the Storie of Noah: Gen: 9:22: of Abraham: Gen 12:19: & 20:2: Of Moses: Exod 4:1: 10:12: Num: 20:24: Deut: 32:51: Of David: 1 Sam: 11: 2 Sam: 24:10: Of Job: 3:3: &c: of Jeremy 20:14: of Peter: Matt: 26:70:72:74:

24: Noah was noe Drunkard (for one action is not enough to give a denomination to the actor, & he was drunke but once): we may hence be warned against trusting a drunkard with a secrett: for a drunkard is as like to tell all when he is a wake, as to shew all when he is a sleepe. | |.

25: Quære: whither Constantines Resolution, To Cast his Robe over
an Adulterous Bishop, if he tooke him in the evill act as Theodoret writes of him: Eccles Hist: lib: 1°: Cap: 11°: did not fayle in
justice, as well as abound in mercy. | |.

26: Beautie is a double Snare: 1: To them that have itt: 2: to them that
love itt:

These very typical entries show not only the absence of a rigid organizing scheme of headings and subheadings typical of the commonplace
tradition as recommended by ancient and contemporary authors but also
several other characteristics.[77] First, we find in these entries a synthesis of
authorities that includes contemporaries such as Peter Heylin, ancient
authors such as Pliny, the Old and New Testaments, and even snatches of
basic folk wisdom, whether true or not (neither "Sinceritie & Safetie meet
always togither," nor "Beautie is a double Snare" seems self-evidently true).
Sacred and secular, ancient and modern, cultivated and homespun often
combine in this way throughout the commonplace section, suggesting that
for Strangways as moral philosopher the ancient past had practical applications to the vicissitudes of life in the 1640s. In the commonplace section, we
are rarely very far from Strangways's overwhelming concerns with asserting
the righteousness of his political and moral positions and with making his
commonplace book a repository of advice for leading the good life within a
political world.

In this way, Strangways is atypical with respect to the mainstream
commonplace tradition of his age. His manuscript contains a preponderance
of entries recorded not as part of a general moral education whose uses were
understood to lie in the varied and unspecified future faced by a moral individual but as specific and timely self-exonerations supported by a variety
of specialized legal texts such as William Stamford's (or Staunford's) *Plees
de Coron,* Coke's *Institutes,* and those staples of the law student, lawyer, and
MP: the published rolls of parliament, statute books, and "sessional" collections of legal statutes. For him, the usual objective of recording and ap-
propriating the culture's received authority becomes instead focused upon
the much narrower object of gathering and (sometimes) framing legal precedents and proofs of his innocence with respect to his imprisonment and,
by extension, his righteousness with respect to the tumultuous events of the
1640s.

---

[77] See Moss, *Printed Commonplace-Books,* vii–viii, for a general distinction between commonplaces and other forms of compilation.

We know from Sir Edward Coke's son that Strangways was thought of as "one of the better lawyers"[78] in the Commons, and one aspect of the commonplace section's value to readers and scholars is that it provides some insight into the workings of his legal thinking. Occasionally, entries serve as nothing more than brief repositories of citations, little more than *pro memoria*, as in entry 44, which reads simply "44: Vide et perlege: 4to: H: 8: Cap: 8." More often, however, he records and frames complex matters of legal theory and precedent and acutely draws from them specific applications to his own circumstances, as in "The Plea of the Lord Hunsdon" (A.76–78) or in his extended reflection upon the legality of his moderate Royalism (A.45–47).

Two final observations concerning Strangways as a commonplace writer deserve some mention. First, as we observe in the excerpt quoted above, Strangways often shows a predisposition for dialectical thought. In this respect, he is quite typical of other commonplace writers in his habit of constructing arguments according to a point-counterpoint dialectical logic that was encouraged, especially, by Ramus and his followers and absolutely fundamental to the general development of the commonplace tradition itself.[79] As a lawyer and experienced MP, Strangways would naturally find dialectical methods congenial, for dialectics was not only the basis of his formal training but also the means by which he would have articulated his beliefs in the institutions of parliament and the English legal system. Finally, many of Strangways's commonplace entries provide the inspiration for and sometimes the actual verbal texture of poems in the verse section—the metaphorical "cut timber" for the eventual project of constructing his verse edifices. For example, the meditative poem dated 13 April 1647 (B.83) that begins "A Man, Lives forty yeares, before he knowes / Himselfe to be a Foole" is based directly upon commonplace entries 220 and 221 (A.55). And in another instance, Strangways appears to do little more than set the matter of one single commonplace entry into rhymed couplets:

> 56: When Zeno the phylosopher reproved one for immoderate feasting he answeared, he spent of his owne & had enough: Zeno replyed if your Cooke should put—2—or—3—handfulls of Salt into your meat more then was fitt, & should he say he had salt enough by him that Cost nothing, should this be a good answeare? (A.11)

---

[78] BL Add. MS 64922, fol. 65 (John Coke the Younger to Sir John Coke, 22 [?] Nov. 1641), quoted in Smith, *Constitutional Royalism*, 83.

[79] Ong, *Ramus*, chapters 8–9.

> A prodigall that Liv'de in huge Excesse
> Was by wyse Zeno counsail'd to goe lesse.
> But he replyde, I spend of my owne store
> And what I spend I can doe, & much more.
> Zeno Return'd: If he that drest your Meate
> Should in that Messe præpar'de for you to eate
> Putt in much more Salt then would well suffice
> Att least three hand-fulls, would you hold him wise
> To say he could well spare itt? I beleeve
> That answeare would but small contentment give.
> Then change the Sceane, & you will plainly See
> You & your Cooke doe in the Case agree.
> per JS:
>
> (B.37)

As will be made clearer in the following section, the correspondence between the commonplace entries and the poems extends beyond merely borrowed subject matter. The quintessentially moralistic and legalistic qualities of the commonplace section carry over as well. The voice which establishes the tone of the commonplace section also sets the tone of the poetry: a vigorous public voice, serious and moralistic, generally free of ironic detachment or delight in exploring perspectives. Strangways drew from his commonplace entries, which probably were, as he implies, written before the majority of the poems. If the poems sometimes lack great range in tone, subject matter, and technique, we can reasonably attribute at least a part of these limitations to their origins as gathered (and sometimes framed) propositions in the commonplace book of a man incarcerated, rightly fearing for his family's material well-being and quite possibly for his own life.

Verse and Versification

The seventy-eight poems contained in Strangways's manuscript treat a rather narrow range of topics, and, though they vary considerably in length, they also remain within a rather narrow set of forms. Strangways favors the rhymed couplet, generally in iambic pentameter, and he eschews most of the formal and dramatic strategies, as well as the modulations of voicing, perspective, and tone that great mid-century poets such as Marvell and the younger Milton employed. Strangways's poems and versifications derive their power not from innovative forms or a wide breadth of experience seen from different points of view but rather from the reiteration of a few central ideas, most of them related directly to—and usually expressions of—his incarceration and suffering. These are Cavalier poems, politically speaking, but without the self-conscious wittiness that the Tribe of Ben brought to the lyric. To see them as pedestrian is perhaps tempting when they are compared with the writings of more inventive and playful poets of Strangways's political outlook—Lovelace or Cowley, for example. But such an assessment would ignore these poems' particular value as heartfelt expressions of disillusionment, an apparent withdrawal from what Strangways calls "this lewd age."

As several recent critics have thoughtfully argued, however, the once-dominant view of "the cavalier mode" misses the richness and sense of political engagement that "cavalier" writing contains, whether overtly or in an encoded fashion.[80] When seen in this larger context, Strangways's poems do indeed merge inwardly directed meditative works with practically oriented explorations of state politics, expressions of disillusioned withdrawal with moments of hopeful advice, and vigorous self-vindication delivered in a hortative, sometimes homiletic, and entirely public voice. According to one argument, the very acts of "composition and dissemination of poetry" in the period constitute "modes of political engagement," not escape from "public disturbance."[81]

Strangways's poetic idiom is fundamentally religio-political, and one feels throughout the poems the verbal articulation of his frustrated political and ideological aims as well as what one scholar has usefully called a "rhetoric of suffering."[82] Broadly speaking, the poems can be seen within four main categories. With due awareness of the shortcomings of any broad system of organizing, I will classify them as, first, "historical poems" such as "Concerning The negative oath" or "Lord how are we from Snarling Come to byte" (B.112 and B.35–36), which engage directly with the political and

---

[80] See especially Earl Miner, *The Cavalier Mode from Jonson to Cotton* (Princeton: Princeton University Press, 1971). For revisions of the Miner thesis, see in particular, Lois Potter, *Secret Rites and Secret Writing: Royalist Literature, 1641–1660* (Cambridge: Cambridge University Press, 1989); Nigel Smith, *Literature and Revolution in England, 1640–1660* (New Haven: Yale University Press, 1994); James Loxley, *Royalism and Poetry in the English Civil Wars: The Drawn Sword* (New York: St. Martin's Press, 1997).

[81] Loxley, *Royalism and Poetry*, 6.

[82] J. Sears McGee, *The Godly Man in Stuart England* (New Haven: Yale University Press, 1976), 13.

military realities Strangways faced; moral "advice poems" on a range of topics related to the pursuit of the good life as both a metaphysical abstraction and a matter of daily life, only sometimes connected to topical politics or the author's suffering; "meditative poems" and prayers which center on concerns more metaphysical than physical; and versifications (sometimes called verse paraphrases or "metaphrases") of biblical passages and previously published meditative works.

First, however, some observations on the general arrangement and characteristics of the verse section may prove useful. In terms of formal variety, the poems range from two lines to almost eight hundred, and most use rhymed couplets. Some have a tight, epigrammatic effect, while several are long meditations extending three hundred or four hundred lines; in general, however, Strangways favored shorter lyrics. Often these are voiced in the first-person and far less concerned with the witty manipulation of language or theme than with establishing firm moral positions that can easily be associated with the author's own circumstances. Of the seventy-eight poems, eighteen are versifications or meditations specifically upon biblical passages; the books of Job, Proverbs, Matthew, and James are especially represented among these. Strangways also versified "The Free Prisoner" and "The Affliction of Israel," two prose meditations by Bishop Joseph Hall.

Many poems are precisely dated, by day, month, and year. The majority of these works were composed during a rush of writing between the autumn of 1646 and the late spring of 1647, though it is worth noting, too, that not all the dated poems fall into a strict chronological sequence (see B.59 and B.70–71). Another ten come from 1665, long after his release, and one poem on the subject of his brief imprisonment following Penruddock's Revolt, erroneously dated 19 June 1685, must have been written in 1655. Strangways's habit of dating his work so precisely has considerable historical interest in itself, for we are left with a record of his literary efforts that corresponds to his incarceration and, we might assume, signals his hopes for some kind of monument of his life as a political prisoner.

Biblical language imbues all the poems, whether topically specific or not, but it is an indication of Strangways's commitment to a reasoned form of government—devout but not zealous—that the language and cadences of the Bible blend so naturally with the language of political advocacy. In this example, Job 33:15, where God speaks "In a dream, in a vision of the night," forms the basis for the political poem that begins:

> Those that oppose themselves against the King,
> And all that doe against his armyes fight,

> That him therby they to distresse may bring
> Shalbe as Dreames & visions of the night.
>
> (1–4, B.57)

Whether cited, paraphrased, versified, abridged, or merely alluded to, the Bible provides the most important poetic and conceptual underpinnings of the entire verse section and, indeed, of Strangways's world view. Politics, the miseries of warfare, the negotiations between parliament and monarch, the moral dilemma posed by coercive practices such as the Negative Oath, all fit into biblical patterns without any jarring discontinuity or artificiality.

Historical Poems

The "historical" poems are most evidently marked by Strangways's need to vindicate his own politics and moral outlook, but they also contain some notable descriptive passages which convey a sense of his direct experience in political negotiation and warfare. In "In Invidum" Strangways prays for an end to "The wofull stirrs, that have or more or lesse / Both in the Church & in the Civill state / Bin raysed from this bitter roote of late" (28–30, B.41). He advises in another poem, "Say what you will, Tis not safe for the State / To make the sword the judge of this debate," and proceeds to weigh the mutually unappealing prospects of military victories on both sides of the conflict ("Concerning the Ending of Our Unhappie differences by peace," 1–2, B.72).

In "Lord how are we from Snarling Come to byte" we hear of the "Hellish fury of Storme / Acted by Souldyers in a warlike forme," "Cytyes and Townes all burning," "channells running all with blood," and "deadly Granados [that] fly / With Fyre in their mouthes" (5–13, B.35–36). Given what we know of the two assaults on his home at Abbotsbury and of the siege of Sherborne Castle, we can surmise that Strangways employed very little descriptive license in such works, and as such, they have some inherent value as records of important political and military events.

Intentionally or not, many historical poems are voiced by a persona who often appears rather naïve in the face of political realities, a centrist constantly outraged by the excesses of the times and forced to resist them as best he can. Often he appeals to more stable times, to tradition, to older ways, or to time-honored precedents as part of a comprehensive strategy of righteous self-vindication. For example, in one short work, Strangways asserts the enduring truths of his "old way" against the coercion or "Might" of those who would seek to make him abandon his principles:

> What I beleeve to be the Right
> Nor hope of Bribe, nor feare of Might
> Shall make me either to forsake
> My old way, or a new to take.
> But Trewth and Reason ever shall
> From myne owne Tenetts me Recall.
> For I resolve & will doe still,
> That they shall rule me, not my will.
>
> (B.56)

This characteristically backward-looking observer also asserts himself in several works devoted to medieval subjects, as in the "discourse betweene King Henry the third & the pryor of Saint Johns Hospitall," "Of the Bishoppe of Herefords sermon at Oxford preached before Queene Isabell," and "Upon the Lord Seaton refusing to deliver Barwicke to Edward the third King of England." The first two examine the relationship between royal and representational prerogatives, the chief political controversy of the 1640s, in terms of previous regimes and earlier times. The third interprets the violent conflicts of the 1640s in terms of historical precedent. As I have suggested above, these concerns with the principles of prerogative and with the horrors of violence emerge as central to both the commonplace entries and the verse. It is not too much to say, in fact, that the two themes exist in almost necessary relation to each other, for central to Strangways's political and poetic thought is the doctrine that principled obedience to law, precedent, and custom permits a people to avoid the extremes which English society in his age was facing.

Religion and politics, of course, were inseparable in the 1640s. Especially for the "activists of the summer of 1642,"[83] who, like Strangways, had by this time moved into ideological party affiliations, a poem was an opportunity to articulate one's own religious politics. In the case of Strangways, meaning proceeds from the perspective of a disaffected and defeated but righteous onlooker. In his third poem, he assails the extremes of both the papists and "our Schismatickes," both of whom "strive for Trewth, but from all peace depart" (3, 6, B.33). In another, he attacks "Formalitie" that calls itself religion but "Tis but a wolfe, that putts a sheep's skin on," concluding with the epigrammatic couplet

---

[83] J. S. Morrill, *The Revolt of the Provinces* (London: Allen & Unwin, 1976), 47.

> Then Looke with Care to your foundation
> Before you sett on Reformation.
>
> (15–18, B.55)

And with equal facility, he also defends holy days ("In Defence of Holy-Dayes," B.61) and applies biblical imagery to topical religious politics ("Those that oppose themselves against the King," B.57).

Despite their topical particularity, the historical poems show imaginative breadth and verbal complexity in some surprising ways. Tonally, however, they almost always proceed from the voice of a defeated, disillusioned first person whose sense of righteousness in a world gone terribly wrong appears to be his only salvation. They serve to remind us that consistency and reiteration, rather than innovation or delight in perspectives or in irony, are the hallmarks of Strangways's verse and that his capture, imprisonment, and suffering were what motivated his poetic endeavors.

Advice Poems

As a category, the moral advice poems present a more serious problem of definition, for nearly everything that Strangways wrote is moral and admonitory. The works I group under this head do, however, have a common concern with what one writer has called "the housekeeping of the soul."[84] These are precepts for godly living but also for the practical or quotidian expressions of the godly life in the affairs of the world: financial and legal transactions, good maintenance of property or friendship, and so forth. Like the historical poems, they are public, hortatory, and admonitory. They achieve an almost homiletic effect because of their subject matter and their tone, as in "The Rules of Trew Obedience" (B.121), which opens, characteristically for this type of poem, "If thyne Obedience thou wouldst have to be / Perfect & Good; Marke what I have to say to thee." He celebrates, both in the verse and in several commonplace entries, the spiritual benefits of correction and reproof (see examples in "Of Reproofe & of the right use therof," B.54, and "De Miserecordia Domini," B.126). Here, his strategy is to remind his fellow human beings (and no doubt himself) of the need for humility and self-mortification. Some advice poems are also epigrammatic, a mode in which Strangways writes with some force, as in the neatly balanced four-line poem:

---

[84] Helen White, *English Devotional Literature, 1600–1640* (Madison, Wis.: University of Wisconsin Press, 1931), 175.

> He that a good thing doth, to a bad end,
> To make god serve a Divell he doth intend;
> But he that to a good end doth doe ill,
> He makes the Divi'll therby to act gods will.
> (B.56)

Although many of these poems concern the "housekeeping of the soul" in a metaphysical sense, others apply the principle of housekeeping rather more literally. Strangways includes meditations on social, legal, and financial dealings, in which, for example, he inveighs against prodigality, counsels caution when offering to stand as surety for others or in transacting financial affairs, advises on the right use of charity, and distinguishes true from false friendship (see particularly "A prodigall that Liv'de in huge Excesse," "Tanti valet, quanti vendi potest," "Against false & pretended Freinds and ffreindshippe," and "Of Freindshipps Break-Bonds," B.37, B.60–61, B.66–67, B.80). In keeping with his status as a member of the religiously centrist landed gentry, Strangways particularly esteems "works of 'material charity'" and "'love of the brethren'"[85] as admirable and obtainable endeavors but not, as he stresses in "Concerning Almes and Suretishippe," to one's own peril:

> . . . See thou take good heed
> Thou doest not fall thy selfe at Length:
> For charitie doth not extend
> To Doe our selves hurt in the end.
> (88–91, B.64)

As a group, the advice poems offer doctrinally, politically, and socially conservative precepts for pursuing the good life, precepts that seem to proceed quite directly from what we can recover of Strangways's own political and moral center. They are often rather one-dimensional, the verse serving to advance and validate rather than question or explore a range of traditional moral positions.

Probably the most tonally interesting of the advice poems draw from the tradition of writers such as George Gascoigne and Walter Ralegh, two much earlier masters of the ironic advice poem (Ralegh's "The Lie" being the example *par excellence*), and, somewhat closer to Strangways's own age, Donne's "Go and Catch a Falling Star." As irony of any sort is rare in

---

[85] McGee, *Godly Man,* 223 and 232.

Strangways's verse, these poems stand out as unusually complex. In "Fayth & Respect are seldome found," the speaker wishes he could offer his unidentified auditor a more positive conclusion concerning the ways of the world, while the poems "Wealth maketh many freinds," "Against false & pretended Friends and ffreindshippe," and "Of Freindshipps Break-Bonds" (B.59, B.66–67, B.80) more cynically explore the limits of true friendship. Presumably, as these poems would suggest, Strangways had occasion during the tumultuous political shifts of the 1640s to explore those limits himself. Friendship, however, is one matter, and submission to authority another, and in a dark meditation on advancement in life, he urges,

> What thing soever itt shalbe
> Thy Governour Commaundeth thee
> I thee advize thyselfe to fayne
> Most willingly to entertayne,
>
> Make it as part of thy belieffe
> To prayse him that Commaunds in cheiffe .
> "Wouldst thou in Quiett gladly Dwell?"
> (4–9, B.70)

The poem "Brute Beastes, which of right Reason want the use," a reflection on the peculiarly human capacity for treachery, is another epigrammatic work which uses the voicing and the situation Strangways favors in the moral advice poems, namely wise counsel delivered by an experienced speaker to someone far less aware:

> Brute Beastes, which of right Reason want the use,
> Their ffeeders serve, off'ring them noe abuse.
> And though untamed, yet Tis understood
> They never harme those men, that doe them good.
> Beleeve me: tis a payne extreamely Smart
> Which Ill Requitall, causeth in the Hart.
> (B.67)

Apart from this more complex subset of cynical observations on the ways of the world, as a group the moral advice poems are reducible to two central, time-honored Christian precepts which Strangways reiterates within fairly narrow creative limits: grace is a mystery not to be plumbed or even attempted, and pride is the great impediment to man's receiving that grace. "By Exper'ience," he claims, "we doe alwayes find / That strife proceeds from haughtines of mind" ("Since BETTER, HOLY'ER, WISER, did encrease," 5–6, B.33).

In the poem entitled "Noli altum Sapere" — glossing Romans 11:20: "be not high-minded, but fear"—Strangways explores the varieties of human vainglory in seeking "things that are beyond thy Length" or "above thy strength" (1–2). It concludes with this injunction, framed in the homiletic imagery typical of this genre:

> Professe not then, thou hast a perfect sight,
> Of those things which noe mortall eyes have seen,
> Nor weare revealed since the world hath been.
>
> (16–18, B.79)

The advice poems are quite consistent with the moral stance and the voicing of the entire verse section and indeed with what we can recover about Strangways's entire system of beliefs and values. They return again and again to basic, time-honored, central themes, and they enjoin rather than delight the reader as part of an overall strategy of repairing a world that, Strangways believed, had come undone. They offer advice, but that advice proceeds from the perspective of the vanquished, incarcerated, and humiliated.

Meditative Poems and Prayers

Given this position as a defeated man and a prisoner of conscience, it is quite natural that Strangways would turn to verse meditations and prayers. Not only did his culture at large provide him with the necessary structures and methods to do so, but his situation all but demanded that he put these into practice as a response to his afflictions. What is fundamental to Strangways's poetic idiom is its occasionality, its engagement with problems of topical importance rather than a "cavalier" withdrawal. What is especially interesting about the meditative poems and prayers, however, is how they combine topicality and engagement with some of the broader cultural forces driving mid-century literature and religious practices.

Since he could not know during his incarceration what he would know by the Restoration, or even by the time of his release, we must assume that Strangways at times quite reasonably feared the worst. As a response, he could also turn away from the slings and arrows of the world to the examination of not only his politics and religion but also the state of his soul. In this respect, he was not atypical of his age, for by the middle of the century

Protestant meditative technique had developed complex systems and structures that drew eclectically upon classical traditions and Christian theology, both Catholic and Protestant, and were in themselves the subject of some controversy.[86] Strangways's generation had literally dozens of popular meditative handbooks and guides upon which to draw as well as a range of sermons, emblem books, and theological writings that also provided direction and rationale for learning the art of interrogating one's soul, pondering the last things, and dying well. In addition, a tradition of Stoic humanism had developed across several generations of English students, readers, thinkers, and, writers, and certainly the group literary historians have come to define as "cavalier" was not exempt from these influences as they faced the "tension between personal and social obligations."[87]

Strangways's ten or so explicitly "meditative Poems" comprise a range of reflections upon worldly and other-worldly matters and include a few works (especially "O God, Thy Nature & thy propertie," "In Invidum," and "A Private Meditation," B.38, B.40–41, B.46–47) that take the more precise form of prayer. As a recent discussion aptly reminds us, "the Bible remained the central cultural text in England, as in the rest of Europe, through the seventeenth century."[88] But the Bible was merely the foundational text, and as others have argued in useful detail, works of popular piety, handbooks, methods, and guidebooks also contributed quite concretely to the formation of popular devotional practices.[89]

---

[86] Frank Livingston Huntley, *Bishop Joseph Hall and Protestant Meditation in Seventeenth-Century England* (Binghamton, N.Y.: Medieval & Renaissance Texts & Studies, 1981), 3–10.

[87] Raymond A. Anselment, *Loyalist Resolve: Patient Fortitude in the English Civil War* (Newark, Del.: University of Delaware Press, 1988), 13, 15; and see his introduction, passim.

[88] Debora Kuller Shuger, *The Renaissance Bible: Scholarship, Sacrifice, and Subjectivity* (Berkeley: University of California Press, 1994), 2.

[89] Something like forty per cent of the total publication in the period was religious in orientation: see Douglas Bush, *English Literature in the Earlier Seventeenth Century, 1600–1660* (Oxford: Oxford University Press, 1962), 294. See the book-length discussions of meditative traditions by White, *English Devotional Literature*; Sister Mary Catherine O'Connor, *The Art of Dying Well: The Development of the Ars Moriendi* (New York: Columbia University Press, 1942); Louis L. Martz, *The Poetry of Meditation: A Study in English Religious Literature*, rev. ed. (New Haven: Yale University Press, 1962); as well as Barbara Keifer Lewalski, *Protestant Poetics and the Seventeenth-Century Religious Lyric* (Princeton: Princeton University Press,

Strangways is specific enough in his meditative writings to permit some comments upon the nexus of beliefs that sustains them as well as some observations upon the sources to which he resorted in order to fashion his religious impulses into literary forms. In matters of creed Strangways clearly followed the doctrine that the majority of English Protestants believed in varying degrees and with varying emphases. In the following prayer, Strangways writes of a grace that is unearned and exists as an inexplicable gift of God, given for faith and not works:

> O God
>> Thy Nature & thy propertie
>> Is to have mercie & forgive:
>> Then put away my sin, that I
>> May be receav'de to Grace, & Lyve.
>
>> O let me live & Grow in Grace
>> And let my hart soe cleave to thee
>> That always & in every place
>> Chryst may be all in all to me.
>
>> In my justification
>> Ther's nothing I myne owne can call;
>> Fayth work's itt in my hart alone
>> Soe Chryst to me is all in all.
>
>> In my Sanctification
>> Gods grace therin is Trewly free,
>> By his meere Grace tis only done,
>> Soe Chryst is all in all to me.

The poem concludes with a reiteration of the same doctrinal point, namely an invocation of the "consensus theology" of the post-Hooker, post-Synod of Dort English mainstream: grace is a free gift, justification is by faith alone, and Christ is the central object of worship.[90] He writes:

1979), especially chapter 5.

[90] Lewalski, *Protestant Poetics*, 13–20; Charles F. Allison, *The Rise of Moralism* (London: William Clowes and Sons, 1966), 186.

> In him shall all I doe be done
> And with his ayde performed be
> And soe I end as I begun
> My Chryst is all in all to me.
>
> The summe is this: Nothing but Chryst
> O make me heare when thou dost call
> And lett me not thy wyll resist
> Soe Chryst shalbe my All in All.
> per JS:
> (B.38–39)

We perceive at this poem's core an Augustinian apprehension of human depravity and, especially in the third and fourth stanzas, a recognition of the mystery of infused grace: "Ther's nothing I myne owne can call; / Fayth work's itt in my hart alone" (11–12). The implicit concerns with self-improvement and the maintenance of an individual's foundations of faith are quite characteristic of the broad Protestant consensus within which Strangways's conceptions of the self operated, and they formed the basis of Strangways's meditative practices, which were in turn quite typical for the period.[91] In his commonplace book, Strangways makes explicit references to Luis de Granada (1504–88) and Bishop Joseph Hall (1574–1656), both extremely popular figures in the development of meditative methods in England and writers whose techniques he followed, sometimes quite closely. Particularly Hall, who wrote meditations over a period of more than fifty years, "set a pattern for his generation, demonstrating both the directions Protestant meditation might profitably take and establishing a standard in style and thought."[92] Stylistically, Hall favored the same Ramist logic that Strangways found congenial, sometimes opposing his and other Protestant writers' Ramism against the stricter sequences and "exercises" of Catholic devotional writers.[93] But despite Hall's (and others') attempts to distinguish Protestant methods from those of continental Catholic writers, there is in fact at least as much common ground between traditions as there are significant differences. Certainly Strangways, who cites Granada and may also have

---

[91] Huntley, *Bishop Joseph Hall*, 3–4.

[92] Leonard D. Tourney, *Joseph Hall* (Boston: G.K. Hall, 1979), 83, 104. Hall's *The Arte of Divine Meditation* (1606), which Strangways seems to have used quite directly, went through ten editions by 1634: see Huntley, *Bishop Joseph Hall*, 59.

[93] Huntley, *Bishop Joseph Hall*, 6.

used Ignatian models alongside those of Hall's *Arte of Divine Meditation* (1606), appears to have cared very little for some of the distinctions Hall and other Protestant writers sometimes emphasized.[94]

"A Private Meditation" (B.46–47) can serve as a paradigmatic example of Strangways's obedience to certain important conventions and *topoi* of Protestant meditation. The poem asks us to imagine something like a dramatic scene, a technique recommended by several authors of devotional methods. The speaker begins by placing himself in a trial or examination, conducted as "an interior drama"[95] typical of the meditative tradition:

> If by my selfe, my selfe weare to be try'de
> I in my selfe can finde noe cause of pryde.
>
> For first I was conceav'de in beastly sin
> And like a beast I wallow still therin.
>
> Most graci'ous God be pleas'd in ev'ry part
> To Cure the plague of my corrupted hart.
>
> Next I was borne into the world in payne
> Wherin I toyle & labour all in vayne.
> (1–8)

The poem then proceeds to a systematic examination of the brevity and vanity of human life, describing, predictably, the horrors of death and physical decay, as well as the promise of grace that has the power to make inconsequential the inevitable effects of death. Among the other conventional elements prominent in this poem, we find Strangways focusing upon a limited, specific topic or scene as an object of meditation, as advised by a number of writers in the tradition. Hall, for example, urges the "bending of the mind upon some spiritual object through divers forms of discourse, until our thoughts come to an issue."[96] Though this particular poem does not follow the most extreme forms such advice could take, some meditative writers went even further in recommending a systematic "composition of

---

[94] Tourney, *Joseph Hall*, 91–92; Huntley, *Bishop Joseph Hall*, 3–4; and Martz, *Poetry of Meditation*, introduction and chapter 4.

[95] Martz, 330.

[96] *The Arte of Divine Meditation*, in Philip Wynter, ed., *The Works of the Right Reverend Joseph Hall, D.D.*, 10 vols. (Oxford: Oxford University Press, 1863), 6:46.

place": a deep, focused process of concentration upon or visualization of a scene as an initial step in structuring a meditation.[97] Strangways obeys convention by posing a problem for debate or reflection, followed by its resolution (he goes on to ask God to "Cure the plague" of the writer's "corrupted hart" and celebrate the creation of a "perfect hart" from its remains). Meditations sought to be dynamic, not static, as they lifted the author out of despair or a debilitating indifference. Moreover, the tradition typically dictated that the rational powers had necessarily to give way to the affective ones. As Hall puts it, through "a hearty and passionate wish," the soul "breaketh through a whole army of doubts, and fetcheth comfort from the well of life."[98] True to the conventions, in "A Private Meditation" what begins as a reasoned survey of human insignificance and bestiality concludes as a celebration of the affections: joy in the expectation of "sure hope, & a Savingsoule beleiffe" (28).

Despite its slightly inverted chronology, the process of birth, life, and death on which this poem is based is also entirely typical of the tradition. Not only did the more general aim of self-mortification encourage reflection upon the course of human life, but the authorities themselves spoke eloquently on the need to structure meditations upon the facts of conception, birth, life, death, and afterlife. Luis de Granada, to take but one example, speaks for a whole tradition in asserting that "our lyfe is no more, but as it were the shotinge of a sterre, that passeth at a trice."[99] His particular image for the frailty of humanity is in this case sidereal, but other authors found different ones. For example, Donne's metaphor in *The First Anniversary* is rather more organic (and somehow more memorable as well) in suggesting that the traditional stages of life are matter for self-mortification and that implicit in birth is the promise of death:

> We are born ruineous: poor mothers cry,
> That children come not right, nor orderly,
>
> Except they headlong come, and fall upon
> An ominous precipitation.
>
> (95–98)[100]

---

[97] Martz, *Poetry of Meditation*, 27–32.

[98] *The Arte of Divine Meditation*, in Wynter, *Works*, 6: 74, 77.

[99] Luis de Granada, *Of Prayer and Meditation* (1584), 342.

[100] John Donne, *The Complete English Poems*, ed. A.J. Smith (Harmondsworth: Penguin, 1971), 273.

Strangways's long meditation entitled "A Motive to Humilitie upon the Conciceration of what thou first was: 2^ly: of what thou now art: & 3^ly: what after death thou shalt be" (B.84–95) participates even more explicitly in the tradition of imagining life itself as a "motive" for humility. It begins

> Open myne eyes O Lord that I may see
> What thing my Body was, till form'd by thee:
> Next what itt is, whiles itt on Earth doth live
> United to the soule thou did'st me give.
> And lastly mind me what thing itt shalbe
> Whenas my soule departed is from me.
> In all these three such Basenes shalt thou find
> Thou wilt with Ease lett fall thy pryde of mind
> If with the Peacocke thou cast downe thyne Eyes
> To see from whence these three things doe arise.

It then enjoins the reader to "first consider from whence all men / Came," concluding that "the Earth from whence all Mortalls Came, / Gave them both their beginning & their name":

> To this End that thou may'st see with thyne eyes
> This Earth from whence thy Body did aryse.
> That when thou shouldest thy beginning find
> Thou may'st be trewly humbled in thy mind:
> Espeacially when thou shalt understand
> Thou Can'st in noe Case meritt at his hand.
> But to be Troad & Trampled on as Earth
> Wherof remember thou had'st thy first Birth.
> As oft as thou this Earth & Dust shalt see
> Concider they Awakeners are to thee,
> Which dayly doe to thy Remembrance bring
> That thy Beginning did from Basenes spring.
> And though they are both, Deafe & Dumbe, they Cry
> Thou hast noe Cause to beare thy selfe soe hie.
> And if their words thou wilt not dayne to heare
> Yet unto those, that God speakes give an eare
> Which unto thee, & to all men speake Lowde
> Why is vile Earth & Mouldring Ashes proud?
> (1–10, 16–28, 47–64)

The poem continues in this manner, surveying the stages of human life over nearly four hundred lines, closely following the traditions of Granada and others, and vividly conjuring images of a "picturesque disesteem for life."[101] It concludes metaphorically, arguing that the "foundations" of the human soul that are necessarily earth-bound (by the terms of his central image) must be laid "both Broad, & Deepe" to reach to heaven (373). Consistent with the genre, it too celebrates an affective triumph after a systematic consideration of human vainglory and divine magnanimity.

Likewise, the work called "Another Motive to Humilitie Upon Concideration Of these three Tymes" (B.97–111) considers the same three-part continuum of birth, life, and death. Unlike the first "Motive," however, this poem begins not with a prayer to God but with an address to an anonymous auditor, more suggestive of public address or disputation than private reflection or prayer:

> Sir I doe here present unto your veiw
> What by my reading I find to be trew
> Concerning Man: And ffirst you here shall see
> What thing man was before he came to be.
> Next what he is whiles his short life doth Last
> Then what he shalbe when his life is past.
> In these three tymes soe manie miseries
> Thou shalt find Lincke'd with Infirmities,
> That we had need of an Æternitie
> To summe them up exactly to your eye.
>
> (1–10)

Consistent with the rather more public voicing of this "Motive," Strangways links stages of this examination of human frailty with the imperative "Concider," which appears at strategic points throughout this long poem. As a verbal marker, the imperative serves essentially the function of Donne's "think" in *The Second Anniversary*: a device to delineate the well-defined movements in the poem but also a means of maintaining the fiction of a colloquy, one-sided though this one certainly is.

The two poems entitled "Of the Meditation of Death" and "A Meditation of Death" (B.115–20 and B.122–25) draw upon Hall's "A Meditation of Death: According to the Former Rules," which he provided as an illustration

---

[101] White, *English Devotional Literature*, 209. See the apt examples in Granada, *Of Prayer and Meditation*, 336–37.

of his recommended methods at the end of *The Art of Divine Meditation*. Here, too, we observe examples of the same "picturesque disesteem for life" but also multiple examples of the well-developed tradition of the *ars moriendi*. As a number of critics have shown, reflections upon death and the last things always amounted to instructions in good living, paradoxically an art of dying as an *ars vivendi*, and Strangways is fully in line with others of his age in this regard.[102]

Both poems participate in the *memento mori* tradition. They are surveys of the reasons that the contemplation of death must humble human beings, specifically how

> The Meditati'on of Our Dying day
> Is the most holesome & the safest way,
> That we into our saddest Thoughtes can take:
> For That alone our life doth perfect make.
> According to that of Saint Gregorie
> A perfect Lyfe thinkes alwayes how to Dye.
> "Of the Meditation of Death," (1–6, B.115)

Tonally, both poems employ the same hortatory voice that Strangways uses in the vast majority of his poems, whether explicitly meditative or not. At times, there seems to be more than a little of the spirit of Donne's sermons in passages such as the following, but the homiletic nature of Protestant devotional writing was so widely diffused and recycled that precise sources are in fact elusive:

> And therfore it is needfull we should have
> Some one who should Continually Engrave
> This lesson on our hartes: to make us know
> How in the way to LIVE WELL we may Goe.
> Now those that teach this art they are the Dead,
> The Church the Schoole is, wherin we are bredde.
> The Sepulchers & Graves, they are the chayres
> From whence we are best taught in these affaires:
> And therfore men them Monuments doe Call
> Because from thence we are admonished All

---

[102] O'Connor, *Art of Dying Well*, 191; Martz, *Poetry of Meditation*, 228; White, *English Devotional Literature*, 209; and see Helen Vendler, *The Poetry of George Herbert* (Cambridge: Harvard University Press, 1975), 165.

> As yesterday alloted was for me
> Soe may to morrow be assign'de for thee.
>   "A Meditation of Death," (25–36, B.122–23)

The various methods for structuring meditation available to Strangways, some of them highly programmatic, often reduce to elaborate schemes for giving form to two age-old central tropes in Christian thought, both of which we see in his meditative poems: an attack upon pride as the mother of all vices and a *contemptus mundi* sustained by a devout faith in eternal things. Both are subjects vigorously treated by the meditative writers of the period, and both are so integral to Strangways's worldview throughout the entire commonplace book that one could well argue that nearly everything he wrote constitutes some kind of meditation on final things, eternal truths, or questions of moral and political righteousness.

Since the published authorities on prayer and meditative writing were so detailed in their instructions and so widely available to readers, it is scarcely surprising that Strangways's efforts at poetic meditation follow conventions as thoroughly as they do. Indeed, even poets as complex and innovative as Donne and Herbert struggled to find room for innovation within the devotional sphere, comprised of what one critic of Herbert has called "the tried and true arguments which lead to foregone conclusions."[103] As with his historical poems and his poems of moral advice, these are works with, fundamentally, a practical purpose. In their narrowest sense, they must have been hedges against the threat of further adversity, which could arrive at any time and in many different forms: fines, sequestration, isolation, prosecution, and perhaps even death. In their broader cultural function, however, they were a means of making the abstractions or minutiae of theology applicable and tangible in a world that, to Strangways the prisoner, must have appeared entirely upside-down.

Versifications

The poems I have classified as "versifications" participate in a tradition of adapting, translating, and paraphrasing biblical writings that had been widely practiced in England since the early days of Protestantism. In the words of Lily B. Campbell, literary adaptation, particularly of the Psalms,

---

[103] Arnold Stein, *George Herbert's Lyrics* (Baltimore: Johns Hopkins Press, 1968), 156.

formed part of "a concerted movement to displace the new love poetry and newly popularized pagan literature by a poetry founded on the Bible."[104] Like many of the commonplace entries and the meditative poems discussed above, the versifications are spiritual exercises, forms of self-discipline intended to keep their author focused upon eternal promises rather than mundane tribulations. By the middle decades of the seventeenth century, such uses of biblical writings were a well-established part of a much larger Protestant imaginative and devotional tradition that also included meditative and devotional writing, hymnology, emblem literature, and pulpit rhetoric.[105]

Eloquently theorized in the previous century by Sir Philip Sidney in his *Apology for Poetry*, versification and paraphrase gained considerable impetus through the works of George Sandys and George Wither in the Jacobean period, but figures such as Thomas Sternhold, William Baldwin, Philip and Mary Sidney, Michael Drayton, Thomas Middleton, and John Donne had also experimented in the genre—to name only a very few.[106] Indeed, even King James paraphrased the Psalms, presumably as one of the "devout who sought consolation or a pathway to heaven by this means."[107] Bishop Hall, for whom Strangways obviously felt great regard, also practiced the technique.[108]

This tradition of versification and paraphrase partakes of the Calvinistic "consensus" of mainstream English theology after the Synod of Dort (1618–1619), in which the fundamental principles of unmerited election and irresistible grace shaped a popular theology perfectly suited to the sorts of free and personalized uses of the Bible that such a tradition naturally encourages.[109] Versifiers such as Strangways sought through their endeavors to bring the spiritual authority of the scriptures into the realm of practical or daily life, particularly in relation to the kinds of extreme affliction and suffering he faced.

Strangways's habit of precisely dating his poems proves very useful in noting some important distinctions between the biblical versifications

---

[104] Lily B. Campbell, *Divine Poetry and Drama in the Sixteenth Century* (London: Cambridge University Press, 1959), 54.

[105] Lewalski, *Protestant Poetics*, 10.

[106] Ibid., 32–36, and see chapter 2, passim; see also Campbell, *Divine Poetry and Drama*, chapters 7–8.

[107] Campbell, *Divine Poetry and Drama*, 54.

[108] Hall offered specific advice on biblical "metaphrasing" in *The Works of Joseph Hall B. of Norwich* (1647), 139.

[109] Lewalski, *Protestant Poetics*, 20.

written while he was incarcerated and those written in 1665, the year before his death. The first group draws upon a broader range of originals (Job 6, Proverbs 30, Isaiah 40, Micah 7, Matthew 25, and the apocryphal Wisdom of Solomon 4), than the latter group, which consists of versifications of the New Testament (Matthew 5–7 and the entire book of James), as well as fundamental statements of basic Christian creed (the Ten Commandments and The Apostles' Creed). The versifications written during incarceration, not surprisingly, focus upon biblical wisdom literature and upon writing for the afflicted, particularly in his selections from Job, Isaiah, and Micah. Collectively, the wisdom literature and "the poetical 'third part' of scripture"[110] were traditionally the most popular sources for versifiers and paraphrasers, and so in this respect, Strangways is quite conventional in his choices of texts for adaptation, especially in light of his general affinity for affliction literature.

What is perhaps more surprising is Strangways's choice of texts in 1665, nearly two decades after his release from the Tower. While Matthew 5–7, The Apostles' Creed, and The Ten Commandments fit comfortably and normally within a broad Christian consensus on matters of faith and basic doctrine, his decision to versify the whole of the Epistle of James defies easy explanation. Beginning with Martin Luther, Protestant theologians struggled with James's explicit emphasis on the efficacy of works, and as a consequence, the book's works-righteous theology tended to be mollified or marginalized among Protestant commentators. However, despite the traditional Protestant objections to James's theology, Strangways does nothing to soften or adapt his source, as, for example, in the second chapter:

> Shew thou thy fayth without thy workes to me
> And I my Fayth by my workes will shew thee.
>   . . . But doest thou o vayne man know
> That Fayth without good workes for Dead doth Goe.
>
> . . . .
>
> You see then that by fayth ther is not one
> Who without workes is justifyde alone.
> For as the Bodie without Breath is Dead
> Evne soe is ffayth wher noe Good workes are Bredde.
>   (143–48, 164–67, B.145–46)

---

[110] Ibid., 32.

The long work entitled "The Ten Commandments" (B.172–85) suggests a different set of questions. While the commandments themselves were not subject to the kinds of theological controversy that the Epistle of James was, there was a distinctly Protestant emphasis upon the commandments of the "second table" (i.e., Commandments 5–10, those concerning relations among human beings) over those of the first four, concerning human relations with God.[111] Strangways's rendering of the commandments, a looser and more personal adaptation than is his habit elsewhere among the versifications, appears quite consistent with this larger Protestant emphasis. What is particularly interesting, too, is that he allows himself the freedom to adapt more freely than he does elsewhere, personalizing the commandments in some revealing ways and, in the process, creating out of seventeen biblical verses a poem of over 350 lines. Like the moral advice poems, which incorporate concrete personal experience into their poetic structures, the Commandments of the second table offer certain insights into Strangways's understanding of the Decalogue and its relevance to his own age. Of the eighth commandment, he begins,

> Thou shalt not plunder, steale, purloyne
> Thy neighbours Cattle, goods, or Coyne:
> Nor in thy Trade shalt use Deceite
> Either in measure or in waite.
> And here it must be understood
> Thou mayst not sell bad ware for Good
> Nor for the buyer's ignorance
> Shalt thou thy selling price advance.
> For in good Sooth I doe thee Tell,
> Tis sinne Good ware to oversell.
> In word & Deed be Trew & Just,
> And doe not falsifie thy Trust.
> To thy poore brother freely Lend
> Who doth not his goods Lewdlie spend.
> Lend, & Looke not for anie Gayne
> But to receave thyne owne agayne.
> And he that borrowes must Repay
> The monie Lent him att his day.
> And if he Trewly keepe that Course

---

[111] McGee, *Godly Man*, 70.

> He may Commande his neighbours purse.
> Now if thy Neighbour be involv'de
> In a Great debte & is Resolv'de
> To sell his Land that debte to ffree
> And offers itt to sale to thee
> And if thou art inclyn'de to buy
> Worke not on his necessitie
> Nor studie him to over-wytt
> Att a low Rate to purchase it
> But give for itt what just & ffitt:
> And if thou art inforc'de to sell
> Make out thy Tytle fayre & well
> And all incumbrances discover
> That he that Runnes may Read them over.
> If in this Case thou thus shalt deale
> 'Twill very much advance thy weale
> For thou therby wilt quicklie find
> A Chapman fitted to thy Mynd
> Who will bring ready monie forth
> And Give thee for itt what tis worth.
>
> (213–51, B.180–81)

Some very obvious elements of the moral advice poem appear here: the literalism, pragmatism, and specificity which Strangways shows in his other works emerge in the biblical versifications, we should understand, as essential parts of any advice rendered to his fellow sufferers and fellow human beings. And indeed, the commandments of the second table are far longer and more detailed than those of the first for precisely this reason: they amount to practical advice wrapped in biblical authority, and in some ways they are among his most imaginative works.

Perhaps most surprising for readers trained in psychoanalytic theories of repression, however, is Strangways's rendering of the commandment against adultery:

> Nor with thy neighbour's wife shall Lye
> And soe Committ Adulterie.
> Nor in thy Lust shalt thou desyre
> Anothers wife to occupyre
> For in that Case itt is all one
> As if that Deed by thee were done
> Nor shalt thou make her an Addresse

44

> To Temp't her unto wantonnesse
> To winne her to give leave to thee
> Her secret parts to feele or see
> Nor yet to clappe her Lovely Hypps
> Nor wantenly to kisse her Lypps
> Nor shalt thou give her thy Consent
> To take with thee the like Content.
> If this of thee she shall desyre
> Spitt in her face & soe denie her.
> Lett not her naked hand once Touch
> Thy naked member, Tis to much.
> And never doe thou her admitt
> With her Bare Buttocks for to sitt
> On thy bare Belly, Tis unfitt
> ffor therby shee meanes to Tempt thee
> Her secret part may entred be.
> You know well if Two fall at Stryffe
> And one hath standing by his wife
> Who as they strive doth playnely see
> Her husband worsted much to be.
> And therupon she waxeth bold
> The others stones with hand to hold
> And 'though shee did that undertake
> Only for her deare husbands sake
> And of that Stryfe an end to make
> Yet God by his Law doth Commande
> That wyfe for that shall lose her hand.
>   (163–96)

An unusually graphic concreteness emerges in this long section, consistent with his attempt in the poem as a whole to render the abstractions of moral prohibition concrete and specific; but his descriptions are also explicit enough to appear voyeuristic or titillating, to suggest a tension between the detailed imagery that fills the lines, and his moral claim at the section's conclusion:

> I doe relate this passage here
> That all may Tremble & forbeare
> To take delight to feele or See
> Those parts which secrett kept should be,

> And doe it that they may therby
> Be made more rype for Leacherie.
>   (197–202)

It must be remembered, however, that Strangways took to heart the advice of guides to meditation such as Joseph Hall, who over and over advised practitioners of the technique to seek out vivid, precise images through which to explore moral abstractions such as human worthlessness or the decay of the body after the soul had departed. Hence, Strangways writes explicitly about adultery not out of prurience, but rather out of the same techniques that he uses in his meditative poems as a means of understanding his suffering and moral being.

Each section of "The Ten Commandements" concludes with a variable refrain, and the poem as a whole ends with one final supplication for grace which must lay to rest any misgivings that later generations of readers might harbor concerning his true purposes:

> Thy Mercyes lord to me Extend
> That I may not in this offend
> To this end Teache me I thee pray
> To know & keepe the good old way
> And gyde me therin soe that I
> May never Treade one steppe Awry
> But may with a most perfect will
> This law in Evry point fulfill.

> And now my Lord I humbly begge of thee
> Thow would'st be pleased to give unto me
> An awfull & a holy Reverence
> Of thyne omniscience & omnipresence
> And lett it worke soe powrefully on me
> That I from Henceforth may as fearfull be
> To Committ sinnes in secrett against thee
> As I would be to Committ openlie
> Great Crymes before an open Enimie.
>   Thus if I live, I trewly shall inheritt
>   The Benifitts of Chryst's soule-saving meritt.
>   (330–48)

Apart from the biblical adaptations, the manuscript also contains two versifications of works by Bishop Joseph Hall, whose considerable influence on Strangways's meditative poetry has already been discussed. In 1646 Strangways rendered Hall's prose meditation "The Free Prisoner: or the Comfort of Restraint" into rhymed couplets, announcing in his headnote that it was "translated by Sir John Strangways Knight . . . for his private Recreation and Meditation" (B.1). Hall had been a prisoner in the Tower between 30 December 1641 and 5 May 1642, some three-and-a-half years prior to the beginning of Strangways's incarceration.[112] The meditation contains precisely the sort of fortifying inspiration that Strangways no doubt sought from an author who, as he claims, was "lodg'd in the same chamber" that he himself occupied. Though Strangways generally follows Hall's original with fidelity and economy, he departs at some significant moments from his source, making the work more personally and topically his own. For example, he revises Hall's original images by taking directly from his own military and political experiences, adding such details as "underworking mynes" and the politically charged line, "The Tyme is Come, the Bishoppes now must downe" (48, 274; B.5, B.13).

Written, according to its headnote, "In Turri Londonensi" and occupying a position in the manuscript between the last poem dated by day and month (24 March 1648) and his reflection upon his brief imprisonment in 1655, Hall's "The Affliction of Israel" is the only other extra-biblical work Strangways versified. It is three-hundred-line meditation based upon Exodus 1 and, like "The Free Prisoner," is Bishop Hall's reflection upon the nature of affliction, the vicissitudes of the world, and the promise of divine redemption. As Hall puts it, "There is no certainty but in the favour of God, in whom can be no change; whose love is entailed upon a thousand generations."[113] The original bears out this message of hope, as does Strangways's verse adaptation, which stays generally quite close to its source.

The two versifications of Hall's writings signal, once again, the constant and abiding motive for all of Strangways's poetic endeavors in this manuscript: they are exercises in meditation and godly self-control, reflections upon the spiritual benefits of affliction, and the healing power of grace. Perhaps most of all, they are testaments to the Christian ideals of pious self-surrender to divine grace and constant resistance to the worldly forces that buffet the godly. Nearly all Strangways's verse (and also a good number of his commonplace entries) seek to articulate these ideals. The poems' power lies less in their originality or mastery of tone, perspective, or technique and

---

[112] A. Davenport, ed. *The Collected Poems of Joseph Hall, Bishop of Exeter and Norwich* (Liverpool: University Press, 1949), xxiv.

[113] Wynter, *Works*, 1:70.

more in their earnestness, their simplicity, and their directness. Like their author, they have a precise historical situation, but they also attempt to link that situation to the quintessentially Protestant problems of faith, to the challenges of endurance in the face of affliction, and to the promise of hope in the face of despair.

The Text

The text (Osborn Collection MS b.304 of the Beinecke Library, Yale University) contains writings from the period 1645–1665. As Strangways announces, it is "A collection of some Notes for my owne private use, gathered out of severall authors as they have bin read by me: JStrangways: wherof most in the Tower — 1645. During the Tyme of my sad imprysonment ther" (A.1).

The manuscript was purchased in 1981 by the Osborn Collection, from Hofmann and Freeman Booksellers of London, who acquired it from Beach Booksellers of Salisbury, Wiltshire. The manuscript contains no internal indications of who might have owned or kept it after Strangways's death; consequently, I have been unable to establish anything conclusive about its provenance prior to purchase by the Osborn Collection.[114] There is slight water damage to some edges, as well as the offset of an earlier binding on leaf B.1, but otherwise the leaves and new binding are in excellent condition. In gold lettering on the spine is written "Compos^s. [i.e., Compositions] in the Tower By Sir John Strangways 1647." Neither Strangways's date of 1645 nor the binder's label adequately describes the true contents, which in fact range from 1645 to 1665.

A particular feature of the manuscript is that the text is arranged in two sections, each inverted and beginning at the opposite end of the volume relative to the other — a relatively common arrangement sometimes called *tête-à-dos* or *relieures jumelles*. What I have called Section A consists of forty-seven leaves and contains numbered and unnumbered commonplace entries,

---

[114] There is, however, one record dating from about 1860, when it was still in the possession of the family. The present binding contains the very faint impression of (probably) an unrelated title, scarcely legible, which seems to read [He ?]odne Choir 1[8?]89, which may suggest a range of dates for its rebinding or sale. Of interest, too, are a commonplace book dating from 1600 and a ledger belonging to Sir John Strangways, dating from 1625, once contained in the same archive. The present manuscript may have been sold at auction in 1960. See the discussion in Keynes, "Lost Cartulary of Abbotsbury," 240–41.

generally in prose, arranged under a variety of headings, such as "Monies Raysed severall wayes never used in this Kingdome" and "The Severall Mottoes of the Severall Emperors ending with Ferdinand the second." Most of these, as discussed above, amount to highly topical self-vindications of Strangways's political and moral positions.

Forty-two blank leaves separate the commonplace entries from the verse (Section B). This second section contains 98 leaves and includes the poems and versifications I have described above. Because of this two-section arrangement, references in the Introduction and Commentary include a section and page number, *e. g.*, A.4 or B.12.

The manuscript measures 19.5 x 14 cm. It is written in a usually clear late secretary hand that becomes more compact and crabbed over time, especially in those poems from B.140 onward, which Strangways dates 1665. It is bound in a later, probably eighteenth-century, brown leather binding with some gold tooling. The leaves are uniform throughout, using paper with watermarks nearly identical to Churchill 469 (a French pot bearing the initials GRO and dated by Churchill to 1645) but also similar to Heawood 3627 (dated 1654 or later).[115]

Clearly, it would be desirable to say with certainty which paper Strangways actually used, for the first would suggest that he did in fact have the manuscript with him "During the Tyme of [his] sad imprysonment" in the late 1640s, while the later type would suggest that the entire manuscript is a copy dating from, most probably, the early or mid-1660s. Since the watermark appears to be much closer to Churchill's than to Heawood's example, and since the compositions do not seem to have been copied for presentation, it is my conclusion that Strangways composed into a blank book, which was once bound in vellum, at a time more or less contemporary with the compositions themselves, and much later bound in the present binding.

Moreover, I think it likely that he did have the commonplace book with him in the Tower during his incarceration: this is what he himself suggests in several places, and I have discovered no reason to doubt his assertions. I base this conclusion upon two additional points. First, the entire commonplace section seems not to have been recopied, and, in general, it is less carefully laid out than the verse section. There is comparatively little overwriting

---

[115] W. A. Churchill, *Watermarks in Paper in Holland, England, France, etc. in the XVII and XVIII Centuries and Their Interconnection* (Amsterdam: Menno Hertzberger & Co., 1935), and Edward Heawood, *Monumenta Chartae Papyraceae*, vol. 1 (Hilversum, Holland: The Paper Publications Society, 1850).

and relatively few cancelations; these characteristics are, as I take it, signs that the commonplace section was a repository of ideas, sometimes roughly laid out, and not a document written to be read by others. Most significant is the fact that his numbered series of entries is frequently interrupted by separate topics or categories, then taken up again; a re-copied version would, one presumes, have regularized this sometimes chaotic organizational scheme in such a way that these entries would run continuously from 1 to 370. Second, internal evidence indicates that he wrote some commonplace entries and poems during the time of his imprisonment, as corroborated by external records. The opening of the commonplace section refers to 11 January 1645/6, and most of the poems are similarly dated from the summer of 1646 through 24 March 1647/8.[116] One is dated 9 August 1645, a date which, if accurate, indicates that Strangways was composing verse during the ten-day siege of Sherborne Castle, where he was taken prisoner, while another was probably written in 1655 and refers to his much briefer incarceration at the time of Penruddock's Revolt. Within the verse miscellany section there is a marked difference in presentation between the first 66 poems and the last twelve. These twelve are particularly worked-over, in several cases showing multiple layers of revisions. Moreover, the hand is noticeably more crabbed, and the ink is different from that which appears in the first sixty-six poems. The fact that Strangways dates six of these poems to his eightieth year of age, 1665, demonstrates that he returned to this manuscript in the last years of his life. Furthermore, this practice of dating by year alone is at odds with his habit of dating his earlier poems more precisely, by day, month, and year.

Taken together, these facts persuade me that the leaves were indeed with him in the Tower. I believe the commonplace entries and most of the poems were written onto these leaves at this time, and that he returned to the manuscript in 1655, and again in 1665, in his eightieth year, to add a few poems, and perhaps also to revise the poems of the 1640s. It appears that he did not return to Section A in the same way.

Editorial Practices

My two guiding principles in preparing this edition are, first, to reproduce the text as written, with as few editorial interventions as possible, and, second, to present a text with as few unnecessary impediments for modern

---

[116] Throughout the Commentary to this edition, I will adopt the modern system of dating, using January 1 as the beginning of a new year.

readers as possible. As any editor will attest, these goals are frequently at cross-purposes. In order to achieve the one without forsaking the other I have had to make a number of compromises.

As a first principle, I have attempted to render the manuscript as it was written, including all matters of spelling, punctuation, and abbreviation. Wherever possible, I have also maintained headings, section groupings, indentations, and Strangways's original spatial arrangements in order to convey a sense of how the manuscript was originally arranged; where emendments serve the purpose of avoiding ambiguity or obscurity, I have made the necessary adjustments and recorded my changes in the Textual Notes.

I concur, however, with Michael Hunter's axiom that "the transfer of a text from manuscript to print entails an unavoidable degree of transformation" (as indeed it would have in the seventeenth century as well), and that "the production of an exact type facsimile of a manuscript document is . . . not a proper ambition, even were it feasible."[117] Hence I do not attempt a page-for-page transcription, nor do I intend anything approaching a "type facsimile." Instead, the page numbers inserted by an archivist and already employed by several scholars who have already cited the manuscript in print[118] are indicated in the right margin of the main text, within square brackets. References in the Commentary and Textual Notes are to the pagination of the present edition.

The following general exceptions to my first principle should, however, be noted:

- I have brought Strangways's i/j and u/v into conformity with modern usage, in both English and Latin. I have left other contemporary usages, such as the ff for F, as written.

- Strangways's signature, which appears as

has been rendered as "JS" or "JStrangways," and his dotted roman numeral "1" has been modernized as arabic: for example, ii7 appears as 117.

---

[117] Michael Hunter, "How to Edit a Seventeenth-Century Manuscript: Principles and Practice," *The Seventeenth Century* 10 (1995): 287.

[118] E.g., Russell, *Causes*; Smith, *Constitutional Royalism*; and Underdown, *A Free Born People.*

- I have not reproduced medial ligatures such as ſt (*st*), but I have retained the diagraphs *æ* and *œ*.

- I have silently separated some ambiguously spaced words not typically joined in Early-Modern usage and which seem incidental to meaning (e.g., "a prince" for *aprince*), but I have left deliberately joined words as written (e.g., *shalbe*).

- I have silently expanded common Early-Modern abbreviations, changing, for example, *w^{ch}* to *which*, *S^r* to *Sir*, and *y^t* to *yet* or *that*, according to context, as well as the various forms of the "tailed" *p* standing for *pro*, *per*, *pre*, and *par*, and the "tailed" *q*, standing for *que*. I have also silently expanded words employing the tilde, or tittle, used to indicate the presence of an omitted or doubled letter, as in *Londō* and *comitt*. I have left other less common abbreviations as written or have indicated in my textual notes where I did expand them.

- When I could be sure whether Strangways was abbreviating in Latin or in English, I have usually silently expanded the abbreviated names of the months, place-names, and the names of persons. When I could not be sure, or where they make up part of his system of legal citations, I have retained abbreviations as written or indicated any changes in my textual notes.

- I have not reproduced Strangways's occasional catch-words and running titles, nor incidental hyphens, nor stray marks, or emendations I judge to be insignificant to meaning. In the Textual Notes, however, I do describe all textual characteristics I judge to be significant.

- Strangways's capitalization often violates modern usage. Following my first principle of accurate transcription whenever feasible, I have retained his capitals as written where they are unambiguous. In deciding the status of ambiguous minuscules and majuscules, however, I have followed modern usage. In the interest of uniformity and clarity, I have also silently capitalized all beginnings of verse lines and new sections where needed and as dictated by context. These instances are so infrequent and so insignificant to meaning that no textual notes are required.

- Strangways used a style of punctuation that often includes the colon or two vertical bars (and sometimes the two in combination) to indicate terminal punctuation. I have retained his system as written, only occasionally silently adding final periods where I felt it necessary to do so. I have also regularized punctuation marks that appear in a series (i.e., converting a period to a colon within a series of propositions otherwise punctuated by colons). These instances are rare, and the emendations do not affect meaning.

- Strangways used double apostrophes (") to indicate both elisions and accentual, or stress, marks, and he did so in an idiosyncratic and sometimes inconsistent manner. As attractive as it is to leave this mark as written, I have decided to forego absolute fidelity to the manuscript in favor of greater readability, silently changing the double apostrophes to single and usually placing them where modern usage would dictate, whether to indicate contractions or to give accentual guidance. I have not, however, added accentual marks where the manuscript does not provide them, even if his metrics would occasionally benefit from such emendation.
- I have left his legal citations as written, though as a result they are nonstandard with respect to modern usage and perhaps somewhat more difficult to read in their original forms.

As indicated above in the section describing the text, this manuscript is generally free of heavy emendation, and I have, therefore, tried to limit editorial intervention to matters of importance. Interlined and deleted sections are described only in my Textual Notes, thus allowing the transcription to flow without unnecessary interruption. My object in preparing this edition has been to produce a readable "clear text"[119] transcription so that the majority of readers who, I believe, are interested primarily in its content can read without unnecessary distractions. I have, however, provided Textual Notes, keyed to the main text, to describe the manuscript's particulars and explain my editorial interventions.

---

[119] See Hunter, "Seventeenth-Century Manuscript," 296–97, citing the approach advocated by Fredson Bowers in his "Transcription of Manuscripts: the Record of Variants," *Studies in Bibliography* 29 (1976): 212–64.

Section A:

Commonplaces

Missel

A Collection of some notes for my owne private
use, gathered out of severall authors as they have
bin read by me, JStrangways: wherof most in the
Tower — 1645. during the Tyme of my sad impry-
sonment ther: | | .

Quid fugiam video: sed quid Sequar non habeo

I have not striven against my hart to make a syde:
    nor hath my Conscience bin oppressed by affection: | | .
                    JStrangways
                      1645.

    Give me O lord hands to my worke: & give
    me worke fitt for my hands. | | .
        Studium partium est Maximà pars Studiorum:
    Non semper in uno gradu; sed in una via:
        Contrarients: Rotul: Contrariensium.
    Animalia Gregalia non sunt Nociva:
    Animalia Solivaga semper Nociva.
        minerva quasi nervos minuens. | | .
    Refellere sine pertinatia: et Refelli sine Iracundia:
Ther is noe pleasing thing in the world that hath soe much
    joy in the welcome, as it hath sorrow in the farwell
In Cases of Necessitie, God regards not the
    posture of the Body, but the affections of the soule. | | .

    Fayth Can remove Mountaynes: But the
    Mountaynes that are Raysed upon fayth are
    unremoveable. | | .

50: Edw: 3: Bonum parliamentum: 6to H: 4: at Coventry
Indoctum parliamentum: Auferat oblivio si potest
Vide et perlege 4 H: 8: cap: 8.   utcunque silentium Tegat
    præcipitatio est Noverca justitiæ: | | .

    A Short prayer before our going to heare the word preached

Most Glorious & most Gracious God I pray thee prepare my hart
    for the hearing of thy holy word, & sanctifie me to this worke

55

& blesse me in itt: Remove my sinnes, & send downe thy spiritt into my hart which may enable me to this great service: Lord blesse the preacher in the deliverie of his sacred message: Direct his tongue to the meeting with my necessityes: Be pleased good God to free my hart from all præjudices & distractions; & keep off from me all Temptations which may hinder the good entertainment & successe of thy blessed word: ffinallie make me Trewly Teachable, & this thyne ordinance the pow're of god to my salvation, through Jesus Chryst our Lord.   Amen:
Soe prayeth   JStrangways   10
11° Januarii 1645.

1:    when a Heathen man prayed unto Juppiter to save him from   [3]
his Enymies, one that overheard him would needs mend itt, with a more needfull prayer: That Juppiter would save him from his freinds: he thought they might doe him more hurt, because he Trusted them. But as for his Enimies, he could looke to him selfe well enough, for receaving harme from them: But the chrystians prayer is more needfull, & to be pressed with greater importunitie, That God would save us from our selves, & not give us up into our owne hands. | |.   20

2:    All the Creatures of God are lawfull for us to use: Soe that it is against Chrystian liberty, either to charge the use of them with sin, or to place Holynes in the abstayning from them: vide Rom: 14:20: & also verse the 14: vide 1 Cor: 10:15 & 27: & verse 23: Tit: 1:15: from all which testimonies we may conclude ther is no impuritie in anie of the Creatures, but that we may with Securitie of conscience freely use them without Sin: But if we use them doubtingly against Conscience; or Indiscreetly against Charitie: or inordinately against Sobrietie, they become indeed in Such Cases sinfull unto us. But that is   30
through our default, not theirs, who sinfully abuse that which we might lawfully use: And that abuse of ours neither defyleth the things themselves, nor ought to prejudice the libertie of another man that may use them well: See Rom: 14:14: 1 Cor: 10:29:30:

3:    We ought as well to Concider what in chrystian Sobrietie is   [4]
meet for us to doe, as what in chrystyan libertie may be done: | |.

56

4:    The Determination of Superiours may & ought to restrayne us in the outward exercise of our chrystian liberty: 1 Pet: 2:13: & ver: 15: & 16: Rom: 13: ver: 1.4.5

5:    Ther are Required to Trew Thankfulnes – 3 – things: 1: Recognition: 2: Estimation: 3: Retribution: He that hath receaved a Benefitt from another, he ought first faythfully to acknowledge itt: 2^{ly} To valew itt: 3^{ly} To Endeavour really to requite itt: And who soe fayleth in anie of these, is (soe far as he fayleth) unthankfull more or Lesse.

              Ut desunt vires tamen est Laudanda voluntas

                Hac, ego Contentos auguror esse deos.

pryde: Envye: Epicurysme: Carefullnes: Security: are the – 5 – Letts & impediments of Thankfullnes. | |.

6:    If for every Idle word spoken: Then by the same proportion for every pennie Idlely spent we shalbe accomptable to god att the day of judgment. | |.

7:    ffor the effectuall furtherance of our Self-dejection itt wilbe requisite to bend our eyes upon a threefold object: 1: to Looke Inward to our selves: 2^{ly} upward to Heaven: 3^{ly} Downe-wards to Hell. | |.

8:    That which David sayd in Hast Psal: 116:11: Saint Paule sayth in full deliberation: Every man is a Lyer: Rom: 3:4:

9:    Qui agit contra conscientiam, qua credit deum aliquid prohibuisse, licet erret, contemnit deum. | |. quod fit contra conscientiam ædificat ad Gehennam: An erronious conscience bindeth thus farre, that a man cannot goe against itt & be guiltlesse: because his practise should then Run crosse to his judgment; & soe the thing done, could not be of ffayth: | |

10:    Mentem in Melius Mutare, non Levitas est sed virtus: I desire to know what is Right, & to Doe itt: | |.

11:    I am BETTER then thou art, rayses the furious and bloody Contestations for præcedency: I am HOLYER then thou art, causes a contemptuous seperation from Companie better perhaps then ourselves: I am WYSER then thou art, is guiltie of all the irregular Opinions that the world is disquieted withall. | |.

12:    Itt was a smart answeare which a witty & learned minister of the Reformed churches of Paris, gave to a Lady of Suspected chastitie, & now revolted, when she pretended the hardnes of the Scripture: why, sayd he, Madame what can be more playne then — Thou shall not Committ Adultery. | |.

13: Paulus Tertius Moriturus, dixisse fertur se iam experturum
veritatem trium quæstionum, de quibus in tota vita dubitas-
set: 1: an animæ sint immortales: 2: an sit infernus: 3: an sit
deus. | |.

14: If you Imagine ther is noe other life but this, then you condemne   [6]
not only the wisest of men of folly: but the comforts, & the
Graces, & the Threates & the promises & the Commaunds, &
directions of god, of Falshood: and that Atheisticall Soule, that
dares imagine the god of Trewth to be a Lyer, shall find that   10
god almightie will give him his portion with Lyers & unbe-
leevers for Ever, in the lake that burneth with fyre & Brym-
stone: | |. Tis a principall of immortalitie, that maketh man to
dispute, whither the soule be immortall: all pietie is founded
in the thoughts of immortality: And it is observed amongst all
the philosophers, that those destroyed all Religion, that held
the soule to be Mortall:

15: 1 Understanding: 2 Will: 3 Memory: in the Soule: 1 Knowledge: 2: Righteousnes: 3: Holines: is the Image of God:

16: Germanorum vivere est Bibere: whence it is that they abound   20
in Brewers; having 777 of the Trade: 40: Bakers: one Lawyer:
one physition in the towne of Hamburge: Heylings Geogra:
pag: 256 & 260.
Lucus: a non Lucendo: mons: a non movendo: Bellum: quasi
minimè bellum. | |.

17: The sun is — 160 — Tymes greater then the Earth (as Astronomers resolve) though rather upon probable conjecture, then
certayne demonstration: the Moone is — 39 — tymes lesse then
the Earth: Some of the fixed starres (as Astronomers affirme)
are — 107 — tymes greater then the Earth: 30

18: Plynie in his Naturall History: lib: 32: Cap: 11: writes that
some whales are — 600 — foot long: & — 360 — foot broad. | |.

19: Sinceritie & Safetie meet alwayes togither   [7]

20: pecora: signifyes great Cattle: pecudes: Small Cattle: Jumentum quasi juvamentum:

21: Betweene the Creation & the giving of the law in Mount Sinay
weare — 2544 — yeares: & 888 — yeares from the Flood to the
rayning of Manna: & the flood was sent upon the world in the
yeare of the age of the world 1656: | |.

22: God Speaketh of himselfe plurally by the word |US| fowre tymes in Scripture: Gen: 1:16: Gen: 3:22: Gen: 11:7 & Esay: 6:8:

23: Note the Impartiallitie of Scripture Storie, which concealeth not the fowlest faults of those it prayseth most: as we may observe in the Storie of Noah: Gen: 9:22: of Abraham: Gen 12:19: & 20:2: Of Moses: Exod 4:1: 10:12: Num: 20:24: Deut: 32:51: Of David: 1 Sam: 11: 2 Sam: 24:10: Of Job: 3:3: &c: of Jeremy 20:14: of Peter: Matt: 26:70:72:74:

24: Noah was noe Drunkard (for one action is not enough to give a denomination to the actor, & he was drunke but once): we may hence be warned against trusting a drunkard with a secrett: for a drunkard is as like to tell all when he is a wake, as to shew all when he is a sleepe. | |. ´

25: Quære: whither Constantines Resolution, To Cast his Robe over an Adulterous Bishop, if he tooke him in the evill act as Theodoret writes of him: Eccles Hist: lib: 1°: Cap: 11°: did not fayle in justice, as well as abound in mercy. | |.

26: Beautie is a double Snare: 1: To them that have itt: 2: to them that love itt:

27: Some Ancient wryters have given the Measure of the height of the Tower of Babell to be — 4000 — paces:

28: Judea contayneth in Length from Dan to Beersheeba but — 160 — miles: & in breadth from Joppa to Beth-lem but — 46: — myles. | |.

29: Thou shalt not Take the name of the Lord thy God in vayne |1| Needleslie; without just & waightie occasions: or Rashly: without Heed & Reverence: or Falslie without Trewth. | |.

30: It is a good Rule in all Gods Commaunds: To concider not soe much what it is, as who it is, that biddeth or forbiddeth anie thing: And it is not a light matter, or little danger to disobey god; Though in a thing (in itt selfe) of noe great waight. | |.

31: It is in gods power to give his people favour in the eyes of Enimyes: therfore when we are to seeke or to sue to any by petition, or other ways: It is good first to present our request unto god, to make us gracious in the eyes of Men: vide: Nehem: 2:4:5: Gen: 33:4: Prov: 16:7: Exod: 3:21: and 11:3:

32: Great mens sinnes are dangerous not only to them-selves but to others that belong unto them: It is not safe to dwell in the howse with such as are wicked: Psal: 101:6: 7:

33: The End of Affliction is to humble our selves with Trew repentance under the hand of God: & soe it is a mercy to be
afflicted. | |.

34: Not only Ingratitude, but too little gratefullnes is a great fault
——2 Chron: 32:25:

35: To bring errors to their first: is to see their Last: Returne, returne, & thinke itt noe shame to have erred: just shame to
continue erringe: Blessed be the amending hand. | |.

36: Eximia est virtus præstare silentia rebus at Contrà est gravior
Culpa tacenda loqui:

37: Dum singuli pugnant, universi vincuntur: nec aliud adversus
validissimas gentes pro nobis utilius, quàm quod in Commu-
ne non consulunt: Tacitus in vita Agricolæ. | |.

38: 9no Edw: 3: when a motion was made for a subsedy to be
granted of a new kind: The Commons answeared; That they
would have conference with those of their severall Countryes
& Places, which had put them in Trust, before that they Treated of any such matter:
Sepe viatorem nova, non vetus orbita fallit.

39: Rot: Par: 11: R: 2: Noe subsedy before the end of the parlia-
ment: because it is to accompanie the pardon. | |.
Auferat oblivio si potest, si non utcunque silentium tegat. | |.

40: These are — 4 — propertyes of a good Counsailor: 1°: parcus
sui: 2: non Cupidus rei alieni; nihil enim ei turpe, cui nihil
satis: 3: avarus rei-publicæ: 4: Super omnia sit expertus:

41: 5to H: 4: An act of Parliament for Beacons and watching of
them: & 8° Eliz: 13° by which if not able to pay the penaltie,
for taking or cutting downe of the same, the partie is Out-
lawed ipso facto to all constructions & purposes. | |.

42: Rot: Parl: 2. R: 2: num: 18: The high Court of Parliament re-
leiveth but such as cannot have remedy but in parliament:
Nunquam recurritur ad extraordinarium sed ubi deficit
ordinarium. | |.

43: Non semper in uno gradu, sed in una via. | |.
Cum Confitente melius est Agendum. | |.

44: Vide et perlege: 4to: H: 8: Cap: 8:

45: Nuncie sis verax, Tacitus, Celer, atque Fidelis
Fœderis orator, Pacis via, Terminus iræ;
Semen Amicitiæ Belli fuga, Litibus hostis. | |.

46: Constable or Cunstable, anciently written Cuning-stable is
Compounded of two Saxon words: videlicet Cuning: per-
contractionem, King; & Stable |1| Columen: quasi columen
regis. | |. præcipitatio est noverca justitiæ. | |.

47: Cronologers accompt itt to be — 130 — yeares from the Creation, to the tyme that Cayn slew his brother Abel.

48: ffrom the name of Tubal-Cayn, as sundry Comentators ob-
serve, might the name |Vulcan| the heathen god of Smyths be
taken: as the name Jove, from Jehovah. | |.

49: Budæus Reports: A custome of the Heathens who in Tyme of
infectious diseases or publique Calamitie, sacryficed certayne
men to their gods, for the removing those evills that weare
upon them: & upon these men they lay the execrations of the
people, as they had bin the causes of all their misery. | |.

50: Trewth & Falshood: Good & evill are at such a distance, as by
the same principle a man cannot apply himselfe to either
syde: But as for Honour, & Dishonour; poverty or Riches: Liberty or Restraint; they are at noe such distance; but that the
same Grace may apply itt selfe, this way, or that way, as occasion serves;

51: We Reade of that Grace |HOPE| somtymes itt is called a hel-
met, somtymes an Anchor: If you be at Land, & meet with
enimyes; Hope is your Helmet: If at sea, & meet with Stormes,
Hope is your Anchor. Lyke Myrtilus his shield, which after
the use he had of it in the feilde having it with him at sea, &
suffering ship-wrack, it served him for a Boate to waft him to
Shoare. | |.

52: Granatensis reports of one Eucrytus, who being asked whither
he had rather be Crœssus or Socrates: he answeared, while he
lived Crœssus: when he dyed Socrates:

53: When Marcus Curio was tould, if he would please Dyonisius
he needed not feed upon Turnepps: he answeared him that
told him soe: If he could but bring himselfe to feed upon Tur-
nepps, he need not please Dyonisius. | |.

54: That which is Reported of Sir Thomas More who was Lord
Chancelor of England manie yeares, was much to his honour:
That when he dyed, he left his heires not above — 25^{li} — per
annum more then the inheritance of his father left him. | |.

55: You would be loath to choose a wife by the painting of her face. It would be your folly to judge of her Complexion according to her paint: Certainly it is as good an argument to prove, the goodnes of the Constitution of her body: as Honors & Riches are to prove the good Condition of any man before god: These things are blessings: but they are Blessings of the left Hand. They are outward blessings: If they be good to you, it must be from some goodnes in you, to use them for good. | |.

56: When Zeno the phylosopher reproved one for immoderate feasting he answeared, he spent of his owne & had enough: Zeno replyed If your Cooke should put — 2 — or — 3 — handfulls of Salt into your meat more then was fitt, & should say he had salt enough by him that Cost nothing, would this be a good answeare?

57: It is a harder Matter to know how to abound, then to know how to want. The warme beames of the Sun, getts the Travellers cloake sooner from him then the wind & stormes doe: Manna could endure the heat of the fyre, but it melted before the sun: Flyes come Thickest to sweet things: Soe Beelzebub which signifyes the god of Flyes, the prince of Divills, loves most to be amongst men, who doe most abound. Ratts, & Mice come to full Barnes, rather then to emptie places: Soe the vermin of Temptations doe more haunt abundance then want: Lay Rattesbane in the window, & the chyld is in greater danger, then if poyson, weare mixed with Aloes:

Difficile est esse in Honore, sine Timore: vide: Hos: 13:6:

58: The Abuse of mercy is the greatest Aggravation of a mans sin: Deut: 32:6: 2: Sam: 12:8: Nehem: 9:25:26: Magnæ fælicitatis est a fælicitate non vinci: we all Complayne much, that in these tymes we cannot receave our Rents, they weare never soe ill payd as now they are: But let us call our selves to accompt how well we pay our Rents to the Lord, of whom we hold all we have. Nulla infælicitas frangit, quem nulla fælicitas corrumpit: Let god be remembred with your goods, & he will remember you for good.

59: If we weare got up to heaven, the Earth would seeme as little to us, as now we being upon Earth the starres seeme to be.

60: In good Things he that speaketh a word, should make it good by his deed: And in evill he that speaketh ill, hath a mind to doe as ill as he speaketh. | |.

61: The way to perfection, is soe to live with men, as to concider god a looker on for all a man doth: & soe to Converse with god, as if men weare spectators of his most private actions. | |.

62: We Reade That Cato the famous Censor was father of a chylde at—80—yeares of age: & King Massanissa at—86—yeares: & that one woman bare a chyld at—60—& another at—80—yeares of age: Plyn: Nat: Hist: lib: 7: cap: 14.

63: When manie are vehemently bent against one, smooth words must serve in steed of Rough resistance: Communitie in Consent is noe argument of a good Cause. 2: Tim: 2:25.

64: Drunkennes drownes both the understanding, the sence, and the Conscience.

65: Restitution of that which is unlawfully taken must be made, before sin be remitted, or punishment removed: Gen: 20:7.

66: When a man is in his declyning age, he must measure his life rather by the Inch of dayes; then by the Ell of yeares. | |.

67: A Godly mans prayer is a Soveraigne Cure for the Kings Evill 1 King: 13:6: wherby the poorest Chrystian may gratifie the greatest: vide the same place. | |.

68: In waightie matters only an Oath is to be taken; as for Ratification of Covenants, & promises of importance: as Gen: 24:5: Gen: 32:53: For removevall of Suspicion: Num: 5:25: Exod: 22:11: For Stinting of Stryfe: Heb: 6:16: For Security of Life: 1: Sam: 30:15:

69: Sighes & Groanes that Cannot be uttered, are the best Oratory with almightie God: & this may be a great Comfort to those whose affections, are better then their expressions: Rom: 8:26:

70: The uncertainty of the day of death, should make us wise to order the tyme of life with a double providence: The one for others in this world: The other for our selves in the next: & soe to sett our selves in present expectation of our parting, or our Masters Comming. | |.

71: Anger is a short madnes: Envye a Long one. | |.

72: The Crosses of this world should make us foreCast for a better Country, the heavenly Jerusalem: & to be willing to remove from Mesheck & the Tente of Kedar Psal: 120:5: the habitation of ungodly men, to enjoy better Companie, in a better place: Heb: 11:10:

73: The Easiest præcept in all the Scripture is that of Paule to the

Ephes: | Be Angry |: And the hardest prohibition that which is joyned with itt: | SINNE NOT | & never more hard for a man to forbeare sin, then when he doth not forbeare Anger: we must not chyde too lowde nor with a sharper accent of Rebuke, then the Cause will beare, & soe fall upon Reproaches, in steed of free Reprooffes. | |.

74: Comminations of Misery, doe not exclude mens Carefull endeavors, either to avoyde or qualifye itt, that it may be tollerable. | |.

75: It was the manner of the Easterne Countryes to bring all [14] 10 mariageable maydes into a publique veiw: & such as wear beautifull, weare bought by those that would give most for them: & the monie payd for them was given in mariage with those that weare not soe amiable as to be desyred meerly for their owne sakes: Soe they made provision for a numerous encrease, that none might be barren by perpetuall virginitie, whether by voluntary resolution, or upon necessity.

76: Cursed be their Anger Gen: 49:7: He Curseth not their persons, but their wrath: we must rather pray against the wickednes of the persons; then against the persons of the wicked: as 20 David pray'd not against the person of Achitophell (as that he might Come to nought, & hang himselfe as he did) but that god would turne his Councell into foolishnes: 2 Sam: 15:31.

77: The Encrease in the Land of Egipt was Commonly according to the proportion of Nylus overflowing: If it overflowed but — 12 — Cubitts deepe, itt was like to be a famine if — 13 — a scarcitie; if — 14 — a Competencie: if — 15 — a Securitye: If — 16: a plentie: Plyn: nat: hist: Lib: 5: cap: 9.

78: Happie is he that hath soe lived, that he can either welcome death as a freind, or defye itt as an enemie. | |. aut pœniten- 30 dum, aut pereundum.

79: Concider in all thy actions these three things: 1: an Liceat 2: an deceat: 3: an expediat. | |.

80: In vayne doth he fly whom god pursues: Ther is noe way to fly from his judgments: but to fly to his mercy by Repenting. | |.

81: Delayed Thankfullnes is not worthy of Acceptation. | |.

82: Sin doth ill in the Eye: but worse in the Tongue: for it can [15] never be blazoned without uncharitablenes; seldome without infection. | |.

83: Noe bond must Tye us to the danger of Infection. | | .

84: Ther is nothing soe miserable as to dwell under the expectation of a great evill: | | .

85: To punish above the offence, is noe lesse injustice, then to offend & to execute Rigor upon a submisse offender, is more mercilesse then just. | | .

86: Good parents have greiffe enough (though they sustayne noe blame) for their childrens sinnes. | | .

87: Afflictions would not be soe heavye if they did not lay us open to uncharitable censures & Conceiptes. | | .

88: He that wilbe safe from the acts of Evill, must wisely avoyde the occasions. | | .

89: Prosperitie doth make us very easily forgett both the deservings & Miseryes of others. | | .

90: Serving & suffering are the best Tutors to Goverment. | | .

91: Ther is noe Sin whose harbour is more unsafe, then that of Malice. | | .

92: Tis noe Excuse for Evill to say I was bidden. | | .

93: Ther Can be noe greater Argument of an ill Cause, then a bloody persecution; wheras Trewth upholdeth it selfe by mildnes, & is promoted by patience. | | .

94: It is a dangerous signe of an ill hart, to feele gods yoke heavie. | | .

95: Doe what May be is tollerable: But doe what cannot be is Crewell. | | .

96: Noe Sugar can bereave a pill of his bitternes. | | .

97: Lawfull policies have from God, both Lyberty in the use, & blessing in the successe: Religion allowing us as much of the serpent as of the Dove. | | .

98: Oppressions may not be righted by vyolence but by Law: The redresse of Evill by a person unwarranted is Evill.

99: The Morall law is Commaunded in both Testaments to be observed: in the old for feare of God: in the new, for the love of God. | | .

100: The sinne of Adultery & Ravishment was before the Law, detested & forbidden: as appeareth by that Revenge taken for the forcing of Dynah: & by the judgment that Judah gave against Tamar, that she should be burnt: & by the Repentance of Pharaoth & Abimelech against whom this sentence was pronounced: Thou art but dead, because of the woman which thou hast taken, for she is a mans wife. | |.

101: Data est Lex quæ non sanaret, sed quæ ægrotantes probaret: The law was given not to helpe, but to discover sicknes: Data est lex ut se homo inveniret, non ut morbus sanaretur, sed ut medicus quæreretur: The law was given that man might find & know his owne imperfection: not that his disease was therby holpen: but that he might then seeke out the physition. | |.

102: Thou shalt doe noe murther: That is Thou shalt not doe the acts following the affections of Hatred. | |.

103: Men from whom God hath withdrawne his Grace, doe always follow those Councells which Cary them to their owne destruction: | |.
Quos perdere vult Jupiter, hos dementat | |.

104: Wher gods warrant will not protect us: it is good for the heeles to supply the place of the Tongue. | |.

105: The Contempt of honest Callings in those which are well borne argues pryde without witt: | |.

106: He hath made an ill use of Mercyes, that hath not learned to be Content with his corrections. | |.

107: Soe must we take our leave of Afflictions, that we reserve a lodging for them, & Expect their returne. | |.

108: Ther can be noe more forceable motive to patience, then the acknowledgement of a devyne hand that strikes us. | |.

109: Bona est substantia, si non sit peccatum in conscientia. Ecclesiasticus: 13:25:

110: He is Rich that wants not Bread: victus et vestitus divitiæ Chrystianorum. | |.

111: He that makes hast to be rich shall not be innocent: & Therfore keepe the beaten Roade, of Honesty: Justice: Charity: & Trewth:

112: Ther are two Maximes that doe usually misleade all the world over: The one is: Res valet quanti vendi potest: The other: Caveat emptor: | | Ther are — 4 — sorts of prizes: 1. Low. 2. meane. 3. Rigorous. 4: Excessive. The last save one is a violation of Justice: The Last differs nought from Theft; but that it is honested by a faire Cozenage. | |.

113: If we wilbe provident Travellers, lett us make over our monies heare, to receave it by Exchange in the world to Come. | |.

114: If you wilbe wise merchants & Thriftie; part with that you   [18]
     cannot keepe; that you may gaine that you cannot Lose. | |.
115: We have jus ad Rem, non dominium in Rem. | |.
116: A non scripto ad factum: a non facto ad non Debitum, non
     valet argumentum. | |.
117: Rerum ordo confunditur, si unicuique jurisdictio non serve-
     tur: as without order all things are but a besome unbound: Soe
     without unitie but Arena sine Calce, Sand without Lyme.
118: Wyse men must Care not only to deserve well, but to heare
     well, & to wipe off, not only Crymes but Censures. | |.   10
119: Every judge should have these propertyes of the Elephant:
     ffirst he hath noe Gall: 2^{ly} he is inflexible & cannot bow: 3^{ly} he
     is of most Ripe and perfect memory. | |.
120: Six Causes of the encrease of Suites: 1. peace is the mother of
     plenty: 2. plentie is the nurse of Suites: 3. monasteryes dis-
     solved: 4. Informers. 5. Concealers. 6. Atturneys. — prius vitiis
     Laboravimus, nunc Legibus. | |.
121: As the north Starre is the most fixed director of the Seaman to
     his desyred port: Soe is the Law of God the guider & Con-
     ductor of all in generall to the Haven of Eternall life. | |.   20
122: A Just Law is like a hart without affection: an eye without
     Lust: A mind without passion: A Treasurer that keepeth for
     every man what he hath: & distributeth to every man what he
     ought to have. | |.
123: Legalia justa, sunt factiva, et Conservativa fælicitatis: because
     by them we are directed ad vitam quietam, yea ad vitam
     æternam:
124: Lex a Legendo: vel a Ligando: Leges quia lectæ et ad populum   [19]
     latæ: for after Lawes weare written and published, all men
     might read them, & behold them, wherunto they weare   30
     bound: & to this agreeth the other Etymologie: a Ligando. | |.
125: Imperium Legis, Imperium dei: The Hebrewes call the Law
     |Thorah| of Teaching, because therby every man is taught his
     duty both to God & Man. The Greeks |Nomos| of distribu-
     ting; because it distributeth to every man his dew: Lex est vitæ
     Regula præcipiens quæ sunt sequenda, et quæ fugienda. | |.
126: Jus hath reference to Men: ffas to God: fas Lex divina: Jus Lex
     humana: To goe over another mans feild is permitted by Gods
     law: not by mans: & therfore in a thing out of Controversie we

use to say: Fas et jura sinunt: God & Men permitt itt. | | .

127: Jus-jurandum came a Jovis-jurandum, in which sence the scripture calls it Juramentum Jehovæ: Justus a jure, et justitia a justo: The right gives name to the righteous: & justice takes her name from the just. | | .

128: To love god by whom we are: And to doe the same justice unto all men, which we desyre should be done to us is an effect of the purest reason: In arce altissima rationis quies habitat In whose highest Turretts the quiett of Conscience hath made her resting place. | | .

129: Nil Turpe Committas, neque coram aliis, neque Tecum; maximè omnium verere teipsum.

130: The acts of Right Reason, are the acts of vertue: & in the breach of the rules of this reason man is least excusable as being a reasonable Creature: for all things else both Sensitive, Growing, & Inannimate, obey the law which God imposed on them at their first Creation. | | .

131: Providence is devided into memorie: Knowledge: & Care: memorie of the past: knowledge of the present: & care of the future: And we our selves doe accompt such a man for provident, as remembering things past, & observing things present, can by judgment, & comparing the one with the other, provide for the future & tymes succeeding. | | .

132: Qui in factis dei rationem non videt, infirmitatem suam conciderans cur non videat, rationem videt. | | .

133: Whosoever shall tell anie great Man, or Magistrate, That he is not Just: The Generall of an Army that he is not valiant: & Great Ladyes that they are not fayre: Shall never be made a Councellor, a Captaine, or a Courtyer. | | .

134: Dum furor in Cursu est currenti Cede furori: He is the author of his owne Miserie that strives in vayne against the Nature of the Tyme wherin he liveth. | | .

135: Noe Freind is soe Commodious in some Cases as an adversarie. | | .

136: Concider not only what god threateneth, but Concider withall why he Threateneth; It is that you may Repent: & withall how he Threateneth; It is unlesse you Repent: He shooteth out his arrowes even bitter words; but as Jonathans arrowes for warning not for destruction. | | .

137: Patience will beare much; mercy for beare much; But being
scorned, & provoked, & dared, patience it selfe turneth furious, & mercy itt selfe Cruell: Læsa patientia sæpius fit furor:
Dividat hæc signis, faciunt discreta, venenum
Antidotum fieri et qui sociata bibet.

138: Take Mercy without Trewth, as a cold poyson itt benummeth   [21]
us, & maketh us stupid with Carelesse Securitie: Take Trewth
without Mercie, as a hott poyson it scaldeth us, & scorcheth us
in the flames of Restlesse dispayre: Take both togither & mix
them well as hot & cold poysons fitly Tempered by the skill of   10
the Apothecary becomes medicinable. Soe are gods Mercy &
Trewth restorative to the Soule: The Concideration of his
Trewth humbleth us: without it we would be fearelesse: The
Concideration of his mercy supporteth us, without itt we
would be hopelesse. | | .

139: The promises of god are Trew as his Threatenings are: but
withall Conditionall, & such as must be ever understood with
a Conditionall clause, of reservation, or exception. The Condition of his Threatening is Repentance: of his promises Obedience: what god threateneth he will doe, unlesse we repent   20
and amend: And what he promiseth to doe for us, he will doe
itt, If we Beleeve and Obey. | | .

140: The Covenant of the Law is a priori Conditionall: Hoc fac et
vives: The Covenant of the Gosple a posteriori, conditionall:
Crede et vives. | | .

141: It is noe small mercy in God, It is noe small Comfort to us: If
either he take us away before his judgments Come: or keepe
his judgments away till we be gone. | | .

142: In the ancient Romane State, the manner was before they
made warre upon any people, first to send Harolds to pro-   30
clayme itt (bellum indicere ne inferrent) To the end that if they
would make their peace by submission, they might prevent
the warre; & not soe only, But be written in Albo Amicorum;
enrolled as their ffreinds and Confæderats. | | .

[22]

That the — 1000 — yeares of Chryst his visible Rayne upon
Earth is against Scripture: And this — 1000 — yeares begin
as they say in the yeare — 1650: or at the furthest — 1695

1:    Against this we say that Christ from his ascension to the last judgment abides in heaven: This is proved from the article of our Creed videlicet, from that place, he shall come to judge the quick & the dead. This is proved from Acts 3:21: Joh: 14:2-3.

2:    Argument: Chryst sitteth at the right hand of God till the day of judgment: vide Ephes: 1:20: Heb 1:3: Heb: 8:1: Psal: 140:1:

3:    Argument: The Godly & the ungodly doe all rise togither at the last day: Heb: 9:28: 1 Thessa: 4:14: 1 Cor: 15:22: Joh: 6:39: 40:44: Matt: 25:31:

4:    Argument: Is builded on chrysts Kingdome which is spirituall & not earthly: Luk: 1:32: 1 Cor: 15:25: Luk: 17:20: Joh: 18:36: Rom: 14:17: Ephes: 1:20.

5:    Argument: is taken from the nature of the church, which soe long as it is upon the Earth is a mixed multitude of Elect & Reprobate: good & bad: A companie of people under the Crosse, & subject to various Temptations: A companie that hath need of the word, and Sacraments, of prayer & Ordinances: That hath Chryst an high preist within the vayle of heaven interceding for them. | |.

For the first That Scripture alwayes makes the church to be a mixed Companie: See Matt: 13:40: & ver: 49: & cap: 24:11: Luk: 18:8 Subject to Crosses: Psal: 34:20: Matt: 5:4: Act: 14:23: Rom: 8:17: 2 Tim: 3:12: Heb 12:6: — Concerning Ordinances that they must continew to the last day: Ephes: 4:11: & for the Continuance of the Sacraments 1: Cor: 11:26: That in the most Godly whiles they live on earth Sin doth remayne, & that they have need of Chrysts intercession in heaven with his father: It is cleare from 1 Joh: 1:8: & cap: 2:1. Heb: 9:24:

6:    Argument: Is drawne from the secresie of chrysts Comming: the Scriptures make itt to be secret & hid not only to men, but to the very **[23]** Angells, & to Christ himselfe as he is man: Mar: 13:32. | |.

7:    Argument: Is drawne from the heavenly & eternall reward of the martyrs: Matt: 5:10: 2 Tym: 4:6: at that day or Tyme when chryst takes vengeance on the wicked: 2 Thessa: 1:6:7:8:9:10:

8:    Argument: The Opinion of the millenaries supposeth the Restauration of Jerusalem: & of the Jewish Kingdome after their destruction by the Romans: But Scriptures denyes this: Ezech: 16:53:55: Amos: 5:2: Gen: 49:10. | |.

9: Argument: Antechryst is not to be abolisht till the day of judgment 2 Thessa: 2:8: Rev: 19:20: Compare it with verse the 7: Noe lyving men are Cast into Hell before the last day: And chrysts marryage with the church is not solemnized with a part of the Elect: but with the whole body at the generall Resurrection. | |.

[24]

Concerning the Necessitie: Choyce & use of particular Callings:

Ther are two sorts of Callings: The one ad Fœdus: The other ad Munus: That ad fœdus is the Generall: That ad Munus the particular Calling: Vocatio ad fœdus is that wherwith god calleth us, either outwardly in the ministry of his word: or Inwardly by the efficacy of his spyritt: or joynctly by both, to the fayth & obedience of the Gosple, and to the embracing of the Covenant of Grace, & of Mercy & Salvation by Jesus Chryst: which is therfore termed the generall calling, because the thing wherunto we are thus called is one & the same, & common to all that are thus Called: The same Dutyes, the same Promises, & every way the same Conditions: Here is noe difference in Regard of Persons: But one Lord, one Fayth, one Baptisme, one Body, & one Spyrit, even as we are all called in one Hope of our Calling: Ephes: 4.4.5.

That ad munus is that wherwith god enableth us, & directeth us, & putteth us on to some speciall Course & Condition of life, wherin to imploy our selves, & to exercise the giftes he hath bestowed upon us, to his glory, & the Benefitt of our selves & others. And it is Called a particular Calling because the thing wherunto men are thus Called is not one & the same to all, but differenced with much variety according to the qualitie of particular persons: Alius sic: alius verò sic: Some Ministers: Some Magistrates: Some Artificers: Some one thing: Some another: as to their proper Callings: with reference to Busines: Office: Imployment.

Of this ther is a necessitie: not de facto, sed de Jure: Noe man should be without one: not ratione Termini: sed virtute præcepti: as a necessarie dutie: The neglect wherof would be a greivious &

10

20

30

[25]

sinfull enormitie: For every man must of Necessitie live in
some Calling or other. | | .

Some of gods Curses are promises: some of his Curses are præ-
cepts: That of Eating our bread in the sweat of our face is all
Three: It is a Curse: It is a promise: It is a Præcept: It is a Curse,
In that god will not suffer the Earth to affoord us Bread without our sweat: It is a promise in that god assures us We shall
have bread for our sweat: And itt is a præcept too in that god
enjoyneth us if we will have bread to sweat for itt.

Adam in the tyme & state of Innocency before he had deserved a
Curse was yet enjoyned his taske: To dresse & to keepe the
Garden: Gen 2:15: And as Adam him selfe lived, Soe he bred
up his first children, his two first borne: The one in Tillage, The
other in pasturage Gen: 4:2: —— working with their hands the
things that are good: Ephe: 4:28: God is the god of order; &
Therfore the Apostle in the 2 Thessa: 3:6:11: blameth inordinate
walkers, & such as walke disorderly. | | .

To whom anie thing is Given, of him somthing shalbe required:
Luk 12:48: The inference is stronger then most are aware of:
from the Abilitie to the Duty: from the Gift to the worke: from
the Fitting, to the Calling: 1 Cor: 7:17: | | .

We Confesse that nature doth not, & therfore we may not think
that the god of nature doth bestow abilityes wherof he in-
tendeth not use: Deus et Natura nihil faciunt frustra: et frustra
est potentia quæ non producitur in actum: Beware of Napken-
ing up the Talent Luke 19:20: vide 1 Pet: 4:10: & 1 Cor: 12:7.

Againe he that hath nothing of his owne to doe, must needs from
dooing **[26]** nothing, proceed to doing naught: nihil agendo
malè agere disces

Idlenes Teacheth much Evill: Some Copies read itt: It hath an Eare
open to Every extravagant notion: Ecclus 33:28:

       Nos numerus sumus et fruges Consumere Nati
—————— Res age Tutus eris:

Non licet: is a verie good, & proper & direct answeare when the
divill would tempt thee to sin: It is Evill I may not doe it: But
non vacat: is the stronger & surer answeare: Semper aliquid
boni operis facito, ut diabolus te semper inveniat occupatum.

Againe life must be præserved: ffamilyes mayntayned: the poore
releived: This cannot be done without bread: for that is the

staffe of life & bread cannot be gotten honestly but in a lawfull Calling: vide 2: Thessa: 3:11:12: & Ephes: 4:28: He that doth not labour he doth steale from Himselfe: from his Family: from the poore: Qui vitat molam, vitat Farinam: Noe myll noe meale: vide Acts — 20:34:35: & Ephes. 4:28: Soe the Idle person stealeth from himselfe, & soe is a foolish theife: stealtheth from his family & his ffreinds, & soe is an unnaturall theife: stealeth from the poore, & soe is a base theife:

Againe a calling is necessarie in regard of the publique: every man ought to conferre aliquid in publicum; put to his helping hand to advance the common good; & in such sort as may be serviceable to the whole body, & profitable to his fellow members in the body: In soe much that diverse commonwealthes weare carefull to ordayne that noe man should live but in some profession, & tooke strict examination who did otherwyse, & to punish them some with fasting, Some with infamie, some with Banishment, & Some with death: | |.

Some Gallants spend their tyme in dooing nothing; or as good as nothing or worse than Nothing. | |. Non otiosè vivit, qui qualecunque utiliter: Quis generosum dixerit hunc qui indignus genere? The Titles which are Given them, & the armes which they beare, doe noe more belong [27] unto them, Then the reverence the good man did unto Isys, belonged to the Asse that carryed her Image: | |.

Againe: as god promised ther should be always some poore: Mat: 26:11 on whom to exercise charitie: Soe he ordayned ther should be noe beggar Deut: 15:4: to make a Trade & profession of begging: Plato allowes not any beggar in his Commonwealth: alleaging that wher such weare tollerated, it was impossible but that state must abound with pylfering & whoring & all kind of base villanie:

The Civill lawes have flat Constitutions against them, in The Titles of de mendicantibus non invalidis: sed quid leges sine moribus? Et vetabitur semper & retinebitur. | |.

Ther are poore indeed that want not only the things they aske, but want also meanes to get itt without asking: Not they that had rather steale, or beg then dig, such a one is noe more to be releeved as a poore man, then a woman that hath poysoned her husband is to be honoured as a widdow. It is pars Sacrilegii

73

rem pauperum dare non pauperibus: for the mayntenance of
the poore is made the spoyle of the loyterer. | |.

Of the choyse of a Callinge.

Iuvat Idem qui Iubet: The Rules are three: ffirst they either con-
cerne the course itt selfe; or else our selves that should use itt:
or else those that have Right & power over us in itt: If ther be
a fayle in anie of these as if either the Course itt selfe be not
lawfull: or Wee not competently Fitt for itt: or our Superiours
will not Allow of us or itt, we may well thinke that god hath
not called us Thither: 10
De 1°: If Diana of Ephesus be an Idoll, Demetrius his occupation
must downe; he must make noe more Sylver Shrynes for Diana; though by that craft he have his wealth: Noe unlawfull
thing can be a lawfull calling; neither make a Calling of that,
which was not made to be a Calling: as to be a Bowler, or
Archer, or Gamester, & nothing else. | |.
The works of our Callings, they are as our Meates & Drinkes; Those   [28]
of delight as sauces, or as physicke: & as sawces, or as physicke they are to be used & not otherways: Ther are somthings
lawfull to doe, which are not lawfull to live by: Sanis homi-   20
nibus publica privatis potiora sunt: Resolve not therfore upon
that Course for thy Calling, which is rather hurtfull to the
Commonwealth then profitable: of which sort are Hucksters,
Engrossers, Forestallers, Regraters, &c: | |.
Againe our Care in our Choyse Must be to inquire into our selves
what Calling is most fitt for us & we for itt: wherin our inquirie
must espeacially rest upon three things: 1: our Inclynation:
2: Our Gifts: 3: our Education: male respondent Coacta in-
genia. | |.

                                                                   [29]
It is But a fancie of Inconciderate Spyritts to dreame   30
That the Soule sleepeth till the day of Resurrection: for
The clearing of this Trewth Concider three Arguments. | |.

ffirst Concider the Soules of the Saints & you shall find That they
doe not sleepe with their Bodyes: ffirst they are gathered to

their fathers: Gen: 25:8: Soe Abraham in that place. 2^ly Chryst promised the pœnitent Theiffe on the Crosse Luke 23:43: This day shalt thou be with me in paradise: │object:│ but ther are some to avoyde this scripture would devyde the words thus: I say unto thee This day; And make a stop ther: Referring the words │This day│ to the person promising, & not to the blessing promised:

To which it is answeared: first to alter Coma's & stops against all receaved coppies is a high presumption: which if Tollerated, wanton witts will wrest the scriptures to their owne perdition: 2^ly his Request is Lord Remember me when thou Comest into thy Kingdome: But Christ immediately that day entred into his Kingdome: none will say his answeare was a denyall; & therfore Christs │Hodie│ must answeare to the pœnitents │Quando│ To think otherwise is to abuse the poore pœnitents fayth: to straiten Chrysts Bountie, & to wrest the words against their Naturall sence: By interpreting them that some 2000 — yeares after, at the day of the Resurrection the Theife should be remembered. ││. 3^ly you read that Lazarus after his death was caryed into Abrahams bosome: Luk:16:22. 4^ly: Concider the saints desyre of dissolution is upon this perswasion: Phillip: 2:23. I desyre to be dissolved & to be with Christ: 5^ly: Concider the saints Confidence upon their departure from Earth to enjoy a glorious life in Heaven: 2 Cor: 5:1: we know that when the Body is dissolved we have a building of god, a house not made with hands, æternall in the Heavens: surely if the soule sleepe to the day of Resurrection, they **[30]** should not have sayed when this howse is dissolved: but when this body is raysed, & this tabernacle restored. ││. 6^ly: The Scripture speaketh expressly, That all the presence the saints have with Chryst whilst the soule is in the body is nothing but a meere absence, in comparison of that neerenes of presence unto Chryst which they shall enjoy when they are absent from the body: 2 Cor: 5:6.8. Knowing that whyles we are at home in the body, we are absent from the lord. ││. 7^ly: Concider that the soule upon itts separation from the Body is perfected, & the saints departed this life are by the holy ghost styled the soules of Just men made perfect. ││.

Secondly Concider the Soules of wicked Men
That att the houre of death they are not Abolished:

God Telling us
> ffirst That they Goe to their owne place: Soe Tis sayd of Judas who fell by Transgression Acts: 1.18:25: Now Judas place was not the Grave, that is the Common way of all flesh: But his place was the State & Degree of Torment that his sinne and Gods justice inflicted on him.

$2^{ly:}$ They are sayd to be in the place of Torment: Soe Dives beggeth of Abraham to send to his brethren that they Come not into this place of Torment: Luk: 16:28.

$3^{ly:}$ the soules of Them of the old world are now in pryson: The Grave cannot be the pryson, to distinguish the just from the unjust that being common to the obedient, as well as to the disobedient:

4^{ly} Tis sayd of the Sodomits, That they now suffer the vengeance of eternall fire: Jude: Verse 7. This cannot be meant of their bodyes, for they weare burnt by fyre to Ashes: nor of that materiall [31] Fyre that fell upon their Cyties, for that many ages since was quenched: But of their soules, which are under the æternall wrath of god, wher the worme never dyeth, & wher the fyre is never quenched. | | .

Thirdly Concider what the Scripture Sayth
Of the Soules of all men in Generall: whither
They feare God, or Feare him Not.

ffirst That the Soule of Man is not Capeable of Corruption: Chryst Biddeth us not to feare him that kylleth the Body, & Cannot Kyll the Soule: Matt: 10:28:

$2^{ly:}$ when the soule & Body part, the scripture telleth us they goe to distinct places: Eccles 3:21: Eccles: 12:7. | | .

$3^{ly:}$ If the soule should sleepe till the Resurrection, then the soule should be as Mortall as the Body. | | .

$4^{ly:}$ If this should be Trew, Then the resurrection of the Soule should be as needfull to be revealed in the Scripture: but of this the scripture is altogither silent. | | .

5[ly]: The Expression of death by the Holy Ghoast is a departure, a putting off of this Tabernacle: & it is a strange mistake, to take the howse for the inhabitant. | |.

6[ly]: This Openeth a gappe to overthrow all the thoughts of æternitie: & soe destructive to all Religion: making men to count the fruition of Carnall pleasures the greatest Good: & to make men to be lovers of pleasures more then God:

See the Arguments brought to the Contrary
On the other Syde. | |.

The Arguments brought to the Contrary
are either drawne from Corrupt nature:
or Taken from Mystaken Scripture.

[32]
10

ffirst for the ffirst I wonder that anie chrystians that enjoyed the light of Scripture should borrow anie Arguments from Galen, & the rest of the Heathen that sate in Darknes & in the valley of the shaddow of death. | |.

ffor the Second Some object, Did not God Threaten Adam Gen: 2:17: In the day that thou eatest therof thou shalt dye & if he dyed then the whole man did dye: for the Body is not the man without the Soule:

Sol: That the death which god did Threaten was not only Naturall but Spyrituall & æternall. | |.

Object: when men are dead the scripture expresslye sayeth that they cannot prayse god Psal: 6:5: & 88:9: Esay 38:8:9:

Sol: The dead qua Tales soe far as they are dead cannot prayse god: Though they Cannot doe itt for an others Conversion; yet they can doe itt for their owne consolation: & those Soules that are with the Lord, they follow the Lambe whither-soever he goeth, & have their Hallelujahs continually in their mouth: Rev: 5:9: & vide Psal: 84:4:

Object: God is sayd only to have immortalitie &c:

Sol: God alone is immortall aparte Ante, from all æternity he is alone, Independently, unchangablely, Infinitely————Immortall. | |.

20

30

Certayne Notes & Rules to Direct us
& Incite us to & in the service of God

[33]

We are Provoked to the service of God

1 by Justice to provoke us
2 By Necessitie to inforce us
3 By easines to harten us
4 Honour to allure us
5 Profitt to Draw us

ffirst it is the most Just whither we respect

1 Right on Gods part
    or
2 equity on ours.

10

Right on Gods part by right of

1 Creation: Esay — 44:21
2 Redemption: 1 Pet: 1:18:19
3 Conquest: Luke: 1.74:75.

And if we may not deny unto Cæsar, the things that are Cæsars: It
is but Right we should also give unto God, the Things that are
Gods, by soe manie and just Titles. | |.
Equity on our Syde: we must doe to others, as we would be done
unto: vis ut tibi serviat cum quo factus es, et non vis servire ei,
a quo factus es? be not like those men that will neither doe
right nor take wrong:

20

Secondly it is the most necessary service

1: Because we are servi nati: & therfore let
us make choyse of best master: I & my
house will serve the lord: Jos: 24:15:
2: ffor Safetie & Securitie: Esay: 60:12:
3: we are bound unto itt by our solemne
vow and promise in Baptisme.

Thirdlie it the most easie service

1. in Regard of the certaintie of the Imployment
2: in Regard of the helpe we have towards
the performance of itt: Phill: 4:13: 1 Cor:
15:10:

30

ffowrthly it is the: { cæteris paribus: he goeth for the better man,
most Honourable   { that serveth the better master: Joh: 12:26:

It is the most profitable service ——— { 1: in Protection
{ 2: in Mayntenance.
{ 3: in Rewarde

Servants owe   { 1: Reverence
to their masters: ———{ 2: Obedience
{ 3: ffaythfullnes

1: Reverence ariseth from an apprehension | 1 Humilitie   [34]
of worthynes: & soe Reverence hath :3: { 2 a feare to offend   10
branches | 3 a Care to please
De 1°:   1: Tim: 6:1: non decet superbum esse hominem servum
De 2do: Mal: 1:6: Psal: 2:11: Heb: 12:18:
De 3^{tio} Tit: 2:9: Gal: 1:10:

2^{ly} Obedience is the second Generall dutie___{ 1 active
Ephes: 6:5: & this is two fold   { 2 passive
Active obedience is the doing of his will: & this must be done in
Auditu auris, upon signification of his pleasure without dis-
puting or debating the matter as the Centurians servant: Matt:
8:9:   20
Passive obedience   { 1 Contenting our selves with his Allowance
Consisteth in   { 2 submitting our selves to his Correction:
{ 1 with meate }
De 1°: He must be Content with: { 2 with Drink | as his master
Having food & Rayment he must   { 3 Livery | can allow
be Content: 1 Tim: 6:8: Phill: 4:11: { 4 Lodging } him. | |.

De 2:$^{do:}$ He must submitt to his holsome   { 1 Fault
dysciplyne since his corrections are for our { 2 Good

The Last Generall Dutie   { 1: By his Hartines of his service   30
is fidelitie: Matthe: 25:21: { 2: By Tender of his masters Honour and
wch is Tryed three wayes {   profitt:
{ 3: By his Dyligence in dooing his Busines

79

De 1°: Coll: 3:22:23: 1 Sam 12:24:
De 3:^tio: noe man would willingly entertayne an idle servant
      Sudant quando vorant, Frigescunt quando Laborant:
They are rightly joyned: wicked & Slothfull: Matt: 25:26:

The poetts give unto Mercury (the messenger as they fayne of
    Jupiter & the other Gods) wings both at his hands & feet: to
    intimate therby what great speed & Diligence, was requisite to
    be used by those that should be imployed in the service of
    princes for the managing of their waighty affaires of State: vide
    Rom: 12:12. Jer: 48:10.   10
Lett us not Triffle away our tyme in unconcerning things, or post   [35]
    of the Repentance of our sinnes, & the reformation of our lives
    till another age: Or anie other way slack our bounden service
    unto God, Either in the Common dutyes of our Generall or in
    the proper works of our particular Calling. Let us pray unto
    god to worke in us both the wyll & the Deed: Phill: 2:13:

Short Notes Concerning Church Goverment

Vide 1: Thessa: 5:12:13: 1 Tim: 5:17: Heb:13:7: & verse 17:
Instruction must goe before observation. | |.
Let dayes speake & Multitude of yeares teach knowledge: Job: 20
    12:12: & 15:10: for this. | |. 1: King: 12:13:14:
The Discipline or goverment is as an hedge or wall about the
    doctrine of Religion: A curbe to Licentious Courses: wherby
    church governors may be enabled to put a difference betweene
    the holy and prophane; & the uncleane & cleane: Ezec: 22:26:
    ffor the rod of Discipline 1 Cor: 4:21: may have a salutarie
    operation in the church, as the rod of Correction in the family:
    Prov: 23:13:14:
Similitudes may illustrate a Trewth proved, or to be proved: but
    they prove nothing: They may be Carryed too far: Similitudes   30
    (as the Common saying is) runne not on fowre feet. | |.
It is the Dutie of a state, that is of them that governe a State not
    only to Try Spiritts, but to rule them: & rather to rule them,
    then to Try them: for the rod of Reproofe sayth Solomon gives
    wisdome Prov: 29:15: And a chyld left unto himselfe bringeth
    his mother to shame: Prov: Ibidem:

Qui monet ut facis, quod iam facias, ille monendo
Laudat: Et Hortatu Comprabat acta suo. | |.

143: Although god hath leaden feet which are long in comming,   [36]
yet he hath Iron hands which when he commeth will strike
home. | |.

144: The wrathfull man, The prodigall man, The lascivious man,
the surfetting man, the slothfull man, is rather an enimie to
himselfe then to god: The Envyous man, the covetous man,
the deceitfull man, the ungratefull man, is rather an enimie to
pryde | men then to god: But the proud man setts himselfe against   10
god, because he doth against his lawes, he makes himselfe
equall with god, because he doth it without god, & craves noe
helpe of him: He exalteth himselfe above god, because he will
have his owne will, though it be contrary to gods will. Therfore god is especially sayd to resist the proude, because the
proude resist him: | |.

145: A man had need to take heed of pryde, for shee will not keepe
pride } counsell: But if he be proude, she will tell that he is proud: &
therfore is called an impudent sin, because she descrieth
herselfe in the Eye, in the speech, in the gesture, in the looke,   20
in the Gate, like the drunkard; soe that a man cannot be
prowde & seeme humble. | |.

146: In patience possesse your soules Luk: 8: as though a man
without patience had noe rule of Himselfe: A mans probing
pati- } wisdome is knowne by his patience: as though he that is not
ence } patient cannot be wyse: Heb: 10: By patience we receave the
promises, as though the promises did not belong unto us
unlesse we have patience: And patience breeds Experience, &
experience Hope: as though he that wanted patience had noe
experience of god, to know the scope of his doings; nor anie   30
hope to Comfort him about the life to Come: Patience is a
physition for all diseases & for all persons: The afflictions of
this world are not worthy of the joyes that succeed them. | |.

147: He which hath but a shew of holynes, hath but a shew of   [37]
wisdome: a little knowledge in his head; but noe knowledge
in his hart: If he speake anie thing that is good, he speaketh by
rote; he that speakes not out of the abundance of his heart is
soone drawne dry. | |.

148: As when Chryst taught in the Temple they asked, how knoweth this man the scriptures Joh: 7:15: seeing he never learned them: Soe it is a wonder what learning some men have, which have noe learning; Like Priscylla & Aquila poore Tentmakers which weare able to school Acts 11:15 Apollos that great clarke, a man renowned for his learning: what can we say to this but as chryst sayd; Father soe it pleaseth thee: Luke. 10:21: Wisdome is justifyed of her children: Matt: 11:19:

149: Crœssus sonne who was borne dumbe, when he saw one going to kyll his father, spake and Cryed out: O Kyll not Crœssus!   10

150: God accounts all those Errors, Heresyes, schismes &c. committed in a land but lett alone, & suffered without punishment by those who have authoritie and power, to be the sinns of those who have power, & he will proceed against them, as if they weare the authors of them: A man comes to be partaker of other mens sinns by Countenancing, Consenting, and suffering without punishment, as well as by formally committing them. | |.

151: Intermissions in Government, are the winter & ill season of a state, wherin the nights are long, & the dayes short. | |.   20

152: —————— Mater erat quondam, nunc est fortuna noverca:
        Sed tamen est Idem, qui fuit antè deus;

153: It is better to doe well, then to doe good: ffor a man cannot offend in doing well; but he may offend in doing good, if he doe not well: | |. Doe good, in a good Sorte. | |.

154: It is written of the Hart that when he lifteth up his eares, he is quicke of hearing, & heareth every noyse: but when he layeth downe his eares he is deafe & hearerth nothing. | |.

155: Trewth will hardly overtake a lye, that is sett out foure — or —5— dayes before itt. | |.   [38] 30

156: Politicke men, as they will reserve themselves, & not speake all their hart: Soe they will not engage themselves beyond their power of Retreat, if they shall after see reason for itt: you know whose it was, That He would Launce noe farther Into the Sea, Then He Might Safely Returne To The Shore Againe. | |.

157: Non est pudor ad meliora transire: Dies diem docet:

158: Tis better to borrow too Soone; Then to pay Too late. | |.

159: Tis not the first blow that makes the quarrell (for that noe wise man will stay for) but the first provocation. | |.

160: The bloudy executioners of Tyrants doe goe to their errands with an halter about their necke, soe that if they performe not, they are sure to dye for itt. | |.

161: These six things doth the lord hate, yea seaven are an ab-homination unto him: 1: a proud Looke: 2: a Lying Tongue: 3: Hands that shed innocent bloud: 4: an hart that deviseth wicked imaginations: 5: Feet that be swift in running to mis-cheiffe: 6: A false witnesse that speaketh Lyes: 7: Him that soweth discord among Brethern:

162: Confidence in an unfaithfull man in Tyme of Trouble, is like a broken Tooth, & a foot out of joynt: Prov: 25:19.

163: He that passeth by, & medleth with strife belonging not to him: is like one that taketh a dog by the eares: Prov: 26:17.

164: Wickednes condemned by her owne witnesse is very Tim-erous & being pressed with Conscience always fore-casteth greivous things: ffor feare is nothing else but a betraying of the succours which reason offereth: Wisd: 17:11:12:

165: He that requiteth good Turnes, is mindfull of that which may Come hearafter: & when he falleth he shall find a stay. | |.

166: Be in peace with manie: neverthelesse have but one Coun-sailor of a thousand. | |.

167: Ther be two things that greive my hart, & the third maketh me angry: 1: A man of war that suffereth poverty: 2: men of understanding that are not sett by: 3: One that returneth from righteousnes to sin: the Lord prepareth such a one for the sword. | |.

168: Who soe discovereth secrets, loseth his Credit: & shall never find freind to his mind: | |.

169: As for a wound it may be bound up, & after reviling ther may be reconcilement; but he that bewrayeth secrets is without hope: . | |.

170: Deliver all things in number & weight, & put all in writing that thou givest out or receivest in. | |. Ecclus: 42:7:

171: In Long waking, a watchfull man may winke now & then:

172: Wickednes condemned by her owne witnesse is very Timerous: & being pressed with conscience always forecast-eth greivous things ffor feare is nothing else but a betraying of the succours which reason offereth: Wisd: 17:11:12: | |.

173: I shall count him my best freind, who shewes me my errors in
    love: and blesse god for that enimie who discovers to me my
    errors in hatred. | |.

174: Fides nequaquam vi extorquetur, sed ratione, et exemplis
    perswadetur;

175: Lett not opinion but Trewth sway your judgments: They are
    but sillie men, who like to animals suffer anie burthen to be
    throwne upon their Backs, & themselves to be governed by
    the opinion of others. | |.

176: Neither Consult with a woman touching her of whom she is   [40] 10
    jealous: neither with a Coward in matters of war: nor with a
    marchant concerning exchange: nor with a Byer of selling: nor
    with an envyous man of thankfulnes: nor with an unmercifull
    man, touching kindnes: nor with the slothfull, of anie worke;
    nor with an Hireling for a yeare of finishing of worke: nor
    with an Idle servant of much busines: Consult not with one
    that suspecteth thee: & hyde thy councell from such as envye
    thee: Harken not unto these in any matter of Counsell: Ecclus:
    37:10:11:

Delinquencie is perpetratio delicti, or derelictio Legis.   20
He is noe delinquent who obeyeth the Law:

7 Ed: 1:
Statutes
at Large
fol: 42:

1:
The power of Armes belongs to the King only: Therfore to
assist that power is noe Delinquencie: That law declareth
further, that the Prelates, Earles, Barons & Communaltie
then assembled in parlament, that they are bound to ayd the
King their soveraigne Lord att all seasons when need shalbe. | |.

25: Edw:
3: Cap: 2:

2^{ly}
To adhere to the King when warre is Levyed against him
in his realme, & to ayd & Comfort him makes noe Delin-   30
quencie. | |.

5to H: 4:
num: 24: act
not printed:

3^{ly}
To execute the Commission of Array is noe delinquencie:
for that Commission of Array is of fforce & noe other:
Vide Cokes Jurisdiction of Courtes fol: 125: published since
    this parlament by the desyre of the howse of com-
    mons: The order printed in the last leafe of the Com-
    mentaries upon Magna Charta. | |.

4$^{ly:}$ To oppose anie change in the established Religion; To op-   [41]
pose anie change of lawes without the Kings assent, To
Remove Councellors, to take the king by force, & to Restrayne him untill he hath yeelded to Certayne demaunds
makes noe delinquencie: Sir Edw Coke in his booke called
Pleas of the Crowne, printed by order ut supra folio 9: et 12:
Subjects are forbidden to take armes by the Law against the
regnant King, being King de facto & an usurper: ibid folio
7°: | |.

11 H:7:   5^{ly} The subjects are bound by their Alleageance to serve their   10
Cap: 1:   king against all power & might reared against him in his
Land: & if the King should happen to be vanquished, the
law declares that in that Case all Actes & processe wherby
they should suffer anie thinge should be voyde. | |.

1 Eliz: 6^{ly} Every member of the howse of Commons of this parla-
Cap: 1:   ment, hath taken a Corporall Oath upon the Evangellists,
5to Eliz: acknowledging the King the only supreame Governour in
Cap: 1:   all causes Ecclesiasticall & Temporall in his dominions:
And the member who hath not taken itt hath noe voyce by
law: nay he is to be deemed & taken to all intents & pur-   20
poses as if he had never bin chosen: This Oath is taken in
Tyme of parlament: If anie power weare above the King, or
Equall, or not from him derived his power weare neither
supreame, nor Only: | |.

That person who keepes his Oath & Obeyes the Law is Noe Delinquent.

The howses are the Kings Counsell: Conciliarii non sunt præcep-   [42]
tores: Concilium non est præceptum: The Councell may be
good, the councell may be ill & therfore may be refused: & he
who is counsailed may approove of itt or reject itt: And soe   30
hath it been done in all parlaments from the beginning of par-
laments to this: | | Le Roy sá visera. | |.

To Say the King is virtuallie with the howses is a delusion: ffirst the
body politique cannot operate but by the body naturall, this is
not with the howses: 2^{ly} will and action make anie thing virtuall: neither the Kinge wills, nor acts with them: If virtually
ther for assent, then Roy ne veult, takes noe place, which ever
did. | |.

Commissions under the great seale, in Case of sicknes, or absence to noe purpose; & the style of acts must change, The houses ordayne by the virtuall assent of the King: In all fore-tymes the King ordaynes by the advise, & assent &c:

In re minime dubia utor argumentis non necessariis: The death of the King alters nothing by this new doctryne; for we have noe interregnum: All adjournaments, prorogations, dissolutions, must be by the virtuall power, contrary to the example of all ages. | |.

The votes & Oathes made this parlament not to adheare to, or assist the King in this warre prove the King is not virtually ther. | |.   10

177: A man may entertayne a Trewth, as well as an error too quick-   [43]
lie: That is, when he entertaynes it upon Trust: or without debate: or because others say itt, or practise itt: or because at first veiw it seemes like a Trewth: Drop by Droppe is the best receaving of opinions. | |.

178: Si sumus inseperabiles; sumus in-superabiles. | |.

179: Nemo sine Crimine, nemo sine errore: Noe man hath an un-erring priviledge. | |.

180: That Cannot be a good judgment, that is passed before evi-   20
dence is brought in. | |.

181: Leo the Tenth that Monster of men: was heard to say: Quantas nobis divitias comparabit hæc fabula evangelii? | |.

182: A fearefull man will never be a faythfull man. | |.

183: It is one thing, judicare, & it is another thing, judicem agere: Ther is a twofold judgment: 1: Forense: this belongs to those that are in publique authoritie: 2: Rationale & this belongs to all whom god hath given a Rationall soule: not by practise, but by precept: not by example but by rule: Honest ends, have honest aymes: The pryde of the head is a dangerous engine   30
for error: | |.

184: If thou wilt passe a right judgment of an opinion; doe not number, but waigh: & weigh not in the false ballance of the multitude, but in the ballance of Trewth, The word of god: for Trewth doth neither depend on many or few:

185: Men of Different Creeds, will hardly be of one Pater Nos-ter. | |. I am not to be bribed nor threatened out of my opi-nion, but to be convinced and perswaded. | |.

186: Tuta frequensque via est, sub amici fallere nomen   [44]
      Tuta frequensque licet sit via, crimen habet.
  The way both safe & common is by freindship to deceave;
  Yet safe & common though it be 'tis Knav'ery by your Leave:
187: Qui dare festinans gratis, ne danda rogentur
    Quod nondum dederat, nondum se credit habere
    Who hastning franckly for to give, for feare that folke
      should Crave:
    He never thought that he had that, which yet
      he never gave.   10

I may pleade a forreigne plea: otherwayes attainted & Convicted   [45]
  in a forraigne Countie: or his Majesties pardon: | |.
An Indictment before two: & one noe Judge is a voyd Indict-
  ment: | |.
The Indictment voyd made before Covenanters. | |. The Rest is two
  Leaves forward at the end of the second page. | |.

---

1   We have ayded the King in this warre contrary to the negative
     oath & other votes: our warrant is the — 25 — Edw: 3: Cap: 2: | |.
2   We have mayntayned the commission of Array by the Kings
     commaund contrarie to their votes: we are warranted by the   20
     statute of 5 — of Hen: 4: & in the judgment of Sir Edward Coke,
     the oracle of the law as they call him:
3   We have mayntayned Archbishopps & Bishopps, whom they
     would suppresse: our warrant is Magna Charta; & 100 statutes
     more.
4   We have mayntayned the booke of Common prayer: they
     suppresse itt: our warrant is — 5 — acts of parliament, in Edw: 6:
     & Queene Elizab: tyme. | |.
5   We have mayntayned the Militia of the Kingdome to belong to
     the King, they the contrary: Our warrant is the statute of 7 —   30
     Edw: 1 & manie statutes since; & the practise of all tymes: | |.
6   We mayntayne the counterfeiting of the great seale to be high
     Treason: & soe of the usurpation of the Kings forts, ports,
     shipping, Castles, & his Revenew, & the Coignning of monie:
     against them we have our warrant by the sayd statute of 25:

Edw: 3: Cap: 2: & diverse other sithence: & the practise of all tymes. | |.

7   We mayntayne that the King is the only supreame governour: they say, they are coordinate: our warrant is the statute of 1° Eliz: cap: 1: & —5$^{to:}$ Eliz: Cap: 1:

8   We mayntayne, that the King is King, by an inhærent Birth-right: They say his kinglye righte is an office upon trust: Our warrant is the statute of 1°: Jac: cap: 1: | |.   [46]

9   We mayntayne that the politicke capacitie is not to be severed, from the naturall: they hould the contrary: our warrant is two Statutes: Exilium Hugonis Le Dispenser patris et filii in Edw: 1: tyme: & in the: 1: of Edw: 3: cap: 2: & their oracle, who hath published itt to posteritie, that it is a damnable, detestable, & execrable opinion. | |.   10

10   We mayntayne that he that aydes the king at home or abroade, ought not to be molested or questioned for the same: They hold & practise the Contrarie: Our warrant is the statute of —11: H: 7: cap: 1: | |.

11   We mayntaine that the King hath a negative voyce, to all bills agreed by the two howses, which they denie: Our warrant is the statute of —2: H: 5: & the practise of all Tymes. | |.   20

12   We mayntayne that parlaments ought to be held in a grave & peace-able manner, without Tumults: They allow multitudes of the meaner sort of people to Come to Westminster to Cry for justice, if they cannot have their will: Our warrant is the Statute of —2: Edw: 2: And their oracle. | |.

13   We mayntayne that to Levye a warre; to remove Concellors; to alter Religion; or anie law established; is high Treason: they hold the Contrary: Our warrant is the resolution of all the judges of England in Queene Eliz: tyme: & their Oracle agrees with the same: | |.   30

14   We mayntayne that noe man should be imprysoned, putt out of his lands, but by dew processe of law, & that noe man ought to be adjudged to death, but by the lawes established in the Land: the [47] Customes therof, or by act of parlament: They practise the Contrary in London, Bristoll, Kent: Our warrant is Magna Charta, Cap: 29: The petition of right 3$^{tio:}$ Cap: & diverse lawes ther mentioned. | |.

For the mayntenance of these lawes we have fought: & will

fight againe if ther shalbe cause: And if they will putt us to death, we will by gods grace dye as becomes constant men, & the Lovers of their Country & the lawes therof: | |.

We of the Kings partie doe detest monopolyes, & shippe monie, & all the greivances of the people, as much as any men living: we doe well know that our estates, lives & fames are preserved by the lawes; and that the King is bound by his lawes: we love parlaments: If the Kings Counsellors, Judges or ministers have done amisse they had from the third of November — 1640 — to the — 10th — of January — 1641 tyme to punish them, being all left to justice: wher is the Kings fault? | |.

———————— Vir bonus est Quis?

Qui Consulta patrum, qui leges, juraque servat:

Lord have mercie upon us, & Inclyne our harts to keepe the Lawes:

> Monies Raysed severall wayes never used in this Kingdome.

1 — Excise — 2: Contributions: 3: Sequestrations: 4: part 20 & 5: 5: meat monie: 6: Sale of plundred Goods: 7: Loanes: 8: Benevolences: 9: Collections upon their Fast dayes & Thanks-giving dayes: 10: Seizing & Selling Delinquents Goods: 11: New impositions upon merchants: 12: Guardes mayntayned at the charges of private men: 13: Fiftie subsedyes at one tyme:

In this Cause & warre betweene the Kings Majestie & the 2 howses at Westminster what guide had the subjectes of the land to direct them but the lawes? what meanes could they use to discerne what to ffollow, what to avoyde, but the lawes? The King declared itt Treason to adhære to the howses in this warre: and the howses declare itt Treason in this warre to adhære to the King: The subjects for a great and Considerable part of them (Treason being such a cryme as forfaites life & estate, & renders a mans posteritie base, beggarly, & infamous) Looke upon the lawes; & find the letter of the law requires them to assist the King as before is manifested: was ever subject criminallye punished in anie age or nation for his pursuite of what the letter of the law commaunds? The subjects of this Kingdom find the distinction & interpretation now putt upon the lawes of Abstractum & Concretum, power & person: Body

politicke & Naturall: personall presence, & virtuall, to have bin
condemned by the law: And soe the Kings partie had both the letter
of the law, & the interpretation of the letter cleared to their judgments: wherby they might evidently perceave what syde to adhære
unto: what satisfaction could modest, and peaceable & loyall men
more desyre? A verbo legis ni criminalibus et pœnis non est rece-
dendum: hath bin an approoved Maxime of law in all ages &
Tymes: If the King be King & remayne in his Kingly office as they
call itt, then all the sayd lawes are against them without coulor: for
they say the lawes relate to him in his office; they cannot say other-   10
wayes; for they make all writts, processes, Commissions & pardons
in the Kings name: & the person of the King & his bodie politike
[49] cannot, nor ought to be severed as hath bin before declared:
vide Collection of ordinances — 727:

    For that of verball & personall Commaundes of the King which
is objected, we affirme few things to be subject therto by the law:
But his Commaund under the great seale, which in this war hath
bin used by the Kings Commaund for his Comissions to leavie &
array men that is noe personall commaund (which the law in some
cases disallowes): but is such a commaund soe made as all men   20
hould their lands by, who hold by pattent: all Corporations have
their charters by, which hould by charters & all judges & officers
their places & callings.

And in all the Bookes of the Scriptures you shall find the letter of
    the Text playne for us: & not one text against us

Witnesses: } 1: Edw: 6: cap: 12: | 5: Edw: 6: cap: 11 4ta pars institut˜
fol: 25: Ther must be two Lawfull witnesses upon the inditment of
Treason & soe upon the arraignment: | | .

Councell } 9: Edw: 4: 2: 1: Hen: 7: 23: Arundells case lib: 6:14: 3^{tià}:   30
    pars institut˜ fol: 137: for matter of Law Councell ought to
    be assigned: The indictment is of a forme not used: The
    indictment comprehendes not matter sufficient to make the
    offence Treason: And I have — 4 — statutes to plead 11: R: 2
    cap: 3: 1 H: 4: cap: 10: 2 Mar: Cap: 10: 11 H: 7: cap: 1: | | .

Challenge } 32: H: 6: 26: 14: H: 7: 19: Stamford 158: 1° et 2° p:
    et m: 10: 3^{tià} pars institut˜ 156: He which is arraigned for
    high Treason may challenge — 35 Jurors peremptorily: &

challenge for Cause every one who hath taken the Covenant to bring malignants to Tryall & Condigne punishment, & therfore not indifferent: for he hath not only
delivered his opinion, but is sworne before hand to find
me guiltie: An Indictor for that Cause cannot be of the Jury
for life & death upon that partie whom he hath indicted,
who ought to be omni exceptione majores: for mens Lives,
Estates, Goodes & Fame rests upon them. | |.

Freehold } 2: H5: cap: 3: 27 Eliz: cap: 6: Every Juror ought to
have — 4^{li} — in Land — Stamford — 156: — a good challenge in
Treason. | |.

Forraigne Plea } Is pleadable in Treason at this day: 3^{tia}: pars in-
stitut˜ fol: 27. by force of the statute of 2°: & 3$^{tio:}$ Phil: et
Mar: cap: 10: | |. Turne to the beginning of this discourse,
two leaves back. | |.

188: A mad man & a chollericke man differ nothing but in Tyme: | |.

189: The Gentiles did paint Angerona the Goddesse of Agonie
with a padlocke on her mouth: & placed her in the Temple of
Volupia, which was the goddesse of Delight: To signifie unto
us that he who can be silent, & hold his peace at such a Tyme
as an injurie is offered him, shall afterwards come to receave
delight & Contentment in this his sufferings: But they who
cannot hold their tongues came afterwards to tast of sorrow
& Repentance: ffor that angry fitt being past they condemne
that which in their choller they approoved. | |.

190: This is to quench fire with water, when by remembring our
owne, we forgive other mens trespasses: ffor he oughte not to
deny pardon to another, who stands in need therof himselfe:
And this is an excellent saying & worthy our often repetition:
Alas why should I not beare, with this one fault, since god
beareth with soe many of myne. | |.

191: Ama Nesciri: Laudet te os alienum, Sileat os tuum: The more
a man commends himselfe, the lesse others reckon of him:

192: The Benedictins boast that of their order ther have bin 18:
Emperors: — 25 — Empresses: — 46 — Kings: — 51 — queenes:

193: Sustine et Abstine: Beare & Forbeare: Beare with patience Adversitie & Tribulation; & Forbeare those things which are of
pleasure & Contentment. | |.

194: The Bodyes sicknes is the soules Allarme: it's Sentinell, itts
watchman which putts him in mind of god, when shee
growes forgetfull of him: & itt is the mistresse which teacheth
man to know himselfe. | |.

195: Avaro quid mali optes, nisi ut diu vivat?

196: Obedience is better then Sacrifice: And the reason hereof is   [51]
That in Sacrifice ther is offered the flesh of beastes: But in
obedience our owne will: | |. Nolite sapere, plus quam opor-
tet sapere

197: A King demaunding of a certayne phylosopher what he   10
would have him to doe, wherby he might make tryall of that
great trust and Confidence which he reposed in him: Answeared: in anie thing whatsoever it shall please your Majestie: Soe as it be not in the disclosing of your secretts unto me.

198: Aristotle holds it a greater distast & fowler affront to be overcome in argumentation, then in warre: In a dispute then in a
duell: for in this is only overcome the force & strength of the
body: but in that the faculties of the soule, as Reason, understanding, & judgment: And for this reason men manie tymes
contest & strive without Reason. | |.   20

199: The Poets fayne that the phylosopher Tyresias was stricken
blind, because he presumed to see the goddesse Minerva
naked: Signifying therby that god useth to punish those with
blindnes of understanding, who with Curiositie seeke to pry
into his Mysteryes, & to see them layd naked & open to their
veiw. | |.

200: Ther are three disordinate affections of the Understanding:
the first is overmuch Curiositie in searching out those things
which are above mans naturall facultie: the second is a
Trusting or relying too much upon his owne judgment and   30
opinion, in those things which he naturally understandeth:
the third is his judging rashly & unadvisedly of his neighbour
in this or that particular upon light inferences & circum-
stances, having noe apparent evidence & prooffe of itt: | |.
Ther are two Leaprosyes in the hart; One a mans owne will:
the other a mans owne judgment: | |.

201:      Magnum opprobrium pauperies!
Quæ Cogit omnia facere, et pati:
Arduamque deserit viam virtutis. | |.

> Quo mihi divitias queis non conceditur uti.   [52]
> Vel mihi da clavem, vel mihi tolle seram.

Load-stone quasi Lead-stone: Lepus quasi Levi-pes. | |.

202: Perditur in puncto quod non speratur in Anno.

203: Upon the — 13th — of May anno — 1304: & in the 31th of Edw: 1: Boniface the Archbishop of Canterbury & — 5 — other Bishopps solemnely denounced this curse in Westminster hall, the king himselfe with a great part of his nobilitie being present: ffirst against them that should wittingly & maliciouslie deprive or spoyle churches of their Rightes: Secondly against those that by anie art or devise infringed the Libertyes of the Church & Kingdome, Magna Charta et de fforesta: Thirdly against all those that should make new statutes against the Articles of these Charters: or should keepe them being made, or bring in or keepe other Customes: & against the writers of those statutes, Councellors, & Executioners therof that should presume to give judgment according to them. | |.

204: In the 42: of Edw: 3: Cap: 1°: It was enacted that if anie Statute weare made Contrarie to Magna Charta it should be voyde: & — 15 — tymes is this Charter Confirmed by parlament in Edw: 3: his Tyme: 8 Tymes in Ric: 2: his Raigne: & 6: tymes in H: 4: his Tyme:

> Heu tot sanctitas per plurima secula leges
> Hauserit una dies! Hora una! et perfidus error:

O utinam fortis tu in Re meliore fuisses. | |.

205: Providere Reipublicæ being but two wordes gave the Dictators of Rome authoritie over every thing. | |.

206: When the Emperor Valentinian required Ambrose to Come & Dispute A point of Arianisme at his Court, he besought him that he might doe itt in the Consistorie amongst the Bishopps: & that the Emperor would be pleased not to be present among them: least his presence should Captivate their judgments, or intangle their Lyberty. | |.

207: Before the Lugdune & Lateran Councells every man might [53] bestow his Tythes upon what religious howse or person he lysted. | |.

208: Stultissimum est existimare omnia justa esse quæsita sunt in populorum insititutis aut legibus: Even experience teacheth us that our Lawes are dayly accused of Imperfection, often amended, expounded & repealed: Looke backe into Tymes past & we shall find that manie of them have bin unprofitable for the Commonwealth: many dishonourable to the Kingdome: Some Contrary to the word of God: & Some verie impious & intollerable: yet all propounded, debated & Concluded by parlament:

209: Ther is jus ad Rem & Jus in Re: jus ad rem makes one rei usufructuarium: but it Cannot make him Rei dominum: All prescriptions, Statutes & Customes against the law of Nature, or of God, are voyd & against justice. Manie things are notoriously wicked in Conclusion, whose beginnings are not suspected: & noe man doubteth that in publique suffrages very manie Tymes, Major pars vincit meliorem:

210: The love of Chryst without Love to his Church, is but an empty maske of an emptie fayth. | | .

211: We must Glorifie god with those externall things we have receaved from him, in the same steppes that the rules & maximes of his owne law have prescribed: videlicet: ffirst we must doe unto him Homage |1| Trew & faythfull service: for it is written — Him only shalt thou serve. 2^{ly} we must not adhære to his enemies, The World, the fflesh, & the Divell: nor suffer them to subtract or incroach upon anie part of that which belongeth to God our Lord. | | . $3^{ly:}$ That we pay dewly unto him all Rightes & Dutyes that belong to his Seignory: ffor it is written Give unto God that which is Gods: ffor all this we must be accomptible at the great Audite: And ther lyes a speciall writt of præcipe in that Case: Redde Rationem villicationis tuæ: That is how thou hast Carryed thy selfe in this his service Committed unto thee. | | .

212: The Ceremonie of unction was not Common to all Chrystian Kings: for they being about Hen: the : 2: Tyme — 24 — in number — only — 4 — of them besydes the Emperor weare annointed: Namely the Kings of England, ffrance, Jersusalem & Sicill. And the first English King that receaved this priviledge was Elfred or Alured the glorious sonne of Ethewolphus King of West Saxonie who about the yeare of our Lord — 860 — being sent to Rome was ther by Leo the 4th annointed and Crowned King in the life of his father. | | . And Clodoveus alias Ludovicus was the first ffrench King that was annointed about the yeare of our Lord — 500. | | .

213: Alexander the great being moved by some about him to goe see the daughters of Darius whom he had overcome: answeared them That he would not see them, least that He that had overcome men, might be overcome of women. | |.

214: Ther are — 5 — things to be observed in our discourse that they may prove fruitfull & beneficiall unto us: 1: what thou speakest: 2: To whom thou speakest: 3: In what manner thou speakest: 4: at what tyme thou speakest: 5: in what place thou speakest. | |.

215: Ther are — 3 — things required in every action: 1: what we ought to doe: 2: the Reasons which invyte us to doe itt: 3: The meanes & manner how it ought to be done: virtus amarissimas radices, fructus verò dulcissimos habet:

216: In all things which thou shalt Thinke: Say: or Doe: let ther precede a dew examination of them, & Try whither they be from god, or for God. | |.

217: By these Signes you may know whither your will jumpe with Gods will: ffirst if you be not Troubled & disquieted with any thing: But take all things as they Come with chearfullnes, as Comming from Gods hand, referring them all to him: The — 2: is the purenes of Intention: when it doth in nothing seeke itts owne; but rather with much purenes seeketh that which is gods; in all things desyring his glory, & the accomplishment of his most holy will: The Third is, when our sword is our suffrance, & our sheild patience: when we have [55] noe afflictions befall us but we thinke our selves worthy of far greater: when we find fault with none but our selves: when we are angry & offended with none save ourselves: when we thinke noe man owes us any thing & therfore whatsoever they doe for us, we take it for a great kindnes and Curtesie: & yet thinke that we owe much unto all others. | |.

218:     ffleres si scires unum tua tempora mensum
            Rides, cum non sit forsitan una dies.

219:     Iam mala finissem letho, sed credula vitam
            Spes alit, et melius cras fore, semper ait.
                But trust not to that:
            Ille sapit quisquis posthume vixit heri. | |.
        Longe erit a primo, quisque secundus erit.
        . . . . Quo justior alter
        Nec pietate fuit, nec bello major et armis. | |.

220: A man lives — 40 — yeares before he knowes himselfe to be a
   foole: & by that Tyme he sees his follie his life is finished: Soe
   men dye, before they begin to live. | |.

221: To dye well is too busie a worke to be done ex Tempore
   Nil miserius morienti, quàm nescire mori. | |.

222: Occidere presbiteros, is nothing soe hurtfull, as occidere pres-
   biterium: when men are taken away, ther is hope that others
   will be Raysed in their places: but if the meanes of Maintenance be taken away, ther followeth the decay of the profession
   it selfe. | |.
   The possessors Title is the best untill he be fairely evicted out
   of itt: | |.
   Quod valdè volumus; facilè Credimus. | |.

223: We have had within the Space of halfe a yeare, one parliament
   proclayming King Edw: the — 4th — an usurper, & King Hen:
   the 6th a lawfull King: & another parliament proclayming
   King Edw: the — 4th — a lawfull King, & King Henry the — 6th
   — an usurper: That we may know in humane affayres, ther is
   nothing certayne but uncertaintie; nothing stable, but in-
   stabilitie. | |.

224: Tis Storyed of King Hen: the — 6th — King of England that he
   was soe devout, that he thought nothing adversitie which was
   not a hinderance to Devotion: And that he had one immuni-
   tie peculiar unto himselfe; That noe man could ever be re-
   venged of him, seeing he never offered anie man injury: And
   that he was soe patient, that to one who strooke him when he
   was taken prysoner, he only Sayd, Forsooth you wrong your
   selfe more then me; to strike the Lords annointed. | |.

225: Tis Storyed of King Hen: the — 5th — King of England, That he
   had Somthing in him of Cæsar, which Alexander the great
   had not: That he would not be druncke; And Somthing of
   Alexander the great which Cæsar had not: That he would not
   be fflattered. | |.

226: These three wayes Rich men offend: 1: in an anxious &
   solicitous desire of getting: 2^{ly} in withholding & keeping that
   close which of right ought to be dispersed & imparted to
   others: 3^{ly} — in augmenting wealth by evill meanes: as by
   Cosenage; usury, oppression & the like. | |. Avaro quid mali
   optes, nisi ut diu vivat?

227: Though the strongest citadell of a King be his peoples Love, & their harts his best exchequer: yet it is observed, that Love without ffeare turnes to Scorne: & ffeare without Love, turnes into Hatred. | |.

228: Moderation is the inseperable attendant of trew wisdome & policie; & shee makes those Councells, & those soveraigne Courtes & Parliaments happie, wher shee sitts in the chayre. | |.

229: The difference betwixt Lybertyes & priviledges is this: pryviledges presuppose the Concession & graunt of some superiour power: But Lybertyes are Originall, & immemorial possessions, & Equall to inheritances. | |.

230: He that hath Theeves to his neighbours, dares not goe farre from Home:

231: A wife is the best, or worst fortune, that can befall a man in the whole Course of his life. | |.

232: Ther is nothing more difficult in the ffait of Armes then to make an Honourable Retreat; nor is it any disgrace to goe away in the night, for preventing of being beaten by day: ffame is not to be esteemed by the Extent but by the Goodnes. | |.

233: They that are inforced to Comply with partyes of severall factions, are oftentymes put to their wytts end, how to put off their Hat to the one, & how to make a Leg to the other. | |.

234: Posterior dies est prioris Magister: | |.

235: Have a great Man for your ffreind, but not for your Neighbour. | |.

236: Populus aut humiliter servit, aut superbè dominatur; They are like Fyre & water: Good Servants but ill masters. | |.

237: Tis the part of a Wise man to Compose troubles: But of a Wiser to prevent that they may not happen. | |.

238: Wisdome & policie though they both agree in their Ends, yet they differ in the meanes conducing to attayne their Ends: The first goes the playne direct high Roade: The other useth now & then, some odde By-pathes:

239: Secrecie & Speed are the two cheiffe poles wheron Martiall Affayres move: — yet — quod fieri debeat, cum Multis tracta: quod facturus es, cum paucissimis: | |.

[57]

10

20

30

A Note of Diverse Remarkable & Strange   [58]
accidents Taken out of Sir Richard Bakers =
Cronicle from the Tyme of William the Conquerour
to the Beginning of the Raigne of King Charles.

Willyam the first: A Great Lord Sitting at a feast was sett upon by Mice: & though he weare removed from Land to Sea, & from Sea againe to Land, yet the Mice still followed him, and att last devoured him: pag 38 of his Raigne. | | .

Wylliam the Second   In the — 4th — yeare of his raigne The rooffe of the church of Saint Mary Bow in Cheape, was soe raysed with a   10 Tempest, that in the fall, six of the beames being — 27 — foot Long weare dryven soe deepe into the Ground (the streetes being not then paved with Stone) that not above — 4 — ffoot remayned in sight: pag: 48

In the — 11th — yeare of his raigne at a Towne Called Finchhamsteed in the County of Bark-shyre, a well Cast out blood, as before it had done water, & this continwed for — 15 — dayes: pag: 49.

Hen: 1: }   In the Raigne of Hen: the first, Ther was an Earth-quake in Lumbardy, that Continewed — 40 — dayes, & removed a   20 Towne from the place wher it stood, a great way off: pag: 58.

Hen: 2 }   In the — 23 — yeare of his raigne a showre of blood rained in the Isle of Wight two howres togither: pag: 79.

In the — 30 — yeare of his Raigne Neere unto Orford in Suffolk certayne fishers tooke in their nett a fish having the shape of a man in all points; which fish was Kept by Bar-tholmew de Glanvyle in the Castle of Orford — 6 — Monethes & more: he spake not a word, all manner of Meates he did gladly eate, but most greedily raw fish when he had pressed out the Juyce: often tymes he was brought   30 to church, but never shewed anie kind of Adoration: at length being not well looked to, he stole to the sea & was never seen after. Pag: 79. | | .

As he videlicet: H: 2 was carying to be buryed, his face being   [59] uncovered & all bare, his sonne King Richard the first, ran in all hast to see him; who noe sooner was Come neere the body but suddainly at his nostrills he fell a bleeding a fresh: pag: 79.

It is storyed that in the family of the Earles of Anjow of whom

98

King Henry the second Came, ther was once a princesse, a great inchauntresse, who being on a tyme inforced, to take the blessed Eucharyst, she suddaynely flew out at the church window, & was never seene after: pag: 82. | | .

King John }   Hugh de Bones Comming to ayde King John with — 60000 men out of Brittannie & fflaunders by misfortune at Sea were all drowned: pag: 103. | | .

In this Kings Tyme weare great Thunders & Lightenings & showers of Hayle stones as big as goose Egges. Pag: 103: | | .

In this Kings Tyme weare taken in England, ffishes armed with helmetts & sheildes; & weare like unto armed Knightes, Saving that they were far greater in proportion: pag: 103. | | .   10

Hen: 3 }   In this Kings ragyne Ther fell out att one tyme noe raine in England from the first of March to the assumption of our Lady: & at another Tyme ther fell soe much raine that Holland & Holdernes in Lyncolne-shire weare overflowed & drowned: pag — 123. | | .

In the — 17 — yeare of his rayne were seene — 5 — Sunnes at one Tyme togither: after which followed soe great a dearth, that people weare constrayned to eate horse flesh, & Barkes of Trees: & in London 20000 weare starved for want of ffood. Pag: 123. | | .   20

In this Kings Tyme ther was sent by the King of ffrance the first Elephant that ever was seene in England: pag: 123. | | .

Edward:2: }   In his — 8th — yeare Ther was soe great a dearth, that Horses, & dogges weare eaten: & Theeves in Pryson pluckt in peeces those that weare newly brought in amongst them, & eate them halfe alive; which Continewing three yeares, brought in the end such a pestilence that the living scarce suffised to Bury the dead. Pag: 154. | | .

Edward 3 }   In his Tyme a ffrost lasted from the middest of September [60] 30 To the moneth of Aprill

Ric: 2 }   In the yeare — 1389 — whilst the King was at Sheene ther swarmed in his court such multitudes of fflyes & Gnatts skirmishing one with another, that in the end they weare swept away with broomes by heapes, & bushells were filled with them: Idem in vita R: 2: pag: 27: | | .

In his one & Twentyeth yeare a River not far from Bedford suddainly ceased his Course, soe as the channell remayned dry by the space of — 3 — miles: pag: 27. | | .

About the yeare — 1380 — The making of Gunnes was found by a germane: The first that used them weare the Venetians against the inhabitants of Geneva. | | . pag: 27. | | .

Henry 4: } In the — 3 — yeare of this King in Danbury in Essex the Divill appeared in the likenes of a Gray fryar: who entring the church putt the people in great feare, & the same howre with a Tempest of whirle-wind & Thunder, the toppe of the steeple was broken downe, & halfe the chauncell scattered abroade pag: 42. | | .

Henry 5 } In the third yeare of his raigne on the feast of the purification seven Dolphins came up the river of Thames — wherof 4 weare taken: In vita H: 5: pag: 59:

Henry 6 } In the — 33 — yeare of his raigne A monstrous cocke came out of the Sea, & in the presence of a multitude of people at Portland made a hydeous Crowing — 3 — Tymes, each tyme turning about clapping his winges & Beckning towards the North, the South and the West: pag: 90. | | .

Henry 7 } In the — 10 — yeare of his raigne In the church of Saint Mary Hill in London The body of Alice Hackeney who had bin buryed in that church — 175 — yeares before, was found whole of Skin & the joynctes of her Armes plyable; which Corps was kept above ground fowre dayes without annoyance & then againe buryed: pag: 160:

In the — 12th — yeare of his Raigne on Bartholmew day at the Towne of Saint Needs in Bedfordshire, ther fell hayle-stones that weare measured — 18 — Inches about: pag: 160: | | .

Henry 8 } In the — 33 — yeare of his raigne on Twesday in Easter weeke, William Foxley pott-maker for the mynt of the Tower of London fell asleepe, & could not be awaked with pinching or burning, till the first day of the next Terme, which was full — 14 — dayes: & when he awaked was found in all points as if he had slept but one night, & Lyved — 40 — yeares after: In Vita H: 8: pag: 66. | | .

Edward 6 } In the — 6 — yeare of this Kings raigne the — 3 — of August at Middleton Storrie — 11 — myles from Oxford a woman brought forth a chylde, which had two perfect bodyes from the Navill upwards: The Legges for both the bodyes grew out of the middest wher the bodyes joyned, & had but one issue for the excrements of them both: They Lived — 18 —

dayes & weare women children. | |. In Vita Ed: 6: pag: 86:

In the Same yeare weare taken at Quinborough — 3 — Dolphyns and at Blacke wall — 6 — more, the least of which was bigger then any horse: pag: 86. | |.

Queene Mary — In the — 2 — yeare of her raigne on the — 15 — of February appeared in the sky a Raine-bow reversed, the bow turned downeward, & the two ends standing upward: pag — 106. | |.

In the same yeare two sunnes shyned at one Tyme a good distance asunder: pag: 106. | |.

This yeare also in the Moneth of August at a place in Suffolke by the Sea syde all of Hard stone & Pybble, lying between the Townes of Orford & Albourough, wher never grasse grew, nor anie Earth was ever seene, ther chanced suddainly to spring up without anie Tillage or Sowing, soe great abundance of Peazon, that the poore gathered above an hundred quarters, yet ther remayned some rype, some blossoming, as many as weare before: pag 106. | |.

In her — 5th — yeare in a marvelous tempest of Thunder that happened, a chyld was taken forth of a mans hand, & caryed two speares length high, & then lett fall two hundred foot off, of which fall it dyed: pag: 106: | |.

Queene Elizab — In the — 3 — yeare of her raigne ther weare manie Monstrous Birthes; a mare brought forth a foale with Two heads, & a long tayle growing out betweene the — 2 — heads: A sow farrowed a pigge with — 2 — bodyes, 8 — feet & but one heade: pag: 117: in vita R: Eliz: | |.

Q: Elizab — In the — 6 — yeare of her Raigne in the moneth of December was driven on the shoare at Grymbesbye in Lincolne-shire a monstrous fish in length — 19 — yardes: his tayle — 15 — foote broad: & six yardes betweene the Eyes: — 12 — men stood upright in his mouth to gett the oyle. Pag: 117. | |.

In her — 14th — yeare a vast mightie whale was Cast upon the Isle of Thanett, in Kent: 20 — Ells long: — 13 — ffoot broad from the belly to the backe bone: & eleven foot betweene the Eyes: one of his eyes being taken out of his head, was more then a Cart with six horses could draw. | |. pag 117. | |.

In the same yeare on the — 24th — of February, being a great frost after a flood, which was not great: Ther came downe the river of Severne such a swarme of fflyes & Beetells, that they were judged to be above—100—quarters: The mills therabout weare dammed up with them above the space of—4—dayes: & then wear cleansed by digging them out with shovells: pag: 117. | |.

King James }   In the yeare—1613—on the 17th of Aprill in the parish of Standish in Lancashyre a Mayden chyld was borne having—4—legges:—4—Armes: 2—Bellyes joyned to one backe: one head with—2—faces, the one before, the other behind, like the picture of Janus. In vita Jac: Regis—154 pag: | |.

In the same yeare on the—26th—day of June in the parish of Chryst-church in Hampshire one John Hitchell a Carpenter, lying in bed with his wife & a young chyld by them, was himselfe & the childe both burned to death with a suddayne Lightning, noe fire appearing outwardly upon him; & yet lay burning almost for the space of three dayes, till he was quite consumed to ashes. In Vita Jacobi regis pag: 154.

These Notes weare taken out of Sir Richard Bakers Cronicle when I read itt over in the Tower in the 1647:

per JS

240: Wyse men are but men: & the best men are but men att the best: subject to the faultes of the Irascible & concupiscible facultyes: | |.

241: Untill the statute of $5^{to:}$ Edw: $6^{ti:}$ all judiciall places weare generally bought & sould, as horses in Smithfeild. | |.

242: Hæc est crede mihi Cunctorum Causa Malorum
    Scripturas Domini non didicisse sacras. | |.

243: Pœnitenda presumtio, non perficienda promissio. | |.

244: By generall rules of physicke noe wyse man can expect to be Cured. | |.

245: The Mayne Ends of Parlaments is to supervise the publique Magistrates: to see that Ministers of Justice be just & execute justice impartiallie. | |.

245: De Cane: } Est Lingua Medicus, Dominoque fidelis amicus:
    Sentit odoratu, fugit eius latro Latratu.

246: To what end should ther be freedome of Debate in a Councell if ther be not freedome of information to the Councell. | |.

247: He breakes the peace that constraynes me to breake itt for myne owne preservation. | |.

248: Sufferance is the greatest wisdome, to prevent a greater suf-
ferance, in matters which are sufferable. | |.

249: If I weare asked who was the most unfeigned lover of his
Country, & the Kingdomes best ffreind? I would answeare in
two things; He that is most forward to goe wayes, which are
most dangerous to himselfe & safe to his Country: wherby I
exclude newters that wilbe sure to sleepe in a whole skin:
when the King of Sweden approached Frankford the citizens
sent unto him that they might be newtrall Till their fayre was
past: what! sayes he are your fayres deerer unto you then   10
your Consciences: By Solons lawes, Newters were to be
Hanged. | |.

250: Lyverie & Seizin made in the night is voyde: If a man be robd   [64]
in the night, ther is noe releiffe for him, it being noe tyme to
travell: noe distresse can be taken in the night for Rent but a
distresse for Damage ffeasant may, for the necessitie that else
the beastes wilbe gone.

251: If man must raigne over the Conscience, wher must Jesus
Chryst raigne? ffor Temporall Kingdome he hath none. | |.

252: A Cannon made in favour of an Angry pope, that he might   20
strike anie man, & noe man strike him, was voyd by the law
of Nature: ffor what is it but to arme sinne against the law. | |.

253: To take away a Mad-mans sword from him, is not to take
away the propertie; but to prevent the mischeiffe.

254: Harry the 8th was wont to say merrilie: If it be a good Religion, it will defend itt selfe: if it be a bad one it is not worth
the defending: Let god alone with Religion.

255: They that have stolen the Kingdomes goose, the feathers will
stick in their stomackes. | |.

256: By the Law of Armes some professions are more priviledged   30
then others in a Tyme of warre, as Preistes, Surgeons, Hus-
bandmen, & those that Keepe vyneyards: & these ought not
to be taken prysoners on either syde, because ther is a neces-
sarie use for them, which party soe ever prevayled. | |.

257: Our Historians tell us, that after Civill warres, ther weare alwayes Commissions graunted, to inquire who had increased
their estates in a publique Calamitie: & out of their superflui-
tyes they weare inforced to releive the necessityes of poore
men. | |.

258: Cui nasci contingit, mori restat: The Hebrewes say ther are —
907 — & sortes of Naturall Deathes. | |.

259: 1: Have death alwayes in thy Remembrance: for therby we   [65]
avoyde vice & follow after virtue: 2$^{ly:}$ ffeare death; because
thou dost not Know in what estate death will find thee: 3$^{ly:}$
Concider that Death is most certayne, But when & How, most
uncertaine: & it is not safe to live secure in that estate, wherin
thou wouldest not dye: 4$^{ly:}$ Mortify thy Affections to what
thou dost disordinately love or desyre, seeing we must leave
& forgoe all at our death, & that which we affect with much   10
love, we forgoe with much greiffe: 5$^{ly:}$ Know, & Contemne thy
selfe, concidering that thou must come to End in Dust &
Ashes: 6$^{ly:}$ Despise the things of this world & the vayne Glorie
therof: & Concider of how small use & worth they are for the
hower of Death: 7$^{ly:}$ Rest Contented with poverty if god place
thee in that Condition; Seeing how poore we shall remayne at
our death: He that will goe in att a narrow wickett, must have
noe big burthen at his backe: 8$^{ly:}$ Take Comfort in all the
troubles & afflictions in this life, Seeing they must be soe
quickly ended: & that those which thou dost suffer for gods   20
sake shall make thy death sweet & Savoury unto thee: | | Hac
animadversione percutitur peccator; ut moriens obliviscatur
sui, qui dum vixerit oblitus est dei: | |.

260: in the yeare — 670: Pope Sylvester the second brought in the
title of Pope: & Pope Gregory was the first that brought into
the popes Style, Servus Servorum Dei: & Boniface brought
into their heads, volumus ac mandamus; statuimus ac præci-
pimus. | |.

261: In the yeare of our Lord — 162 — : in the tyme of King Lucius
the Brittaynes receaved the Chrystian ffayth. | |.   30

262: Wyllyam the Conquerour caused to be inrolled in his Treasury Every Hyde Land & the owner therof: what fruit & Revenewes of Every Lordshippe, of Every Towneshippe, Castle,
feild, village, River & wood within all the Realme of England:
moreover how manie parish churches, how manie Living
Cattle ther weare: what & how much Every [66] Baron in the
Realme could dispend; what fees were belonging what wages
were taken &c. The Tenour & Contents wereof yet remayne in
Rolles: | |.

104

263: Wyllyam the Conquerour Graunted to the city of London, the first charter that ever they had, written in the Saxon Tongue, with Greene wax sealed, & Contayned in few lines. | |.

264: In his Tyme The bishoppes see of Shirborne was translated to Salesbury: & the first Bishoppe ther was Hermannus a Norman, who first began the new church & minster of Salesbury; after him succeeded Osmundus who finished that worke: He first began the Ordinall which was called, Secundum Usum Sarum in anno 1067. | |.

265: After the raigne of William Rufus the name of Kings ceased in the Country of Wales amongst the Brittans since King Rys who in the yeare — 1093 was slayne in Wales. | |.

266: The Bishoppes in ancient Tyme made — 4 — partitions of all that was given: one to the Bishoppe for Hospitalitie: Another to the cleargie: The Third to the poore: The — 4th — to the Repayring of churches. | |.

267: Tully sayd Trewly, out of Asia to live a good life is noe god a mercy: But in Asia wher soe great occasions of Evill abound, ther to live a good man, that is prayse-worthy. | |.

268: King Ethelbert was the first founder of Saint Paules church in London: & of Saint Andrewes in Rochester; which Tower was soe called of one Rott:

269:     Linquenda est Domus, Tellus, et placens uxor
    Et harum quas Colis arborum
    Nulla præter unam Cupressam
    Te brevem Dominum sequetur. | |.

270: In the yeare — 747 — in the moneth of September & in the raigne of King Egbert: Cutbert being Archbishop of Canterbury at a great Synode neere the place Called Clonesho amongst other decrees it was enacted:

1: That None should be admitted to orders before his life should be Examined. | |.

2: That they should Teach the lords prayer & Creed in the English Tongue. | |.

3: That all should joyne togither in their Ministry after one uniforme Right & Manner. | |.

4: That the Sabboath Day should be reverently observed & Kept. | |.

5: That publique prayers should be made for Kings & Princes. | |.

6:    They disputed of the profitt of Singing of psalmes. | |.

271: } To Pipinus the ffrench King was first sent into France the In-
vention of Organes out of Græcia by Constantine Emperour
of Constantinople anno Domini — 757. | |.

272: Noe Bishoppe was to be Condemned under — 72 — witnesses. | |.

273: King Ethelstane made the Law that such as stole above 12^d &
weare above 12 yeares old should not be spared. | |.

274: He ffounded the Abbey of Middleton in Dorsett, & of Michil-
ney in Somersett:

275: King Edgar ordeyned certayne Cuppes with pynnes or Nayles
to be sett in them, adding therunto a law; That what person
dranke past that marke at one draught, should forfaite a
certayne pennie, wherof one halfe should fall to the accuser,
& the other parte to the ruler of burrough or Towne wher the
offence was done. | |.

276: King Edgar founded the monasterie of Nunnes at Shaftesbury
in Dorsett anno 969.

277: King Edgar Pacificus ordayned that the sunday should be
solemnized from Saturday at 9 of the clocke, Till munday
morning: Fox: pag: 206.

278: It is reported of King Edgar by diverse authors that about the
— 13th — yeare of his raigne being at Chester eight Kings
(called in Historyes subreguli) |1| pettie Kings Came & did
Homage unto him of whom the first was the King of Scottes
called Kynadius: Malcolinus of Cumberland: Machus or Mas-
cusinus King of Monia: & of diverse other Islands: & all the
Kings of Wales, the Names of whom weare Dufiall or Dunck-
waldus; Syfreth: Huwall: Jacob: Uykyll: Inchell. | |.

279: Pope John the 14 brought in first the chrystening of Belles
anno 971: | |.

280: Pope Gregorie the 5th: By the consent & Councell of Otho the
3 ordayned — 7 — princes of Germanie to be Electors of the Emperour: which order yet to this day remayneth: what be the
names of these — 7 — Electors & what is their office these verses
expresse:

    Maguntinensis; Treverensis: Coloniensis
    Quilibet imperii fit Cancellarius horum:
    Et palatinus dapifer; Dux portitor Ensis
    Marchio præpositus Cameræ: pincerna Bohemus.

<u>These</u>—7—he ordayned to be electors: 3 Bishopps: 3 Princes videlicet the Palatine: The Duke of Saxonie: The Marquesse of Brandenburgh: To whom also was added the King of Boheme, if the even voyces could not agree. This Constitution being first begun anno—997—was afterwards established in Germanie by Otho the Emperour in anno 1002. | |.

281: It is storyed of King Egelred or Elred that when Dunstane the Archbishoppe should christen him; as he did hold him over the Font, he Fyeled therin: wherupon Dunstane Sware by the mother of Chryst, that he would be a prince untoward & Coward like. | |.

282: The Tribute of Danegelt, which was first payd by this King Egelread or Elred amounted at first to—10000^{li}—& within—5 —or 6 yeare to 40000^{li} yearely. | |.

283: Nullus hostis acerbior, Nulla pestis efficatior quàm familiaris inimicus: & evill judges are worse in a Common wealth, then Bloody Enimies: Susceptio muneris et dimissio veritatis, non enim opera, sed munera Conciderant: They Spare the divill the paynes in Courting them, by preferring themselves to his service. | |.

284: Though I know that I am not to live for my selfe, I am to dye for my selfe; & may now at this age justly challenge to my selfe a writte of Ease from all worldly Imployment. | |.

285: Power never wants pretences & those Legall to Compasse what it doth desyre. | |. Quicquid eis placuit Juris ad instar erit: | |.

286: Tis just that they should dye of the physicke, who made a god of the physition: But ther is noe such tourment as to dye of the Remedye. | |.

287: In the Councell of Laterane in the yeare—1059—under Pope Nicholas the second, was Transubstantiation brought into the church: | |.

288:　　　Ac veluti magno in populo cum sæpe coorta est
　　　Seditio Sævitque animis ignobile vulgus,
　　　Iamque faces et saxa volant; Furor arma ministrat
　　　Tum pietate gravem ac meritis si forte virum quem
　　　Conspexere, silent: arrectisque auribus astant.
　　　Ille regit mentes, dictis, et pectora Mulcet. | |. &c:

289: Every man hath his owne busines in hand, when his neigh-bours howse is on fire:

290: Punishment dew to Malefactors & Rebells is not to be Called
persecution, but dew Correction:

291: If anie Bishoppe shall institute or Consecrate such a preist as
shalbe unmeet & unconvenient, if he scape with the losse of
his owne proper dignitye yet he shall lose the power of In-
stituting anie more. | |.

292: Whom they ought to have obeyed, though he had bin Evill
(speaking of the Barons Behaviour against King John) even for
very Conscience sake: Fox: pag: 333. | |.

293: Augustus presented before the people of Rome Lucius a young [70] 10
gentleman well descended: only for to shew that he was lesse
then two feet in height: seventeene pound in weight; & of an
immense voyce. Suetonius in Augusto. | |.

294: In the yeare 1224 By virtue of a certayne parlament, was
graunted of the lords & Baronie of the Land, the King & his
heires to have the ward & Mariage of their heires: which was
then called & after soe proved Initium Malorum The Begin-
ning of Harmes. This was as I take it in 6to Hen: 3$^{tii:}$ | |.

295: Great Riches stoppe not the taking of Much; but a Mind Contented with a little: 20
    Quod virtus reddit non Copia sufficientem
    Et non paupertas, sed Mentis Hiatus Egentem:

296: Benignus animus, dubia in melius interpretatur:

297: King H: the 3: in the yeare 1227: & in the 20th yeare of his Age
graunted the Citizens of London should passe Toll-free throughout all England: And if of anie one City, Burrough, or Towne
they weare Constrayned at anie Tyme to pay their Tolle, then
the Shreiffes of London to attacke every man Coming to London of the sayd City, Burrough, or Towne, & him & his goods
to with hold till the Londiners weare agayne Restored of all   30
such monie payd for the sayd Tolle: with all Costes & Dam-
ages sustayned for the same. | |.

298: Stephen Langhton Archbishoppe of Canterbury did first distinguish the chapters of the bible in that order & Number as
we now use them.

299: Noe Man Can see anie Spotte in his owne face, without he
looke in the Glasse: or else be toulde by some other whither
his face be blotted or Noe. | |.

300: We ought to doe good even to them that be ungratefull: ffor [71]
soe doth the sea participate her calme & smooth Tides even to
the pyratts: And soe god causeth the sunne to shyne upon the
just and unjust: But (alas for sorrow) what bitter division is
this, that hath thus sequestred us asunder? one of us detract-
eth another, & shunne the Companie of one another, as the
damnation of his soule. If you thinke we are fallen, then doe
you helpe to lift us up: & be not unto us as a stumbling blocke
to our Bodily Ruine: But helpers unto the spirituall resurrec-
tion of our soules: | |. But if the Blame & first offence proceede   10
from you, Then read the wordes of Saint Paule to the Gal:
Cap: 2: ver: 11: when Peter Came unto Antioch Paul with-
stood him in the face, because he was to be rebuked &c: yet
this Resistance was noe cause of anie disorder or breach betweene them, but Rather the cause of further search & pro-
founder disputations, provoking Temporall agreement; For
they weare not separated by Ambition or Avarice. But you
scrape togither all that you can scratch or Rake, you heape up
gold & sylver, & yet you pretend that you be the disciples of
him which sayd Golde & Sylver have I none; And Soe you   20
unteach by your deedes, that which you Teach in wordes. | |.
I write this unto you not for anie instruction, but only to putt
you in remembrance: ffor I know how god hath endewed you
with all wisdome & knowledge: Solomon sayth, Give only
occasion to the wise, & he will learne wisdome; Teach the just
Man, & he wilbe glad to take instruction. | |.
301: Qui non vetat peccare cum potest, Iubet: nil enim inter est
sceleri an faveas, an facias: | |. Malum est sui diffusivum.
302: In magnis ingeniis, magnis errores: and the greatest talkers
are not alwayes the wisest men.   30
303: One syde makes Religion a marke of Rebellion: And the other
side make rebellion a marke of Religion: And I feare they both
hate Loyaltie & Religion. | |.
304: The more Knave, the better Lucke: & I Know noe Reason, but [72]
that proverbe is still as Trew as Ever. | |.
305: Ima permutat brevis hora Summis: Hodiè mihi, Cras Tibi: | |.
306: Tis the word of God that is ordayned to suppresse false
religions, & not the Sword of Man: ffyre, Swordes, & pistolles
are the weapons of Antichryst, & not of Chryst. | |.

307:   Eius Avaritiæ Totus non sufficit orbis
       Eius Luxuriæ Meritrix non sufficit omnis:

308: Although the waters in the Generall Flood rooted up all the
Trees, yet the Olyve remayned still standing, ffrom which the
Dove brought a greene leafe, or little Branch in her Bill; now
this Olyve is a simbole & Embleame of Peace: And therfore
although in this life the waters of Gods chastisements & the
ffloods of his wrath arise never soe high, yet shall they never
be able to overwhelme gods mercie: In thy wrath thou re-
membrest Mercie: Hab: 3:2.   10

309: If Almesdeeds shalbe judged, what shall become of Theftes?
& Extortions, of Briberie & Corruptions? If Fasting shalbe
Examined, what shall Gluttonie & Surfeiting be? If accompte
shalbe taken of good wordes, what reckoning shall we render
for those that be Idle? What of our perjuries & Blasphemies?
If the chaste shalbe censured, for his slacknes in Casting out
an Evill thought, how shall the Carnall & Loose wanton be
Taxed who hath Committed a thowsand filthy Actions? &c: | | .

310: He that shewes himselfe thankfull for one benifitt, makes
himselfe worthy of Manie: The unthankfull Man is a Mon-   20
stere, for he is a man without Eyes, Mouth, or Handes. | | .
       Beneficiorum inventor, Compedes invenit. | | .

311: Tis great ffoolishnes, if not Madnes to offend him, whom thou   [73]
Knowest must be judge of thy Cawse. | | .

312: The way which is playne & all upon a Levell, wearieth a man
more, then that which is not soe: & varietie even in punishments is a Kind of Comfort, though a poore one.

313: In these three Adverbs, Sobriè; justè; piè: we are taught how
to Cary our selves towardes our selves: videlicet: Soberly:
Towards our Neighbours: justly: & Towards God: Godly: 30

314: Ceremonia, quasi Cereris mœnia: now Ceres was reputed to
be the goddesse of Corne & ffruites: Customes and Cere-
monies ordayned in the church by the ancient ffathers, are
that Counterscarffe wherwith the ffort of Sacred Religion is
secured & made good: It is the hedge which gardeth the
Garden of the Bridegroome, that the Boare of the fforest may
not enter in to destroy itt: It is like to the leafes of a Tree which
beautifie itt, shelter itt, & Season the ffruite therof: It is that
Barke & Rinde of the Tree, which although it may seeme to be

Superfluous, yet it concerves itt & keepes itt in itts verdure and Bravery: By breaking of these things, enter those little Foxes, of whom the Bridgroome sayth, that they wast & destroy the vyneyard.| |.

315: In rebus-publicis benè Temperalis, providendum est in primis, ne quid preter instituta moresque fiat: Sed Maximè omnium quod exiguum est Caveri debet. Detrimentum enim latenter obrepit, quia non totum simul contrahitur: ab his enim rebus decipitur intelligentia, et ratio illa Captiosa est: Si unumquodque parvum est, erunt et omnia parva: quod est quodammodo verum, quodammodo secus: Nam totum et omnia non [74] sunt res parve, sed ex parvis Constituuntur. Qui minima negligit, paulatim defluet, He that Contemnes small things shall fall, by little & little. Ecclus 19:1:

316: Lett us offer unto God, Gold, ffrankencence & Mirrhe: Deedes of Charitie are figured by Golde: Of prayer by Incense: of Mortification & Sorrow for our Synnes by Myrrhe:

317: Quia dilexit movere pedes suos, et non quièvit domino non placuit: Jer: 14:10: Cella sit tibi Cælum qua cælica mediteris: Cælum et Cella are derived from the verbe Celo, Celas; which signifyeth to Cover.

318:    Ut sis nocte Levis, sit tibi cæna brevis:
    Not Supping Cures more men: Then ever did Avicen:

319: Obedience must be wayted on by these seven Adverbes. 1 Diligently: 2: Willingly: 3: Cheerfully: 4: Simply: 5: Strongly: 6: Constantly: 7: Humbly:

320: Amici sunt fures Temporis:

321: Quia factum legimus, non ideo faciendum Credimus: sectando enim exemplum, violemus præceptum.

322: Misera est servitudo ubi jus est vagum et incertum:

323: In the Parlament of 39 of Q: Eliz: the queene refused to passe —48—Bills, which had passed both howses.| |.

Concerning the Covenant [75]

We will endeavour to mayntayne the Trew reformed protestant Religion in the church of Scotland, in Doctrine, Disciplyne, worshippe & Goverment according to the word of God.| |.

These words Imply that the worshippe, disciplyne & Goverment of the church of Scotland is according to the word of God, which is more then I dare subscribe, much lesse confirme by an oath. | | .

1: I am not perswaded that anie plat-forme of Goverment in each particular circumstance is Jure divino.

2: Admitt some weare, yet I doubt whither the Scotts presbiterie be that

3: Although somwhat may seeme to be urged out of Scripture for the Scotts goverment, with some shew of probabilitie, yet farre from such evidence as may convince a mans conscience to sweare, itt is agreeable to god's word. | | .

    I shall endeavour the extirpation of prelacie out of the
    Church of England &c:

I dare not sweare that:

1: In Regard I beleeve Episcopacie is an Apostolicall Insitution

2: That the church never soe flourished as within — 500 — yeares after chryst, when it was governed by Bishoppes.

3: That our English Episcopacie is justifyed by the pryme devynes of the Reformed churches beyond the Seas.

4: That our English Bishopps now & Ever since the Reformation have disclaymed all Papall dependencie. | | .

5: That the fowre Generall Councells (confirmed in England by Act of Parliament 1°ᐟ Eliz:) assert Episcopacie. | | .

6: The Ministers of the church of Scotland ordayned according to a forme (confirmed by act of parliament) at their ordination take an Oath, that they will reverently obey their ordinarie, & other cheiffe Ministers of the Church, & them to whom the charge is Comitted over them.

This Oath I & all cleargie men have taken: & if we shall sweare the [76] extirpation of prelacie, we shall sweare to for-sweare our selves. | | .

    I will defend the Rights & Priviledges of Parliament &
    defend his Majesties Person and authoritie in defence of
    the Trew religion & Lybertyes of the Kingdome.

Here the Members are putt before the head: The Parliaments priviledges before the Kings prerogative: & the Restraint of Defending the King only in such & such Cases, seemes to imply Somthing which I feare may be drawne to ill Consequence.

The Plea of the L: Hunsdon.

By the Law of the Land noe peere ought to be questioned for his life; but by Indictment at the Common Law for Treason, misprision of Treason, ffelonie or misprysion therof, by Jurors of that Countie wher the offence was Committed: The Lord Hunsdon stands not indicted by Jurors: After such Indictment a Lord Steward is to be made under the Great seale to proceed upon that Indictment Secundum Legem et Consuetudinem Angliæ: & the sayd L: Steward is to proceed therupon, & to award his precept to a Number of peeres for the Tryall of that offence: which Number must be Twelve at the Least: 1: Hen: 4: fol: 1°: | |. 10° Edw: 4: fol: 6$^{to:}$ 13° Hen: 8: fol: 13° The Lord Coke his — 3 — parte of Instit⁻ fol: 28. Published by the order of the howse of Commons this session of parlament.

Ther is noe such Indictment nor Steward Constituted: nor noe such precept awarded for anie such Number of Peeres or more: & therfore the L: Hunsdon ought not to answeare by the Law & Custome of England to the pretended Cryme charged upon him in anie other way. | |. And the L: Hunsdon farther sayth that all the offenses charged upon him by the sayd Articles weare Committed between the — 26th — of July & the 10th of August last: all which Actions now pretended to be Treason, Crymes & Misdeameanors weare directed & avowed by the parliament then sitting: In which tyme ther was either a Parliament or Noe Parliament: If a Parliament, the offences charged by the sayd Articles can be noe Treason, Nor Cryme, nor Misdeameanor: If Noe Parliament, then it was Ended, & being Ended, without a new summons, ther Can be noe Parliament assembled. | |.

And the sayd L: Hunsdon farther sayth that the votes, Orders & Ordinances of this present Parliament are in force untill they be repealed: and that the sayd Votes, Orders & Ordinances, approoving & directing the actions now pretended by the sayd Articles to be Crymes, weare justifyed & Justifiable be-tweene the sayd 26th of July & the sayd — 10th — of August: which Votes, Orders & Ordinances weare not repealed till after the sayd 10th Day of August. | |.

And the sayd L: Hunsdon farther sayth, That by the law of the
Land, Custome of Parliament, & Common Reason, Noe man
is punishable for obeying the Votes, Orders & Ordinances of
the sayd Parliament in Being, or doing or acting anie thing by
the Commaund of anie Legall power in force: for that it is his
dutie to obey the same, & ought, & is compellable soe to doe:
howbeit afterwards the sayd votes, Orders & Ordinances or
anie of them be repealed. | | .

By the statute of Magna Charta & other good Lawes of the Realme,
noe peere or other person ought to be proceeded against, but
according to the Establisht lawes of the Land: & Not otherwise, nor in anie other Manner: And therfore sithence the law
of Land for the Tryall of a Peere [78] is as aforesayd: To which
Lawes all the peeres of the Realme have consented & bound
themselves unto, in all succession of Tymes & Ages: The howse
of Lords att this tyme ought to proceede against the L: Hunsdon accordingly, & in noe other Manner: Mag: chart' cap: 29
25: Ed: 3: Cap: 4: | 25 Edw: 3: cap: 2: | 28 Edw: 3: cap: 3: | 37
Edw: 3: cap: 8: | 42: Edw: 3: cap: 13: | 1 & 2 Phil: & Mar: cap:
10: | The Petition of Right & 3^{tio} Caroli: | | .

Judicandum est Legibus, non Exemplis: Albeit in Tumultuous &
Troublesome Tymes, some Examples may be alleaged or
produced of an other way: yet Constant practise & establish't
Lawes are & ought to be the guide & Rule of all proceedings
in Judicature: otherwise settled Lawes wilbe of Noe effect: ffor
all which Causes, the sayd L: Hunsdon prayeth to be discharged of his Imprysonment & further Trouble, & to goe
without Delay. | | .

Finis.

324: Symonides being demaunded why he had noe more Enimies
& Envyers of his Estate? answeared, quia nihil fæliciter gessi:

325: The Birds have their Captayne: & the seely Bee their King: But
you will come under noe Governement, & through your default it perisheth: Soe that wher Nature hath placed the sence
& the understanding, That parte like a Monster remayneth
with you both sencelesse & head-lesse. | | .

326: Honour & Authoritie are in love with such a man as refuseth
them, & yett abhorres them not. | | .

114

327: He is a man of Good report & a worthy Man, who knoweth better how to doe other men good, then to receave a good Turne of another. | |.

328: Heresye is a sentence taken & chosen of Mans owne Brayne; Contrary to holy Scripture openly mayntayned & stiflie defended: He that can resist him & doth not, he sinneth; & seemeth to be a favourer therof: according to the saying of Gregory He lacketh not Conscience of secret societe, which ceaseth to resist open impietie. | |. [79]

329: In King Henry the 3 his Tyme, The Revenewes of forrayners placed here in England by Innocentius the—4th—amounted to the summe of 70000 Markes & above: wheras the meere Revenews of the Crowne came not to—30—Thowsand. 10

330: In the yeare 1247 in the raigne of King Edw: 1: the statute of Mortmayne was first enacted: which is to say, That noe man should give unto the Church anie Lands or Rents without a speciall licence of the King. | |.

331: The Blacke ffryars by Ludgate weare first founded in the 7th yeare of King Edw: 1: And the same yeare the Jewes weare Banished this Realme of England. | |. 20

332: At ffankyrch on Saint Mary Magdalenes Day King Edw: 1: in the yeare 1298: had with the Scotts a sore fight: but the victory through gods providence fell to the Englishmen: Soe that of the Scottes weare slayne in the feild—32—Thowsand & more: & of the Englishmen barely—28—persons. | |.

333: In the Tyme of Hely & Samuell the Prophett, Brutus Came from Troy to this Isle called then Albion, after Called by him Britannia: He had three sonnes: Locrynus to whom he gave that part of the Land called Loegria; now Anglia: Albanactus his second sonne, To whom he gave Albania, now Called 30 Scotia: & his third sonne Camber, to whom he gave Cambria, now Called Wales: | |.

334:     Dum viguit Rex et valuit tua magna potestas,
     Trans Latuit, pax magna fuit, regnavit honestas. | |.

335: Gods Love is a love with hands, not a bare affection: Soe that to love us, to wish us well, & to doe us good is all one: | |.

336: Love is the uniting of Two soules & two harts into one: & therfor the thing which is most proper unto love, is to desyre this union. | |. The Measure to love god is to love him without Measure. | |.

337: Giftes Breake the hardest Rockes: [80]

338: As Man Naturallie loveth himselfe: soe likewise ought he to love anie whatsoever parte that is his: A Kinsman is nothing else but a peece of that person who is of his parentage & Kindred: which the Latine word doth more significantly expresse, which calles a Kinsman Consanguinem that is to say, one that hath the same blood running in his veynes. | |.

339: Sapere et Amare vix deo Conceditur. | |.

340: The Egiptians did poynt for a Symbole or Heiroglyphick of god a hand with a Scepter: placing on the Top therof a vigilant eye: giving us therby to understand that god hath alwayes the Scepter of his Goverment in his hand: & the eye of his divyne providence still open for to watch over his servants, & to see they want nothing. | |. — 10

341: All Things worke togither for the best unto them that love god, who by the divyne providence of our lord god from their owne sinnes draw humilitie: & from other mens a fayre warning: & from pardon of them, they draw love & thankfullnes for this great mercie Towards them: & from chastisements draw a feare & Reverence of his divyne justice. | |. — 20

342: The shippes of Mirmicides weare much celebrated & very renowned which having all their sayles & Tacklings, weare soe small that they weare hid under the wings of a Bee, of that ordinarie bignes as Bees now a dayes be. Plyn: lib: 36: cap: 8: & Cicero lib: 4: Academ: quæst͂:

343: It is storyed that Constantine the Emperour when certayne of his subjects presented unto him libells accusatory against the Bishopps receaved them at their hands: but calling before him those Bishops: which weare accused therin cast in their sight those libells in the fire, saying, departe you hence, & discusse these matters within yourselves: ffor it is not Convenient and meete that we judge gods, because it is written, God stood in the Synagogue of Gods, & in the midst of them he did judge Gods. | |. — 30

344: Noveltie & Alteration doth engender discord: & therfore in making new Alterations ther ought to be both evident utilitie, & urgent Necessitie. | |.

345: In matters of waight & of Greate Importance, next after Conscience, we must have regard to name & fame: as it is written [81] in the 22th of Proverbs: A Good name is better then Riches. | |.

346: He that offereth up unto god a proud hart, & killeth it with
the Axe of Humilitie: giveth unto him the best & fattest bul-
locke he hath in his whole heard. | |.

The Severall Mottoes of the
Severall Emperors Ending
with Ferdinand the Second:

1: Semel quàm semper: Better once to dye, then to live alwayes
Languishing: | |. Julius Cæsar

2: Festina lentè; Sat cito, si sat benè: which hinders not a speedie
resolution of that which is deliberately resolved upon: | |.
Augustus Cæsar.

3: Melius est Tondere, quàm deglubere: Tyberius. | |

4: Oderunt dum metuunt. | | Caius Caligula.

5: Generis virtus Nobilitas: It is vertue, not Scutchions of aun-
cesters that makes men noble. | |. Claudius. | |.
It would doe well that this Emperours law against ffreed men
ingratefull to their patrones should be retracted to their for-
mer Slavery weare severely executed in these tymes. | |.

6: Quævis Terra artem alit: All Countryes yeeld a being to a man
of partes & artes. | | Nero.

7: Legendus est miles, non Emendus; Galba. | |.

8: Unus pro multis: He had rather dye himselfe then draw on
the death of a multitude | |. Galba

9: Bonus est odor Hostis, Melior Civis Occisi: The smell of a
dead Enimie is good; But better of a dead Citizen: Vitellius. | |

10: Lucri bonus Odor ex re qualibet: Vespasian
Of Gaine Contenting is the smell
If Gotten & Disposed well. | |.

11: Princeps bonus orbis Amor: All the world falls in Love with
a good Prince: Titus

12: ffallax Bonum, Regnum: A Kingdome is a deceiptfull good | |.
Domitian

13: Mens bona, regnum possidet: my mind to me a Kingdome
is. | |.

14: Qualis Rex, talis Grex: Subjectes prove good by a good Kings
example: Trajanus. | |.

15: Non mihi sed populo: Salus populi suprema Lex, esto: The
 peoples good, must be the supreame scope of the Ruler. | |
 Adrianus. | |.

16: Satius est Servare unum Civem, quàm multos hostes perdere:
 Antoninus Pius. | |.

17: Regni Clementia Custos: Antoninus Phylosophus.

18: Pedetentim: Commodus. | |.

19: Militemus: Let us march on. | |. Pertinax. | |.

20: In pretio, pretium: Monie Getts anie thing: Didius Julianus. | |.

21: Laboremus: Lett us be dooing: Septimius Severus. | |.   10

22: Omnis in ferro Salus: Bassianus Carucalla

23: Ferendum, et Sperandum: | | Macrinus:

24: Suus sibi quisque hæres optimus: Heliogabalus

25: Quod tibi, hoc alteri: Alexander Severus:

26: Quo major, hoc laboriosior: Maximinus Thrax

27: Princeps miser, quem latet veritas: Gordianus:

28: Malitia Regno Idonea: wickednes fitts to Governe: Phylippus   [83]
 Arabs. | |.

29: Apex Magistratus Authoritas: Fugitiva nulla Corona: Decius. | |.

30: Nemo Amicus idem et Adulator: Noe Flatterer can be a trew   20
 ffreind: | | Trebonianus Gallus. | |.

31: Publica Fama, non est vana: Volucian. | |.

32: Non Gens, sed Mens; non Genus sed Genius: nor Race, nor
 place, but Grace trewly setts out a Man: Emilianus. | |.

33: Non Acerba, sed Blanda: Not Bitter, but Flattering words doe
 all the Mischeiffe. | | Valerianus.

34: Propè ad Summum, propè ad exitum: Neere the Top neere the
 end: | | Gallienus.

35: Rex viva Lex A King is a living Law: Claudius. | |.

36: Quò major, eo placabilior: The greater the Gentler: Aureli-   30
 anus. | |.

37: Sibi bonus, aliis malus: he that is too much for himself fayles
 to be good to others. | |.

38: Pro stipe Labor: Noe fight, noe pay: Probus. | |. Sure free
 quarter was not then in use. | |.

39: Bonus Dux; bonus Comes: A Good Leader, makes a good
 follower. Carus. | |.

40: Esto quod audis: Be as good as thou art reported to be.
 Numerianus. | |.

41: Cedendum multitudini: Most voyces must Cary itt: Carinus.

42: Nil Difficilius est Quàm benè imperare. | |.

43: Virtus quæ patitur vincit: In suffering vertue overcomes; Con-   [84]
stantius Chylorus: | |.
Note: not rebellious opposition, or deluding projectes; or
hypocriticall tergiversations: But prayers, & Tears, & resolute
profession & Martyrdome proved at length victorious &
Celsus, Porphyrie, & Heirocles, with his Appollonius, Tya-
næus & the like mountebanks, how palpably weare they
Convinced & made ridiculous, by Justine Martyr, Tertullian,   10
Origen, Eusebius &c.: in their Apologies remayning unto this
day. | |

44: Immedicale vulnus Ense recidendum est; when ther is noe
hope of Curing, we must fall to Cutting: Constantius Magnus.

45: Patiens sit principis auris: A prince must have a patient Eare:
But to faythfull Counsailors not to fawning flatterers. | | Con-
stantius.

46: Pennis propriis perire, Grave: Julyan.

47: Scopus vitæ Chrystus. | |. Jovianian.

48: Princeps Servator Justis: A prince by Justice preserves his   20
people — Valentinian.

49: Alienus ab Ira, Alienus a Justitia: He wilbe slacke in justice,
whom anger somtyme prickes not forward. Valens~.

50: Non quàm diu, sed quàm benè; Gratian

51: Amicus veterrimus optimus: An old ffreind is the best:
Valentinianus.

52: Eripere Telum, non dare Irato decet. Theodosius. Magnus | |.   [85]

53: Summa Cadunt subito! Arcadius.

54: Tempor parendum: we must fitt us (as far as may be done
with a good Conscience) to the Tyme, wherin we live with   30
Chrystian prudence: Theodosius the second.

55: Pax Bello potior: Give me peace, let others quarrell: Marti-
anus. | |.

56: Regis Clementia Virtus: Leo Trax. | |.

57: Malo nodo, Malus Cuneus: Zeno: An ill wedge must be fitted
to an ill blocke. | |.

58: Mellitum venenum, blanda Oratio: Smooth talke proovs often
sweet poyson: Anastatius Dicorus.

59: Quod pudet, hoc pigeat: Justinus

60: Summmum jus, summa iniuria: Justinian. | |. Quem virtus ex-
tulit invidia depressit: These weare the words of Bellisarius
the great Captayne of this Justinian: | |.

61: Libertas res inestimabilis: Justine the second

62: Stips pauperum Thesaurus divitum: The trewest Treasure of
the rich, is the Almes they give unto the poore. | |. Tyberius
the second. | |.

63: Quod Timidum Idem et Crudele: None soe Cruell as Cow-
ards. Mauritius. | |.

64: Fortunam citius reperias, quàm retineas: Phocas. It is Easyer
to get then to hold an unlawfull Bootie. | |.

65: A deo victoria: Heraclyus: The Emperor (like Senacharib) had
52000 men of his Army found dead in one night without any
apparent execution. | |.

66: Insania læta voluptas: excessive pleasure is but a kynd of
madnes: Constantyne the third. | |.

67: Parendum Necessitati: necessity must be obeyed. | |. Constans~:

68: Quod citò fit; citò perit: Quickly Come: Quickly gon: Hast
makes wast: Constantyne the 4$^{th:}$ | |.

69: Multi Nimium, Nemo satis: Manie have too much none is
Content: Justinian the − 2 − :

70: Fortuna cito reposcit quæ dedit: That which fortune gave, she
will soone agayne have. | |. Phylippicus Bardanes. | |.

71: Si non des, accipit ultra: If thou give not to some, they will
make bold to take itt. | |. Anastatius. | |.

72: Patientia Remedium Malorum: Theodosius the 3:

73: Occulti inimici pessimi: Leo Isaurus

74: Quid sine pectore Corpus: Constantyne the − 5th. | |.

75: Quo fortuna si non uteris: Leo the − 4th. | |.

76: Mulieri Imperare res desperata: Constantyne 6th

77: Vive, ut vivas: was his Mothers Motto. | |.

78: Chrystus Regnat, vincit; Tryumphat: Carolus Magnus:

79: Omnium Rerum vicissitudo: & Seldome Comes a Better.
Lodovicus Pius. | |.

80: Ubi mel, ibi fel: Lotharius. | |.

81: Par sit fortuna Labori; Lodovicus the − 2.

82: Quod pastori, hoc Ovibus: The fflocke never thryves, in the
pastors Miseryes | |. Charles the Bald:

83: Miles Legendus, non emendus: Lewys the Stammerer & it was also Galba his motto. | |.

84: Os garrulum intricat omnia: Charles the fatt: | |.

85: ffacile vocabis Cacodæmonem, sed non facilè repuleris: Arnul-phus; | |.   [87]

86: Multorum manus, paucorum Concilium: few directors, will guide many hands. | |. Lewys th—4:

87: ffortuna cum blanditur ffallit: Conradus. | |.

88: Tardus ad vindictam, ad Beneficentiam velox: Itt is a princely mind to be readyer to gratifie, then to take revenge. | |.   10

89: Aut mors, aut vita decora: Otho the first; | |.

90: Pacem cum hominibus, cum vitiis Bellum: Otho the 2:

91: Unita virtus valet. Otho the—3.

92: Ne quid Nimis: least overdooing proves undooing: Henry 2

93: Omnium mores, tuos in primis observato: Commodus: 2

94: Qui litem aufert, execrationem in benedictionem mutat Henry the: 3.

95: Multi, Multa sciant se autem nemo: Henry the 4:

96: Mortem optare Malum, Timere pejus: Henry the 5:

97: Audi alteram partem: Lotharius the 2. | |.   20

98: Pauca cum aliis, tecum, multa: Conradus 3:

100: Qui nescit dissimulare nescit regnare: Frederick the 7:

101: Qui nescit tacere, nescit loqui: Henry the 6:

102: Satius est recurrere quàm male Currere: Phylippe:

103: Minarum strepitus Asinorum Crepitus; He that dyes with Threates, deserves the funerall of an Asse: Fredericke the 2:

104: Melius est Imperare, quam imperium Ampliare: Radulphus Auspurgensis: | |.

105: Animus est qui divites facit: Adulphus. | |

106: Quod optimum, illud et jucundissimum: Albertus: 30

107: Calix vitæ, Calix mortis; The Cup of life is made my death: Henry the 2: being poysoned in the Eucharist by one Bernard an hyred Moncke. | |.   [88]

108: Sola Bona quæ Honesta: Get you such Goodes as in a Ship-wracke may be Carryed away with you: Lewys of Bavaria. | |.

109: Optimum est aliena frui insania: Charles the—4th:

110: Morosophi, moriones pessimi: None are more pernitious fooles, then those that are betweene hawke, & Buzzard. Wen-ceslauus: | |.

111: Miseria res digna miserecordia: Rupertus: Misery is to be
pytied, from what fountayne soever it aryseth:

112: Cedunt munera fatis: Rewards doe not alwayes attend
desertes, but fortune. Sigismund:

113: Amicus optima vitæ possessio: Albert the 2 of Austria:

114: Rerum irrecuparabilium felix obliviò: Fredericke: 3

115: Tene mensuram, et respice finem: Maxmilian: 1:

116: Plus ultra: A pious Contemplation must not be be bounded:
But seeke farther for a safer haven:

117: Fyat justitia et pereat Mundus: Ferdinand the .1.

118: Dominus providebit: The Lord will provide for all such as
depend upon him: Maxmilian the -2^d.

119: Omnia ex voluntate dei: All things must be as God will have
itt: Rodolphus the: 2:

120: Concordia lumine major } Concord is more then light
To sett things Right: Matthyas

121: Legitimè Certantibus: Noe warre must be undertaken but
upon just Groundes: & itt is the better for them that doe Soe:
Ferdinand the: 2:

Fynis.

347: Nescire quid antea quàm natus sis acciderat id semper est
esse puerum.

348: Fælix quem faciunt aliena pericula Cautum;
Fælix quem faciunt aliena præmia promptum

349: Ne te quæsiveris extra: Domi Talpa foris
Lynceus: — Abroade Let not thy Fancie roame;
Untill thou know what's done at home.

350: Hoc quid sit pulchrum, quid turpe, quid utile, quid non
plenius et melius, Crysippo et Crantore dicit. | |.
This informes us better for our Compleate behaviour then Cry-
syppus or Crantor, or the excellent Athenian phylosophers:

351: Etsi parendum est patri in Omnibus, in eo tamen non par-
endum, quo efficitur ne pater sit. | |.

352: A mans Lively voyce moveth more: A mans writing Teacheth
more: more throughly, because it giveth a man leave to Concider & pause on itt: more generally because it reacheth not
only to them that are neere, but also to them that are far off:
not only to them that are alive, but also to them that are yet

unborne. He that speaketh profiteth for the hower: but he that writeth profiteth for ever. | |.

353: Never lesse alone, then when not alone;

354: Three good mothers, bring forth 3 bad Chyldren: Trewth, Hatred; Familiaritie, Contempte: & Riches — Pryde. | |.

354: Fredericke Duke of Saxonie being on a day hawking in the feildes, & seeing his servants carelesslie to ryde over the Corne, & spoyle itt: when he Came home commaunded their meate should be sett before them as plentifully as ever yea & better if it might be; But not one morsell of Bread: The service being strange & noe way knowing the Cause, the good Duke sent them word, that if they saw anie use of Bread to their Comfort, they should learne to take more Care of Corne hereafter, & not for anie pleasure to ryde over itt, & spoyle itt as they had done that day. | |.

355: Rich mens Chyldren are the most part fully & Costly fed, yet prosper not; & poore mens chyldren are seldome soe, but ever courslie fed; & yet for the most part they are fatt, fayre, & healthy: This teacheth us that man liveth not by bread only, but by every word that proceedeth out of the mouth of God: | |.

356: Non tibi datur soli quod habes, sed per te dat deus aliis: And it wilbe a joy unto thee if thou canst say with Job, I have not Eaten my morsells alone, but the fatherlesse hath Eaten with me. | |.

357: Whiles wisdome makes art the Ape of Nature: Pryde makes Nature the Ape of Art. | |.

358: The Reason that Manie want their desyres, is because their desyres want Reason. | |.

359: Wyse men buy desert with the Hazard of Reputation, & choose rather to loose opinion then Meritt. | |.

360: I had rather not know the good I should doe, then not doe the Good I Know. | |.

361: He was never soe good as he should be, that doth not strive to be better then he is. | |.

362: Jesus Chryst had one priviledge in his birth, which never anie prince had; That he chose his owne mother. | |.

363: It is but a shallow & narrow honestie to be noe better then the law forceth him to be. | |.

364: We read but of one childe Zoroaster, that Laughed at his birth:

365: Let not an ignorant or distempred Zeale silence thee; for to induce or occasion a silencing upon our selves is as ill as is an ignorant & Lazie silence: | | .

366: Every mans Knowledge makes him a ffoole, when it makes him to undervalew & despise another: ffor a ffoole is noe more a man, then an Idoll is a god: | | .

367: fforaigne helpes, are Rather Crutches then Legges. | |

368: Gardiners that husband their Groundes well to the best Advantage, sow all their seeds in such order one under another that their Garden is Always full of that which is then in season:

369: Saint Jerome Reportes when he was in Rome, he saw a man that had buried 20 wives, to marry a wife that had buryed Twentie & Two husbands. | |

370: Since we are Commanded to love our Enimies, as our selves; we must be sure to love our selves as we should doe.

Of Anger   [92]

Pryde Robbes me of God; Anger of my selfe; Envye of my Neighbour; Our Anger offends, when the Cause is unjust; or the quantitie is excessive: The Cause is unjust when we are Angry with a man for a thing which is good: For an indifferent thing: ffor a thing which is Tryviall:

Whiles the Blood is up, That Anger which a Man should turne inward upon himselfe for his sinne, he spends outwardly upon his reproover. | | To be angry for good is Devilish, To be angry for that which is neither good, nor Evill, or that which is slight & fryvolous is Idle, & absurd. The Jewish Doctors tell us that Pharaoth was Angry with his Butler & Baker for noe other Cause but that ther was a ffly in his Cuppe, & a little grayne of Gravell in his bread.

He that is Angry with his brother without a Cause, shalbe in danger of the judgment Matt: 5:22. The well governed man must be like a strong Oake which is not moved, but with a blustering wind: Not like an aspen Leafe, that shakes with the least styrring of the Wind:

Anger is excessive, if either too long or too vehement

The charge of the Apostle is, we should not lett the Sun goe down
    upon our wrath: much lesse then may we with the Sun lett it
    ryse agayne: Nightly Anger is like the serene in hott Coun-
    tries: unholsome, if not deadlye.
Our Anger must be Tempred with Mercie, & Charitie, otherwise itt
    is like to a fyre under an Emptie Kettle, which burnes the Ves-
    sell to noe purpose.
As wise princes are wont in the midst of peace to provyde for war: [93]
Soe must we in the Calmest estate of our myndes prepare against
this Inward Turbulencie. Anger quasi anger, vexation. It is like vin-   10
egar which discoulers the vessell it stands in. Thou canst not take
up a Cole to throw at another, but thou shalt burne thyne owne
fingers: And soe that of Solomon shalbe verifyed of thee; Anger
Resteth in the bosome of ffooles. | | .
Looke to the effectes of itt, thou shalt find itt utterlye disables thee
from Good: The wrath of man doth not worke the righteousnes of
God: James the .1.20. It exposeth thee to all Mischeiffes, for he that
hath noe Rule over his owne spryritt, is like a Citie that is broken
downe & without walles Sayth Solomon Prov: 25-28. And therfore
Saint Paule Ephes: 9-26 when he chargeth us not to suffer the Sun   20
to goe downe upon our wrath: Adds give noe place to the Devyll
as if the Continewing passion did open the gates of the Hart, for
Satans entrance & ffree possession. | | .
Archytas sayd to his Bayliffe, I had punish't thee if I had not bin
    Angry: A phylosopher sayd to Xenocrates whippe this boy for
    I am Angry. | | .
Another phylosopher when he had discoursed Against Anger, &
shewed how unfitt the passion is for a wise man, one of his audi-
tors purposely spitt in his face, from whom he Receaved noe other
answeare but this: I am not Angry, But I doubte whither I should   30
not be soe.
Pysystratus being rayled upon by his Adversarie, sayd he was noe
more Troubled with those rayling words, Then if an Hoodwinck't
man, had reeled upon him heedleslye in his way. | | .
Cato would usually say he pardoned all offenders but himselfe: &
when Lentulous spitt in his face, ther fell noe other language from
him [94] Then, I will say now those men are deceaved that denie
Lentulus to have a mouth. | | .

Cleanthes being called Asse, he only sayd, he should then be fitt to
Cary Zeno's Budgett. | |.
All these weare pagans: And shall meere pagans that were without
god in the world, have such rule over their passions; & shall a
Christian whose first lesson is to denie himselfe, & to mortifie all
Evill and Corrupt affections, give the Raynes to the wilde & Rude
Eruptions of his Rage?
Lastly Good Chrystian looke upon the Termes wherin thou stand-
est with God: how greivouslie dost thou provoke him Every day to
his face? One of thy offenses against that infinite Majestie is more
then thou canst be capable to receave from all Thyne Enimies upon
Earth: yet how silently doth he passe over, all thy silent affronts, &
bids his sun to shyne, & his Rayne to fall, as well upon thy
Grownd, as the holyest ownors? How Graciously doth he invyte
thee to Repentance? how sweetly doth he Labour to wynne thee
with new mercyes? Doest thou daylie pray unto him to forgive thee
as thou doest others, whilst thou resolveth to forgive none, whom
thou Canst plague with Revenge? Looke upon thy Redeemer, &
heare him, even whiles his Crewell Executioners were Tormenting
of him, Crying father forgive them for they know not what they
doe. | |.

Section B:

Poems

Perlege quæ regni clarissima Conciliorum
Sunt monumenta: aliter nil præter somnia cernis:

M^d That the — 17th — day of August — 1647. The most glorious, gracious, pious & just King Charles, = = sent abrace of very fatt Buckes to the prysoners in the Tower of London being — 22 in number, who weare all Committed, by the two howses of Parlament for high Treason, vizt, for bearing Armes, & adhæring to his Majestie in this unnaturall Warre: The first & only præsident I beleeve that ever was knowne of this kind to be done by a King of England to subjects Soe accused: And is an = undenyable testimonie of their Loyal-tie & ffaythfullnes to his Majestie their Soveraigne Leige Lord & King: And the 24th of August another brace:

10

Their names are hereunder written:
1:   The Lord John Pawlett Marquesse of Winchester: 2: Sir ffrancis Howard: 3: Sir Edward Hales: 4: Sir Benjamin Ayloffe: 5: Sir ffrancis Wortley: 6: Sir John Strangways: 7: Sir Lewys Dyve: 8: Sir John Hewett: 9: Sir Thomas Lunsford: 10: Sir Winckfeild Bodenham: 11: Sir Henry Bedingfeild: 12: Sir Walter Blunt: 13: David Jenkings Esquire: 14: Gyles Strangways Esquire: 15: Sir John Marley: 16: Sir Wyllyam Moreton: 17: Thomas Coningsbye Esquire: 18: 19: Michael Hudson: 20: Sir Henry Vaughan: 21: Thomas Violett esquire: 22: Thomas Slaughter esquire: 23: To bind all fast, The right Reverend ffather in God Doctor Wrenne Bishoppe of Elye.| |.

20

[2]

Quicquid propter Deum fit, æqualiter fit: Trew obedience as it dis-puteth not the Commaund, but obeyeth cheerfully: Soe neither doth it devyde the Commaund but obeyeth æquallie:
JStrangways: 18° Augusti — 1647.

1647

The ffree Prysoner: or the
Comfort of Restraint: written
Some whyle since in the Tower
by Doctor Joseph Hall the
Bishoppe of Norwich:

30

And Translated by Sir John Strangways
Knight A prysoner in the same place;
& lodg'd in the same chamber wher itt
was first penn'd, into this forme for his
private Recreation and Meditation: 1646

per JStrangways   40
1646

Section the First   [3]

Sir whiles you pittie my afflicted State
Take heed lest you the same doe aggravate,
And in your thoughts itt greater seeme to be
Then anie wayes itt can appeare to me.
Tis trew I am restraind, what's that to me
Who in the Tow're know well how to be free?
And whersoever I make my Aboade
I cannot but a prys'ner be abroade.
Such is the State wherin you doe me see
And all my fellow — prysoners here with me.   10
And weare my walkes much straighter then they are
They cannot me of this trew freedome barre
I cannot; I will not, a prysner be,
It is my soule that makes me to be free.
My flesh my partner is, & if that itt
Be not my servant, Sure then tis not fitt
It should my selfe be: Though my body Lye
Immured, yet that Agile Sp'ryte shall fly
Abroad, & visit all in heav'ne above,
And what below upon the Earth doth move.   20
Who shall it hinder to mount up on hye
Unto that place of Blysse? Who shall denye
Her ther to see by fayth's Soule saving eye   [4]
What blest Saint Paule saw in his Extasye?
And when to Heav'ne itt hath made her advance
And view'd that Blessed Hierarchy, to Glance
Through the innumerable globes of Light
Which doe distinguish betwixt Day and Night:

And then into this lower world descend
Ther Lands, & Seas to Compasse doth intend   30
And in a Trice, & without ship-wrack to
Which Expert Drake, or Candish could not doe
But with great Danger & Vexation
By spending yeares in Navigation.
And if my Thoughts would stay & Cast an eye
But in their passage, what varietie
Of Sev'rall Objects can take up my soule?
Here in darke Vaults some prysners doe Condole
And ther in Dismall Dunge'ons of Restraint
Others doe make disconsolate Complaint.   40
And to fetch from their greater Misery
A perfect Cure of my Calamitie.
Ther Looking into howses of Excesse
I pitty that which fooles call happines.
Then stepping into Courts of princes, wher
I doe observe some great mens fawning Feare;
The base observance, Treacherous designes;   [5]
Of others, & their underworking mynes.
Their hollow freindshipps, faythlesse promises,
Smooth Tongues, Fayre Faces, Rich Suites; viewing these   50
And all except their harts (which cannot be)
And censures nothing which it doth not see.
Then calling in, I enter att the doore
Of the low-homely Cottage of the poore
And ther out of their Emptie Cupboords find
My selfe to furnish with a thankfull mind.
Here I the Courts of Justice Overlooke
And see the just judge guided by his booke.
But in noe Case it can indure to see
Rigour to sway or Partiallitie.   60
Ther Listing in those meetings what they say
Which would for Sacred passe: God graunt they May
And greatly wondring at what things itt Heares
Is much affrighted with some suddayne Feares.
Thus Can, & Shall, & Doth my nimble Sp'rite
Bestirre it selfe still in a Restlesse flight,
Making the highest heav'ne the only Bound
Of all itt's moving: & itt is not found
Unto that Moti'on more to putt an end

Then heav'ne it selfe, from whence it did descend   70
Into my Soule if that the Iron should   [6]
Enter as it did Josephs, yet itt Could
Noe wayes unto me an affrightment be
Yet shall it not, itt cannot fetter me.
My Spiritt can noe more unto one place
Confined be, then I can runne a Race
In manie at one tyme: perhapps therfore
You are mistaken in the state before
That I liv'de in: ffor what is't Sir I pray
That makes a prysner? Tell me if you may!   80
Is't an allotment unto the same Roome
Without Remove, & wher noe change doth Come?
Why should that Trouble either you or me?
Or what is that unto a mind that's free?
Why is my body more a prysner, then
The soule of him who is the best of men?
That, you know is assigned to the day
Of dissoluti'on, to this howse of Clay.
Why more then fixed starres, which remayne ther
In their first Stations, ever since they weare?   90
Why more then those great persons, which have been
Kept up, for State, or beawtie, & not seen?
Why more then those Anachorites which have
For meritt bin coop't up as in a Grave?
How much more larger Scope have we then they?
Who with the freest Tra've-Lers on the way
Doe see the Beautie of the Heavens fayre   [7]
And with all men we breath the Common Ayre.

The Second Section.

But you'l say we have bounds for our Restraint
And that's a good Cause for a just Complaint: 100
Which the free Spyritt hates, as never eas'de
Till with full prospect, or free passage pleas'd
Since anie Barre to him of Lybertye
Is death unto his foote, or to his Eye:
O vayne & foolish Curiositie   —   —   —   — ⎫
If their desyres cannot soe bounded be   —   — ⎬
Their Moti'ons must, when they above them see ⎭

The heav'ne, they cannot into itt ascend
Nor see from one, unto the other End:
And when the whole earth doth before them lye   110
They can but measure some small peeces by:
Then let me know how they can quiett be
Till Tycho Brahe's prospective they see
A Trunke of thirtie two foote Long, wherby
A better face of Heaven they discry,
Some lesser planetts round about the sunne.
How Moonets about Jove & Saturne runne,
And in the Moone the Mountaynes, Vallyes, Seas
And Thousands of such fantasies as these.
How can they rest untill they know right well   120
And can the very Constellati'ons tell
Of our great Hemisphere? Till they have past   [8]
The Equinocti'all, & have seene at Last
The Crosse, Triangle, Clouds & Starrs that move,
(To us unknowne) the other pole above.
And when all this is done, I dare say they
Are in noe better, or more wiser way.
Perhapps they far lesse happines have felt
Then those, who none but their owne smoke have smelt.
The Morning Starre & Sev'ne starrs they know well   130
But noe Starre else, save Char'les-wayne Can they tell.
ffor me, I wonder, but doe not Envye,
The pleasing freedome these men happilie
Themselves think to injoy: And doe it hold
A weaknes in those minds which are not bold
In their Confinement and Retyrednes;
And shall I count the benifitt the lesse
Or but a small one to be placed ther
Wher Blasphemyes nor Oathes offend my Eare?
And wher my Eyes noe wounding Objects see   140
And wher my Eares are from Invectives free;
Nor yet false Doctrines Taught, nor sermons made
By ignorant Mechanicks: Men by Trade
Felt-makers, Broomemen, Coachmen, Cookes, & Groomes
And Iron-mongers, who supply those Roomes
Now in their Tubbs abroade: nor anie Kind
Of those that boast of their inspyred mind.

Noe Ribaldryes, noe Curses vex my Eare
Noe over-drunken men doe I see ther
Noe obscene Mirth, noe hard oppression   [9] 150
Noe Routs, noe Ryotts, noe Rebellion.
Nor aught that may my quiett soule affright.
This is the freedome wherin I delight:
And whiles I sitt lock't up in Quiett here
Can pittie the distempers eve'ry wher
And Turmoiles now abroad: And joy to See
My selfe from these too-Common Evylls free.

The Third Section.

Is it the force, & the Necessitie
Of the Restraint? Since things done willingly   160
For the most part, we with delight Embrace
But with Regreet when forced from us passe.
Why should not I soe over-pow're my mind
That I in itt a willingnes may find
With Cheerfullnes that thing to undergoe
Which by another I am forc't to doe?
The soule that is subacted unto Grace
Doth frame it selfe to beare in any place
What itt must suffer: & with such a sence
That itt contentment finds in patience.   170
Thus to our god we dayly doe, whose will
By our submitting to itt we fulfill,
And make it ours: this Trewth all wise men know
And dayly pray to god they may doe soe.
Without him all our Labour is in vayne,
And without him what Man can us restrayne?
If therfore my wyse god shall think itt best   [10]
To Cage me up, & in that Cage to Rest,
By Lawfull power and Authoritie
Upon what cause soever, Tell me why   180
I should not thinke this shutting up to be
A far more better Lyberty to me?
Since I know, (& not in a strayned sence)
Ther's perfect freedome in Obedience.

If then Constraint, & power make me one
I meane a prysner; Know Sir I am none
Who am Resolv'd most willingly to be
Ev'ne wher God is best pleased to have me.
And if my will seldome brought me abroade,
When at my owne howse I made myne aboade;   190
Why it should not confine (I cannot tell)
Me, to the Compasse of the Tow're as well.

The Fowrth Section:

Is't Solitude & want of our freinds sight?
This may perhapps to him, that knowes not right
To entertayne himselfe, be troublesome:
But to him that into himselfe can Come,
And can hold constant discourse with his hart,
Noe favour can be greater on his part.
Nothing more Comfort to the soule doth bring   200
Then doth selfe-Conf'rence: physick for a King:
Other mens speech may make us more to know   [11]
Of Learning or of Myrth: But none can soe
The inward profitt of our soules advance
As selfe-discourse against proude ignorance.
And when all's done the Greeks did well advise
Not MUCH but USEFULL tis that makes us wise.
Besydes we have not th'Opportunitie
As when alone of soe good Companie.
God & blest Soules we then for Comforts have   210
Which in a Throng of Visitants we Wave.
When the Great God his favours would expresse
Unto his Church; Into the wyldernes
I will her bring in great Retyrednes
And ther will her (sayth he) with Comforts blesse.
With other men, we cannot, as, a-part,
Send up to God the secretts of our hart:
To be alone, & know how soe to be
Wher is the man that benifitt can see?
What worldly hart can find itt to be soe?   220
Since none can valew what he doth not know.
What can the sight of Mortall men please me,

When I may him that's invisible see?
And what Care I, for chatting with my freinds
When I with God that all good Blessings sends
May talke famili'arly? What doe I Care
For entertayning guests that Mortall are,
When I with Abr'am, & his nephew Lott
May feast the Angells? which (if god had not
Soe spoken) weare a word too great for me   230
And in my wayes by them attended be.

The Fifth Section   [12]

Is't the Reproach, the Scandall, or the Shame
That of a pryson doth attend the Name?
Weake minds at ev'ry thing take discontent:
But with the wise tis not the punishment
But Cause; That Crownes the Martyr at the Stake
And att the Gallowes Malefactors make.
Blessed Saint Paul's Bonds very famous weare
And Peters weare solemniz'd e'vry yeare   240
T'weare Hard if Martyrs & Confessors who
For Trewth's sake have both liv'de & dyed to
In prysons; should not in some Creditt bring
That place, for sure the Cawse must be the thing
And not the Pryson that begetts the shame
Back't with foule guilt that blasts a fairer Name.
For Haynous Crymes may be at liberty
When innocence doth in close pryson lye.
And as those crymes are not free from offence
Soe the Jayle cannot staine trew Innocence.   250
Besydes (perhapps itt was not in your Thought)
Restraint is not for punishment still brought.
Ther is a safe, & straight imprysonment;
And each from other differs in Intent:
Somtymes a pryson serves for our defence,
Although the word beares still an Evill sence.
And then it serves their persons to secure
Who must the justice of the Law Indure.
For my part, I, doe God, for these walls blesse   [13]
Without them I doe not know more or lesse   260

Wher I my selfe had bin safe from the Rude
Rage of the incensed multitude.
O poore seduced soules how weare they taught
'Twas Crueltie to be with pitty fraught
And mis-perswaded |us| not to endure
For that (which should their Reverence procure)
Ev'ne for that holy Stati'on which we hold
In Gods Church; & to Curse us they grew bold
Calling us Trewths-destroying Fy-er-Brands
When we noe ill deserved att their hands   270
But Thankes & Prayers: Rayling in the Street
On our professi'on, & tell whom they meet
With Great rejoycings throughout all the Towne
The Tyme is Come, the Bishoppes now must downe.
Father forgive them I thee humbly pray
They know not what they either doe or say.
Here we the danger of Mis-raysed Rage
Having past over; pray'd God to asswage
Their Cause-lesse Malice: & soe we went on
To quench the wilde fyres of Contention: 280
Which to our greater greiffe we did behold
Incendyaryes, men wickedly Bold
Amongst gods deare well minded saints to Cast:
Here happilie & well we have at Last
Approved with th'Apostle That (though we   [14]
Are Close restraind) Gods word is alwayes free.
With what zeale & Successe did we preach ther
The word to all that thither Came to heare?
And let them say whither the Tow're had Store
Of such guests, or such Blessings heretofore.   290
And if this place hath rendred us secure
We spar'd noe paynes to make itt's welfare Sure.
Wherin our best performances did reach
To Confute that Cornelius did Teach
Bishop long since of Rome: That the sad mind
Which Troubles did with heavy burthens bind
Could not that service doe, nor soe well please
As it can doe, when 'tis free and at Ease.
Our Troubles by gods mercie have made more
Effectuall, our Labours then before.   300

The sixt Section

Adde hearunto the honour of this place
Able to give Captivitie some Grace.
In tyme of yore itt was the antient seate,
Of kings wher they for safetie did retreate:
Their Treasury, ward-robe, & Magazyne
Wher all their preti'ous things weare to be seene.
And all are under the same Custodye   [15]
Sent hither to a safe Reposito'rie.
Why should we then the prysners of this place
Conceave our selves to be in other Case?   310
Within these walls; how manie doe we see
Not knowing wher they happyer may be
To make choyse here to fixe their whole aboade
Not knowing how they may be safe abroade.
The place the same is unto them & me
If that my will with theirs could but Agree.
They dearely purchase by suites & decrees
That which Costs prysners nothing but their fees.
And what Is't makes the diffrence seeme soe hye?
But meerly the conceite of Lyberty.   320
Which whiles that I unto my selfe can give
In my best thoughts; why should men think I Live
Oppressed here with wofull wretchednes?
While other men applaud their Happines.
In that which you my pryson doe miscall
You see how free I live from Slavish thrall.
How little cause to think my walks are scant
Or to beleeve tis Lyberty I want.
Since I shalbe wher I make my aboade
None other then a prysner when Abroade.   330
Much Diff'rence ther of prysons is: one's straight
And soe close lock't, & watch't, that you may waite
Somtymes a yeare, & not admitted be
To speake with him, or yet his person see.
And if the Order be stric't from the Slate   [16]
The sun scarce looks into his Crosse-Bard grate.
One larger is & fairer of Addresse
Yeelding both pleasant walks & ffree accesse.

When from these walls I shall discharged be
You both these wayes will me a prisner see.   340
My Body doth my soule in pryson keepe
The world will both, till in my Grave I sleepe.

The Seventh Section

Now with the former thus I doe begin
Noe prysner ever was shutt up within
A Closer pryson, then my Soule, whiles shee
Within my Body must a prysner be.
Close, in Respect of th'essence of that Sp'ryte
Which since it first gave to my Body Light
Never stird out the roome wher it did lye
Nor can doe, till my Goale Deliverye.   350
If you thi'mprovement of that soule would see
In itt's effects, you'l find itt then to be
Successively by moti'on ev'ry wher
Noe place can hold itt, either here or ther.
If you thi'mmortall substance doe regard
And immateri'all of itt, then tis Bar'd
And fast lock't up within these walls of Clay
Untill my changing Come, & ther must stay.   [17]
Ev'ne as the closest Captive to his freind
May letters wryte & them unto him send,   360
Though far Remote, whyles he in Durance lyes,
I know & feele the Symptomes how they Ryse
Of my trew Native Jayle; To my great payne
I too much Reason have thus to Complayne.
What Darknes here of Sorrow have I found?
What Melancholy Lodgings? How unsound
With Little Ease? What Shackells doe I beare
And Manacles of Crampes & Tort'ring feare?
If some ther be find lesse Cause of Complaint
Yet such good Soule finds æqually Restraint.   370
That Devyne substance which within us we
Doe find impryson'd would fayne flying be
Upp to that Heav'ne from whence it did descend;
These walls of fflesh forbids them to intend
To make that flight (as Socrates of old

Did call itt) & itt will not leave that hold
Untill that God who plac't it ther shalbe
Well pleas'd by death to sett the prysner free.
He that Infus'de life into Lazarus
And call'd him from the grave must take from us   380
This life when he out of the pryson shall
Of this Dull Lumpish flesh, us to him Call:
O Chryst thou know'st that I desire to be
Dissolved here that I may live with thee.
Whiles we unto this flesh here chayned are
This chayne our passage doth to Heaven bar.
Nor doth it us this priviledge affoord   [18]
How to converse with Jesus our deare Lord:
Although it was the priviledge of Paule
Who to the Trew fayth did the Gentills Call   390
That he was often in a vysion
In Heav'ne before his dissolution.
But whither in his body ther or noe
He doth himselfe confesse he did not know.
Nor wher it did to both extend; If he
Did not himselfe know this, then how can we?
But when this visi'on was in him, we know
His soule did not out of his body goe:
Which if another shall hope to attayne
He's in the wrong, & he shall hope in vayne.   400
And for him, though he, — did this Glorie see
He could not yet partaker of itt be.
Before that either he or we be blest
With Christs fruiti'on; we must be at Rest:
That is before that we with Chryst can Raigne
We must be free'd & loosed from the chayne
Which makes the soule a prys'ner to Remayne.
What but my pryson walls can be a blynd
To hinder my free prospect? what can bind
Myne eyes from Seeing God? Nought but this wall   410
Of flesh can doe itt: Therfore now I shall
See for the present tyme ev'ne as I may.
Nothing can enter but must passe the way   [19]
Through sence into my soule, & in some sort
Must stoope & yeeld unto this Earthy fort.

When thou great Lord from them shalt set me free
As I am seene I then shall althings see
In an abstracted and a heav'nely way
As one Sp'rite sees another Night & Day.
I now at Best doe see that Glori'ous Light   420
As in a glasse, but darkly as by night,
By th'eye of fayth, & that not very cleare.
What Dym sight is it I attayne to here
Of Majestie which makes me blessed? Ther
I shall once see, & be seene face to face,
My blessed soule shall then see in that place
The Glori'ous face of that Great Deitie
And happie be therin æternallie.
But for a prysner in this howse of Clay
To know & fore-expect that happie day   430
It is enough: wherof these earthly Gyves
Uncapeable him renders while he Lyves.

The eight Section

Woe, woe is me what prysons doe we meet
When our devyne soule doth the body greet
And is infus'de? It is a prys'ner still
Nor can it passe out of this skin, untill
This frame of Nature be demolish't: and   [20]
You may be pleased heare to understand
That as the soule is in the Bodyes Tombe
Impryson'd: soe the Body in the wombe   440
Wherin 'twas formed is a prysner: Here
What Darknes? Closenes? What un-ease is Ther
In Natures Dunge'on? wher he must remayne
In uncouth posture till he doe attayne
To his appointed Mon'th till native bands
Be-ing all Loosed, he shall by the hands
Of Skilfull Midwives, the Doores forced ope'
Into the world be drawne: wher he more scope
May in that lightsome & Large pryson have
Then the Straight Womb of his deare Mother Gave.   450
Indeed ther Larger Elbow roome hath he
But all that Large Scope Cannot sett him free
From a right Trew Incarceration

Attended with full great vexation.
What man is he that knowes not and May see
The sev'rall wayes we may Restrayned be?
A Symeon may Impryson & Enchayne
Himselfe within a pillar: & disclayme
Allowance by his owne Intentions
For Easing of his whole dimentions.   460
Peter may in a larger Jayle be lock't
And ther betwixt Two Leopards be stock't.
Although Saint Paule the favour doth attayne   [21]
For two yeares Space a prys'ner to Remayne
In his owne howse, tis not without his Chayne.
Some ther are, that upon just Causes may
Be kept Close up, fast under Lock & Kay.
Others ther are we prisners call at Large
But yet they are under a keepers Charge:
And though they have the Lybertie to walke   470
Within the Tow're, & each with other Talke
And may at pleasure take the fresher Ayre
Walking in Gardens Spatious & fayre,
Yet this allowance doth not sett them Free
But prysners are acknowledged to be.
Such is my State, Such to the world am I
When I am att my fullest Lyberty.
Tis trew indeed when I doe meditate
Upon the straightnes of my first Estate
And therupon doe elevate my Thought,   480
Unto that Large Extent I now am brought:
With Isaacks Heards-men I say Rehoboth
For now the Lord hath made me Roome enough.
When I this world, wherin I am, Compare
With that above, & with the joyes ther are
Which I look to enjoy: I can see here
Nothing but Walls, Bolts, Fetters, Racks, & Feare.
Soe that the │All│ I in this world Can see   [22]
Cannot from straight endurance sett me free.

The Ninth Section

If the whole world as Varro sayd of old   490
Was Little Man's great House; I shalbe bold

To adde of what kind tis: & without fayle
It is noe other then a loathsome Jayle
Yea a darke Dunge'on: From me be it far
To vilifie the works that Glori'ous are
Of my almightie Lord: To looke on Heav'ne
I weare not worthy, were I soe un-even,
Nor of these earthly Land-scipps with my eyes
To see the pleasant strange varietyes
If I that pow're & wisdome saw not cleare   500
Which in this goodly Fabricke doth appeare.
And god for that Majesticke beauty blesse
And that Transcendent woorkmanshippe Confesse;
Rather when I the Moone & Starrs see: than
I with the Psalmist say, Lord What Is Man.
But Lord tis noe dishonour unto thee
Although that this a very fayre howse be
That thou hast one that beares from itt the bell
More Then a pallace doth a jayle Excell.
This beautie may in part please, & Controule   [23] 510
In some respects; That ravisheth my soule.
Here's Light but tis but Dymme & Duskie Light
Being Compar'de to that which shines soe bright
Wherin thou dwellest: Here's a glorious sunne
That day by day about the world doth runne
And gives it Light & Life: but Lord thou art
The Trew sunne which enlightnest ev'ry part
Of that most Great & Glori'ous world above,
To whom this sun will but a Shadow prove.
Here we Converse with Beasts, or att the best   520
With men; but ther with saints & Angells blest:
Here vayne delights are Mixed with Alloy
Ther in thy presence fulnes is of joy.
Lett then that Hart his paradise misplace
Who doth the pleasures of this world embrace;
The world for other shall not passe with me
Then for my pryson: Soe it still shall be.
Why can itt? nay why should itt not be soe?
What other Termes doe I find here or know?
What blind Light lookes in? How doe I Condole   530
Here at these narrow Loop-holes of my soule?
What Darknes is't of Ignorance that soe

Possesseth me? What Bolts & Shackells doe
Of heavy Crosses I about me beare?
How with the bread of Teares Am I fed here?
How am I watch'd, & with ill Sp'rytes besett?   [24]
What is the Cause my brethren me forgett?
And how Traduc'de? how Look'd on with disdayne?
How with the worst offendors drag the Chayne?
& How Restrayned from that Lyberty   540
Injoying of my home, & God am I?
Which dayly in my dissolution
I doe expect: when therfore I am gon
And from these walls I shall released bee
Me in a larger pryson you will see.
And soe I shalbe: Till th'almighty Lord
Of the pure Spyritts of all flesh accord
(Who putt me ther) to sett me free: And all
The Dayes of my appointed tyme I shall
Wayte Carefully, untill my changing Come;   550
When I shall passe to myne æternall home.

The Tenth Section

By this tyme then you easily may see
How little Reason I have now to be
Too much aflicted with Imprysonment,
Or my freinds for me to be discontent.
But yet some sort of prysoners ther are
To whom we owe our best & greatest Care.
And those upon a faythfull search I find
To be but two, yet of a sev'rall kind.
The first are those that too much greive & pyne   [25] 560
With outward bondage, and will not enclyne
Their eares to Comfort: Th'other who noe whitt
In Synfull thraldome have, of Feare, or Witt.
The first are those who shrinking att the waight
Of their great Fetters, thinke them too too straight.
Poore soules that under Turkish Thraldome moane,
Or under Spanish inquisition groane.
Wanting Fayths Helmett for a sure defence
Against their most impetu'ous violence.

I sorrow for their suffering, tis soe bad,   570
But for their fainting am extreamely sad.
I wish they Could the Crowne of Glory see
For their victori'ous patience, which he
The righteous judge doth ready for them hold;
They could not then but be like Lyons, bold:
To contemne payne, & Crewell death despise,
And all their torments seeme light in their eyes:
(Which are but for a Moment): Soe their Story
Should end in an exceeding waight of Glory.
But their eyes have, soe long in Darknes been   580
They only looke at those things that are seene.
Close walls, strong Fetters, & Tormenting Racks,
Engins of dreadfull Torture, Saucie Jacks
I meane Insulting warders: These they see,
But are not as they should acquainted be
With Things that them with victorie should blesse
And crowne them with æternall Happines.
Had they unto Saint Stephens Knowledge Come   [26]
They would have striven for his martyrdome.
But whosoever shall the storie read   590
Of that brave mother, & seav'ne brothers dead
Related in the Machabees: And then,
That of the forty bold Armeni'an men
Who dyed Martyrs frozen unto death
And shall ther see the false revolters breath
Fayling for feare within him, & soe dye
In the Hott Bath most miserably lye.
Whiles Thirty nine are (with their keeper found)
Converted newly by an Angell Crown'd
From Heav'ne: he cannot choose, but needs must find   600
Within himselfe a noble Hart and Mind
Of their great Courage to be emulous
And of their Honour most ambitious.
But we alas by dayly proofe doe see
What e're desyres & purposes may be,
That it is not for Ev'ry man to Come
Unto the Glorie of Trew Martyrdome.
He must be more then man, whom death & payne
Cannot from Holy purposes regaine.
Espeaci'ally if heightned in their growth   610

By Lingring executi'on of them both.
If one age can one |Mole| yeeld itt is well:
O blest Confessor how shall I thee tell
To future tymes? & how Commemorate
The great example of thy Constant state
In these Back-slyding tymes? If att the least   [27]
Thy rare perseve'rance be not more increast
For wonder, then for Imitation;
Whom thirty yeares, when fully past & gon
Of Tedious durance could not weary thee   620
Out of thy fayth, nor make thee disagree
With thy sincere professi'on: all this while
None durst looke on thee with a freindly smile.
And thyne endurance soe extreamely hard
All weare from speech, or sight of thee debar'd
But persecutors: ther weare none that would
Once pittie thee, nay ther weare none that could
Exhort thee Trewly: & if either force
Or Threats, or Favours, could have wrought remorse
For thy perversion, wherin Dayes & Howers   630
Weare fully spent: Thou had'st not Dyed ours.
But Blessed be the god of Comfort, who
Hath stood by thee, & made thee faythfull to
The very death: & now hath given thee
A crowne of life & immortalitie.
Leaving thy patterne of Trew fortitude
To teach us how our Troubles to Conclude.
Which Soe much more should well observed be
By how much itt lesse practis'de we shall see.
Whither I looke upon the former tymes   640
Or on the present, they are black with Crymes:
The world I full of Tyme-professors find
And that they weare a multiplyed Kind
Whom persecution did discover soe   [28]
That by fowre sev'rall sorts they did them know.
The first of them & without doubt the worst
Weare those whom they then justly stil'de, accurst
Idolaters; who did give publique way
To worship false gods, & to them to pray.
The second sort weare Sacryfycers, who   650
Did condescend soe far with them to goe

145

As to admitt some kind of Sacryfice
Unto those false & feigned Deities.
Or at the least to this they did Agree
That things thus offer'd might well tasted be.
The third Incensers weare, these came soe far
(whom Marcellinus precedent did mar)
That they beleev'de they might without offence
Into the Idolls fyre cast Frankinsence.
The last weare the Lybellaticks, such men   660
As did in private by them selves, or then
By some allowed proxey did deny
The trew fayth: yet with monie did out-Buy
This Ignominie, & this fearfull sinne
Of foule Idolatry they Lived in.
I will not of those manie Thowsands Treat
Which did fall downe to Solyman the Great
And held their finger up to signifie
That by that acti'on they would certainly
Make good the fruites of their Conversion   [29] 670
To his Mahometan Religion.
For easing of their great Taxations:
And some doe dayly of all Nations
And manie (which I shame & Greive to say)
Of our owne English Run the selfe same way;
Their fayth renounce in gods soule saving Sonne,
And doe receave their Circumcision.
How Lamentable is the State of those
Distressed Chrystians? for if they stick close
To their professi'on, they shall then remayne   680
Whiles they live heare in a perpetu'all Payne.
If they Revolt, then danger is their hyre
Of Restlesse paynes in everlasting fyre.
Ev'ne this restraint of mine within the Tow're
Brings unto my remembrance ev'ry howre
Their hard endurance: And I meditate
Why Christi'an Harts with sence of their estate
Doe not all bleed? why our Compassion
Is like the Summers Morning Dew, soone gon?
O lett it ryse in each Degree as hye   690
As is the Depth of their great Misery.
What are our Bowells made of? Tell me why

They doe not yearne at their Calamitie?
Yee Merchants under whose imployment these
Poore soules have past the dangers of the Seas
And have at last bin thus unhappie made
How Can you blesse your selves in your rich Trade?
Whiles you the members of your Savyour see   [30]
For want of Ransome unre-deem'de to be?
And that a pettie one: yee great men whom   700
God hath advanced to such pow're & Roome
How Can you on your beds in quiett sleepe?
Whiles you thinke what cold lodgings ther they keepe.
The hungry bellies, & the naked Backs
Of these poore Chrysti'ans, & their manie Lacks.
Lastly what fervent prayers should we make
That doe professe Chryst's name, for Chryst his sake
Unto the God of Heav'ne? To give them Strength
Their fayth & patience may hold out at Length,
Against the feirce assaults of violence;   710
That he would please to be their strong defence
And them from Thrall & Bondage to sett free;
From which good Lord deliver them; & Me.

The Eleventh Section

These prysners doe deserve our cheifest Care
And deepe Compassi'on, as those soules who are
Under a wofull, hard Captivitie
Too sensible of their owne Misery.
Some worthy are of much Compassion
Because they have lesse apprehension
How they doe need itt: These contented lye   720
Under a high spiritu'all tyrannie;
Whose very wylls are in Captivitie   [31]
To powers of Darknes everlastingly.
That if it should be left to their owne choyse
They would be bondmen clearly by their voyce
Pleasing themselves in those Curst chaynes to dwell
Whose waight's enough to sink their soules to hell.
Such, Such are they who doe themselves give o're
To be enthrall'd in sinns they knew before:
None under heav'ne doe more applaude the way   730

147

To freedome; but, none greater slaves then they.
If this trewth be not by phylosophy
Enough Evinc'd, tis by Dyvinitie.
Here's one fast fetterd in his Lust, that he
Rot's whiles he lives: Another ther I see
Soe over drunken with Excesse of Wyne
He metamorphys'de is into a Swyne:
And hath indeed himselfe soe much un-mand
That he cannot Speake, Heare, See, Goe, nor Stand.
Ther's one whom Golden fetters doe soe gall   740
He cannot Eate, nor Drinke, nor Sleepe at all:
Nor can himselfe enjoy: Envye dwells By.
A more Curst neighbour none can have: And why?
He is soe pyn'de & over-vext with need
That he's enforc'd on his owne hart to feed.
Here one with Anger is Tormented soe
That he stark mad doth for the present grow
And Cares not how he doth himselfe offend
Soe it may to anothers Hurt extend.
Ther Lyes a man much strayn'd above his Strength,   [32] 750
And although rack't & strech't beyond his Length:
Yet is possest soe by Ambition
He feeles noe payne of Selfe Extention.
These of all prys'ners we the worst doe hold,
Having themselves to base affecti'ons sold:
And soe much better worthy of your Care
By how much they, of themselves carelesse are.
Good Sir spend your Compassi'on upon these,
These are fitt subjects for itt if you please:
But as for me, pray wish me if you will,   760
As free from imputati'on of all ill
As I was from the Thought, am, & Wilbe:
But in your Champi'on wish me to be free:
Ev'ne in those Spacious feilds of yours, wher I
May have noe Hedge that may Confine myne Eye.
And in the Meane Tyme good Sir thinke of me,
None otherwise, then as in pryson free:
And your most thankfull & Devoted ffreind
In all observance faythfull to my End
        JStrangways
        1646

Since BETTER, HOLY'ER, WISER, did encrease   [33]
The world hath lost her old Contented peace.

For when they meet, they alwayes doe Contest
Who shalbe held most HOLY, WISE, or BEST.

Thus by Experie'nce we doe alwayes find
That strife proceeds from haughtines of mind

For what is that begetts this Confidence
But over-weening hight of Insolence.

I am far BETTER then thou art: Stand By!
Here's one that breakes peace for præcedency.   10

I am more Holy doth another Cry
That makes him seperate from Companie

Better (perhapps) if he could clearly see
Then such with whom he doth in that agree.

A Third man sayth I WYSER am then thou;
Oh! that's the man that doth disquiett now

And guiltie make with his proud-Jeering eye
The whole world of Irregularitye.
           per JS:

The Papists cry up blind Obedience
To such a height they make it playne-Nonsence.
Our Schismatickes high-Disobedience
Doe Open-Eyde mayntayne with Confidence;
Those without Trewth love peace with all their Hart   5
These strive for Trewth, but from all peace depart.
           per JS:

By Death my Ill's had ended long agoe   [34]
But that vayne Hope unto that end sayd Noe:
Telling me that to Morrow I should see

That all things fairely would amended be:
But trust not that! Remember what I say   5
That man is wise that liv'de wise yesterday.
ffor he that on Right-Principles doth build
Shall see his ends with Good successe Fulfild.
          per JS:

Lord how are we from Snarling Come to byte   [35]
To take noe wrong, nor willing to doe Righte.

The Father hates his sonne, the sonne his brother
And all like Dogs doe worry one another:

Ah! what a sad sight is itt: woe is me
Cytyes and Townes all Burning thus to see:

To see the channells running all with blood
Of Men & Horses mingled in that Flood:

To see the Hellish fury of a Storme
Acted by Souldyers in a warlike forme.   10

Those clambring up the high walls to assayle,
These Tumbling downe not able to prevayle.

And then to see deadly Granados fly
With Fyre in their mouthes; & to heare the Cry

The Horror doth of their alighting make:
Which whiles I speake of, I with Terror quake.

To heare th'infernall Thunder of a Myne
Now blowing up the strong-works of the Lyne:

The Roaring Cannon, & the Ratling Drumme
The Hoarse noyse of the Trumpetts, sounding Come   20

Come on, charge home; & then the Groanes to heare
Of Dying Men; wives shrikes, & chyldrens Feare,

Augmented by the murd'rers Hellish Noyse
Kyll, Kyll; Spare none, nor men, wives, Maydes, nor Boyes.

And in a word the great Confusion
Of Soules engag'de in that Destruction.

What meanes this Rage? What ay'les you that professe   [36]
The name of Chryst? In peace your soules possesse.

Deare brethren looke upon bruit beastes & Blush
Did ever Lyon yet a Lyon crush   30

With's Hungry Jawes? or did you ever see
The Savage Beares togither disagree?

Nay wher a Legi'on of Ill Spiritts weare
In one man Lodg'd, they did not quarrell ther.

Oh let us then in tyme learne to be wyse
And cease to doe the worke of Enymyes.

Soe shall the fruites of Righte'ousnes encrease
To them that sowe them in the feilds of peace.
———————— per JS: ————————

Lewes de Granado doth relate
One ask't of Encrytus, which he
Had rather choose: Rich Crœssus State,
Or else wise Socrates to be.

He answear'd Crœssus: Soe that I   5
Might whiles I live his plenty have;
But I would when I come to dye
Goe Socrates unto my Grave.
                    per JS:

A Lady of suspected Chastitie   [37]
Revolte'd from the Trewth to Popery:

And being ask't what mov'de her to doe soe
Answear'd, she knew not what, nor how to doe;
For such sence and soe hard that church doth give   5
Of Scriptures, she could not with Comfort Lyve.
To which he forthwith made this sharpe Reply:
Madame noe Text is playner to the Eye
Then thou shalt not committ Adultery.
           per JS:

A prodigall that Liv'de in huge Excesse
Was by wyse Zeno counsail'd to goe lesse.
But he replyde, I spend of mine owne store
And what I spend I can doe, & much more.
Zeno Return'd: If he that drest your Meate   5
Should in that Messe præpar'de for you to eate
Putt in much more Salt then would well suffice
Att least three hand-fulls, would you hold him wise
To say he could well spare itt? I beleeve
That answeare would but small contentment give.   10
Then change the Sceane, & you will plainly See
You & your Cooke doe in the Case agree.
           per JS:

O God   [38]
    Thy Nature & thy propertie
    Is to have mercie & forgive:
    Then put away my sin, that I
    May be receav'de to Grace, & Lyve.

    O let me live & Grow in Grace
    And let my hart soe cleave to thee
    That alwayes & in every place
    Chryst may be all in all to me.

    In my justification   10
    Ther's nothing I myne owne can call;
    Fayth work's itt in my hart alone
    Soe Chryst to me is all in all.

In my Sanctification
Gods grace therin is Trewly free,
By his meere Grace tis only done,
Soe Chryst is all in all to me.

In all Respects my Chryst above
My wife, or him my ffreind I call
Or chyld, or Brother doe I love: 20
Soe Chryst to me is all in all.

When I some good Thing doe desyre
I first on him for that doe Call
Without him I Noe-Thing Require
Soe Chryst to me is all in all.

I am Resolved to be free   [39]
My profitt & my pleasure shall
Be slaves not masters unto me
Soe Chryst to me is all in all.

In Trouble & Adversitie   30
What-ever shall to me befall
My fayth wypes all Teares from mine Eye
Soe Chryst to me is all in all.

In him shall all I doe be done
And with his ayde performed be
And soe I end as I begun
My Chryst is all in all to me.

The summe is this: Nothing but Chryst
O make me heare when thou dost call
And lett me not thy wyll resist   40
Soe Chryst shalbe my All in All.
        per JS:

In Invidum.   [40]

Wher Envye raignes ther is noe roome for peace:
Hatred to persons, always doth encrease

Dislike to Causes: My great Enimye
Advanced is, & I neglected lye.

Am I soe Tame to suffer itt? whiles he
My Puisnè, far unæquall unto me

Gaynes Reputati'on by his meane desertes;
And noe man lookes at my much abler parts.

Whiles he is all shall I Noe Body be?
Shall Jacob with the birthright scape Scott-free   10

And with the blessing too doth Esau say?
Shall Moses us and Aaron over-sway

Sayth Cursed Corah? Noe! wee'le rather Dye
With wyves, & chyldren & our Companie:

Good Josuah what mov'de thee to Envye
That Eldad should, or Medad prophesie?

Shall David be sung up for victoryes
Sayth Saule; whiles me, my people doe despise?

And therupon such under-mynings grow,
Which cease not till they worke their over-throw.   20

Such Secret, open Contestations
Such Dreadfull, deadly Concussations,

Doe Breake out with such Horror, that itt blowes
A mountayne up, or downe a City Throwes

If it be in the way: And who can stand   [41]
Sayth Solomon wher Envye doth commaund?

What Mortall Tongue is able to expresse
The wofull stirrs, that have or more or lesse

Both in the Church & in the Civill state
Bin raysed from this bitter roote of Late?   30

Therfore as we would willingly eschew
The worst of Evills, or enjoy the Trew

And best of Comforts; lett itt be our Care
To ffree our Soules from this infernall Snare:

By peace the Church, the King & Kingdome's blest:
Instruct us Lord to entertayne this quest. | |.
            per JS:

Short is the sentence of the greatest Doome
Two words expresse itt at the fall: Goe: Come.
Goe is a Cursed word: A Blessed Come
Each sending man to his Eternall home.
Goe Cursed live in Restlesse Greiffe & payne   5
And in that state for Evermore remayne.
Come blessed live in Endlesse blisse and joy
Which neither Tyme nor Sorrow shall alloy.
Lord grant me Grace in this world to live soe
I may be Call'd to Come, not bid to Goe.   10
            per JS:

The State wherin I stand is now soe bad   [42]
That I must take such Termes as may be had:

And if that I shall find them such to be
That under them I may live well & free;

I am Resolv'de my reason & my wyll
Shall both Concurre how I may keepe them still.

Mercy begetts Love in an honest mynde
And good deeds alwayes good men firmely bynde.

If these conditi'ons shalbe held too much,
My obligati'on then will not be such;   10

For Crueltie breeds feare, & feare breeds Hate;
Two ill supporters of a New-rays'd State.

And then If I shall doe all that I Can
I shall but doe, what fitts an honest Man.

Only I must patience perforce obay
Till Tyme & Trewth shall find me out a way

How from this Bondage I my selfe may free.
And if you aske what's dew for that to me,

I say the same that he deserves to have
That was borne free & hates to dye a slave.   20
     per JS:

In Decium Curium   [43]

Great Curius that thrice Tryumph'de in Rome
Retyres from thence unto his Country home

God wot it was a poore & homely Cell
And far unfitt for him therin to dwell.

Yet he with itt was well Content: his meate
Weare Roots which he himselfe did dresse to eate.

The Samnites heard this, & to him they sent
Ambassadors with Gold, that to him went

To visitt him; whom by the fire they find
Dressing of parsneps, or some other kind   10

Of Roots wheron he sup't; They him present
With all the Gold their Masters had him sent:

Which he refus'de on anie Termes to take
But unto them that brought itt thus he spake:

He that can eate my supper with Content
Wants not this gold by you unto him sent:

And I a greater honour doe it hold
To Commaund men that Masters are of gold:

Then to have all these golden heapes I see
Left here by you to be dispos'de by me   20
         per JS:

My person's seiz'd, my howse, my goods, my Land   [44]
Are all Ta'ne from me by the States Commaund

My wife & children soe oppres't with Need
They know not wher to eate their dayly bread.

My eldest sonne doth in close pryson lye
My younger sonne unsure of Lyberty
And I my selfe fore-doomed am to dye.

My freinds & kindred know this yet they stand
Farre off, & feare to Lend their helping hand.

But I have found that man's extreamitie   10
Is alwayes god's best Opportunitie.

In this distresse I pray'de unto my god
Beseeching him to Cast away his rod

To give me Comfort in this tyme of greiffe
And in my need to blesse me with Releiffe.

Draw out thyne arrowes that stick in my hart
And heale those wounds with thy soule-Curing art.

And be thou pleas'de myne enimies to move
That I may find their Hatred turn'd to Love;

Abate their Malice & their pryde asswage   20
To pitty change their furie & their rage

Inclyne their harts to be right good & kind
That I may from them Grace & Mercy find
Such as may Comfort my perplexed Mind.

And guide all those that right unto me stand
With their whole harts to yeeld their helping hand.

Direct the Meanes & blesse them Lord I pray   [45]
That I may not miscarry in the way,

Without offence, with favour & successe
To purchase from the parlament my peace.   30

Which I resolve by gods good leave to doe
Lord in this way doe thou before me goe:

And be thou pleas'de to speake & pleade for me
And then shall I in peace & Safetie be.

If anie man at this shall take offence
I leave him freely to enjoy his sence

Nor will I care though he shall angry be
Soe I doe good, or Good be done to me.

And soe that I none Evill feele or feare
I care not what from Evill Tongues I heare.   40
          per JS:

A Private Meditation   [46]

If by my selfe, my selfe weare to be try'de
I in my selfe can finde noe cause of pryde.

For first I was conceav'de in beastly sin
And like a beast I wallow still therin.

Most graci'ous God be pleas'd in ev'ry part
To Cure the plague of my corrupted hart.

Next I was borne into the world in payne
Wherin I toyle & labour all in vayne.

Lord Teach me Tymely to be Trewly wise
And worldly wealth & glory to despise: 10

For I must leave them & perforce must dye
When, wher & how god only knowes not I.

Be pleased Lord thy servant to defend
Both from a shamfull & untymely end.

Then after death become a loathsome worme
Such pow're hath mighty death man to Transforme

Then Horror, stinck, & filthy rottonnes
Shall seize me, & for ever me possesse.

And thus by proofe I dayly find & see
How all men come at last noe men to bee.   20

Lord Graunt that I may trewly ready be
When thou by death shalt please to call for me.

In meane tyme graunt that whiles I heare shall live
I for my sinns may trewly mourne & greive.

Because by them I have offended thee   [47]
Whom I have found a grati'ous god to me.

Adde Lord I pray thee to this holy greiffe
A sure hope, & a Saving-soule beleiffe

That by the mercyes of thy blessed sonne
My sinns shall all be pardon'de & undone.   30

To this adde grace that I sincerely may
Feare to offend thee: & may run the way

Of thy Commaundments with a perfect hart
Untill my soule shall from my body part.

And when on Earth I may noe longer be
Then grant me Lord a place in Heav'ne with thee.
                    per JS:

The sixt chapter of Job Translated
into Verse per JS: 9no Augusti: 1645.

To Eliphaz thus answear'd Job & sayd
O that my greiffe & Miserie weare layd
In a just ballance & Togither wayd.

For now itt would appeare more heavy far
Then the huge Mountaynes of the sea sand are

And you would know how much I need Releiffe
In that I want words to expresse my greiffe.

The arrowes of th'Almightie stick in me   [48]
And from their poyson my soule is not free.

The Terrors of th'Almightie in array   10
Doe stand against me: Doth the wild asse Bray

When he hath Grasse? or doth the dull oxe low
Over his fodder having meate enow?

Will anie man for Meat unsave'ry beg
Or without salt eate the white of an egge.

The things my soule refused once to touch
Are as my meate I dayly feed on such.

O Lord who art in power great and strong
Grant me the thing for which I soe much long:

O let itt please thee to destroy me; And   20
To cutt me off: Soe lord lett loose thy hand.

Then should I yet have Comfort, yea I would
Harden my selfe in sorrow all I could.

Lett him not spare, for I have not conceal'd
The words th'almightie hath to me reveald:

What is my strength? What is my end that I
Should hope I should prolong my life therby?

What is my strength, the strength of Stones? or is
My flesh of Brasse? Sure you are much amisse

If soe you think: Is not my helpe in me?   30
Is wisdome driv'ne quite from me? Can that be?

To men afflicted ffreinds should pittie beare
But of th'almightie they have lost the feare.

Ev'ne as a Brooke whose streames we dayly see   [49]
To passe away; my brethren deale with me.

Which blakish are by reason of the Ice
Wherin the snow is hid; But in a Trice

As soone as it growes hot in their owne ground
They are consumde & can noe wher be found.

The Large pathes of their wayes are turn'd asyde   40
They goe to Nothing & noe wher abide.

The Troopes of Tema looked for them: And
The men of Sheba did amazed stand.

Waiting for them: Nay they confounded weare
Because they hop'de, but found noe water ther:

ffor now unto them you are like; yee see
My casting downe and are affraide of me.

Did I say to me bring, or to me give
Part of your substance wheron I may live?

Or from my Cruell Enimyes me free?   50
Or from the hand of God deliver me?

Teach me my freinds & I will hold my Tongue
And make me know wherin I have gone wrong.

Right words are of great force & much they move
But tell me what your Argui'ng doth reprove?

Doe you Imagine him with words to bind
That desp'rate is, whose words move as the wynd?

Yea yee ore-whelme the fatherlesse, & you
Doe dig a pitt for him that is your trew

And faythfull freind: now therfore be Content   60
Looke upon me, for itt is evident

Unto you If I lye: Returne I pray   [50]
Lett not iniquitie be in your way:

Returne againe, In this thing I am right
And doe desire to stand soe in your sight.

Returne I say: Is folly in my tongue?
Cannot I judge what's Right? & what is wrong?
     per JS:

The fourth Chapter of the booke of Wisdome: [51]

I Rather would vertue then children have,
For that's Long-livde, when these lye in the grave.
Because it is approov'de with god and men:
When that is present, we example then
Doe take of itt: & when that itt is gone,
Tis more desyred then the preti'ous stone.
It weares a Crowne & doth Tryumph for aye;
And for rewarde strives, having gott the day.
But the increase of the ungodly brood
Shall never thryve, nor shall the roote be good   10
From Bastard slipps: nor their foundati'on fast;
For though they flourish for a tyme, at last
Their branches shall not grow, but they shalbe
Soe shaken with the wind, that we shall see,
Them with the force of winds, (without all doubt)

In a short tyme to be cleane rooted out.
Unperfect branches shall ffall from the Tree,
Their fruit with all mens tast shall disagree;
Noe Summer sun can make it ripe to eate.
Doe what you can, for nothing 'twill be meet,   20
For children gotten of unlawfull bedds,
Witnesse their parents sinnes against their heads.
Though death prevent the righte'ous, he is blest,
And shall for ever be in perfect rest:
For honourable age, it doth not stand
In length of tyme, nor yet by yeares is scan'd.
Tis wisdome, not gray hayres that makes men old,
Tis a good life, not fiftie yeares twise told.
Enoch pleas'd god, and was of him belov'de
And amongst sinners Living, Soe approv'de   30
That he Translated was, yea speedily;   [52]
Least wickednes should alter on the bye
His understanding; or deceite beguile
His soule: for Sin bewitching but a whyle,
Doth much obscure things that are honest; and
Doth those destroy that little understand.
He in a short tyme being perfect made,
Ful-fild a long tyme: It was his soules Trade
To please the Lord: Therfore he hast did make
Him from among the wicked hence to take.   40
This by the world was seene, not understood;
Nor was it Layd up in their minds for good:
That with his saints his mercie is, & Grace;
And that he them Respectes in every place.
Thus shall the righteous that is dead condemne
Th'ungodly Courses of all wicked men:
And youth that is soone perfected, The yeares
Though Long & Manie, of's unrighteous peeres:
For of the wise they shall the End see, And
What god of him decree'd, not understand.   50
And By noe meanes can they the knowledge gett
To what end God hath him in safetie sett.
They shall despyse him when they shall him see;
But God shall laugh att them, & they shall be
Hencefforth a stinking Carcase, & a sore
Reproach, among the dead for evermore.

For he shall rend them, & shall headlong Cast
Them downe, that they shall speechlesse be at Last:
And by his Glori'ous greatnes he shall make
From the foundati'on them to shrink & shake: 60
Soe that they shall be utterly Layd wast
And their Remembrance in Oblivi'on plac'de
And when th'Accompts of their sinns they shall Cast   [53]
With ffeare they shall be overcharg'd att Last
And their Iniquities shall them disgrace
Convincing them with shame unto their face.| |.

Comfort for an afflicted Soule

What ill soever is upon thee brought
By noe meanes cherish an uncheerfull thought.
Be patient, (though thou had'st great plentie late)
When thou art changed to a low estate.
ffor as men in the fyre, pure gold doe Try:
Soe god doth good men in Adversitie.
Although that they be punish'd in our Eye,
Their hope is full of immortalitie.
And those that here we doe chastized see,
In Heav'ne hereafter surely crown'd shalbe.   10
For god did prove them, & they proved sound:
Thus for himselfe those men he worthy found.
Behold how happie is the man whom God
Corrects for sin with his soule-saving Rod.
Give eare therfore to what I thee advise
Doe not the chastning of the Lord despise.
For whom the lord doth love he doth correct
As fathers doe their sonnes they best respect:
            per JS: 20 Julii—1646

Of Reproofe & of the right   [54]
    use therof:

I alwayes shall him for my freind approve
Who showes to me my errors in his Love.

And I shall blesse god for that Enimie
Who doth my faultes to me in hate descry.
This by gods Grace shall Teach me to take heed
That I noe more doe sin in word or deed.
Nay itt shall cause me hence-forth to grow wise
With Holy care my selfe to exercyse
In all my words & Deeds without offence
To God & Men in all good Conscience.   10
Thus Sin may prove a blessing; not a Curse
When by Reprooffe we better grow; not worse.
                    per JS: 5$^{to:}$ Sept⁓: 1646

Tis not a Fast proclaym'de can Countenance
Nor Ahabs Title anie wayes advance
To Naboths vyne-yard; nor can justifie
His unjust Act in making him to dye.
It is the height, & depth, the bredth & Length,
Of pryde & follie in their greatest strength
To take much paynes, & to be at great Cost
(ffor charge & Labour therin is all-lost)
To beawtifie the Outsyde, when we see
Nothing within but Rottennes to bee.   10
This att the Toppe doth only heale the wound   [55]
When att the Botome 'twilbe fest'red found:
And I must tell you that profession
Was never held till now possession.
Formalitie is not Religion,
Tis but a wolfe, that putts a sheep's skin on:
Then Looke with Care to your foundation
Before you sett on Reformation.
                    per JS: 7° Sept⁓ 1646.

Nor Length of Tyme, nor multitude of men,
That follow error: nor the Learnedst pen
Can make that Error to be free from blame:
Nor can they change the nature of the same.
As in beginning 'twas soe still itt is,
And in the end will alwayes be amisse.
Soe that the more men, that shall give itt vent,

Doe therby make it far more pestilent.
As is the stomacke to the body, Soe
Religion's to a man: which if it grow   10
Corrupted, doth all other parts infect
Therfore tis fitt we should itt not neglect:
But that with Care it be examined
And if that it be found replenished
With peccant humors, (fantasyes I meane
Of mad-mens braynes) those must be purged cleane.
Else Shall your soules & bodyes live togither
In Restlesse paynes 'mongst damned soules for ever.
               per JS: 8° Sept͂ —1646.

He that a good thing doth, to a bad end,   [56]
To make god serve the Divell he doth intend;
But he that to a good end doth doe ill,
He makes the Divi'll therby to act gods will.
               per JS: 10: Sept͂: 1646.

All that thou hast is not too deare,
Nor yett too Good a Trewth to buy:
But nothing is soe little here
That is not too much for a Lye;
The Income cannot be soe great   5
To make it recompence the sweat.
               per JS: 10: Sept͂ 1646.

What I beleeve to be the Right
Nor hope of Bribe, nor feare of Might
Shall make me either to forsake
My old way, or a new to take.
But Trewth and Reason ever shall   5
From myne owne Tenetts me Recall.
For I resolve & will doe still,
That they shall rule me, not my will.
               per JS: 11° Sept͂ —1646.

Those that oppose themselves against the King,   [57]
And all that doe against his armyes fight,
That him therby they to distresse may bring
Shalbe as Dreames & visions of the night.

It shall ev'ne be, as when a hungry soule
Doth dreame he eates, but when he doth awake
Himselfe doth empty find & doth Condole
He knowes not wher his next meale he shall Take.

Or as a thirstie man that dreames, & he
Beleeves he drinkes: but, he is very dry   10
When he awakes; & then by sence doth see
His soule is faint through want, & like to dye.

Thus all the people of the land shall fare
That up in armes against their Soveraigne are.
                    per JS: 30: Sept~: —1646.

When wickednes condemned is
By itts owne witnesse for sin past,
When Conscience tell's us tis amisse
Then Greivous things itt doth forecast.

The Succors Reason doth declare,   5
Base slavish Feare doth them betray:
Affirming that they dange'rous are
And lead the cleane Contrary way.││.
                    per JS: 30 Sept~: 1646.

In Adulterium et Adulteros   [58]

Adulterie & Ravishment
Before the Law forbidden weare
And did receave sharpe punishment
As doth by that revenge appeare
     Which Dynah's brethren for her sake
     Upon the Shechemites did take.

For when their father did them call
And chyd them for what they had done,
Shewing the ill might them befall
For killing Hamor & his sonne: 10
    They answeard thus, & Sayd noe more
    Should he our sister make a whore?
And by the judgment Judah gave
That Tamar should for whoordome dye
Though afterwards he did her save
When he knew who did with her Lye:
    Doth prove before the law was made
    Unlawfull 'twas to use that Trade.
Abimelech & Pharoah, take
The wives of Abram & his sonne,   20
Minding them Concubines to make
Which they thought lawfull to be done;
    For each to save her husbands life
    Deny'de her selfe to be a wife.
But in the visions of the night
The lord god did to them appeare
And told them they had not done right
Because the women marry'ed weare
    And therfore as you love your lives   [59]
    Restore unto the men their wives.   30
For they are Prophetts & they shall
Make prayers for you unto me;
And when for you to me they Call
I will by them entreated be,
    That your owne wives may be noe more
    Barren, as they weare heretofore:
    But if you persevere therin
    You surely shall dye for your Sin.
        per JS: 6ᵗᵒ Octobris—1646.

Fayth & Respect are seldome found
In our Lost fortunes safe & sound:
Shame & Reproach accompanie
Alwayes our Infœlicitie:

I wish I could not say to you   5
That by good proofe I find this trew.
      per JS: 12:^{mo} Octobris
        1646.

Wealth maketh many freinds: but he that's poore
May noe Tyme come within his neighbours doore.
The brethren of the poore man doe him hate
Then much more may his ffreinds their love abate:
And though with words he doth them still pursue   5
Yet their denyalls dayly they Renew:
      per JS: 14° Octobris — 1646

1:      Tanti valet, quanti vendi potest: [60]
2:          Caveat Emptor:

Two Maximes make most men mis-treade
That sell by whol-sale, or re-tayle
Nay they all those men doe mis-leade
Who by their Compasse steere or sayle:
    For all their wares well worth they hold
    The price, for which th'are bought & sold.
Next they regard not what they sell,
Soe that the price be high enough:
They thinke they have done very well,
Although they sold base-rotten stuffe.   10
    For tis a cheiffe part of their Creed
    The buy-er always must take heed.
Now ther — 4 — sorts of prizes be,
Of which all men should Notice take;
Low, Meane and Rigorous are three,
Excessive, doth the Fow-erth make.
    The first & Second Meane & Low;
    Are those by which Good men doe goe.
The third of them we rightly may
Without offence Injustice call: 20
But he that feeles the — 4th — may say
He in the hands of Theeves did fall:

For ther is nothing in itt left
To diff'rence it from downe-right theft;
Though in this Lewde age we doe all
The same fayre & Honest Couz-nage Call.
        per JS: 12° Octobris — 1646.

Good Counsaile & Safe for these Tymes   [61]

Keepe farre from him that hath the power to kill,
Soe thou shalt have noe Cause grym death to feare;
And if thou come unto him 'gainst thy will
In word or deed make noe fault to appeare,
Least he thy lyfe take from thee presently: 5
Remember thou in midst of snares doest goe
And walkst on Battlements narrow & high;
ffrom whence if thou shalt fall, for certayne know
Without all doubt thou instantly shalt dye:
        per JS: 13:° Octobris — 1646.

In Defence of Holy-Dayes

Why doth one day another soe excell
When as the light of all dayes we know well
Proceeds through-out the whole yeare from the Sunne?
This by the knowledge of the Lord was done:
Distinguishing according to his will
Both feastes & Seasons: Therfore we doe ill
If those which he hath made high-holy dayes
We shall not in them celebrate his prayse.
And those which he hath ordinarie made
In them we ought to use our dayly Trade.   10
ffor as the Clay is in the potters hand
To ffashi'on it, for what use it shall stand:
Soe God who made Tyme, at his pleasure may
Order itt; and, we stand bound to obay.
        per JS: 13° Octobris — 1646

Concerning Almes & Suretishippe: [62]

In Tyme of need, thy neighbour Lend,
And in dew season him repay;
Let promise, in performance end
Soe thou shalt never want a stay:
    Deale faithfully & thou shalt find
    Thy neighbour freindly, free, & kind.
Manie when as a thing was lent
They did it reckon to be found
ffor they had never an intent
That their repayment should be sound: 10
    But oft-tymes them great trouble give,
    Who did soe freindly them releive.
Hee'l kisse your hand till he receave
And for your monie humbly speake;
But he will surely you deceave
And will his day of payment breake:
    ffor when he should repay againe
    Then of the tyme he will complayne.
If he prevayle you hardly shall
Receave the halfe; & Count he will 20
As if that he had found itt all
And thinks you deale extreamely Ill
    Him of his monie to deprive,
    And sweares you bury him alive.
Therfore you may be well assurde
Without a Cause, an enimie
You have unto your selfe procurde
Who will rayle on you bitterly;
    Soe for dew honour, to your face
    He will repay you with disgrace. 30
For this cause manie doe refuse [63]
Oft-tymes to men in want to Lend
Because such men ill dealings use
Fearing they'le cheate them in the end:
    Yet to the man that's poore & low
    Tymely and Trewly mercy show.
Helpe him for the Commaundments sake

And turne thou not from him thyne eye:
But lett him of thy store partake,
Denie him not for povertie.   40
    For if that this be rightly done
    The Lord wilbe thy Sheild & Sunne.
To Lose thy monie, be content
Both for thy brother & thy freind
And think it not to be ill spent
Which for their want thou doest expend:
    For better tis, soe to be found,
    Then Rust or be lost underground.
Lay up thy Treasure as the Hye-
— Almightie Lord Commaundeth thee   50
And when thou giv'st lett not thyne Eye
In anie case repyning be:
    Soe itt shall bring thee to be hold
    More profitt, then the fynest gold.
If thus thou keepe thyne Almes in store
It shall from evill sett thee free:
Against thyne Enimyes much more
Att all tymes itt shall fight for thee,
    And keepe thee better in the ffeild,
    Then a strong Speare, & Mightye Sheild.   60
An honest man will undertake,   [64]
And for his neighboure suretie be;
An impudent, will him forsake,
And will him helpe in noe degree.
    The freindship of thy surety mind,
    For he his life for thee did bind.
A Lewd man will the good estate
Of his good suretie overthrow:
Not fearing, what all good men hate
That they should him unthankfull know;   70
    For him that sav'de him hee'l deceave
    And in great danger will him leave.
Manie good men of great estate
By suretishippe have bin undone:
The rich mans strength it doth abate
And from his howse it makes him runne;
    Soe that he wanders here & ther

And dares noe more at home appeare.
He that doth not these Rules obey
Which god the Lord doth him Commaund   80
By surtishippe shall pyne away:
And he that busenesse takes in hand
    Of other men for gaine: he shall
    Into great suites & Troubles fall.
Yet helpe thy neighbour in his need,
According to thy power & strength;
But hearin See thou take good heed
Thou doest not fall thy selfe at Length:
    For charitie doth not extend
    To Doe our selves hurt in the end: 90
The cheiffest things that life mayntayne   [65]
Are Howse-Rome, Clothing, Bread & Beere
And sure we need not to Complayne
If we have them in plenty heere.
    These are the Rules by which I Give
    When others wants I doe Releive.
        per JS: 17° Octobris — 1646.

Feare not (my Sonne) if that we be made poore
And are inforc'd to beg from dore to dore:
For if thou feare god thou aboundst in wealth
Depart from sinne, and thou art sound in Health:
Doe that which is, well-pleasing in his sight,   5
Soe, thou shalt find great Burthens wondrous light.
And having try'de thy patience, fayth, & Love
He will from thee his punishments remove:
And in the end with Comfort will restore
To thee that good thou didst enjoy before.   10
        per JS: 17° Octobris 1646:

Against false & pretended =   [66]
Freinds and ffreindshippe

I doe in publique here protest
That he shall never with me close

Who Cares not, soe he wynne his jest
Though he therby his freind doe lose:
    Sure this mans booke can-not him save
    ffrom being judg'd a Foole or Knave.
Nor will I ever him forgive
That shall his freind in earnest byte:
Such men for freindshippe whiles they live,
Unto the world may bid good-night: 10
    Noe Booke can anie such man save
    From being judg'd a Foole or Knave.
Some men ther are must beare such sway
With those whom they to Love pretend,
That you must them in all obay
Or else their love is att an end:
    I'le say noe more, these cannot have
    Their Booke by law themselves to save.
But he that freindly doth me show
The wrong way I have walked in;   20
And therby makes me fairely know
That I have in an error bin.
    Sure such a man his Booke will save
    From being judg'd a Foole or Knave.
And those that thankfull are for good   [67]
That hath bin done them here-to fore,
They cannot monie want nor food,
When they have Layd out all their store:
    And if they aske itt they may have
    By Law their Booke themselves to save.   30
For he that shall beare such a mind,
When Fortune shall upon him frowne,
He shall not fayle a freind to find,
To helpe him up when he is downe:
    This man needs not his booke to have
    For he is neither foole nor Knave.
          per JS: 31° Octob: 1646:

Brute Beastes, which of right Reason want the use,
Their ffeeders serve, off'ring them noe abuse.

And though untamed, yet Tis understood
They never harme those men, that doe them good.
Beleeve me: tis a payne extreamely Smart
Which Ill Requitall, causeth in the Hart.
            per JS: 3:^{tio} Novembris 1646.│ │.

5

Begin well: & End well   [68]

He that intends a howse to build
      He must prepare
      With his best Care
To have his baggs & Cofers filld.
Else when that he one halfe hath done
      He shall with shame
      Leave of the same
And greive that ever 'twas begun.
Soe he that doth a warre intend
      He must foresee
      By what meanes hee
May bring it to a happie end.
He must provide, How, Wher, & When
      Powder and Shott
      Is to be Gott
Cloathes, Monie, Victu'alls, Armes & Men.
But if these things cannot be had
      Doe not neglect
      Peace to effect
Although the Termes be somwhat Bad:
He that his worke hath well begun
      In this fayre way:
      I may well say
The best halfe of his worke is done.
A Good Begin: makes a good end:
      And will doe still
      Say what you will
The actors of itt well Commend:
          per JS: 2:^{do} Novembris
             1646:│ │.

10

20

The Parable of the Ten Virgins: Matthew the 25th [69]
Or Take Tyme, whiles Tyde serves

When Jesus Chryst himselfe did preach
This parable he did us Teach
And therby taught us Heav'ne itt selfe to reach.

Ten virgins in one howse weare found
Five of them weare with wisdome Crownd;
And five of them with folly did abound.

The wise did Timely Oyle provide,
Against the Comming of the Bryde,
Wherwith their Lampes might fully be supplyde.

The Bridgroome Came: they are prepard: 10
He entertaynes them with Regard
Bestowing on them great & large Reward.

The other having kept none; Try
Wher for their monie they may buy:
And having bought, returned presently.

But when they Came the doores weare barrd
They knock't Long, Lowde, & wond'rous Hard,
Yet all their knocking getts them noe Regard.

And though theratt they much Complayne,
Yet their Complaints are all in vayne,   20
Those doores can never ope-ned be agayne.

The use hereof is! Watch & Pray
And not to sport our tyme away
For noe man knowes his certayne dying day.

Yet that's the day when god will Call
Us, to accompt with him for all:
By which we must for Ever stand or fall.
                    per JS: 5to: Novembris — 1646:││.

Wouldst thou in Quiett gladly Dwell? [70]
Then doe the Things I heare doe Tell

The world is bad! I, tis god wott
Able to make an old wife trott
Yet if affaires passe but Soe, Soe;
Be not thou troubled how they Goe.

What thing soever itt shalbe
Thy Governour Commaundeth thee
I thee advize thy selfe to fayne
Most willingly to entertayne.

Make it as part of thy beleiffe
To prayse him that Commaunds in cheiffe.   10
If these three things thou canst doe well
In Wales thou may'st in Quiett dwell.||.
               per JS: 22do Januarii—1646

Virtus ipsa, sibi præmium:

He that for doing well, seekes recompence;
Knowes not the worth of a good Conscience.
          per JS: 22:^{do} Januarii 1646:

Noe Humane Reason can amend his sence   [71]
That with his fayth beleeves he may dispence.
Noe Law, nor wisdome can his fayth assure
That holds itt Lawfull to stoope to that Lure.
Great Benefitts are very narrow where
Vayne-Glory presseth Meritt first was ther.
By dayly proofe I now doe playnely see
Favours & Meritt seldome doe Agree.
    For, Benefitts are not Religious, noe
      Though they be great, If they be not held soe.||.   10
         per JS: 22do Januarii—1646

The man that good is, hardly will
Suspect another to be ill;
But he that's Evill scarcely Can
Judge one to be an honest man.

A Good man ought always to be
From Cryme & from Suspition free;
And not to have an easie eare
Back-biting & false tongues to heare.
     Nay what you are not pleas'd to know
     Beleeve itt hardly to be soe.   10
         per JS: 22:^{do} Januarii 1646:

Concerning the Ending of Our Unhappie   [72]
differences by Peace: — — — — —

Say what you will, Tis not safe for the State,
To make the sword the judge of this debate.
If in this warre the parlament prevayle;
To us & ours, they doe the warre intayle.
And if the King regayne his Crowne by Armes
Then we may thanke our selves for all our Harmes.
For having soe gott all into his hands
He is made Lord of all our Lives & Lands.
And we our Lawes & Lybertyes (which Cost
Our fathers soe much English blood) have lost.   10
But if by Treatie it receave an End,
We may with safetie our affaires attend:
And we agayne a glorious state shall see,
If King & people, by this meanes agree.
O would to God this warre, this way might cease
And we injoy the fruites of peace in peace.
If not, our peace-foes, we must sacrifice
To law & justice, for our Lybertyes.
Howe're I hope none wilbe found soe mad,
To Hazard all, for what cannot be had.   20
Nor yet appeare in Armes agayne to fight,
For that to which they can pretend noe Right.

If this workes not, Then in Conclusion
'Twill us & ours bring to Confusion.
          per JS: 23° Novembris—1646.

The Misery of Warre [73]

Armyes & pow'res know noe inferiour freinds;
Publique pretences, have their private ends.
And in the verie Cause of pietie
They doe injustice & great injurie.
Both Good & Bad they æquallie doe strike
And ffreinds & ffoes they plunder all alike.
Can god that State blesse? wher the innocent
Shall with the guiltie share in punishment?
Thus a good Cause ill mannag'de, getts the name
Of a bad Cause; & meritts æquall blame.   10
And justly soe: For in Conclusion
'Twas this brought England to Confusion.
          per JS: 28° Novembris 1646.

In Sacriligos

It is a snare, to him, that shall, devoure what holy is
And then vowes an accompt to make, for what he did amisse.
The seed of such who are soe bent, we never yett did see
To prosper to the Third descent: nor shall renowned be.
          per JS: 29° Novembris 1646.

A discourse betweene King Henry the third & the pryor of Saint Johns Hospitall [74]

The Grand Commaunder of the Hospitall
Which we Saint John's by Clearken-well doe Call
Came to the King & boldly did Complayne
His servants did their Lands & goods distrayne.

And on themselves weare served many writtes
Against their Charters, Lybertyes, and, Rightes.
To whom the King in Anger thus replyes,
Too great your charters are, and Lybertyes:
Your Riches make you proud; pride makes you mad
And since by these meanes you are growne soe bad   10
I am resolv'd that hence-ffoorth I will all
Your charters and your Lybertyes recall:
Which with good Conscience I may justifye,
Being first graunted unadvisedlye.
Then tells him how the Pope did commonly,
With |non obstante| his graunts nullifie;
And therfore he did know noe reason why
Those graunts which weare made Inconcidrately
Should not revoked be; sith they did give
A deadly wound to his prerogative,   20
To which the pryor boldly did reply,
Sir God forbid you should my suite deny;
Or such a word purporting soe much wrong
Should once be spoken by your sacred tongue.
Tis great injustice Sir to doe this thing
And doing itt, you doe your selfe unking:
        per JS: 4to Decemb: 1646

The — 7th — chapter of Micah Translated   [75]
into verse the — 6th — of December — 1646.

Woe is me, for, I am, ev'ne as when they,
Have gather'd all the Summer fruites away:
As the Grape-Gleanings of the vintage: ther
I found noe cluster to eate anie wher.
My soule desyred much the first ripe fruite
But I by noe meanes could obtayne that suite.
The good man is destroyde out of the Land;
Ther's none amongst them that upright doth stand.
ffor Blood they wayle & labour till they sweat;
And each man Hunts his brother in a nett.   10
That they with both hands may much evill doe,
The prince doth aske, & the Judge asketh too,

For a Rewarde: and the great man doth tell
His Lewde desire: Soe up they wrappe itt well.
The best of them doth as a Bry-er Teare
The most upright is far more sharper Geare,
Then a Thorne hedge: Thy watchmens day is Come:
Now shall they be perplexed in their doome.
Trust yee not in a freind, for he will slyde;
Nor put your Confidence in any Guyde.   20
With Care the doores of thy mouth from her keepe,
That in thy Bosome lyes & takes her sleepe.
The father is dishonor'd by the Sonne,
The mother by the Daughter is undone:
The Sonnes wife doth against his mother rise
Those of our howse are our worst Enimyes.
Therfore I will looke to the Lord: I will   [76]
For god my Savyour wayte: hee'l heare me still:
Myne Enimie, against me when I fall
Rejoyce thou not: Aryse agayne I shall: 30
When I sitt in the darknes of the night
The Lord shalbe to me a Glorious Light.
per JS: 6:^{to} Decembris — 1646

Of the Bishoppe of Herefords sermon
at Oxford preached before Queene Isabell

A Trayt'rous Bishoppe, hystoryes record
At Oxford preach'd, and from god's holy word
Out of the booke of Kings this Text did take
Before Queene Isabell, MY HEAD DOTH AKE.
Queene Isabell that was King Edwards wife
When he from her did flye to save his life.
From which he did most undevinely draw
This for a certayne Maxime of gods law
That a sicke and an aking head must be
Of a great Kingdome, of necessitie   10
Cutt off: & farther he did then assure
Itt could not otherwise admitt a Cure.
A Cursed doctrine, which doth not accord
By anie Rule unto Gods sacred word

Which in Corrupted Tymes ill men produce
The judgments of unsounde men to abuse.
Therby confirming mens Credulitie   [77]
To justifie their damn'd impietie,
In all that Malice or Ambition
Dares doe 'gainst Kings in low Condition.   20
       per JS: 9:^{no} Decembris 1646:

Upon the Lord Seaton refusing to deliver Barwicke to Edward the third King of England:

In Tyme of yo're, when Barwicke was Scotch Land,
And the Lord Seton did the towne commaund:
Edward the Third Great Englands King came then
And blockt itt up with an hugh hoast of men.
The seidge was straight; vittaylls within grew hard
ffor all releiffe was utterly debarr'd:
Seton a parlee sounds, & did agree
That if the Towne should not releived be
By such a day; he would the same resigne:
To which the King did readily inclyne;   10
But for performance hostages would have,
To which he yeelded; & his two sonnes gave.
Before that sett Day Came, the King did heare
That Succors weare approaching very neere.
And doth demaund the Towne: Sweares, Instantly
If he the Towne to render shall deny
Hee'l hang his Sonnes: Honour & Nature strive
Which of the Two he stands bound to Repryve.
And thus perplext his wife unto him Came   [78]
A Lady worthy of immortall fame   20
Who humbly doth to his remembrance bring
The fealtie he had sworne to his King:
Then to his native Land, his charitie:
Lastly the honour of his familye.
Then tells him they had other children left,
If they of these unjustly weare bereft:
Besydes themselves weare not soe aged yet
But that he might of her more sonnes begett.

How those, if they should be preserv'd that day
Might shortly perish by some worser way: 30
And what a stayne he should lay on the name
Of Seton: & how great would be the shame
Which he on his posteritie should lay
By a base act this Towne soe to betray
Committed to his Trust: nor could he know
Whither he should his children save or noe:
For how could he hope, that this King who had
In his performance been, soe extreame bad
By violating what by Oath he past
Would trewly with him now performe at last: 40
And therfore beg'd him to give eare to her
Beseeching him that he would not preferre
A momentarie & uncertayne gayne
Before a Certayne & eternall stayne.
Thus shee Confirmes his Resolution:
And his sonnes brought to Execution
Before the Walles; wher by the Kings Commaund   [79]
They both weare strangled by the hang-mans hand:
Their parents doe withdraw themselves, unwilling to behold
That Spectacle, which without Greiffe for Shame cannot be Told: 50
        per JS: 15:^to Decembris 1646:

Noli altum Sapere

Strayne not at things that are beyond thy Length:
Nor search the things that are above thy strength:
But what thou art commaunded think upon,
And take good Heed with Reve'rance itt be done.
For itt cannot be needfull unto thee
Things that are secrett with thyne eyes to see.
Nor be thou Curi'ous to search out with Care
The matters which un-necessarie are:
For manie things are shewed unto thee
Which few or none know how such things should bee.   10
For manie by their vayne Opinion,
And by their false and ill Suspition,
Deceaved are; & itt is too well knowne

Therby their judgments have bin overthrowne.
Without eyes thou canst not discerne the light:
Professe not then thou hast a perfect sight,
Of those things which noe mortall eyes have seen,
Nor weare revealed since the world hath been.
per JStrangways: 16to Decembris:
1646

Of Freindshipps Break-Bonds [80]

Birds fly away when stones are att them Cast
And ffreinds up-brayded, ffreindshippe breake in Hast:
But though against thy freind thou draw thy sword
Despayre not; That, may have a fayre accord.
Nay though thy ffreind feele thyne intemp'rate Tongue
Yet feare not; he may pardon thee, that wrong.
Except ther be up-brayding, & base pryde;
Or thou his secretts didst not fayrely Hyde.
Or else for giving him a Treache'rous wound:
ffreindshippe thus crack't, noe sodder can make sound: 10
These things indeed doe alien'ate the hart,
And for such things a freind will soone depart:
per JS: 17:^{mo} Decembris 1646:

Three Good: Three bad: Ten Happie things
The Author in these verses sings.

Three things ther are that doe delight my mind
And I in them doe great Contentment find:
1:2: The unitie of Brethren: Then the Love
Of Neighbours; which noe slanders can remove;
3: When man & wife soe well in all agree
Nothing can make them Disunited bee.
Three sorts of men I with my soule doe hate;
For they are in a Damning-soule Estate.
1: A poore man prowde; poore both in wealth & witt:
This man Can be for noe imployment fitt: 10
2: A Rich man that will for his profitt Lye,   [81]

184

     And Loves to cheat, whither he sell or buy:
3:   Next when an old Adulterer soe doates
     His health & wealth he to his whore devotes.
     Nine things ther are which I doe Happy deeme
     And those which have them, happy I esteeme.
     But for the Tenth I'le witnesse with my voyce
     He hath just Cause, that hath itt, to Rejoyce.
1:   A man that of his children hath great joy:
     And never yett was mixed with Alloy.
2:   Next he that lives to see with his owne eyes,
     The Downefall of his proudest Enymyes.
3:   ffull well is him that dwelleth with a wife
     Of understanding all dayes of his life.
4:   That hath at noe Tyme slipped with his Tongue
     Unto his owne, or to his neighbours wrong.
5:   That unto him hath not a servant been
     Whom he of good men hath despysed seen.
6:   Well is him, that a prudent freind hath found
     For all his dayes with Comfort shalbe Crownd.
7:   Happy is he that speaketh in the Eare
     Of understanding men That will him heare.
8:   How great is he that doth Trew wisdome find?
     Wisdome, that gives Light to Men, that are blind.
9:   Yet above all is He that feares the Lord;
     And walkes with Care according to his word.
10: But Last of all God's Love doth happie make
     All sorts of men that doe therof partake.
     The man that takes Sure-hold-fast of itt: He
     Unto Gods Angells may well likened bee,
     For knowledge & Illumination
     For practise & for Conversation:
              per JS: 17° Decembris
                 1646:

Fowre sorts of men discourage me to Crave
Monie from them, who store of monie have.
First ther are some who will not give at all;
If Some give, tis, but only to a few,
Some give to manie, but their giftes are small.
If Some give much, they will up-brayd itt you:

20

30

40

[82]

5

The tymes are hard, & Monie's very scant
Yet none of these men shall releive my want.
          per JS: 21° Decembris — 1646.

What Better Thing, in my hart Can I beare?
What better wordes from my mouth can you heare?
Or what can from myne owne pen better passe?
Then this Sound-Soule word: Deo Gratias.
          per JS: 4to Januarii — 1646:

A Man, Lives forty yeares, before he knowes   [83]
Himselfe to be a Foole; & when he Growes
To see his folly, his life's att an End;
Soe most men dye, 'fore they begin to mend.
If one should tell thee that thou Canst not Lyve
To see one mon'the more ended, Thou wouldst Greive:
Yet thou art Jollie, when perchance death may
Take thee from hence whilst itt is Call'd To Day.
Therfore take Notice when Grimme Death is nie;
Ther Can befall noe greater Miserie,   10
Then not to know the Right way how to Dye.
To Dye well, is Too hard a Worke to be
By anie Man Well Done ex Tempore.
          per JS: 13° Aprilis — 1647.

He Dares not far from Home goe, who beleeves,
His neerest neighbours to be arrant Theeves.
Those warres abroad to good passe seldome Come,
When we doe feare Combust-ions at Home.
When armyes marshall'd are, Tis a wise feate,
If Cause require, to make a safe Retreate.
And better tis, to steale away by night
Then Tary, & be beaten in the Light.
Trew fame is not esteemed by extent,
But by the Goodnes, that doth give it vent.   10
For wisemen oft tymes clearly see, that they
May wiser be to Morrow then to Day.
          per JS: 21° Aprilis: 1647.

A Motive to Humilitie upon the Concideration of what thou first was: $2^{ly:}$ of what thou now art: & $3^{ly:}$ what after death thou shalt be. per JS:

[84]

Open myne eyes O Lord that I may see
What thing my Body was, till form'd by thee:
Next what itt is, whiles itt on Earth doth live
United to the soule thou did'st me give.
And lastly mind me what thing itt shalbe
Whenas my soule departed is from me.
In all these three such Basenes shalt thou find
Thou wilt with Ease lett fall thy pryde of mind
If with the Peacocke thou cast downe thyne Eyes
To see from whence these three things doe arise.   10
And heare be Carefull that thy thoughtes thou place
Upon that Matter man first formed was.
Now sith that things we Commonly doe know
By their Beginnings from whence they doe flow
Lett thy proceedings be the very same.
And first concider from whence all men Came.
They weare not made of Heaven Chrystallyne
Wher Starres are wrought & wher they brightly shyne:
Nor yet form'd of the Watry Element
Wherof the fishes weare, & therin pent: 20
Nor of Transparent matter Fayre & Cleare
Wherof the Rubyes & the Dy'amonds weare
But man was formed of the basest Earth
The first man Adam had noe better Byrth.
The Latine tongue doth this earth Humus Call   [85]
Thence Homo Came: A Common name to all.
Soe that the Earth from whence all Mortalls Came,
Gave them both their beginning & their name.
From this mould yt doth ytt's descent derive,
And from thence itt tooke yt's Appelative.   30
He likewise was Call'de Adam that is Earth
And seeing he forgott whence was his birth
He was Call'de Enosh, which doth signifie
Forgetfulnes: joyne these togither nye
And tis as much to say, as if that he

Forgott himselfe, base & vyle Earth to be:
Concider then (deare brother) that thou art
The sonne of Adam: Lay this to thy Hart,
That thou art made of Earth as Adam was
Call not thy selfe Enoch: in anie Case,   40
Forgett not thou art Earth: Cast off all pryde
Since thou art form'd of matter on one syde
Soe base & vyle; & on the other part
Of what may be both Seen & Felt thou art
In all partes formde: not of Noe-thing, as he
The Soule Created, which he plac'd in thee:
To this End that thou may'st see with thyne eyes
This Earth from whence thy Body did aryse.
That when thou shouldest thy beginning find
Thou may'st be trewly humbled in thy mind: 50
Espeacially when thou shalt understand
Thou Can'st in noe Case meritt at his hand.
But to be Troad & Trampled on as Earth
Wherof remember thou had'st thy first Birth.
As oft as thou this Earth & Dust shalt see   [86]
Concider they Awakeners are to thee,
Which dayly doe to thy Remembrance bring
That thy Beginning did from Basenes spring.
And though they are both, Deafe & Dumbe, they Cry
Thou hast noe Cause to beare thy selfe soe hie.   60
And if their words thou wilt not dayne to heare
Yet unto those, that God speakes give an eare
Which unto thee, & to all men speake Lowde
Why is vile Earth & Mouldring Ashes proud?
Had thy base Body formed bin of heaven
It had not then bin halfe soe much uneven,
That then thou shouldest Bigger looke & higher;
Or of that supreame Element of Fyre.
But being formed of an Element
The Basest which God unto Man hath Lent,   70
For to be Troad & Trampled on by All:
And being but vyle Earth & Ashes small
Why art thou now become soe vaynely bold
Thy head above all other men to hold?
That he himselfe might Trewly humble; marke
How Abraham that Holy Patriarck

His meanes did make, by his concidering
He was but Earth a Contemptible thing:
With this he doth himselfe to God addresse
And at his Entrance did this Trewth Confesse   80
Most mannerly, & in an humble way
That he was nou'ght but Ashes, Dust & Clay.
A moderne author offers to our sight
What Gods word doth in this sett downe aright:
Telling us that the scripture Calls not Man   [87]
Earth only: why? what doth it call him than?
Itt Calls him Earth & Ashes; & therfore
That he therby might humbled be the more.
ffor Earth alone is & hath always bin
Of some good use for to sowe seedes therin: 90
And when for this It is not good att all
Yett at the worst 'twill serve to make Mud-Wall.
And Ashes by itt selfe alone make Lye
But Being mixt they make greene grasse to dye.
Therby the Earth is not made good to sowe
And Ashes mixt make not good Lye we know.
Then joinctly Earth & Ashes Man to Call
Is to tell him, when you have summ'de up all
Though he be Earth, yet therby he may find
'Tis of such barraine & such fruitlesse Kind   100
Itt will not be made usefull fruite to beare
Nor with itt can you a good Mud-Wall reare.
That Earth which Chryst clap't on the blind-mans Eyes
Did serve to cure all his darke Maladyes:
Soe shall thy soule recover well yts sight
If on thyne eyes thou shalt but clappe on right
That Earth wherof thou didst thy being take
ffrom Thy first parents whom God first did make.
Tis usu'all with physiti'ons to advise
A sicke man that's opprest with Maladyes   110
If he out of his Native Soyle abyde
That thither he returne, & ther resyde
For to recover health: Doe thou ev'ne Soe
Returne, & into thyne owne Country Goe
Thy Native Soyle: ffrom thence By going Out
Thou shalt be Cur'de of pryde: ffor without doubt
Itt makes thee sick, Because thou doest not see   [88]

The base Beginning of thy pedigree.
They weare wont in a pothecaries shoppe
T'have powders small as Dust the blood to stoppe   120
And to Cure woundes & other Maladyes
Which doe from sundry accidents arise.
O then what healing powder have we here
What holsome dust, wherof we formed were.
If it with Care thou to thy head apply
'Twill forthwith Cure the ayre of vanitie.
He that resydeth in a howse of Dust
He needs himselfe therwith besprinkle must.
Mans Body Job doth Call a howse of clay
    And he who lives in such a howse one day   130
    And sees by little & by Little How
    This clay goes drying & is mouldring now
    And in a Disposition to fall
    Not only in the rooffe, but sydes & all
    And to be Turned into Dust: sure he
    Ought not unmindfull of this dust to be
    But dayly to pow-der his memorie
    Therwith to dry up his great vanitie.
    And to procure that Temper which doth Cause
    Our dis-deceaving by such holsome Lawes.   140
    God wylls thee to the potters howse to goe
    And tells thee that his words thou ther shalt know;
    Thyne Error ther thou shalt in ev'ry Case
    Much better see then in another place.
    By seeing that vyle matter wherof Man
    Is Form'de, The potter makes an Earthen Panne.
And if that thou shalt here unto me Say
    'Twas only Adam that was form'de of Clay,
    Not his Successors, I must say to you   [89]
    That which you doe object is very Trew,   150
    If of thi'mmediate matter of their Birth
    You speake to me: But did they want their Earth?
    Noe certainly; as wilbe made most cleare
    By bodyes of Earth formed to appeare.
    Soe Adams Body was nam'de by the Lord
    Which did with ours in Kind & Forme accord.
    And in the End when we decayed Goe
    Unto our graves, It turnes to Earth we know:

And had not this Beginning giv'ne it birth
It would not have bin turned into Earth.   160
But Dust thou art, & to Dust thou shalt be
Transform'de, when god by death shall Call for thee.
That Matter wherof Adam was first made
Manie & Great Advantages itt had
Over thy Body, formed of such stuffe
Soe Loathsome, none can thinke itt soe enough.
Nor can we itt: without great Horrour name
Nor think on itt but we doe blush for Shame.
That Second Adam Chryst our only Good
Would have this thing soe to be understood.   170
ffor Howsoever he did not disdayne
To undertake our Miserie and payne
That soe he might disburthen us therby
Of all those Evills which on us did Lye.
Yet sure the manner of our Being Gott
He worthy of his Greatnes held itt not
Wherby the Basenes thou mayst plainely See
Of that vyle Mettall God hath formed thee.
Then how much Reason hast thou to debase   [90]
Thy selfe at all Tymes & in Ev'ry place: 180
And having entertaynd this in thy thought
With Thankfullnes lift up thyne Eyes aloft
And blesse that God with humble joy & myrth
That hath mans Body formed of Base Earth;
Having Ordayn'd an Antidote therby
To Cure thy Pride & Foolish Vanitie.
Beseeching him thee to inlighten soe
That thou thy soules Malignitie May'st know
That he would Cure with this pow-der of Dust,
Thy Soule from pryde, thy Body from foule Lust.   190
Then what thy body is, Concider next
Whilst that unto thy soule it is annext:
And thou shalt find thou hast small cause to Bragg,
'Tis but Lyve Earth impryson'de in a Bagge.
And if in itt you anie Beautie find,
Tis not its owne, but borrow'de of the mind.
Then when the soule doth from the Body passe,
The Body turnes to Earth from whence it was:
Appearing then abhominably foule,

Having now Lost the Nature of itts Soule.   200
Ev'ne as a Cloude when touched by the Sunne
Though it a bright thing seeme, when soe tis done
Yet in itts Nature doth not Cease to be
A Darke Cloude, &, this thing we dayly See:
Soe Bodyes when inform'de by Soules, they may
Seeme far more beautifull; yet always they
Their foule, vyle & base Being doe retayne.
In the next place, Concider we agayne
This Beautie of Mans Body Borrow'de is
Tis only owtward, & not trewly His: 210
Hadst thou Lynx Eyes, then wouldst thou see & know,   [91]
Tis but a Dung-hill Cover'de o're with Snow:
Which though without it seemeth wondrous white,
Yet is within, with all uncleanenes dight.
What Dung-hill in the whole world can be found
That doth with Loath-some Savours more abound
As doe those ill Fumes which from man proceede?
What part is ther from Foote unto the Head
Wherin ther are not pores from whence doe spring
Fountaynes which filth & uncleane Ev'ry thing?   220
Glori'ous Saint Austen putts it out of Doubt
That from mans Body are exhaled out
Fumes pestilent, as from a standing Lake
Which doe of Stinke & Loathsomnes pertake.
A slaughter howse which from a thowsand Sinkes
Doth rid away the off-Scummes of all Stinkes,
Which Come from yt: A publique pitt wherin
All men doe throw their Refuse things: A Skynne
That's full of poyson: Tis a vault full fraught
With Rottennes; & what is Ill & Naught: 230
And to say all in one word, Death Transformes
Att Last our Bodyes into Beddes of Wormes.
These are the Leaves & fruit which this Tree beares,
And if yts pestilenti'all Savour reares
Some noysomnes, stoppe thy Nose, Ope thyne Eyes
And Looke what from thy Stomacke doth aryse:
Which to the end thou may'st the better See
Tis placed in th'Anteri'our part of thee,
Neere to the Hart; That thou thyne Eyes migh'st place
Upon itt, & in thyne owne Eyes seeme base   240

By such Trew motives: To this doth Agree
What Micah spake; Thy Casting downe shalbe
Ev'ne in the middst of thee: Ther is noe-thing   [92]
Can sooner to Humilitie thee bring
Then to Concider with thy selfe what thou
Within thy selfe doest beare about thee now:
A Case soe foule, soe tainted all within
That whatsoever Liquors thou putt'st in
It Sowers & Corruptes them By & By:
A Living Grave of Dead things: for all Dye   250
That enter therinto: Things of high prize
And Sa-vory it forthwith putrifyes:
Say what I can, I cannot Say inough
It Turnes all into Nause'ous-stinking Stuffe.
A Sepulcher the Greekes doe Syma Call
A Body Soma therby Teaching all
That still the Body of the Lyving head,
Is nought but the Sepulcher of the dead:
Since then within thee thou hast such a one,
That without thee, a greater can be none;   260
Doe not persist in following of this chase
Out of thy selfe, in anie other place
To seeke for motives humbled how to be;
Thy Casting downe is in the midst of Thee.
Begge then of the Almightie-saving Lord
That he this mercie would to thee affoord
That of thy soule he would inlight thy Eyes
Therby to see thy Bodyes Miseryes:
And that thou mayst be humbled by that Sight
Ceasing to seeke for Bodily Delight   270
And Daintyes for thy Body, noe wayes Fitt;
And for those yt hath had; chastizing itt
Because injoy'd to thy soules præjudice
With rigor'ous pænance, & with weeping eyes.
Thirdly Concider what Thing thou shalt bee   [93]
When as thy soule departed is from thee:
Then thou shalt find, itt playnely will appeare
The sight of itt doth horrour Cause & feare.
Wher is the man that can be found soe bold
As to indure Dead Bodyes to behold?   280
O see how foule & black they doe Remayne

When God from them doth take their soules agayne.
Though whiles they Liv'de & breathed in this Ayre
They weare exceeding beautifull & ffayre.
Concider how at him they stand Agast
Whom they most dearely Lov'de unto the Last:
Thinking the Tyme exceeding long till they
Be from the Howse, Lodg'd in their howse of Clay.
Concider next as in the Grave yt Lyes
How wormes goe in & out at both their eyes   290
Out of their Mouthes & all their inward partes
Devouring Back & Bellie, Lungs & Hartes.
Ther needs noe wormes Come to them from without
They are ingendred in them, all through-out.
And therfor Job our Kynsfolkes doth them name,
Because from our owne fflesh & Blood they Came.
Nay he doth them our neerest Kinsfolkes Call
As ffather, Mother, Brother to us all.
This is that ffamilie which in the Grave
Their sustenance from our Dead Bodyes have;   300
Till all of them are Turned into Dust
Wherof they all weare formed at the ffirst.
Heare in the Grave those words now once agayne,
Which the wyse Syrach doth sett downe soe playne
O why is Earth & Ashes growne soe proud!   [94]
And this you see he doth proclayme alowd!
As if 'tweare not inough to humble thee,
That thou & all, which in the world now bee,
Weare of the Dust, of the Earth, wholy made
And that all of them this Beginning Had.   310
Lett it suffice thee yet to see the End
Wherunto Death at last doth all men Send:
And when thou se-est Earth, & Dust & Clay
Suppose they Cry Alowde to thee, & Say;
Remember that thou shalt be Turn'd to Dust
And then be Troad & Trampled on thou Must:
English men, Graves a Monument doe Call
And Rightly; for it doth admonish all
Of our last end, & wherunto we must
When all is done Trust to be payd: with Dust: 320
A Holy Father tells us that the End
And Haven wher all men to Land intend

After that in Great Tempestes they have sayld
And amidst Rockes & Perills ought have fayld
Both of the Body & the Soule; are those
Sepulchers which our Bodyes doe enclose:
Which although they without, seeme Glorious Stones,
Are yet within full of stench, wormes & Bones.
Since then of stinking wormes thou Brother art
Why art thou then Soe vayne & proud in Hart?   330
And Syth that thou in Earth soe soone must end
What moves thee to such high things to pretend?
Unlesse thow wouldst thy fall the Greater make
Why doest thou thus of Emtie ayre pertake?
And doest thus Hurry up thy selfe on hye   [95]
By the false-feather'd wings of vanitie?
But know this ffoolish & vayne Tumour must
Be Cured by this powder of thy Dust.
Present thy selfe strew'de therwith unto God
That he may pittie thee, & spare his Rod;   340
As Holy Job did, when he sayd, If Thou
Should'st with my Sin O Lord upbrayde me now
Saying; Remember that but Dust thou art
I should Remember then an other part
Saying; Remember I thee humbly pray
That thou hast made me as the potters Clay;
That I am form'de of Earth, & therfore Weake;
And tis noe wonder if I fall & Breake:
Nor that Temptations rayse me up Amayne,
And then that they doe drive me downe agayne.   350
Present this Dust with humble Confidence
Unto thy God, thy Buckler & Defence;
And that Almightie Lord will presently
Take pittie of thy great Infirmitie:
According to that, which King David sayth;
(If on him onlie thou doest build thy ffayth)
What pitie parents to their children beare
The like doth God to those that doe him feare;
He knowes our Mould, our Forme & Fashi'on just
How weake & frayle, & how we are but Dust: 360
Forgett not what thou art, But Carefully
Lay up this Dust fresh in thy Memorie.
To this End: That thou Having before thee

What first thy Body was: & now doest See
Both what it is: & shall hearafter be.
Thou mayst thy selfe both Humble & Condemne   [96]
And for thy haughtines thy selfe Contemne.
Lastly Saint Austen doth this lesson Teach,
If thou wouldst have thy buildings heav'ne to reach;
Thou must endeavour to be humbled soe,   370
As is the Earth on which men Treade & Goe.
For they that will upright, High Buildings keepe
Must their foundati'ons Lay, both Broad, & Deepe.
        JStrangways
        6° Maii 1647.

The voyce sayd Cry! He sayd, What shall I Cry?
All fflesh is Grasse, & like the Grasse shall Dye.
Yea all the pleasant Beautie yt doth yeeld,
Is as the fading fflower of the ffeild.
The fflow're doth fade; Grasse withers, we doe know;
Because god Spiritt doth upon itt blow.
Soe that we may conclude right well this Case
And safely say, THE PEOPLE IS BUT GRASSE.
The fflow'res doe fade, & the fresh grasse doth wither;
But the good word of God stands sure for ever.   10
        per JStrangways
        8 Maii 1647

Another Motive to Humilitie upon Concideration   [97]
Of these three Tymes. vizt:

1   What Man was before he was borne.||.
2   What he is all his life Long, after he is borne.||.
3   What he shalbe after this his life is Ended.||.

Sir I doe here present unto your veiw
What by my reading I find to be trew
Concerning Man: And ffirst you here shall see
What thing man was before he came to be.
Next what he is whiles his short life doth Last
Then what he shalbe when his life is past.

In these three tymes soe manie miseries   10
Thou shalt find Lincke'd with Infirmities,
That we had need of an Æternitie
To summe them up exactly to your eye.
And speaking first, of what man was before
That he was borne; we must a vayle cast o're
Taking into our Contemplation
His Loathsome & vyle Generation.
Great Aristotle Long agoe did say
Man is ingendred in a shame-full way
In manner soe immodest, tis not fitt   20
Either to thinke, to heare, or speake of itt.
ffirst weigh the place whence he beginning had
And you shall find 'twas dismall, Darke, & Sad.
Soe straight & Loathsome was his mothers wombe
When he nine mone'ths lay clos'de up in that Tombe
That all that Tyme he had perpetuall Night,
Without the use of anie Sence or Light.
Nor Had he other Nourishment or food   [98]
But poyson-some & putride menstruous blood:
Which from th'effectes we clearly Come to know   30
Besides expert physitions tell us soe
That if a Man by chance shall therof tast
His life forthwith would as with poyson wast.
Nay if a Dog therof but tasted had
He therupon would presently grow Mad
That manie men had by Experience found
Wher it doth fall, noe Grasse growes on that ground.
Trees, & Quicke plants, doe wither & Grow dry
And Soe by Little & by Little Dye.
Wine sharpe as vinegar it is avow'de   40
That it doth turne: & Looking Glasses clowde
Edges of Swordes it Dulls; Iron & Steele
The force of Rust are therwith made to feele.
Looke what this fare is with a Seeing eye
To Create pryde & nourish vanitie.
His Byrth with paynfull Throawes & deadly payne
Of his sad mother, minister agayne
Far lesse occasion of this foolish pryde
And from presumption to be trewly wyde.
A chyld cannot be borne & draw his breath   50

But putts his mother in great feare of Death:
And the poore infant manie tymes we see
Ev'ne in the Byrth doth not escape Scott-free.
But by his entrance doth receave some harme
With hurting of a foote, or of an Arme.
Working his way into the Light to Come
Out of that Darke & Miserable Roome.
All which a father breifly doth expresse   [99]
Yet toucheth all these things or more, or lesse.
We all begotten are in filthy Lust   60
And therfore itt is most extreamly just
We should in Darknes in the wombe remayne
And be brought forth in Anguish & in payne.
Agayne that holy father doth invyte
All men, that they Concider should aright
This their beginning, to the end that they
Might be ashamed therof every way.
Loe to thy sad thoughts I doe recommend
Thy first beginning, Middle, & thy End.
The first will cause shame in thee to appeare   70
The Second Sorrow, & the Third will Feare.
Thinke whence thou Come'st & Blush: Weepe wher thou art
And Tremble whither thou art to depart.
Then in that second tyme wherin we live
Lett me this, unto your Remembrance Give.
And first I pray Concider in what sort
That little Body Comes out of its port
Soe foule, that without Nauseousnes none Can
Receave him, or but touch this little Man.
Soe weake that on its Leggs he Cannot stand   80
Nor move himselfe but by anothers hand.
Soe poore, that he into the world noe-thing
To keepe himselfe but warme doth with him bring.
And soe unable that he doth not know
Which way unto the Nurses Breast to Goe.
Which he must sucke; unlesse that some the nutt   [100]
Into the childes mouth of the Brest doe putt.
In all these things if you them rightly scanne
All Creatures have advantages of Man.
For they Come Cloathed forth, & then they know   90
As soone as they are brought forth how to Goe.

Seeking out that which for them fitting is
Wherof they doe, seldome or never misse.
Only this our poore little chyld doth know
How to doe one thing, which none doth him show
That is to weepe, to shed Teares & to Cry
Which witnesse his unhappie miserie.
But now Concider the Calamityes
Which on this poore weake chyld most heavy lyes.
    And thou shalt them innumerable find.   100
    Ther is noe flower soe mixt with frost & wind
    Nor Blighted with heate of the scorching sunne
    Which noe Care can prevent from Being done.
    For being Tender Eve'rie Cold or heate
    Or but an Apple that his nurse doth eate
    Which hurtes her milke; The poore babe for it payes
    With Losse of health, or shortning of his dayes.
    Nay only with a Looke but Indirect
    It somtymes is strooke dead with that aspect.
    You see how strong this Castell is ev'ne wher   110
    Our life is kept? & only Treasur'de ther?
    Syth that by Casting only a Bad Eye
    ffarre off on itt, it pyneth & doth dye.
    Some yeares it lives thus, (without diff'rence   [101]
    In anie thing from beastes) only by sence.
These miseries of poore mans Infancie
Are the beginnings of those Constantly
    Which follow him in those his other yeares,
    As he growes, they grow, plainly itt appeares.
    And therfore are the greater in old Age   120
    When ther is lesse strength to indure their Rage.
    ffor to recount the manie Maladyes
    Of life though short, Long tyme will not suffice.
    Looke but into the Inward partes aright
    And thou shalt find th'are almost infinite
    Soe manie are the great infirmityes
    And from within Diseases that arise.
    And all phisitions doe avouch it Soe
    That we the number of them Cannot know.
    Galen affirmes that only in the Eyes   130
    Ther are six-score seve'rall Infirmityes.
    Physitions bookes are with diseases fraught

And with their Remedyes which they have Taught
And this their Doctrine dayly doth increase
By some or other new found out Disease.
Our present Evills soe in number Grow
That they the witt of all that's past outgoe.
If but upon those Myseries you thinke
Of which all men but outwardly doe drinke
They likewise are as infinite, as are   140
The Cawses, which afflict us with such Care:
The Heavens with their Influences, And
Th'Aspectes of plannetts, if we understand
Th'Ecclypses, & th'Effects which from them ryse   [102]
The Elements, mixt with their Qualities.
Beastes with their hooffes, their hornes, their teeth; nay fflyes
And Gnatts, sting & offend man in his Eyes.
Yea Ev'ne those things which verie little are
And without life, It is not very rare
To heare they doe him harme: As may be seen   150
In a small thorne, which if it doth within
A mans throate but a verie little crosse
His life is straight in danger of a Losse.
Nay if a small hayre gett into his Eye
Itt paynes, if not putts it out presently.
Soe that we may say that our Miseryes
As manie are, as things seene with our Eyes.
And tis noe small meanes for a man to know
His weaknes to see what weake things doe Soe
Afflict him, & doe Take his life away.   160
A Little Colde fresh ayre doth in one Day
An Ague Cause: A little heate him putts
Into a Feaver, & that forthwith Cutts
The Thread of's life: If soe it doth not move
It oftentymes freniticall doth prove.
And Fruites eate out of Season we are Sure
Castes us into a deadlye Calenture.
Much after this all Cawses are almost
That sicknes brings & death into our Coast.
What Thing is sorrow & the Greiffe we have   170
Which Layes a man both in his Bed & Grave.
And when it Cometh from some bad successe   [103]
Though in it selfe it be nought more or lesse:

Yet somthing then it always Comes to be.
What shall we say of those men whom we see
Themselves disquiet inwardly: & Soe
Loosing their health; from Life to death they Goe
For things Imaginarie: & which have
Noe powre at all, if had, our life to Save.
Hence nothing doth another nothing Cause	180
And this nothing, doth give that nothing lawes,
Tormenting Man, & doth him overtake
Who of himselfe doth such great reck'-ning make.
Concider likewise all the Remedyes
Which for these Evills are found by the wyse
Since that in them our Myseryes we know
Noe lesse then in the Ill from whence they flow.
ffor they are few, & of uncertaintie
Or of much Cost, & Small Efficacie.
Or more distastfull, or more paynefull then	190
The greiffe, they bring upon the sonnes of Men.
Soe that from one payne we Cannot be free
Without induring what we know to be
ffar greater; nay in things ev'ne that are good
Our Evills likewise may be understood.
ffor nothing is soe pure but more or Lesse
Itt Comes unto us mixt with Bitternes.
Or if the same thing we doe Trewly mind
Itt Leaves oft-tymes a bad relish behind.
Health, which we soe much study to mayntayne	[104] 200
With Easines is Lost; & with what payne
Is it recover'd? & then what great feare
Doth man possesse, when sicknes doth appeare?
Great Beautie is but like a fading flowre
Which flourisheth & dyes both in one howre.
Our parents, brethren, Kinsfolkes & our Freindes
The more in life we Love them, in their Ends
The more our selves we doe afflict: Somtymes
We suffer greater harmes by our ffreinds Crymes
And greater mischeiffes unto us arise	210
From them, then from our greatest Enimyes.
With what great Labour, & what store of Sweat
Doe we our worldly Goods & Riches gett?
And with what great Solicitude & Care

Those Temp'orall Goods & wealth conserved Are?
And with what Sorrow & Anxietie
Doe we forgoe them when we are to Dye?
Of Dignityes & offices we may
Without Offence the very same thing say.
With what great charge a King is made a King?   220
What Cares doe beate his braynes? What sad thoughts bring
Disquietnes to his Contented Minde?
What great suspici'on doth he dayly find?
One while he feareth that his Enimie
Will warre upon him: & then By & By
That his owne subject will a Traytor prove
Whom he before did alwayes dearely Love.
That fortunes Thunderboltes at last will light   [105]
Upon the mountaynes eminent for hight.
What goods are these which all men doe deceave   230
And in the end a bitter Relish leave?
This doth the wise man in these words expresse
The End of Myrth is alwayes heavines.
Ther is noe Good, nor ever was ther weale
Wheron Ill hath not sett his marke & Seale.
The End of a Great Supper, marke it Right!
Is the Beginning of an Evill Night.
This man at Tilt runnes, & the next ill newes
He from his Horse fell, & receav'd a Bruise.
And Soe you shall of other good things find,   240
Both in their Manner, & their severall kind.
These Evills which the Body doe befall
Will if Compared nothing prove at all
With those which dayly doe the soule perplex
And itt like home-bred Enimyes doe vex
In that perpetu'all war which it doth wage
With itts owne passions in most furious Rage.
Mans hart is as a troubled Sea, with winds
Still tost & beaten of Eleven kyndes,
Contrary passions, Crossing one another   250
That tis a wonder how they live togither.
Love, Hatred, Dislike, Desyre, Sorrow, Joy
Then Hope, Despayre, Feare, boldnes doe annoy
And Lastly Anger: These the fflesh doe Arme
Against the Soule, & therby doth itt harme.

And by assaultes doth force itt oft to doe
That unto which she rather should say Noe.
And to Hate that, which shee is bound to Love   [106]
To Love that, which in us should Hatred move.
Then to Dislike that, which it should desyre   260
To Desire what doth great Dislike require.
And to Rejoyce for what it ought to Greive,
To greive for that which should us Comfort Give.
Perverting what we ought to understand
Right Reason & gods Lawes doe us Commaund.
Itt happeneth in this troubled Sea likewise
One passion doth against another ryse.
For Delight makes us to desyre that Thing
Which the Desyre of Honour finds a sting.
And the Desyre of Honour to pursue   270
That thing which Ava-rice seekes to eschew.
Soe that poore man with these Contrary waves
He is soe tost himselfe he never saves,
Nor from the one, nor from the other Ill,
For in one breath he will not, & he will.
His inward passions likewise Cruellie
Torment him with their strange varietie
When without, ther wants one, him to Torment
Then they within deprive him of Content,
Making those Cordes wherwith the Enimie   280
His snares doth sett Cause him fall therby,
Into most Greivous Sinnes: Soe every man
As it seemes unto me Doth all he Can
His Enimie to furnish with those Armes
Wherwith he setts upon him, & him Harmes.
And this it was Made Holy Job to Cry
Unto my selfe a Burthen now am I.
That he might therby Teach us right to know   [107]
That his Afflictions did not soe much grow
ffrom those his outward Enimyes, which he   290
By keeping all his Doores close shutt might be
Enabled alwayes himselfe to Defend
As against what his home foes should intend,
Which he within him had, 'Gainst which noe power
Can save him, or secure him but one hower.
Nor will it serve, once them to overcome

Noe nor an hundred Tymes: For on they Runne
Soe manie Tymes againe, & doe Renew
The Fight, which they with Courage soe pursue
That neither Tyme, nor Place can end this Jarre   300
Which made Job style itt, A PERPETUALL WARRE.
This is the Cause the wyse man sayd itt then
A heavie yoake is on the sonnes of Men.
From that day they goe from their Mothers wombe
Untill they Lodge in their perpetu'all Tombe.
How just & meet it is we should Despyse
This Life from which such myseries arise;
God having putt theron such Bitternes
To weane our Hartes from yts Love more or Lesse
That we might sett them on that Life of Rest   310
Wherby we shall for evermore be Blest.
Concider likewyse with a Seeing eye
A Greater then the former Myserie.
Which is the weak-nes of our Faculties
And Great Disorders, which from thence Arise.
Inherited by our first parents Sin   [108]
Inclyning us more unto vice: wherin
With pleasure we love better to remayne
Then to make Godlines our greatest Gayne.
Whence all those diffi-culties doe arise   320
Which they must suffer who adhære to vice.
What stumbling blockes are ther found in this way
Which makes it Rough & Toylesome Every day.
Againe how manie are ther to be found
Who like right well to walke upon that ground
Which unto vice doth leade; This pleaseth still
Because the way is Easie, All downe hill.
ffrom this Ill Nature & weake Faculties
Ther doth provene far greater myseryes.
That knowing what is good, we doe confesse   330
To follow it, Consistes our happines:
And our best Reason shewing us this way,
And what that doth Comaunde, we should obay.
Yet notwithstanding without knowing why,
We doe forsake this cheifest Remedie:
Omitting to doe what we understood
Yea what we judge to be our greatest good:

Suiting with what Saint Paule Sayth; what I would
That I doe not, & Love not what I should.
Doing those things we Care not when, nor How   340
Which in our judgments we doe disallow.
From this ground springs another Miserie
Noe lesse then this, Mans Mutabilitie.
Which he hath in that good he hath begun: [109]
How soone doth he strike sayle & leave undone
Those good desyres which he did undertake
When he hoys'd Sayle, his way for heave'n to make?
For he had scarce begun his Barque to Sayle
With a fayre Gale, but forthwith that gan fayle;
And presently a suddayne storme doth ryse   350
Which either backe into that port him drives
Whence he put forth; or else it alwayes Leaves
Him to the mercie of the Raging Seas;
Wherin he shall well weather-beaten be
If he sinke not, & Land noe more shall see.
Lastly Concider that Soe miserable
This life is, that by noe meanes we are able
But therin to offend God more or Lesse
Without his Ayd; Such is our wretchednes:
Soe manie are the stumbling Blockes withall   360
Which in our way doe Lye to make us fall.
The just man as the Holy Goast doth say
ffalleth seven Tymes, that's manie Tymes a day
Wher first of All note, That he sayth the just
Not speaking of those who in sin doe Rust;
But of the just, who doth strive & endeavour
To doe what just is, & to doe it Ever.
And then observe seve'n tymes seve'n dayes will beare,
And seve'n Dayes, all the dayes of the whole yeare.
Yea all the yeares of Mans Abiding here   370
In this world, although they æternall weare
Then in the Day he sayth, not in the night   [110]
But in the Day, in those workes which seeme bright,
And cleare & good, The Best man of us all
Ev'ne in those workes, he oftentymes doth fall.
Now had this life noe other Miserie
Save this alone, our Great Inconstancie,
Wherby we loose our God: This would suffice

To make us throughlye this life to despise.
Touching the third tyme, what man is when he   380
Shall cease 'mongst Mortalls anie more to be
    'Twill not require Conciation
    Because he is just Nothing when he's gon.
    For Man implyes a perfect union
    Of Soule & Body: This Communion
    By Death dissolved is: you may from hence
    Gather with Ease the patt & proper sence
    Of those significant Comparisons
    And those most rare divine Expressions,
    Which some Saints & phylosophers have made,   390
    Of Man, who style him fresh Grasse in the Blade;
    Which being Cut downe forthwith waxeth Dry,
    And in an instant withers & doth Dye.
    Unto a Leafe you him compar'de shall find
    Which is Blowne off with Every Blast of wind:
    A Smoake that Soone doth vanish quite away;
    A Shaddow Constant noe part of the Day.
    A Spyders webbe; A vapour from the Earth;
    A water Bubble from his very Birth.
    The Spoyle of Tyme; Blind ffortunes Tennis-Ball: [111] 400
    Nay some men doe him not unaptly call
    The totall summe of this worlds vanity
    Subject alwayes to all Calamitie.
    And as he is a little world, ev'ne Soe
    He is a world of vanitie we know.
    All whatsoever is in man doth ffly
    Just like a shadow, and fades instantly.
    How soone doth youth & Beautie passe away?
    How soone our golden hayres are turned Gray?
    How soone the Rubyes of our Lyppes wax pale?   410
    How soone our Rozie cheekes blast with a Gale?
    Our faire white Skinnes, the azure of our veynes
    Neither of them their coulor long retaynes.
    How soone doe our fayre Teeth of Ivory
    To our great greiffe Turne into Ebonie?
    And if you well Concider itt you may
    See how they rott, & how they fall away.

How soone our nimble feet doe weary Grow?
How soone the strength of our armes failes us Too?
How all in man growes weake & doth decay   420
In such a pace it stands not att a stay!

In the Tower of } per JStrangways 10: Junii — 1647.
London______
    1647

Concerning The negative oath   [112]

I am Resolv'de I will not breake my Troth
By taking of the new denying Oath;
ffor first it forfeites all my Lyberty
And rather then I will soe doe, Ile Dye.
With which I doe conceave itt cannot stand
That on the Subject should be Layd a Band
Ev'ne by an oath, which is not by Consent
Established by act of Parlament.
Next my allegiance I therby forsake
 Breaking the Oathes I formerly did take   10
 Both of Allegiance & Supremacie
 By which my selfe I did most strongly Tye
 With th'utmost of my pow're to helpe the King.
 By this I sweare the cleane Contrary thing.
Lastly itt plainly doth appeare by this
 His Majesties just pow're & greatnes is
 Much Lessened; & therby I clearely breake
 What the third Branche doth of the Cove'nant speake
 By owning that the house of Parlament
 Can use a pow're without the Kings consent: 20
 For I confesse I cannot understand
 How any pow're in England can Commaund
 By anie Rule of a pretended state
 Which is not to the King subordinate.
Who will Condemne him that grounds his defence
Upon the Rules of Law & Conscience?
    per JS: 6ᵗ Augusti: 1647.

The — 30 — Chapter of the Proverbes of Solomon   [113]
Beginning at the — 7th — verse — to the end therof

Two things have I requir'd before I Dye
Blessed lord god doe not me them denye.
ffarre from me Lyes, & Vanitie remove;
Nor poverty, nor Riches lett me prove.
Feed me with food Convenient day by day
Least I be full & thee denye; & say
Who is the Lord? or least I poore remayne
And steale, & take the name of God in vayne.
Anothers servant Hurt not with thy tongue
Tell not his master he hath done him wrong   10
Least he thee Curse & thou be guilty found;
Thy doo-ing Soe, to doe it gives him ground.
Ther are some men that doe their father Curse,
Nor doe they blesse their mother; & that's worse!
Ther is a man that's pure in his owne eyes
And yet unwash't in his uncleanenesse Lyes.
Yea ther are some men that are very proud
Their eyes are loftie, & their Tongues speake Lowd:
Ther are some men whose teeth are very swordes
And their jaw Teeth as knives; whose deeds & wordes   20
Ev'ne from the Earth devoure the very poore
And make the Needy beg from doore to doore.
The daughters of the Horse-leach cry: Give, Give;
Three things you may know whiles on Earth you Live
Yea ffowre that endlesse are in their Desyre,
The Grave, The Barren Wombe, Water & Fyre.
The eye that mocketh at his fathers way
And doth despyse his mother to Obey.
The Ravens of the Rocke shall picke itt out,   [114]
And the yong Eagles Eate itt out of doubt: 30
Three things, yea foure, which I know not ther be,
And they are all to Wonderfull for me.
An Eagles way that in the aire doth ffly,
A serpants way that on a Rocke doth lye:
A shippe i' the Sea with all his sayles arrayde
And the way of a young man with a Mayde.
Such is the way of an Adulterous wife

Who Loves a Knave, as she doth love her life,
She Eates, & then she wypes her mouth & sayth
I To my husband have not Broke my fayth.   40
The Earth for three things troubled is with Feare,
And for a fowrth thing which itt cannot beare.
When Servants to Rule princes doe grow great:
And for a Foole, when he is fill'd with Meate.
For a Base whoore when shee is marryed
And for a mayd, heire to her Mistresse bed.
Ther be fowre things which are in all mens eyes
But Little, yet they are exceeding wyse.
The Ants a people are, not strong, nor great,
Yet they in Summer doe provide their Meate.   50
The Conies are but feeble, yet they take
Refuge in Rockes, & ther their Howses make.
The Locustes have noe King; & yet they Doe
In Bands well ord'red all of them still Goe.
The Sillie Spyder takes hold with her handes
And her Howse in the Kings great palace standes.
Ther be three things which goe exceeding well
And the ffowrth doth, the other much excell.
A Lyon whom the strongest Beastes obey   [115]
A Greihound next for Beauty beares the sway: 60
A Goodly Horse right in his propertyes;
A King 'Gainst whom noe Subjectes dare to ryse.
If thou hast err'de in lifting up thy hand
Or hast thought Evill? Doe not therin stand!
Churning of Milke doth alwayes butter Bring,
And Blood comes from the Nose we hard doe wring
Soe, much enforced wrath doth bring forth strife
Betweene the dearest Husband & his wife.
        per JS: 1°: Augusti — 1647.

Of the Meditation of Death.
Or a præparation to Death:

The Meditati'on of Our Dying day
Is the most holesome & the safest way,
That we into our saddest Thoughtes can take:
For That alone our life doth perfect make.

According to that of Saint Gregorie
A perfect Lyfe thinkes alwayes how to Dye.
Death is a cleare Glasse, wherin Looking; Wee
The Spottes which Sin makes in our soules may see:
And doth by cleansing take them all away:
Soe we with vertues doe our selves array.   10
The prophet David tells us these two things
Eschew ill, & Doe good perfection brings.
And can ther be a stronger remedie   [116]
Then to be mindfull that we are to dye
To take us off from this vayne world's delight
And to forsake what's Evill in god's sight?
What Alo-es more bitter can we find
To weane us from the Teate we soe much mind,
Of all the daintyes that we now possesse
And they are great and manie I confesse: 20
Then well to weigh that he who takes great paynes
To pamper his base Body, hath noe Gaynes
For all that he therin doth undertake
Is for the wormes himselfe a Cooke to make.
What physicke can more coole us, & allay
Our high desyres to gayne by anie way
Great wealth & Riches; then to understand
That death from them will take us with his hand:
That with us we shall nothing beare away
But one poore winding sheet to lodge in clay.   30
ffor being dead we nothing shall receave
Our wealth & Glory then will take their leave.
This Holy David as a sovereigne balme
Delivers in the nine & forty'th psalme.
And what Receite more powrefull Can ther be
Att all tymes rightly for to temper thee
From the insatiable appetite
Of Honour wherin men soe much delight
Then to Concider be it ne're soe great
That Death will shortly plucke thee from thy seat   40
And thence thou shalt be Hurrye'd to thy Grave   [117]
And ther be trampled on by eve'ry Slave.
He that beleeves death forthwith will him bring
Unto his grave, despyseth eve'ry-thing
And nothing more Can us from Sin withdraw

Then still to mynd w'are Subject to death's Law.
That Holy King Josias did Commaund
When he against Idolotry did band
That Idolls from the Altar should be Cast
And dead mens bones should in their roome be plac'd   50
Teaching us therby from our harts to Chase
Those things which we as Idolls doe embrace
Therby to move us to depart from pryde
And Cast the love of wyne & wealth asyde.
Which Paule doth Idolls Style: Nor can therbe
A Better Remedy præscrib'de to thee
Then in this large feild dead mens bones to sow
And to perceive this seed doth therin grow.
Remember thy end doth the wiseman say
And then be sure thou canst not goe astray   60
Or as by some it hath translated bin
Remember death, & thou shalt never Sin.
Let deathes remembrance thy mind still possesse
And thou shalt not be Sin's Slave more or lesse.
Most admirable & Soule-saving things
The minding of Death always with it brings.
The Sacraments serve cheifly for things past
But the Remembrance of our Death doth blast
All Sinnes By-past, Sinnes present, & to Come;   [118]
Soe sending us to our æternall Home.   70
ffor thou shalt never sin if thou dost spend
Thy short life here in thinking on thy End.
Death doth not only us restrayne from vyce
But in the wayes of vertue makes us wise.
He who bethinkes himselfe he soone shall dye
And that this life once ended, presently
The Tyme of working therwithall doth end;
That in that other life none can amend
Though it æternall be: but must sustayne
Himselfe with that, which he in this did gayne   80
And had hard Labour'd for: he would not be
As Idle, as we manie men doe see.
Soe short a life on Earth God did us give
That we might Heav'ne obtayne, & therin Live.
Our Savyour tells us ther will Come a Night
Wherin noe man can worke for want of Light

When god by Grimme death Calls us hence away
All our worke's done, we may noe longer stay.
If a great King should to a poore man say
All shalbe thine thou canst gett on this day: 90
And know that what thou shalt on this day gayne
Must all thy life long serve, thee to maintayne:
Doubtlesse that man would not sleepe on the ground
Nor be with's hands in's bosome Idle found:
But would worke hard, & with great diligence
ffinding how neerly itt did on him Trench.
In such like Manner we are to beleeve   [119]
The King of Heave'n this short life did us give
That we therin might labour & take payne
And by gods goodnes life æternall gayne.   100
Now since this working day growes to an End
Ther is noe Loitring, but we must Contend
And Lay about us with what hast we may
Not Loosing anie part of this short day.
But as the wyse man doth advise us right
All that we doe, Lett's doe with all our might.
Ev'ne like the Norway hawke catching his pray
With Nimble wing, because the winters day
Is ther but short, & he quicke worke must make
Or else noe pray can for his Supper take.   110
If then the Thoughtes of death doe make us wyse
To follow vertue & declyne all vyce.
Which are the steppes wherby we doe ascend
Unto perfection, which all men pretend.
It was well sayd of Great Saint Gregory
To thinke on death is to live perfectly.
ffor as they on the Gallowes hanging leave
Part of the Halters which did those bereave
Of life, which dyde for malefactors ther
That they who looke theron may looke & feare.   120
If then Death be for this disease the Cure
It is good for us that we make all sure,
That whither we doe walke, or sitt, or stand
We soe may have Death ready still att hand.
That as the hurt Comes to us frequently,
We may in like sort have the Remedy.
ffrom hence we likewise may the reason know   [120]

Why the wyse God ordayn'de it should be soe;
That when mans soule doth from the body part
If he hath serv'd God with a perfect hart   130
It forthwith doth partake of Endlesse joy
Which neither Tyme nor sorrow shall annoy.
But if he hath Liv'de here in deadly sinne
And did without Repentance dye therin:
His soule is forthwith sent to Restlesse payne
Wher 'tis Confin'de for ever to remayne.
And Though their bodyes ne're soe holy be
Yet they of Heav'ne are not forthwith made free.
Nor presently are punished in hell
Though ne're soe sinfull as divynes doe tell.   140
ffor neither of them shall receave their doome
Untill the great & gen'rall judgment Come.
Tis wonderfull the Body having bin
A great helpe to the Soule, wherby to win
That Crowne it weares, that yet the soule alone
Should sitt rejoycing at gods glorious throne:
And that the Body when tis dead & gon
Should only serve for wormes to feed upon.
But know all this if rightly understood
Our wyse God did ordayne it for our good.   150
To this end that we might good masters have
To Teach us how to live well in the grave.
    Read more of this subject in the   =   =   =
    next page after the Rules of Trew Obedience
            per JS:

The Rules of Trew Obedience   [121]

If thyne Obedience thou wouldst have to be
Perfect & Good; Marke what I say to thee.
ffirst Diligence use without all delay
And drive not off the Tyme, from day to Day.
Next Willingnes, not forced therunto,
Nor Minded When, or How, thou should'st it Doe.
Thirdly performe with Cheerfulnes this thing,
Without all Muttring or base Murmuring.

ffowrthly discharge itt with Simplicitie,
Without Excuses, & without Reply.   10
ffifthly with Strength & with brave ffortitude
Be Carefull thou this Dutie doe Conclude.
Sixtly ther's nothing Can it more advance
Then an unwearye'd strong Perseverance.
Lastly, Humilitie must lett you know
He is not proude that he hath done it Soe.
ffor he will Trewly represent to you
He hath not done the halfe of what was Dew.
And therupon craves pardon for his Sinne,
That in's Obedie'nce he hath faultie bin.   20
              per JS: 17° Januarii — 1647.
   Turne over and read more of the meditation of Death:
or the preparation to Death: JS:

A Meditation of Death   [122]
or a preparation to Death.

Wyse Seneca the questi'on asketh why
Ther being Masters for Each facultie
And for all Trades & artes, that none ther were
To Teach us how to live well any wher:
Yet could he not to his remembrance bring
Soe necessarie, & soe hard a Thing.
But God in's goodnes would not wanting be
In things of soe great Consequence to thee.
Doubtlesse ther are good Masters too for this
Learne to doe WELL & FEARE TO DO DOE AMISSE.   10
If we must learne then some ther needes must be
That must this lesson Teach, to you & me.
And must we schollers be? Then Sure ther are
Some masters whome we must observe with Care.
But who are those? Not your Cathedrall Men
Which in their schooles doe teach but now & then.
They may a Lawie'r make or good Devyne,
But these men seldome doe a Man Inclyne
A good & ffaythfull Chrysti'an to be.
Nor are your preachers always such we see;   20

ffor though in pulpitts they the Trewth may preach
Yet out of them the Contrary they Teach:
These masters doe their Tymes & Seasons take
In which they doe few or noe sermons make
And therfore it is needfull we should have
Some one who should Continually Engrave
This lesson on our hartes: to make us know [123]
How in the way to Live Well we may Goe.
Now those that teach this art they are the Dead,
The Church the Schoole is, wherin we are bredde. 30
The Sepulchers & Graves, they are the chayres
From whence we are best taught in these affaires:
And therfore men them Monuments doe Call
Because from thence we are admonished All
As yesterday alloted was for me
Soe may to morrow be assign'de for thee.
Nor did God rest with what is sayd before
But he hath give'n us many Masters more
And this he was well pleas'd to bring to passe
Because a thing it soe important was. 40
And therupon made Eve'rye thing a Booke
To Studie Death when we theron doe Looke.
Soe that when as our eyes are open, We
Some one booke doe or other, forthwith See
Which wilbe to us a Memoriall
That God likewise by Death will for us Call.
If on the Rising of the sunne we Looke
And on the setting of itt, tis a Booke
That tells us we must dye: The like doth Say
The Opening & the shutting of the Day. 50
Th'increase & wayning of the Moone, they Doe
(Adde the Eclypses of Both therunto)
These plannetts lively represent Mans Birth
And eke his Death: Then looke upon the Earth
It mindes us of our Death: ffor ther we see [124]
What is our End: Att last we Earth shalbe.
The ffeildes in winter naked are & Bare
The Trees then stript of ffruites & Leaves all are.
And now if Man wilbe but pleas'd to Come
And make Inquiry somwhat neerer Home: 60

Memorialls he a Thowsand ther shall find
Presenting Death right Trewly to his mind.
The Dayly changes in himselfe doe prove
That long he Cannot in one Being move.
By Little & by Little he doth know
He to the Age doth of perfection Grow
And when he doth unto that height attayne
ffrom thence he falls backe to decay againe:
And in his strength diminishing doth Goe
Till he without itt, findes itt to be Soe.   70
And is incompassed on eve'ry Syde
With Aches, which Noe physicke, Though oft Tryde
Nor med'-cynes can o'recome, although far Sought
And att Deere Rates from forraigne partes are brought.
And if this Man a great-rich office have,
That, putts him in remembrance of his Grave;
When he his predecessor dead doth See
And mindes him, who, must his Successor be.
Then in the Garments thou dost dayly weare
A MEMORY OF DEATH thou mayst find ther;   80
Since from DEAD BEASTES thou hadst them: & thy sleepe
DEATHES IMAGE, makes thee, DEATH in mind to keepe.
Thy howse wherin thou dwellest did descend
ffrom thy DEAD parents, when ther life did End:
And by their DEATH thou hadst thy Land & gold   [125]
Which in their life, they did possesse & hold
The Tales thou tell'st; The Bookes which thou dost read
Are for the most parte alwayes of the DEAD.
In your Contractes of Mari'age Eve'ry wher
Memorialls of DEATH are written ther.   90
Wherin tis worded ordinarily
That if the husband shall first chance to DYE
The wife shall such a Joyncture then enjoy:
And Soe before that they have anie Boy
The eldest shall possesse his fathers Land
And if he DYE; the second then shall stand
Posse'st therof: & Thus by prooffe we find
Almost all things of DEATH put us in mind
And yet therof we soe forgetfull are
As if in nothing it concern'd our Care   100

Nay I Beleeve should men speake as they meane
They would say death weare nothing but a Dreame.
                Finis   per JStrangways
                                1647 Feb: 14.

De Miserecordia Domini.   [126]

The Mercyes of the Wicked Crewell are
Their Sauce is Sharpe, And Bitter is their fare
But I by Sweet Experience doe find
God's punishments are of another Kind.
When he Corrects, he doth Instruct therby
To ffollow vertue & ffrom vice to ffly.
If his Rodds—Sin-destroying things doe prove
In midst of wrath he doth Remember Love.
By pard'ning all that we have done Amisse
And from thence-forth he ownes us to be his.   10
All you that reade this, marke well what I say
Returne to God whiles itt is Call'd to Day:
And you shall mercyes find both Sweet & Sure,
Mercyes that shall for Evermore indure.
                per JS: 24° Martii—1647.

The Affliction of Israell Translated   [127]
by Sir John Strangways out of Doctor Hall
Bishoppe of Exeter into verse: during his
      imprysonment in the Tower: whither
      he was committed by the parlament the
      29th of November 1645 & Continewed
      to the 15th of May—1648:

Egipt a long tyme had to Israells Men
An Harbour bin: But now a Jayle to them.
And Jacobs issue now to late Can tell
What 'twas for their Great Grandfathers to sell
Joseph a Slave: Those whom they did Before

Honour as Lordes & like their gods Adore
They now Contemne as drudges: Thus whom one
Phar'aoth doth rayse, another doth pull downe.
One man oftymes doth change of Copyes Give
But if his favours doe one Age outlive,   10
They Hartlesse & decrepit prove; Tis Rare
To find a sonne that is th'undoubted heire
Of's ffathers love: How should mens favours be
But like themselves, inconstant? certainly
The dearest ffreinds doe manie tymes looke strange
But in Gods ffavour ther can be noe change
Whose Love & Mercy doth itselfe Display
To Thowsand Thowsands that doe him obey.
If they to Pharaoth Traytors had bin found
Of this Great Change ther had bin some just Ground.||.   20
Now that they prosper is their cheiffe offence;   [128]
That which should motive be of their defence
Is of their malice cheiffest Cause: ffor why?
Unto a wicked man their Cannot be
A Sight more hatefull then for him to see
Gods dearest chyldren in prospertie.
Only John Baptist with Content can say
He must increase but I must fall away.
And what if Israell be full rich & Strong,
If ther be warre they may ere it be Long   30
Themselves Conjoyne with such as hate us; And
Then safelie may gett them out of the Land:
Behold they are affrayd to part with those
Whom they are greiv'de to entertayne God knowes.
It is offence Inough to stay or Goe
To those that quarrells seeke: They did not know
What Warres might unto Egipt bring Dismay
And yet their king (if ther be warres) doth say.
Israell had never given Cawse of Feare
ffrom Pharaoth to Revolte, yet he sayth here   40
Least they joyne with our Enimies! Base Slave!
With those he meanes they may hearafter have.
And soe his certayne ffreinds he slaves doth make
ffor feare they part with unknowne foes might take.
Sure wickednes is alwayes Cowardlie
It makes a man whom none pursues to ffly.

ffull of unjust suspicions, breeding Feare
Wher noe feare is! What Difference is ther
Betwixt Two Kings: The fayth of one doth say
I meane King David: 'Twould not me dismay
If Thowsand Thowsands should besett me round
But Pharaoth's feare sayth, Least they should be found
If ther be war with our foes to Combyne
Therfor to shew them Grace he should inclyne
To make them trewly his: How could he Tell
Why they for him might not stand foorth as well.
Thus weake & Base mindes we by prooffe doe find
Unto the woorse are evermore inclynde.
And rather safetie seeke when once they smurt
In an impossibilitie of Hurt,
Then in the hopes of just advantage: More
Had smallest favours binding bin, then sore
And Crewell bondage: yet to serve their Ends
They had rathe' have weake servants then strong ffreinds.
Pharaoth a mischeiffe unto Israell owes
Only for their weldooing: & he knowes
The way to pay itt: & he doth itt; How?
He Calls a Councell, Lets worke wysely now.
Lewd men their wicked counsailes wisdome Call
And their successe brings happines withall:
But hearin sathan wiser is then they
Who both the plott by guilfull craft doth lay
And such fooles makes them that they doe mistake
Madnes & Lewdnes for a vertue take.
Injustice still by violence growes bold
But Kings by love just Goverments uphold.
Task-masters o're them must be sett: they Could
Not be the seed of Jacob if they should
Not wrestle with God in Affliction;
Most heavye burthens now must be lay'd on,
The Destinie that did upon one fall
Of Jacobs sonns, is Common unto All.
Betwixt their Burthens to Lye downe; If they
Had seem'de to Breath somtymes, whiles they did stay
In Goshen; yet the greiffe Could not be small
That they weare strangers, & Converst withall
Amongst Idolaters: But now the Name

50
[129]

60

70

80

[130]

219

Of Slave is added to encrease the same.
In Ægipt they some Rust had gather'd, now
They must be scoured; God had made them bow   90
Under the burthen of his wrath, if they
Under this burthen had not fainting lay.
As Gods affliction tended to redresse
Their sinfull lives; Soe Ægipt to suppresse
Their growing greatnes; who would not have thought
Such miserie should them unfitt have brought
ffor Generation, & Resistence too?
That Exercise we moderately doe
Quickens our Spyritts, addes unto our strength
But Extreame, Nature doth destroy at Length: 100
That God which is the searcher of the reynes
Doth manie tymes worke by Contrary meanes;
When they with persecution weare brought Low
With their depression he made them to grow:
How Can Gods church but fare well, since the spight
Of those who hate them, brings them benifitt.
God Turnes our poysons into Cordyall wyne
With Bleeding still the better prooves his vyne.
And now the Ægiptians Could offended be
With their owne malice, which the Cause they see   110
Or their encrease whom they did hate & feare
And that this service greater gaynes should reare
To workmen, then their Masters: And therfore   [131]
The stronger grew the Isralites the more
Decrepit grew oppressing Malice: And
Since their own Labours strengthens them to stand
Now Tyrannie will try what can be done
By violence: which now in place doth Come.
Since they their present strength cannot subdew
The hopes that by succession may accrew   120
Must be prevented: weomen they suborne
To murther Infants 'soone as they be borne:
And those whose office 'tis to helpe the birth
Must now destroy itt, to make Ægipt myrth.
Ther lesse suspicion was of Creweltie
In that sex; & more opportunitie
Of dooing Mischeiffe: All the males must dye
After their birth by Mid-wives presently.

What can more Innocent then that chyld bee
That hath not liv'd to Cry, or light to see?   130
And now tis fault inough for anie one
To be of a Trew Israelite the sonne.
The daughters may for Bondage live, for Lust
And wyll they, nill they this turne serve they must.
A Qualitie far worse then death: at least
Making a woman worser then a beast.
O Crewelty unheard of, that a Man
Should for his sex-sake seeke anothers bane.
He that letts loose the raynes to Crueltie
With Ease doth runne to all extreamitie.   140
From Burthens they to Bondage doe proceed
And then from Bondage to this bloody deed.
From vexing of their Bodies they goe on
To a most inhumane destruction
Of the fruit of their bodyes: As the sinnes
Of Lust which from slight motions first beginnes
Growes on to foulest executions; soe   [132]
Those of the part Irascible doe to:
Ther is noe sin in which ther lurkes more Ill
Then that of Malice: But oft-tymes the will   150
Is greater then the pow're; And Ill Commaunds
Doe not meet always with ill acting hands.
Gods feare doth teach midwives to disobey
Pharaoths Commands: They knew they might not say
I bidden was, & soe excuse their ill,
God sayd unto their hartes, Thou shalt not Kyll:
Pharaoths lowd voyce could not be heard soe far
Their Great obedyence I commend; I dare
Not their excuse Commend: Surely ther was
As much of weaknes in their answeare, as   160
Strength in their practise: for as they did feare
God, in not kylling: Soe they fearfull weare
Of Pharaoth in Dissembling: Oftentymes
Those that make Conscience of the Greater Crymes
With lesse are taken: And tis rare if wee
Of dangerous actions can come forth & be
Free from all soyle: And if we scape the storme
That after droppes nor wett, nor doe us harme.
What man would not expect the midwives should

Not be soe simple to thinke that they would   170
Be Trustie: yet his indignation
Had not the power to punish what was done.
God doth the midwives prosper, who can then
In anie thing or harme or injure them.
Behold gods goodnes who with blessings will
Reward all such as feare to doe what's Ill.
The midwives prosper'd, And Ile tell you why,   [133]
Not for dissembling, but for pietie.
Soe God their mercie did regard that he
Regarded not this their Infirmitie.   180
How fondly doe men lay the thankes upon
The Sin, which is dew to the deed well don
Gods actions to distinguish, wisdoms lawes
Doe teach, & them to'ascribe to the right Cause:
Pardon belongs unto the Midwives lye,
Remuneration to their pietie:
And to their feare of god prosperitie.
But that which now the Midwives will not doe
The multitude enforced is therto.
'Tweare strange if wicked Rulers should not fynd   190
Some Instruments agreeing to their Mind.
Their Crueltie made but a Smoke before
Now it flames up, & rageth more & more.
Secret practising hath it shamelesse made
And Tyrannie now dares sett up a Trade.
It is a state most miserable wher
Each man is made an executioner.
Ther Cannot be a greater Argument
Of an Ill Cause, then wher Mans blood is spent,
By bloody Tyrants: But by Mildnes, Trewth   200
Upholdes her selfe: & is advanc'de in Sooth
By patience: Thus you trewly have their Act;
What was their issue? just like to their fact.
The people drowne their Males, themselves are drown'd
And by the selfe same meanes they dead are found,
By which they Caus'de, Israells poor Infants dye
That Quitting Law which God doth us denye,
Because all men here fellow Creatures be   [134]
In us he wisely practiseth; & hee
Would in our judgment have us read our sin   210

That we might both Repent & Turne to him.
King Pharaoth, greatly was inrag'de before
      That he receav'de a message, now much more
      Because they must goe, doth he Rage & Curse
      Gods warnings alwayes make the wicked worse.
      The waves doe noe wher soe much rage & beat
      As at the Banke which God for bounds hath sett.
      Corruption when it checked is doth Grow
      Starke mad with Rage: The Vapours schoolmen know
      In a Clowde: that Report be full of ffeare   220
      Would not make, if noe opposition weare:
      Gods stillest voyce Conquers a good mans hart:
      But though unto the wicked he impart
      His Gratious Motions, they Continew still
      Hard Harted & delight in Dooing Ill.
      Manie would not soe settled be in sinne
      If by gods word they had Controuled bin.
      How mild a message was this to pharaoth
      And yet how sharpe, we pray thee lett us Goe.
      That which he fear'de God him Commaunds, for hee   230
      The men of Israell did oppressed see
      With Bondage, & therwith was greatly pleas'de,
      When God Commaunded they should be releast:
      Had the suite bin for Mitigation
      Of Labour, or for preservation
      Of their young chyldren, ther had bin some Ground   [135]
      Of Hope: & soe some favour might have found:
      But God requires that which will discontent
      Pharaoth as much, as ever Pharaoth ment
      His crueltie should Israell: Lett us Goe   240
      Gods præcepts alwayes are Repugnant to
      Mindes meerely voyd of Goodnes: And as they
      Doe love to Crosse him in all that they may:
      Soe he doth Crosse them in their wylls before,
      And afterwards doth plague them more & more.
      It is a signe that hart is very ill
      Which 'playnes that Gods yoake he doth heavy feel.
      Pharaoth of worke talkes when of Sacryfice
      Meeke Moses tells him: Saving Gods service
      All things seeme dew worke to a carnall mind   250
      Which only good deeds doe superfluous fynd.

Chryst sayth but one thing needfull is for blisse,
Nature that Nothing but that needlesse is.
Moses speakes of Devotion, he of sloth,
It hath of auntient tyme bin used, both
Fayre Coulors on our vicious acts to lay,
And vertue with foule scandall to repay.
That Divill which in Pharaoth spoke, speakes still,
In all our scoffers & for ever will.
Who doe Religion Call Hypochrysie   260
And Care of Conscience singularitie.
Each vice a title hath it selfe to Grace
And Everie vertue's cloathed with disgrace.
Whiles they such taskes as might be brought to passe
Imposed on them, ther some Comfort was:
Their diligence their backes from Stripes might save   [136]
For the conceite he that Commands may have
Of profitt: & hope of Impunitie,
To him that Labours, some pretence might be
For difficult Imployments: But to Call   270
For Taskes not possible's Tyrannicall,
And only doth a Quarrell pycke: They Could
Neither make Straw, nor find it, if they would,
Yet they must have itt: Tollerable 'tis
Doe what may be done: But it Cruell is
Doe what can not be: They which are in place
Far above others, & in Greater Grace
Must measure their Commands not by their will
But by the strength of their inferiors still.
Tis Inhumane as all the world doth know   280
More to require of Beastes then they Can doe.
The Taske's not done, Taske-masters beaten are
Wher the charge is, the punishment Lyes thear.
They must exact it of the people, And
Pharaoth the king of the taske-masters hand.
They which are Trusted with Authoritie
Doe oftentymes incurre this mysery
That they for their inferiours faults doe pay
Though for their owne parts they keepe the right way
'Twas not the fault that they did it Require   290
Of the Taskmasters without anie hyre,
But by them of the people; 'Twas a wrong   [137]

224

For which god meanes to plague them ere be Long:
With Thowsand hands, Kings Good or ill doe give
And with noe few-er they shall itt receave.
                     per JStrangways: In Turri Londonensi:

When I was Taken up by the [138]
Souldyers & Kept At Dorchester
& Weymouth by them: June 19th 1685:
Upon a Private & Retyred life:

He that shall seeke lost Creditt to regayne
Shall lose his Laboure & spend tyme in vayne:
Honour once Lost, on just or unjust ground,
Though 'tweare well sought, was never yet well found.
Could I doe soe, my selfe I should not please,
It would soe greatly præjudice my Ease;
And might my safetie hazard too perhapps
By manie unexpected after-clapps:
Therfore for Ease & Quyett I will Trade
From hence-forth in the darke & silent shade;   10
'Tis a safe way in this distemper'd tyme,
To keepe me from suspition of a Cryme.
He that from all men hydes, none seekes to find,
For he that's out of sight, is out of mind.
Nor am I out of hope I may therby
Avoyde the Stroakes of publique Emnitie.
Wheras if I lye Busking in the Sunne,
Tis ten to one, but I shalbe undone.
And yet I dare not to be wedded soe
To Ease & Quiett, as with Guilte to Goe   20
And by Dull sloath, or by base Cowardize
To Court them: That would them much overprize
Nor dare I soe Indifferent to be   [139]
Whither good Men, speake well, or Ill of me
Nay all good Men's good thoughts I love to meritt
And soe to Lyve that I may them Inheritt.
But Soft! me thinkes I heare itt is resolv'd,
That I shall in new troubles be involv'd:
If itt be soe, I know they must aryse

ffrom Base-ffalse feares, & feigned Jealousyes: 30
And Tis my Comfort they will find noe Cause
To warrant their proceedings by the lawes.
Trew Dealing may be sicke & bleeding Lye
'Twill not miscarry, neither will it dye.
Pure Innocence is long Breath'd & itt will
Runne Long, & strong against a Craggie Hyll.
Then by Gods Grace I'le soe keep Rancke & Fyle
That on my sufferings I may sitt & Smile.
           per JS:

[140]

The Epistle of Saint James in verse by
Sir John Strangways Knight in the 80th Yeare   1665
of hisAge: in the yeare of our Lord

Chapter the ffirst
       A servant of god, & of Chryst the Lord
       A Teacher of Gods Trew soule Saving word
       To the Twelve Tribes which scattered are abrode
       James Greeting sends, in the name of the Lord.
My Brethren Count it great Joy when ye shall
       Into Temptations great & diverse ffall.
       Knowing therby that with a perfect sence
       The Tryall of your fayth workes patience.
       And lett your patience then worke perfectlie,   10
       Being Intire, nothing wanting therby.
If anie man want wisdome lett him then
       Aske it of God who giveth to all men
       Most Liberallie without upbrayding, And
       It shalbe Giv'ne him on right grownd to stand.
       But Lett him aske in fayth without wavering
       And he shalbe sure to obtayne that Thing.
       But he that wave-reth is like a sea wave
       Not knowing how to Aske, what he would have:
       Being soe Tos't & Driven of the winde   20
       That he knowe not the right way how to find.
       But if that man doth thinke he shall receave
       What he doth aske he doth himselfe deceave
       A double minded man unstable is

In all his wayes, & all things doth amisse.
But lett the brother of a low degree
Rejoyce, he doth himselfe exhalted see,
Soe lett the Rich, in that he is brought Low
Because he like the fflowre of Grasse doth Goe,
Which vanisheth, & shalbe seen noe moe.   [141]   30
ffor when the sunne is rizen we doe see,
With Burning heate grasse, ceaseth greene to be.
And we doe see A Gallant spreading fflowre
Dead, Dry, & Withered, all within one Howre.
Soe shall the Rich man fade in all his wayes
And soe an End shall putt unto his dayes.
But he who doth Temptation indure
Is Blest, for when he's Try'de he shalbe sure
The Crowne of life from his hand to receave,
Which he hath promis'de, who cannot deceave.   40
Ev'ne god who dwelleth in the Heav'nes above
To give to them who Trewlye doe him love.
Let noe man say when he is Tempted, I
Am Tempted by God, for God Cannot Lye
Nor yet with Evill can god Tempted be,
Nor anie man with Evill Tempteth he.
But Everie man is Tempted when he is
Intised of his Lust to doe Amisse.
Then when lust hath Conceav'de it brings forth sin;
And sin brings death if you remayne therin.   50
My Brethren doe not Erre I doe you move
For every perfect gift Comes from Above
From God the ffather with whom more or Lesse
Ther's noe Shaddow of variablenes.
Who with the word of Trewth of his owne will,
Begat us that we might therby fulfill
The first ffruites of his creatures: & therfore   [142]
My brethren I doe heare adde one thing more
Be swift to heare, & be you slow to speake,
And slow to wrath, for that noe peace doth breake: 60
ffor man's wrath worketh not the righteousnes
Of god, wherwith he doth his servants blesse.
Wherfore Lay ye apart all ffilthynes
And superfluitie of Naughtines

And soe receave you the Ingrafted word
With meeknes, which is able to affoord
Unto yourselves perfect salvation,
And sett you ffree from soule-Damnation.
But of this word see that you Carefull be
Hearers & Dooers; & in this Agree,   70
If anie of the word a Hearer be
And not a Dooer, like that man is he
Which doth beholde his owne face in a glasse
And By, & By forgetts what man he was;
But he that looke's into the perfect Rule
Of Libertie, & studies in that schoole,
Not being a forgetfull hearer, he
Will doe what he hath heard, & he shalbe
A Right good man alwayes esteem'de by thee.
But if among you anie seeme to be   80
Religious, & would soe be held by thee
And yett is of a most unbrideled Tongue   [143]
He's a false brother & will doe thee wrong.
And here one word more I shall adde Againe
This Mans Religion's wicked, Lewde & Vayne.
Religion pure & undefiled is
What God Commaunds yee doe it not Amisse
Nor anie parte yee leave undon of This.
That ffatherlesse & widowes you Assist,
In their distresse, It is the will of Chryst.   90
And from the world your selves in all things keepe
Unspotted like t'a meeke & Harmlesse Sheepe.

The Epistle of Saint James Cap: 2:

Lett not Trew fayth in Chryst worke this effect
Rich men to Honour, poore to disrespect
For if to your assembly ther Come one
Who on his finger hath a pretious Stone
Or doth a suite of Rich apparrell weare
And a poore man ill cloath'de is likewise ther
And to that man who cloathed is soe Gay
Thou say'st sitt thou in this good place today   100

And then unto the poor man thus dost say
Stand By, & unto this man come not neere   [144]
Or doe thou sitt under my foot stoole here.
Are you not in your selves then partiall brought
And become judges of an Evill Thought.
I pray you my beloved brethren heare.
God chooseth them who are poore Eve'ry wher
If rich in fayth, & doe to him adhere
And promiseth the kingdome shalbe Theires
And therof he will make them his right heires.   110
But yee the poore dispised have! Doe not
Rich men accuse you for a dangerous plott
And by their most unjust & dangerous feates
Draw you by pow're before their judgement seates.
And doe they not Blaspheame that Glorious name,
By Blaming you for acting by the same.
If you the Royall law of God fulfill
Which is the summe of his most holy will.
Then in Two wordes I will unto you tell
In dooing soe you verilie doe well.   120
But if you have Respect to persons, yee
Doe committ sin & shall Convinced be
By breaking Gods Law he hath Giv'ne to thee.
For he that keepes the whole Law if he shall
Offend in one point, Guiltie is of All:
For he that sayd see thou doe not Committ   [145]
Adulterie, to kyll held it unfitt.
Now 'though thou commit not Adulterie
Yett if thou kyll thou doest deserve to dye,
For breaking Gods Law soe presumptually.   130
If That a Brother or a Sister be
Hungry or Naked & soe comes next To thee
And therupon thou doest unto him say
Eate & be warme, & in peace Goe your way
And yet those things he doth not to them Give
Their Nakednes or Hunger to Releive,
He must needes be a false hard Hearted Knave
And shall his Tytle carrye to his Grave
And shall his judgment without Mercie have
He well deserves itt, for he Nothing Gave.   140

Soe speake & doe as they shall certainely
    Be judged by the Law of Lybertie.
    Shew thou thy fayth without thy workes to me
    And I my Fayth by my workes will shew thee.
    Thou doest beleeve that one Trew god ther is
    Thou doest well: & the Divills beleeve this
    And Tremble: But doest thou o vayne man know
    That Fayth without good workes for Dead doth Goe.
    And soe of Fayth, if good workes ther be none   150
    Without thy workes, thy fayth is Dead Alone.
    By fayth was Abr'aham justifyde we say
    When Isaacke bound upon the Altar Lay   [146]
    Seest thou how fayth wrought with his workes! & By
    His Workes, his fayth appeared perfectlye
    And thus Gods word fulfilled was which sayth
    That Abraham beleeved God: And's ffayth
    Imputed was to him for Righteousnes
    And with the name of ffreind God did him Blesse.
    Was not the Harlott Rahab justifyed   160
    By workes when shee the Messengers did hyde
    And when shee sent them out another way
    Wher in the mountaynes they did Rest & Stay
    Soe the pursuers mist them in their way.
You see then that by fayth ther is not one
Who without workes is justifyde alone.
For as the Bodie without Breath is Dead
Evne soe is ffayth wher noe Good workes are Bredde.

The third Chapter of Saint James

My Brethren be not Manie masters! Why?
Because we know we shall receave therby
The Greater judgment if we steppe Awry.   170
In manie Things Ev'ne all of us doe wronge
But if a man offend not in his Tongue
He shall passe for a right good Honest man
Since the whole man soe well he Brydle can
For as by Byttes our Horses we Commande;   [147]
And turne their Bodyes with an Easie hand.
And as our Shippes 'though they be wondrous Great

And are by Rough & high windes dryven; yet
By a small Helme, they Turned are About
And are from Dangers safe deliver'd out   180
Ev'ne soe the Tongue although itt Little be,
Boasteth great Things, & we doe daylye See,
One word makes all men Apt to disagree.
The Tongue a world is of Iniquitie,
And soe among our members it doth lye,
That the whole Body is defil'de therby
And the whole Course of Nature sett on fyre.
I want a word to sett it one point higher
For 'Tis a Trewth which I can safelie Tell,
The Tongue it selfe is sett on fyre of Hell.   190
Both Byrdes, & Beastes & Serpents of Each Kind
And in the Sea Things Tamed are we find
And soe have bin, & to itt are Inclyn'de.
Yet sure the Tongue of man, can noe man Tame
Soe fraught with deadlye poyson is the same.
Therwith our God & ffather doe we blesse
And against men with Cursing we Transgresse,
Although the Image of God they Expresse.
Blessing & Cursing from one mouth proceed,
Brethren these things should not be soe Indeed.   200
Can a figge Tree your Olive berries beare   [148]
Or on a vyne are figges found anie where
Or from one spring did ever anie know
Both bytter & sweet water thence to fflow.
The man who with Trew wisdome is Indu'de
His workes with meekenes alwayes are pursuide:
But in your Hartes if strife & Envye dwell,
You sure are in the Readie way to hell.
That wisdome which descends not from above
Is Earthly, sensu'all, & doth Dyvilish prove   210
But the Trew wisdome which Comes from above,
Is Gentle, pure & peaceable in Love:
And doth right without partialitie,
And yeelds good ffruites, without Hypocrysie:
For sure the fruites of Righteousnes increase
When they are sowe'n by men who doe love peace.
                    ffinis

The Epistle of Saint James Cap: 4: [149]

From whence Come warres & Brawlings Amongst you
Ev'ne from your Lusts, that most accursed Crew.
Yee Lust & have not, yee desyre to have   220
But obtayne not the Things which you doe Crave.
Yee fight & warre but have them not I wys
You have them not, because you Aske amisse.
Adulterers I know you know it well
Adulteresses I need not to tell.
The ffreindshippe of this world is Enmitie
And this world's freind is gods knowne Enimie.
Doe you thinke that in vayne the scripture sayth
The Spyritt which to Envye Lust's want's fayth.
But god more Grace doth give, & therfore he   230
Resistes the prowde, which always envy'ous be
But to the Humble gives his Grace most ffree.
To God therfore doe you your selves submitt;
And he will make the Dyv'le to ffly for itt
Draw nigh to God & Hee'le to you draw nigh
Yee Sinners cleanse your Hands most perfectlie.
Yee double minded your hartes purifie:
Be you afflicted, sigh & Greive, & Mourne:
And Lett your Laughter into sorrow Turne.
And doe not Cease soe to make your Addresse   240
That your joy may be Turn'd to Heavines.
Thus Humble your selves in the sight of God   [150]
And Hee'le withdraw from you his scourging Rod.
My Brethren speake not ill of one another
ffor he that speaketh Evill of his Brother
Doth judge him; & doth of the law ill speake,
And soe a just Law, doth unjustly breake:
For not a dooer of the Law thou art,
But thou therin doe'st act the judges part.
Ther's one law Giver to save & destroy,   250
And neither of them is mix't with Alloy.
Who art thou then that holdest thy selfe fitt
In judgment on another man to sitt.
Goe to now yee, who Confidently say
We will to morrow, if not on this day

To Such a citie goe, & wee'l stay ther
To buy & Sell, & Traffique One whole yeare.
Wheras you know not, what next day shalbe;
Nor doe you know whither you shall itt see.
For what's your life? A vapour of short stay,   260
Which in an Instant vanisheth away.
Soe that you ought to say, if the Lord will,
And we shall live, we'le this or that ffulfill.
But in your Boastings you doe now Rejoyce,
Though therby you much prejudice your choyse.
ffor surely he that knoweth to doe well   [151]
And doth it not he is the Chylde of Hell.

The 5th Chapter

Goe too ye Rich men, now sigh, Mourne & weepe
ffor miserie both when you wake & sleepe
Lyes Heavye on you: And your riches are   270
Corrupted, & your Garments are not farre
From being eaten by the Moath: your Gold,
And sylver Hydden under Ground untold
Is Canckared, & therof shall the Rust
A witnesse be against you Trew & Just
Which shall devoure & Eate your flesh like fyre
For keeping Backe the Labourers just Hyre:
Who have Reap'de downe your feildes, & is by you
Kept backe by fraude, although you know tis dew.
And those their Cryes, Ile speake all in one word   280
Are entred into the Eares of the Lord.
You have in pleasure lived on the Earth,
And wanton bin in the mid'st of your myrth:
And nourished you have yourselves with Laughter
As in a Day of Extream joy for slaughter
You have Condemn'de & kylled the just man
Who gave you noe offence, though you began.
Be patient therfore Brethren I you pray   [152]
Unto the Comming of the Lord's great Day
The husbandman doth with great patience waite   290
To make the ffruites of the Earth his Receite.
And doth beleeve he waiteth not in vayne

Both for the Earlie & the Later Rayne.
Soe be you patient, & waite Constantlye
ffor Sure the Comming of the Lord drawes nigh.
Brethren doe not 'gainst one another Grudge,
Behold before the doore doth stand the judge.
Gods antient prophets your Example make
Who in the name of God most boldly Spake
And with great patience suff'red what was done   300
When they weare Loaden with affliction.
Beholde we count them Happie who endure
Of Job's Great patience you have heard I'me sure
And therin have seene the end of the Lord
Who doth great mercies to such men affoord.
But above all things keepe yourselves soe Ev'ne
You sweare not by the Earth, nor yett by Heav'ne
But let your yea, be yea; & your Nay, Nay,
Least you to Condemnation fall away.
Is anie man Afflicted? Let him pray,   310
If merry, Let him sing a psalme that Day
Is anie sicke amonge you? Let him Call
For the Church Elders, & lett them Come all
And over him lett them pray: & with Oyle
Anoynt him in Gods name, & him assoyle   [153]
ffrom his sinnes, & the pray're of ffayth shall Save
The sicke, & god will keepe him from the Grave.
And if he hath Committed sinns they shall
By gods greate mercie be forgiven all:
Confesse your sinnes to one another; and   320
Pray that you may be heal'de & healthy stand:
A fervent pray're which is Trewly such
And by a good man made availeth much
Elyas was a man, as we are all
Subject to passion: & to god did Call
And earnestlye he pray'de it might not Rayne
For three yeares & six monthes: & then agayne
He pray'de, & the Earth brought forth fruites amayne.
If anie doth from Trewth departe & Goe;
And one convert him: then lett that man know   330
That he who doth Converte a sinner Soe

Shall save a soule from death: for he doth Hyde
Those Heynous sinnes, for which he else had Dy'de.
per JStrangways In The eightieth yeare
1665 — of his Age: 1665. | |.

The sixt Chapter of Saint Mathew [154]

Take heede you give not your Almes before Men,
Nor Lett itt be know'n how much you give then;
ffor soe from men you shall have your Reward,
ffor god doth not that Sacryfice Regard.
And therfore when thyne Almes are Giv'ne by thee
Lett not a Trumpet by thee sounded be:
Nor in the Synogogue, nor in the street,
That thou from men may'st not with Glorie meete.
But what thou giv'st let not thy left hand know
At anie Tyme what thy Right hand doth doe. 10
Then by thy God which doth in secret see,
Thou openly, shalt sure Rewarded be:
When you fast be not as an Hypochrite
Of a sad Countenance in all mens sight,
For they disfigure themselves that they may
Appeare to men that they doe fast & pray
But thou, when thou dost fast anoint thy head
And doe not Looke as if thou wer't halfe dead:
That thou appeare not unto men to fast,
But to thy father, who know's what is past: 20
And he that see'th in secrett, Openly
Will thee Reward for thy Sinceritie.
Noe Treasures upon Earth, for yourselves Gett;
Wher Rust & Moath shall them Consume & Eate:
But Treasure for your selves in Heav'ne privyde
Wher they always wyll sure and safe Abyde
And noe Theeves can Amongst themselves devyde: [155]
ffor wher your Treasure is, all men doe know
Your hart wilbe found to be ther also.
When thou dost pray avoyde with holy Care 30
To be such as the Hypocrytes still are
For in the Synogogues they stand & pray,
And this they fayle not to doe Every Day:

Lykewise at Every Corner of the street
In this sort praying you shall with them meet.
And verely I doe say unto you
They dayly doe for this receave their Dew,
Which is the prayse of men for their Reward
ffor God doth not vayne Glorious actes Regard.
But thou, when thou dost pray, enter into   40
Thy closet by thy selfe; & then this doe,
Shutt fast thy Doore, & to thy father pray
To heare in secrett what thou then shalt say
And he that doth in secrett heare thee, will
What thou dost begge, most openly fulfill.
But doe not use vayne Repetition
For tis a Heathenish Superstition
Who thinke for their much speaking they shalbe
In all their prayers better heard by thee.
For God doth know the things you need to have   50
Before you them doe by your prayers Crave.

    After This Manner Therfore doe you pray   [156]
    And in these verie words thus to him Say.
Our Father by Right of Creation
And by Right of my preservation
Of soule & Body from Damnation
And by Right of Provision, wherby
Thou doest all my necessities supply:
Which art in Heav'ne thy Throne of Majestie
Their Heretage who serve thee faythfully   60
Which they are Sure when this life Ended is
They shall inherit with Æternall Blisse.

Give me the Grace to hallow thy Great Name,
And by my Thoughtes, Wordes, Deeds to doe the same
In such a way I may be free from shame
With such a will I may incurre noe blame.

Thy Kingdome Come of pow're I thee desyre
And lett it slay all deadlye sinne in me
Thy Kingdome Come of Grace me to inspyre
That I may serve noe other God but thee   70
And soe this Mercie to me Lord extend
It may be well done too & in my end.

Thy wilbe done in Earth as tis in Heavene
Then Guide the feet of my soule Lord soe Even
That in thy Lawes I may walke Right & Straight
Without a Rubbe of murmure or deceite.
Give unto me this day my Dayly Bread   [157]
And being thus in soule & Body fed
Lett me by precept & Example Too
Teach myne their duties how they ought To doe   80
To God and man with a sound Conscience
In all their words & deeds voyde of offence
And with more Care to keepe them sound from sinne
Then how to sleepe or wake in a sound skinne
With this give me a hart & hand That I
Thee poore with food & Rayment may supply:
And keepe me ffree in acts of Charitie
ffrom Pryde, Vayne Glorie, & Hypochrosie
And ffrom a Grudging & Repining Eye
& If my deeds of Charitie be such   90
My god will me repay seav'ne Tymes as much
For he who for chryst's sake releives the poore
Chryst for the poore's sake will increase his store.
My Trespasses Committed Against Thee
Pardon them Lord I pray thee unto me
As I doe those who Themselves prowdlie boast
To be my foes, although unto my Cost
I feele their wounds in Body, Goods, & Name
Yet freely I doe pardon them the same.
For if to such my pardon I denie   100
Thyne Giv'ne to me is wholy voyd therby.
And Leade us not into Temptation
By the Lust of the fflesh, or of the Eyes:
Or by sinnes which from pryde of life Arise

   All which are Hatch't by malice of the Div'le,   [158]
   Therby to Shipwracke my salvation:
   But doe thou me deliver from all Evill

Forgive what's past, what's present Lord Remove
And in thy service lett me soe improove
That Tymely I, Soe Trewly may Repent   110
That I thy future judgments may prevent
And never may meet with my punishment

For thou art that Great King who Gove'rnest all
And at thy word downe fall's the strongest Wall
And thou hast pow're to Commaund & doe all
And then for Evermore the Glory shall
Be thine in all, & by all, all in all:
      Amen: as thou dost Say, tis trew we see
      What thou doest promise itt shall always be
      And what I now have prayd for unto thee,   120
      Signe itt my God with Thyne AMEN to me:

      Now if men you their Trespasses fforgive
      Then in Gods favour you shall surely Lyve.
      But if you shall not rightly doe this Thing
      Then on your selves gods judgments you shall bring.
      The Trew sight of the Body is the Eye
      If that be single thou see'st perfectly.
      But if the light that's in the Darknes be   [159]
      Then Great must be the darknes thats in thee.
      Noe man can serve Two masters, for he will   130
      Either love one & his worke well fulfyll
      Or else the other hee'l hate & despyse
      & he shalbe contemned in his eyes:
You cannot serve your God & Mammon too
For 'Tis impossible for one to doe.
      Wherfore I say unto you take noe thought
      What meate or drincke shall for your life be sought.
      Nor for your Body what Clothes shalbe bought.
      Mans life is more then meate & drincke I wys
      And sure his Body more then Rayment is.   140
      Behold the fowles they neither sowe nor Reape
      Nor wher they Rest doe they Lay uppe their meate:
      But by your father are fed Every day:
      And are you not much better then are they?
      Which of you Can by taking thought adde one
      Short Cubite to his Length: 'Twill not be done
      And why for Rayment doe you take such Care
      Concider How the Lyllies cloathed are,
      How they doe Grow: They Toyle not, nor doe spynne
      Yet in the Glory Solomon liv'de in   150
      Array'de like one of those he was not seen.
      Wherfore if God soe cloathe the Grasse to day   [160]

Which in an Instant vanisheth away
Then shall he not (marke what to you he sayth)
Much more Cloathe you, O yee of little fayth.
Wherfore take noe thought! nor yet doe yee say
What shall we eate, or drincke, or weare to day?
For after these things doe the Gentiles seeke,
But god your father knowes you doe them lyke:
And that of them in great need you doe stand: 160
But first of all seeke you at anie hand
Gods Kingdome, which in Righteousnes doth stand;
And all those things shall added be to you;
And you shall find what here is sayd is Trew.
Take therfore noe Thought for the Morrow day
To morrow thoughts for themselve well will pay
Sufficie'nt is the Evill of the Day.
          per JStrangways   in fine octogesimi
             1665   anni, ætatis suæ:

The fifth Chapter of Saint Matthew   [161]

When Jesus saw the multitude, he went
Into a mountayne, wher some Tyme he spent,
And when he was sett, his disciples came
Unto him, whom he in his fathers name
Did Teach; & thus unto them he did say:
1: Right Blessed, yea Thrice blessed sure are they
    Who are of a most meeke & humble Spyritt
    For they the Kingdome of Heav'ne shall inherit.
2: Blessed are they that mourne, for they shalbe
    Comforted in a very high degree.   10
3: And Blessed are the meeke, for they shall finde
    The good things of the Earth in Every Kind:
    And their delight shall very much increase
    In the Aboundance they injoy of peace.
4: And Trewlye they who after Righteousnes,
    Hunger & Thirst, god will them fully blesse.
5: And blessed are the mercifull for they,
    Shall obtayne mercie, in gods judgment day.
6: And blessed are the pure in hart, for they
    To their great Comfort, see god Eve'ry day.   20

<pre>
7:   Blessed are they who persecuted are
     For Righteousnes; for that's the Trew North Starre
     Which guides us unto heav'ne wher surely we
     Shall of that Kingdome be for ever ffree.
8:   Blessed are yee when men shall Revyle you
     And speake against you things which are untrew
     And falsely for my names sake those things brew.
     Rejoyce & be exceeding Glad, for Great
     Shall your Reward be for that Cursed Feate.
     For soe the prophetts which before you were,   [162]   30
     They in this sort did wrong them Eve'ry wher.
     Salt's good, but if it be unsavory Growne,
     Then to all men by these lett it be knowne
     Tis fitt it should be on the Dunghill Throwne.
You are the light of the world: If a Towne
Be on a Hill built 'Twilbe seen & knowne;
Neither doe men a Candle light & then
Sett it wher it Can not be seen of Men,
But on a Candlesticke that it may give
Light to all those who in that Howse doe live.   40
     Soe lett your light before all good men shine
     That they may be seen to be Trewly thyne.
     And then lett them be alwayes kept soe Ev'ne
     They may your father glorifie in Heav'ne.
     Thinke not that I bring with me anie wyll,
     The Law or prophetts to destroy & kyll.
     But I am Come them wholy to fulfill.
     For verelye I doe unto you say
     Untill that Heav'ne & Earth shall passe away
     Not one Jote or Tytle shall you see   50
     Passe from the Law till all fulfilld be.
     Then whosoever shall breake one of these
     Commandments, & thinkes men therby to please
     He in gods Kingdome shalbe cal'de the Least:
     But whosoever then shall doe his best
     And shall Teach others soe to doe it, sure he,
     Great in gods Kingdome shall esteemed be.
     But if your righteousnes shall not exceed,
     That of the Scribes & Pharises in Deed;
     Then into Heaven you shall in noe Case   60
     Enter, nor ther shall you have anie place
</pre>

By men of Old Tyme you have heard & know [163]
Thou shall not kyll, & he who shall doe soe
He shall in Danger of the judgment be
But I doe say that whosoever is
Angry with one who hath not done amisse
In danger of the judgment he shalbe
And whosoever to his brother shall
Say RACHA, they shall him to judgment Call.
But whosoever shall say this to thee 70
Thou Foole, for this he shall meet with his hyre
That he shalbe in Danger of Hellfyre.
If thou thy gift unto the Altar bring
And ther dost mind thy Brother hath something
Against thee: doe not thou thy selfe deceave
But ther thy gift before the Alter leave
And to thy Brother reconcyled be
And then lett thy gift off'red be by thee.
When thou dost with thyne adversary Goe
Unto the judge, then quickly thy worke doe 80
And doe thou not fayle with him to Agree
Least that the judge doe then deliver thee
Unto the Jaylor by whom thou shalt be
In pryson kept, Till all be payd by thee.
You have heard that of old tyme it was sayd
Thou shalt not lye with wyddow, wife, or Mayd,
    But I doe say, who with a Lustfull eye
    Lookes upon these, commit's Adultery
    And hath already done itt in his hart;
    God grant we may all from this sinne depart. 90
If thy right Eye offend thee plucke it out [164]
And Cast it from thee, for without all doubte
Itt is more better for thee with one Eye
To live with God in Heav'ne Æternally;
Then with Two eyes to be Cast into Hell,
And ther in Endlesse Myserie to dwell.
Cutt off thy Right hand if it thee offend
And Cast it from thee: 'Tis for a good End.
ffor better Tis I doe thee Trewly tell
Then thy whole Bodie should remayne in Hell: 100
It hath bin sayd who putt's away his wife
At anie Time for the Terme of her Lyfe,

A writt of Dyvorce he shall to her Give
During the Tyme shee in this world shall live.
But I say to you whosoever shall
Putt of his wife for anie cause att all
Excepte it be for fornication
(And for that it may lawfully be done)
Doth cause her to Commit Adulterie:
Againe you have heard & you have bin Tolde,   110
Forsweare not thy selfe: Be not thou soe bolde.
But pay thy vowes, & oathes unto the Lord,
And Lett thy words & Deeds with that Accord:
But I say to you, An oathe doe thou ffeare
And neither by Earth nor by Heav'ne sweare
ffor Heav'ne sure is god's most Glorious throne,
And the whole Earth is for his ffootstoole knowne.   [165]
Nor anie oath by thy head shalt thou take,
For not one Hayre blacke or whyte canst thou make.
Therfore to Avoyde condemnation   120
In your Course of Communication
Let your yea, be yea; & your Nay be Nay:
For more then that putt's you in an ill way.
A Tooth for a Tooth; An Eye for an Eye
Was sayd of old: But now to this say I,
Resist not Evill, But if one smite thee
Upon one Cheeke, let Th'other Smitten be.
If anie man for thy Coate shall thee Sue,
Lett him thy Cloake take likewise for his due
And he that shall Compell thee for to goe   130
A myle with him; doe thou goe with him two.
To him that Asketh Give; & say not Nay;
From him that Borrowes turne thou not away.
This speech in old tyme passed Currantlye
Thy neighboure love, & Hate thyne Enimie;
But I say to you love your enimies,
'Though in All things They seeke your præjudice.
Doe good to them that hate you, & then pray,
ffor those that persecute you every day,
And with despight abuse you Eve'ry way: 140
Soe of your father who in Heaven is
You shalbe know'ne & owned to be his.   [166]
Who makes the sun to sett & Ryse Agayne

Who gives us Ease & free's us from our payne
And on the just & unjust sendeth Rayne.
ffor if you love them, who love you, then what
Reward have you? The publicans doe that:
And if your brethren only you salute
Doe not the Quakers therin with you suite.
Therfore soe perfect be, in doing this;   150
Ev'ne as your father which in Heaven is.
per JStrangways   in fine octogesimi
1665   anni ætatis suæ.

The 7th Chapter of Saint Matthew   [167]

Judge not, & soe you shall not judged be,
ffor as thou judgest, they will judge for thee.
Then give noe Cause of Measure to Complayne
ffor as you mete, you shall receave againe.
Thou see'st the Mote that's in thy brothers eye
But not The beme which in thyne owne doth Lye.
Then how canst thou unto thy brother say
Doe thou give leave to me, that soe I may
Pull out the mote which Troubleth soe thyne eye
And yet in thyne a greater Beame doth Lye.   10
ffirst Cast thou out thy beame, thou Hypocryte
Which lyes in thyne eye & doth blind thy sight
And then thou shalt see clearly how to Cast
The mote which in thy Brothers eye is plac'de.
That which is Holy give not to the Doggs
Nor Cast your pearles before the Nastie Hoggs;
Least they doe Trample them under their ffeet,
And Turne againe & Rent you when yee meet.
Aske right it shall unto you be giv'ne
What you shall soe Aske of the god of Heav'ne   20
Then seeke & you shall be sure then to find
Those things which trewly shall Content your mind
Then knocke & itt shall opened be to thee
And then within thou glori'ous things shalt see;
Now what man is ther of whom if his sonne
Shall Aske bread of him, will give him a stone?
Or if from him he shall desyre a ffish

243

Will Give to him a serpent in a dysh?
If being Evill, you know how to give,   [168]
Good gifts unto your children well to live   30
Shall not your father then give them much more,
(Who aske of him) out of his Heav'nely store.
Ev'ne soe all things, you would that men should doe
For you; I wish, for them you should doe soe:
The Law & prophets bids us this way goe.
Into the strait gate strive to enter in.
ffor the Great, & Broade way leads us to sinne;
And most men with delight doe walke therin.
But straight's the Gate & narrow is the way,
Which lead's to life: 'Tis not found in one day;   40
Of Prophets in sheeps clothing doe beware
ffor Inwardly Most Ravening wolves they Are.
But by their fruites these men you well may know:
Doe Grapes & ffigges upon the Bryars Grow?
Ev'ne soe a good Tree, Good ffruit bringeth forth;
But a Corrupt Tree beares fruit nothing worth.
That Tree which beares not the ffruit we desyre
We cutt itt downe & make therwith a Fyre.
Not Ev'ry one that Sayth Lord, Lord to me,
Shall enter Heav'ne, & therin placed be.   50
But he that keepes in all his wayes soe Ev'ne
And doth fulfill my fathers will in Heav'ne.
Then manie at that tyme will to me say
Lord, Lord we trewlye have kept thy right way.
And in thy name we Devills have cast out
And wond'rous Things we have done round about,
But unto those who these things to me presse
I never knew them I shall then professe.   [169]
Therfore yee workers of Iniquitie
Depart; & unto me draw you not nigh: 60
But he that heares these words, & doth them Too
Is a wyse man; & like to him doth doe
Who built his howse upon a Rocke, & when
The rayne descended, & the winds blew, Then
That howse fell not, for it was founded Sure,
That it was Able all stormes to indure.
But he that heares, And doth not what I say
Is like him, who did the foundati'on Lay

Of his howse in the sand: & the winds blew
And Great Raynes fell: & then be't knowne to you   70
That howse fell, & the ffall of it was Great.
And having sayd this, he rose from his seat
And then Astonish'de all the people were
When they these Doctrines from his mouth did heare.
ffor he Taught them not perfunctorilie
As doe the scribes; but with Authoritie.

per JStrangways   in fine octogesimi anni
1665   ætatis suæ.

Looke for the Lords prayer thus Turned into   [170]
verse by Sir John Strangways in the 6th Chapter
of Saint Matthew: in octogensimo anno
Ætatis suæ

The Apostells Creede:

In God th'almightie father I beleive
Who life & Beeing doth to all men Gyve.
Who did the Heav'ne & Earth & Seas Create,
And all the Creatures that to them Relate.
And I beleive in Jesus Chryst his sonne
Who perfectlye his fathers will hath done:
That he was by the holy Goast Conceav'de
And from a virgin pure & chast Receav'de
His humane Birth: That he was Crucifyde,
By Pontius Pylate's judgment & soe Dyde.   10
That dead & burye'd in his Grave he Lay
Three Nights & Dayes: That upon the Thyrd Day
ffrom Death to life, by's owne pow're did Aryse
And was seene by more then five Hundred Eyes:
That after that he did to Heav'ne asscend
Wher he Remaynes untill this world shall End:
And then attended with God's Glorious hoast he shall
Both Quicke & Deade, All men to judgement Call
And unto those who here did Holy Lyve
A crowne of Endlesse Glory he shall Give: 20

245

But unto those who did his Lawes Disdayne
And held his service Labour spent in vayne,
He shall adjudge them unto Restlesse payne   [171]
And in that State for Ever to Remayne.
And I in God the Holy Goast beleive
ffrom whom I my welbeing doe derive
ffor he doth Grace & Vertue to me Gyve
A Godly, Righteous, Sober life to Lyve.
Who proceeds from the father & the sonne
And 'though in Name three Gods are yet but one.   30
And that God hath a Trew Church I beleive
Holy & Catholique, which doth us Give
All those old Trewthes God's prophetts did us Teach
And Chryst & his Apostles since did preach.
And I beleive the sainctes Communion
In Heav'ne & Earth doth keepe a union.
Which by Trew ffayth, Trew Love, Trew Hope in Chryst,
Is perfected; & therin doth Consist.
And I beleive my sinnes shall pardened bee
And I from Gylt & punishment sett free   40
By Chryst's soulsaving mercies unto me:
And I beleeve this fflesh agayne shall Ryse,
From Death to Liffe; & I shall with these Eyes
Behold my God: & I shall after this
Remayne with him in Endlesse joy & Blysse.
     Finis

The Ten Commandements   [172]

  Almightie God to whom all harts Alone
  Are open, & all their desyres are knowne,
  ffrom whom noe secretts are or can be
  Soe cleanse my soule I humbly beg of thee
  That noe lewde thoughts may harbour ther with me
  But perfectlie I may love thy great Name,
  And worthylye may Magnifie the same.
1: God spake these words & sayd I am
  The Lord thy God, I am the same
  Who when thou did'st in pryson lye   10
  And wert unhear'd Condemn'de to dye

And excepted from all mercie
Did from that pryson sett thee ffree
And from that death deliver'd thee.
And then I gave thee perfect health,
And Taught thee wisdome to gett wealth
And how to gett, & keepe, & spend,
And in none of this to offend
And when to thee I did give these
I gave thee with them peace & Ease.   20
Then see that thou most faythfull be
To serve noe other god but me.
    Thy mercie to me Lord extend
    That I may not in this offend
    To this end Teach me I thee pray
    To know & keepe the good old way   [173]
    And guide me therin soe that I
    May never Treade one steppe awry.
2: Thou shalt noe Graven Image make
Nor yet the liknes shalt thou take   30
Of anie thing in Heav'ne above
Or on Earth or in waters move
Before them thou shalt not bow downe.
All Idoll worshippe I disowne
ffor I am a most Jealous god
And will not spare my stinging Rod,
Unto the Third & ffowrth descent
That shall breake this Commandement
But will to Thowsands Gratious be
Who Trewly love & Honour me.   40
Nor shalt thou seeke by Hooke & Crooke
To gett fyne Gold on itt to Looke
For in one hart I must thee Tell
God & thy Mammon cannot dwell.
For Tis a Trewth none Can denie
It is downe Right Idolatry.
    Thy mercie Lord to me Extend
    That I may not in this offend:
    To this end Teach-me I thee pray   [174]
    To know & keepe the good old way   50
    And Gyde me therin soe that I
    May never Treade one steppe Awry

But may with a most perfect wyll
This Law in Every point fulfill.
3:   In vayne thou shalt not take my Name
ffor I will not him Guiltlesse hold
But will him Bring to blame & Shame
That shalbe soe profanelye bold.
My Covenant thou shalt not Breake
Nor therin shalt thou spring a Leake.   60
Thy Oathes & Vowes made unto me
Must be sincearely paid by thee
Then feare an Oath, & Hate a Lye
And keepe this Rule most faythfully
Without Æquivocation
Or mentall Reservation
Or Papall dispensation.
    Thy mercie to me Lord Extend,
    That I may not in this offend:
    To this End Teach me I thee pray   70
    To know & keepe the good old way
    And guide me therin soe that I   [175]
    May never Treade one steppe Awry
    But may with a most perfect wyll
    This Law in Every point fulfill:
4:   Remember thou the Sabacth day
To keepe it holy to the Lord
Goe to his Temple then to pray
And with great Reverence heare his word
Six dayes thou may'ste labour and   80
Doe all thou hast therin to doe,
But on the seventh day understand
I doe forbid thee to doe soe.
On that day my worke must be thyne
And thy worke that day must be myne
The words thou speakest must be knowne
To be my words & not thyne owne
And in my wayes walke thou that day,
And see thou walke noe other way.
On that day noe worke may be done   90
Nor by the husband nor the wife
Nor by the daughter, nor the sonne
On payne of forfaiture of life.

Nor by thy Man nor by thy Mayd;
Nor by thyne oxe, nor by thyne Asse;
The Stranger that day must be Stayde [176]
Out of thy Gates he may not passe
ffor in Six dayes the Lord of Hoastes
The Heav'ne & Earth & Seas did frame
And all that in their Sev'rall Coastes 100
Doth Live or move he made the same.
Then on the seave'nth day he did Rest
None other workes he made therin
Wherfore the Lord God that day blest
And since that day, 't hath holy bin.
 Thy mercyes lord to me Extend
 That I may not in this offend
 To this End Teache me I thee pray
 To know & keepe the Good old way
 And guyde me therin soe that I 110
 May never Treade one steppe Awry
 But may with a most Ready will
 This Law in Every point fulfill.
5: Unto thy parents Naturall
To Civill & Spirituall
Dew Honour doe thou always Give
That in the Land God giveth thee
Thou may'st with Comfort Long Tyme live
And never ther a Stranger be,
And this must noe Lippe Labour be 120
But it must from thy hart proceede
And must be well perform'de by thee, [177]
In Thought, in word, in wyll, in deede.
 Thy mercies Lord to me Extend,
 That I may not in This offend:
 To this end Teache me I thee pray,
 To know & keepe the good old way:
 And guide me therin soe that I
 May never make one steppe awry
 But may with a most perfect will 130
 This Law in Evry pointe fulfill.
6: Thou shalt noe wilfull murder doe
Nor give thy Consent therunto
Nor shal't conceale it when 'tis done

'Though it weare by thy only sonne.
Let Rancour, Hatred, malice be
Alwayes meere strangers unto thee
Revenge is gods peculiar
Then doe not Thou Remove that Barre
But leave it to him to Repay   140
In his owne Tyme & his owne way.
ffrom men of Disposition
ffroward & peevish get thee gon
And Leave them by themselves alone.
Be Swift to Heare, be slow to speake
And slow to wrath noe peace doth Breake.
An Angry man doe thou not know   [178]
Nor with him on the Highway Goe
For Anger a short Madnesse is
And alwayes speakes & doth Amisse.   150
Then with Care keepe Chryst Jesus Rule
And doe not Call thy Brother ffoole
ffor if thou cal'st him soe in Ire
Thou art in Danger of hell fyre.
      Thy mercie Lord to me Extend
      That I may not in this offend
      To this End Teach me I thee pray
      To know & keepe the good old way
      And gide me therin soe that I
      May never Treade one steppe awry   160
      But may with a most perfect wyll
      This Law in Eve'ry point fulfill.
7:   Nor with thy neighbour's wife shall Lye
     And soe Committ Adulterie.
     Nor in thy Lust shalt thou desyre
     Anothers wife to occupyre
     For in that Case itt is all one
     As if that Deed by thee were done
     Nor shalt thou make her an Addresse
     To Temp't her unto wantonnesse   170
     To winne her to give leave to thee
     Her secret parts to feele or see
     Nor yet to clappe her Lovely Hypps
     Nor wantenly to kisse her Lypps
     Nor shalt thou give her thy Consent

To take with thee the like Content.   [179]
If this of thee she shall desyre
Spitt in her face & soe denie her.
Lett not her naked hand once Touch
Thy naked member Tis to much.   180
And never doe thou her admitt
With her Bare Buttocks for to sitt
On thy bare Belly, Tis unfitt
ffor therby shee meanes to Tempt thee
Her secret part may entred be.
You know well if Two fall at Stryffe
And one hath standing by his wife
Who as they strive doth playnely see
Her husband worsted much to be.
And therupon she waxeth bold   190
The others stones with hand to hold
And 'though shee did that undertake
Only for her deare husbands sake
And of that Stryfe an end to make
Yet God by his Law doth Commande
That wyfe for that shall lose her hand.
I doe relate this passage here
That all may Tremble & forbeare
To take delight to feele or See
Those parts which secrett kept should be,   200
And doe it that they may therby
Be made more rype for Leacherie.
For God's sake whilst tis Cal'de to Day   [180]
Breake off that synne & dayly pray
    Thy mercie to me Lord extend
    That I may not in this offend
    To this end Teach me I thee pray
    To know & keepe the good old way
    And gyde me therin soe that I
    May never Treade one steppe Awry   210
    But may with a most perfect will
    This Law in Every point fulfyll.
8: Thou shalt not plunder, steale, purloyne
Thy neighbours Cattle, goods, or Coyne:
Nor in thy Trade shalt use Deceite
Either in measure or in waite.

And here it must be understood
Thou mayst not sell bad ware for Good
Nor for the buyer's ignorance
Shalt thou thy selling price advance.   220
For in good Sooth I doe thee Tell,
Tis sinne Good ware to oversell.
In word & Deed be Trew & Just,
And doe not falsifie thy Trust.
To thy poore brother freely Lend
Who doth not his goods Lewdlie spend.
Lend, & Looke not for anie Gayne
But to receave thyne owne agayne.   [181]
And he that borrowes must Repay
The monie Lent him att his day.   230
And if he Trewly keepe that Course
He may Commande his neighbours purse.
Now if thy Neighbour be involv'de
In a Great debte & is Resolv'de
To sell his Land that debte to ffree
And offers itt to sale to thee
And if thou art inclyn'de to buy
Worke not on his necessitie
Nor studie him to over-wytt
Att a low Rate to purchase it   240
But give for itt what just & ffitt:
And if thou art inforc'de to sell
Make out thy Tytle fayre & well
And all incumbrances discover
That he that Runnes may Read them over.
If in this Case thou thus shalt deale
'Twill very much advance thy weale
For thou therby wilt quicklie find
A Chapman fitted to thy Mynd
Who will bring ready monie forth   250
And Give thee for itt what tis worth.
Thy Covenant keepe faythfully
'Though thou art sure to loose therby: [182]
ffor Evry knave will doe the same
When he is dealt a winning Game
And Lowdely will Cry, Fye for Shame,
To breake your word you are to Blame.

252

Thy servants wages duly pay
And those that Labour by the Day
And lett them know likewise that they 260
Must earne the wages thou dost pay
Nor may they Loyter Tyme a way
But whiles the sunne shynes must make Hay.
The widdow & the ffatherlesse
Thou shalt Not Injure nor oppresse
But shalt be their freind in distresse
The naked Cloath, the Hungry feed
And give thyne Almes to those that need
But Among'st them doe thou not fayle
To helpe poore pr'ysoners in the Jayle. 270
But if a Beggar shalbe found
Who in his Wytts & Lymbs is sound
And will not worke, but Idle sitt
I then doe hold it very ffitt
Hym to some working howse to send
Wher he his Tyme may better spend
And for his Idlenes he may
Att whipping post receave his pay:
If this Almes thou shalt to him give [183]
He by his hands will learne to live. 280
 Thy mercies lord to me extend
 That I may not in this offend
 To this end Teach me I thee pray
 To know & keepe the good old way
 And guyde me therin soe that I
 May never Tread one steppe awry
 But may with a most perfect will
 This Law in Evry point fulfill.
9: Neither shalt thou false witnesse beare,
 For Love or hate, for hope or feare: 290
Trewth, whole Trewth, nothing but Trewth Sweare.
Nor shalt thou wound thy neighbours Name
By Raysing Slanders on the same
For verilie a Slaunderous word
Wounds deeper then a Cutting sword
Nay if thy neighbour be defam'de
Defend him & be not asham'de
Tell them thou dost the man well know

And dost beleeve he did not soe
Nay I beleeve who inform'de this   300
Was Certaynly informde Amisse.
But if that he hath step't awry
Sure it was done unwittingly.
But if doth avow to doe itt
Then know the Cause that mov'de to itt
And in the meane Tyme doe forbeare   [184]
To sensure him Till you him heare
Or judge him by his life forpast
And not by this one act at last
For 'tis a very Certayne thing   310
One suallow doth not make a spring:
    Thy mercies lord to me Extend
    That I may not in this offend.
    To this End Teach me I thee pray
    To know & keepe the good old way
    And guide me therin soe that I
    May never Tread one steppe awry
    But may with a most perfect will
    This Law in Ev'ry point fulfill.
10: Thy Neighbours wyfe thou shalt not Covett   320
   Nor's howse I charge thee doe not move itt.
   Nor in his Tytle seeke a fflaw
   To gett them by a Tricke of Law
   Nor give him just Cause to Complayne
   Thou wouldst his servant from him gayne.
   Neither lett thy Hart Inclyne
   To make his oxe or his asse Thyne
   For thou shalt highly doe Amisse
   To Covet anie thing that's his:
       Thy Mercyes lord to me Extend   [185] 330
       That I may not in this offend
       To this end Teache me I thee pray
       To know & keepe the good old way
       And gyde me therin soe that I
       May never Treade one steppe Awry
       But may with a most perfect will
       This law in Evry point fulfill.

And now my Lord I humbly begge of thee
Thow would'st be please to give unto me
An awfull & a holy Reverence   340
Of thyne omniscience & omnipresence
And lett it worke soe powrefully on me
That I from Henceforth may as fearfull be
To Committ sinnes in secrett against thee
As I would be to Committ openlie
Great Crymes before an open Enimie.
        Thus if I live, I trewly shall inheritt
        The Benifitts of Chryst's soule-saving meritt.

Upon the Oxford monie Coyned   [186]
King Charles the ffirst

1:   The protestant Religion
     Is the sure Rocke I build upon
2:   And by the just & Righteous Lawes
     Of England I'le mayntayne my Cause.
3:   The Pryviledge of parlament
     Hath always had my full consent

     I wish it may to all be knowne
     That I these things did rightly owne
     And therupon I thought itt fitt
     Upon my Coine it should be writt.   10

Appendix 1

Commendatory verses by Sir John Strangways

[from Thomas Coryate, *Coryats Crudities hastily gobled up in five Moneths travells* (1611), d^v-d2]

Thou crav'st my verse, yet do not thanke me for it,
For what rimes can praise enough *Tom Coryate*?
Kemp yet doth live, and onely lives for this
Much famous, that he did dance the Morris
From *London* unto *Norwich*. But thou much more
Doest merit praise. For though his feete were sore,
Whilst sweaty he with antick skips did hop it,
His treadings were but friscals of a poppet.
Or that at once I may expresse it all,
Like to the Jacks of jumbled virginall.   10
But thou through heats and colds, through punks and trunks,
Through hils and dales hast stretcht thy weary stumps,
Feeding on hedge-row fruits, and not on plum-trees,
Onely through zeale to visite many countries.
But stay a while, and make a stand my Muse,
To thinke upon his everlasting shoo's.
Come to my helpe some old-shod pilgrime wight,
That I of you may tread the way aright
Which leads unto his fame, whilst I do stile
How he did go at least nine hundred mile.   20
With one poore paire of shoes, saving alone-a
He onely once did sole them at *Verona.
So that it grew a question whether
Thy shoes or feete were of more lasting leather.
Which at that time did stand thee in most use,
When as the Jewes would cut off thy prepuce.

But thou that time like many an errant Knight,
Didst save thy selfe by virtue of thy flight.
Whence now in great request this Adage stands;
One paire of legges is worth two paire of hands. 30

  * You should have said Zurich.

APPENDIX 2

Sir John Strangways to the Commons, 1 April, 1647

[BL Harl. 158. f.270, abbreviations expanded, as per editorial principles]

To the right Honourable the Knightes, Citizens, & Burgesses of the howse of Commons in parliament assembled. | |.

> The humble petition of Sir John Strangways Knight now a prysoner in the Tower of London.

Humbly sheweth

That he is oppressed with abundance of greiffe & sorrow of hart that he hath incurred the displeasure of this honourable howse: And that he is very far from justifying anie of his unhappie actions by which he hath drawne the same upon him.

That by the order of this honourable howse he hath bin a prysoner three-score & ten weekes in the Tower of London; wher his ordinarie charge for his chamber rent & Dyett amountes to one hundred & thirty poundes per annum for himselfe & his servant that attends him, & he is allowed but one meale aday: That all the profitts of his Landes are sequestred, & his whole personall estate seized, & disposed of by the order of this honourable howse; Soe that he hath bin enforced to live during all the tyme of this his imprysonment by the mere almes & charity of those few freindes adversitie hath left him, who are not able in these hard Tymes anie longer to mayntayne him:

That he is growne into great yeares, & besydes the weaknesses which usuallie accompanie old age, he is also oppressed with diverse other infyrmities, as without good & Carefull attendance (which will not be had without Cost & charge) will in a short tyme putt an end to his miserable life.

10

20

That as he is verie far from justifying of himselfe in the anie of his doings by which he hath given offence to this honourable howse: Soe he hopeth that he hath soe behaved himselfe during the tyme of his imprysonment, that neither by word or deed he hath given anie further Cause to increase your disfavour towards him.

Lastlie he hopeth it is not unknowne to this honourable howse that he voluntarily endeavoured to cast himselfe wholy into your pleasure & protection, & thereupon willingly rendred himselfe into your power. ||.

Wherfore he most humbly beseecheth you to Commiserate him in this his extreame necessitie, & out of your goodnes to allow unto him such mayntenance, wherby he may be enabled to provyde for himselfe convenient food & Rayment, with such other necessaryes as shalbe requisite to support him in this tyme of his misery: And that you would be graciouslye pleased to inlarge your goodnes towardes him by graunting him his liberty upon Bayle, to render himselfe againe a trew prysoner, when this honourable howse shall please to remaunde him: & in the meane Tyme not to act, nor to Consent to the acting of anie thing which shall or may tend to the disservice of the proceedings of this most honourable howse. ||.

And your petitioner (as in duty bound) shall dayly pray &c:

JStrangways
1° Aprilis: 1647

APPENDIX 3

A poem by Sir John Strangways

[from Dorset R.O., Ilchester Deposit, D124/Box 263: a nineteenth-century MS
copy, whose punctuation has been slightly modified here]

1ˢᵗ May 1650

The Lands which do belong to me
I did Resolve this spring to see.
But since the State hath me denyde
Above five Miles from home to ride
This Note declares the Lands I have
Which my forefathers to me gave
Or which for Monie I did Buy
And in what places they do lie
When in my last Survey I went   10
To make some fines and gather rent.
First I have in Southampton Town
An Entyre third part of the Crown
From thence I into Purbeck came
Where I a little Landlord am.
In Brenscombe my lands do lye there
In Corffe in Wolgarston and Beere
In Sturminster and Spetisbury
And Mapowder some Lands have I.
Cawsway Mill belongs to me   20
I[n] Dorchester I have the fee
Of Burgages some two or three.
To Munckton Church I do present
That Right came to me by decent.
Woodsford Strangways is well known

And Bolmeston to be myne own.
Of Stinsford Farm I have the Fee
That Right my ancestors gave me.
In Forthington Mead they Confesse
Three yards I have be't more or lesse.   30
And those three Yards which ther I clayme
Doe unto Stinsford appertayne.
In Burton Strangways all the Lands
I have from my forefathers Hands.
And Charlton Strangways which I Clayme
Doth by like Right to me pertayne.
In Charminster Mead there doe lye
Eight Acres I of Ryckes did buy.
Which I to Carlton Strangways adde
For Mead is there scarce to be had.   40
Loverd Walterson are Myne
By a Recovery and Fyne.
In the Rich Meads of Puddle Town
Twelve Acres yearly I cutt down.
Besydes in Moreton three there are
Of which I yearly take the Share.
And Shepton Gorges tis well knowne
I have by purchase made myne owne.
Of Balston Bragge & Hebbes did I
Buy three Freeholds which ther do lye.   50
From thence along by the sea syde
To Abbotsbury I did ride,
Where all the Dwellers in that Towne
Me only for their Landlord Owne.
The Personage Mills & Demayne Lands
Pay all their profitts to my Hands.
And here before I farther go
I think itt fitt to lett you Know
Though I that personage hold in fee
That Right by purchase came to me.   60
Neer this one Tenement have I
Which doth in Puncknoll parish lye.
And is well knowne to be the same
Which Strangways Bexington some name.
I[n] Portesham and Looke Meade Stake
The Hay Six acres yearly make.

To Mayden Newton next I went
Where I unto that Church present
I[n] Stockwood, Halstocke Evershott
Some Lands in each fall to my Lott.   70
Which came not to me by Decent
My Monie bought that Land & Rent.
And by my Monie tis well knowne
That I have made Burle Farm myne owne.
Whe[r]to six acres now are lay'd
Which in Frome Quintin lye tis sayd.
In Melbury Osmond wher ther are
Three Lords I have a Double Share
Besydes some Houses & some Grounds
For which I paid full Eight score pounds.   80
I cannot Melbury Sampford wave
Wher my fore fathers lye in Grave.
And wher all those of my surname
Liv'd since into the west we came,
And wher by God's Leave I intend
The Remnant of my Life to spend.
This makes me keepe ther in my hands
All former leased demayne Lands.
Besides to make the place more fitt
I added have Leggs Land unto it.   90
For which when they weare to me sould
I pay'd Twelve Hundred pounds in Gould.
With Dorsetshyre I now have done
From thence I went to Somerton
Wher all my Lands which ther doe lye
I of the Rosses late did Buy.
In Littleton some Land I hold
Which Edward Merryott to me sould.
To Compton Dundeyne thence I went
Which hath bin myne by longe Decent   100
Wher Great Freeholders do Resort
To do their service at my Court.
And such of them that are away
Are for their Absence fyn'd & pay.
Thirteene of those ther hold of me
Their Lands by one intyre Knights fee
Which all have pay'd me once; some twice

And one of them hath pay'd me thrise.
And twenty more of them ther are
That of a Knights fee pay some share.   110
To Pen in Zelwood next I ryde
Which Lyes upon the Forest syde.
In that place ther belongs to me
An intire third parte of the fee.
From thence to Hardington I came
Whereof one half I Landlord am.
Besydes my Manor I have ther
One Moytie of Hewingbere.
To Middle & West Chynocke then
I next did goe wher all the Men   120
Unanimously did Accord
That I was ther the Rightfull Lord.
Wolington Marshall: Lawrence [S]lade
My Monie ther Lands mine have made.
In Chelisberg which next doth lye
I have an intyre Moytie.
In Mer-ri-ett the Fee Farm Rents
I have of all the Tenements.
This Rent for Monie I did Gett
From Robert Earle of Somersett.   130
I[n] Montague & Hasilbere
Some Quilletts of my lands lye there.
In Stratton & in Cudworth rents
Are pay'd me for 2 Tenements.
In Wyke which doth neere Lamport lye
Halfe of one Tenement have I,
South Braydon & Sad Merfield
Doe yearly me some profitts yeeld.
Some Lands that ther belong to me
Within Whitlackington they be.   140
In Ilton, Ashill & in Pyle
Some are & some in Abbotts Ile.
And in all these wher ere they are
I have a third part for my share.
I[n] East Coker one Tenement
Pay's me a Half Crowne for chieffe rent.
From thence I to West Coker went
Wher I have but one Tenement.

Some Lands I have in Kingsdon Carie
In Bicknell and in Buckland Marie.   150
Here I with Somersett have done
And thence to Devon I ride on.
Wher the first place that I did see
Was Newcott that paid rent to me.
From thence to Cullampton I went
Whose Fayres & Marketts pay me rent.
Besydes some Tenements there lye
Wherof I have a Mo-y-tye.
Next I to Silferton Resort
Wher forthwith I did call a Court.   160
And ther some Tenements I sold
For which I was well paid in Gold.
In Rew which next to that doth lye
Some Tenants new Estates did buy.
From Rew to Exeter I past
But going thither made such haste
That to survey I almost mist
Two Tenements with in Broadclist.
Which when I return'd and seen
At Exon I took up my time   170
Wher I have land & Houses Manie
But no sole propertie in Any.
In most I have a Sixth part ther
In some a third falls to my share.
And ther some Houses & Good lands
By Death are in the Landlords hands.
For which I had my parte in Rents
And of all other Tenements,
When that was paid I went away
And next at Houghton I did stay   180
Wher all the Lands are passing Good
For by some ther I understood
That every Acre take them Round
In yearly Rent was worth a pound.
I wish I the like could say
Of Lustleigh wher next night I lay.
For ther two thousand Acres are
Att least in which I have my share.
But sure that land will not be found

To yeeld the 5th parte of a pound   190
Of yearly profitt to the taker
If it were all set by the Acre.
I Chalenge here in one part in three
Which rightly doth belong to me.
Before I went from thence I sould
A new Estate in one Leasehould,
Which yeelded me one Hundred pound
And Thirtie for which none were bound.
For I must let you understand
Twas forthwith paid me all in hand.   200
Some lands I have unstated ther
Which yeeld me thirtie pounds a year.   } this is since estated
In this noe Lord shares with me here
From thence I rode by ways unknown,
To Wadham where I halfe doe Owne.
Whereof the yearly profitt grows
I[n] Knowston some, Some in Ash Rose.
These Lands although they barraine are
Yett for my half parte I did share
Six score & Five pounds for a State   210
Which all the Lords sould there of late.
By purchase here now in my hands
For one life I have the Farme lands.
And when that life shoulde chance to dye
I shall have still one Moitye
When that fine was unto me pay'd
I took my horse & no where stayd,
Untill I unto Widcombe came
Wher of three Landlords one I am.
A little Fine I ther did make   220
For which I fortie six pounds take.
Then Sydmouth next I went to see
Wher some lands did belong to me.
But I found whiles I ther did stay
The sea had wash'd my land away.
From thence I unto Branscombe went
Wher Lewes French holds one Tenement.
Pome Roy doth in another dwell
Which doe Maintayne them very well.
The demayne of Edge which lie here   230

Which ninety five pounds pay each yeare.
Seven parts of 12 doe of the fee
Of these Demeasnes belong to me.
But of the foresayd Tenements
I have but one half of the Rents.
The fee of Branscombe [S]heaffe I wave
Yett during three lives that I have
Which by the yeare yeelds sixscore pound
And Good Men for that rent stand bound.
Of this Sheaffe Twelve whole parts ther are
Of them six parts and half I share.
From thence I went to Culliford
Wher half a Burgage calls me Lord.
To which ther doth belong one Acre
Which lately was held by In[dig]o Baker.
To Melbury Sampford thence I come
And blest be God am ther at home.

      per   JStrangways
             1st May 1650

240

These notes describe textual characteristics such as cancelations, additions, marginal glosses. The lemma or the phrase containing the lemma is in boldface roman type, placed to the left of the square bracket. To the right of the bracket, I use roman type for material from the manuscript; my own comments are given in italic.

Notes are arranged according to the following system:

- A cancelation within the line or lines in question is indicated by pointed brackets < >, empty if that cancelation is illegible, but containing full or partial transcriptions where I could discern the canceled word(s) or letter(s):
    - **God regards]** God <requires> regards
    - **we reserve]** we <s > reserve

- I describe the placement of cancelations and additions with a descriptive word or phrase:
    - **am to dye]** <to misery> *below*
    - **without]** *inserted with a caret*
    - differs **nought** from Theft] <nought> *below*

- I indicate doubtful readings with a question mark inside the pointed bracket:
    - **our]** <thy?> *below*

- Words or parts of words written over others are indicated with only the over-written section placed between pointed brackets, followed by the descriptive phrase *written over*:
    - **he]** <soe?> *written over*
    - **fantasies]** fant<i>sies *written over*

As described in my statement of editorial principles, I have ignored emendations I judge to be inconsequential, these being principally stray marks and some single-letter over-writes in which the original letter is illegible. As noted, I have not reproduced catch-words and running titles in the main text, but they are noted here:

- Catch-words occur at the bottom of pages 26, 29, 30, 65, 76, and 92 of Section A and at the bottom of pages 3–11, 13–29, 31, 51–52, 54, 58, 62–64, 66, 78, 80, 84, 86, 88–95, 98, 100, 102, 104, 106, 108, 110, 114–18, 122–24, 138, 140–46, 150–52, 154, 157–59, 161–64, 168, 172–82, 184 of Section B.

- Running headings or titles occur on manuscript pages A.93–94 and B.41, 47, 63–65, 128–31, 134–37, 141–85.

Section A: Commonplaces

Numbering refers to running page and line numbers in the main text.

55/23	**God regards]** God <requires> regards
56/17	himselfe **well** enough] well *inserted with a caret*
24	**1 Cor: 10:29:30]** 1 Cor: <12 1> 10:29:30
58/29	**(as Astronomers affirme)]** (as Astronomers) affirme *in MS*
33	**Sinceritie & Safetie]** Sinceritie & <S > Safetie
60/19	**Sepe]** < > Sepe
23	**−4−propertyes]** −4−<p > propertyes
61/24	**your anchor]** you anchor *in MS*
64/13	by those **that]** <such> *below*
18	**Cursed be]** Cursed <by> be
66/21	**we reserve]** we <s > reserve
36	differs **nought** from Theft] <nought> *below*
38	**provident]** prov<ed>ent *written over*
68/27	**Generall]** <g>enerall *written over*
69/24	**Gosple]** *sic*
71/14	**Gosple]** *sic*
72/21	**1 Cor: 7:17:| |.]** *Here JS uses a dotted version of his habitual terminal punctuation mark (| |.).*
31	**notion]** motion *in MS*
74/4	**Idem]** <i>dem *written over*
9	**well** thinke] will thinke *in MS*
24	**Engrossers, Forestallers]** Engrossers Forestallers *in MS*
76/19	that **materiall** Fyre] <naturall> *below*
31	If the **soule** should sleepe] <Body> *below*

33–34	**Soule should be as needfull]** Soule <flesh?> should be as needfull
80/34	**sayth Solomon]** <hath?> *below*
81/7–8	**to himselfe then]** to himselfe <to himselfe> then
23	**possesse your soules Luk: 8:]** Luk: 8: *written above* your soules
25–26	he **that is not** patient] <had > *below*
26	**cannot be wyse: Heb: 10:]** Heb: 10: *written above* cannot be wyse
82/2	**Joh: 7:15:]** *written above* scriptures
5	**Acts 11:15]** *written above* Apollos that
16	**they weare the authors]** they weare <they> the authors
21	nights **are** long] < >re *written over*
27	written of the **Hart]** <h>art *written over*
35	**Launce]** *the letter* u *is inserted with a caret*
83/36–39	**Wickednes . . . 12: ‖.]** *This entry is crossed out and the phrase* Enter^d before} *is written in the left margin, in reference to CP 164, above.*
84/10	**176:]** 1<6>6: *written over*
21	**who** obeyeth the Law] <that> *below*
85/30	may be **ill]** <bad> *below*
32–33	the beginning **of** parlaments] <of> *below*
87/20	**warranted by]** warranted < > by
88/10–11	**our warrant is two Statutes]** our warrant is two < > *below*
89/7–8	**is bound]** is < > bound
23	**Westminster]** *expanded from* west *in MS*
23	**subjectes of the land]** subjectes <of the > of the land
33–34	**subjects of this Kingdom]** subjects <find> of this Kingdom
90/10	**him** in his office] <the>m *below*
10	him **in his** office] < > *below*
12	**in the Kings name]** Kings *is inserted with a caret*
12	King & **his bodie** politike] his bodie *written over* <both>
91/20	who **can** be silent] <cannot> *below*
92/16	**a dispute]** adispute *in MS*
93/23	**Heu tot sanctitas]** Heu tot sancitas *in MS*
94/13	**210]** 2<0?>0 *written over*
26	**writt of praecipe]** writt of <p > praecipe
95/23–24	**our sword is our suffrance]** our <s > sword is our suffrance
96/34–35	**anxious & solicitous desire]** <anxious> *below*
98/30	**Juyce]** <Juce>ce *written over*
101/10	**pag 106]** p<g>g *written over*
102/18	**in the 1647]** *sic*

33	**245: De Cane:}]** *sic: entry number 245 is repeated here*
36	**information to]** <D ll> *below*
37	**247]** 24<6> *written over*
103/6	**safe** to his Country] < > *below*
37–38	**out** of their superfluityes] out *inserted with a caret*
104/1	**nasci]** < > *below*
106/8–9	**Milchilney]** *written over* M<a>lchilney
107/10	**a prince]** aprince *in MS*
17	**Susceptio muneris]** Susceptio< > muneris
26–27	made **a** god of] a *inserted with a caret*
33	**ignobile]** ignob< >ile
108/12	pound **in** weight] in *inserted with a caret*
22	**Hiatus]** tus *written above* < >
109/3	**god causeth the sunne]** the sunne *inserted with a caret*
12–13	**Paule withstood him]** Paule *is expanded from a tailed* P *in MS.*
27	**Qui non]** Qui < > non
27	**inter est]** interest *in MS*
29	**magnis errores]** magni errores *in MS*
111/6	**Temperalis]** *sic for* Temporalis
12	**quodammodo]** *sic for* quondammodo
12–13	**et omnia non]** et omnia non <su>
17	**Golde]** G< >lde *written over*
112/11	yet **farre** from such] <sure?> *below*
26	**confirmed]** *the* r *is inserted with a caret*
31	**to for-sweare]** to <forswea> for-sweare
113/3	**Jurors]** <Jur > *below*
35	**& the** sayd] <t? > *below*
114/27–28	**goe** without Delay] < > *below*
28	**Delay]** Day *in MS*
116/10	a **hand** with a Scepter] hand with *inserted with a caret*
117/23	**himselfe]** himsefe *in MS*
118/13	**Heliogabalus]** Helioga< >lus *written over*
16	**latet]** l<u?>tet *written over*
16	**veritas]** verit<u>s *written over*
119/1	**Cary itt: Carinus]** Cary itt: <Carinus> Carinus
5	**opposition]** opposion *in MS*
9	**mountebanks]** mounteban< >s *written over*
15	**auris]** < > *below*
120/27	**Isaurus]** I< >uarus *in MS*
121/6	**Multorum manus]** Multorum <C s > manus
10	**then** to take revenge] the *in MS*

13	**Unita]** *sic for* unica
22	**100:]** *there is no item* 99
25	**strepitus]** <C>repitus *written over*
122/23	**Fælix]** Fæl< >x *written over*
26	Let **not** thy Fancie] <no>t *written over*
123/6	**354:]** *the entry number* 354 *is repeated*
10	**not one morsell]** not < > one morsell
13	learne to take **more** Care] more *inserted with a caret*
124/28	**The Jewish doctors . . . Baker]** *A device resembling the sun appears in the left margin.*
37	**too vehement]** too <short> vehement
125/20–21	**not to suffer the Sun to go downe]** not to suffer the Sun not to go downe *in MS*
32–33	**noe** more Troubled] < h > *below*
126/9	**dost thou]** dost the *in MS*

Section B: Poems

Numbering refers to running page and line numbers in the main text.

128/17	**6]** <v> *written over*
21	**18:]** *illegible cancelation follows*
22	**22]** <25 > *below*
129/5	that **to me]** to *inserted with a caret*
6	in **the** Tow're] th<is> *written over*
10	**fellow-prysoners here]** divyne phylosophers *below*
23	**Soule]** <solile> *below*
27	**innumerable]** inume<l>able
130/53	**Then calling in,]** Then calling, in, *in MS*
131/75	no **more** unto] <wher> *below*
80	if **you** may] <my> *below*
94	up **as** in a Grave] < > *below*
98	**Common]** <same fresh> *below*
132/119	**fantasies]** fant<i>sies *written over*
131	**Can** they tell] <th>an *written over*
139	**nor** Oathes] <and> *below*
133/183	**Know]** Kn<e?>w *written over*
134/188	**wher God]** wher <my> God
188	**God is]** God<">s *written over*
218	**how soe]** how < > soe

135/229	**which]** < (> which
231	**And in]** <In all> *written over*
256	**beares]** be<r>res *written over*
136/262	**incensed]** <mis > incensed
270	**we noe ill]** <had> *below*
270	**att]** <nothing> att
283	**well]** < > *below*
288	**The]** written over Th<at?>
299	**by]** <have> *below*
138/361	**lyes,]** lyes. *in MS*
139/388	**our]** <my> *below*
394	**confesse]** *inserted with a caret*
395	**wher it]** wher < > it
401	**though]** *inserted with a caret*
401	**did this]** did <see> this
408	**a blynd]** ablynd *in MS*
409	**prospect]** <passage> *below*
413	**nothing can enter]** < > *canceled above*
140/429	**But for]** But < > for
title	**The]** <S >he *written over*
450	**Womb]** < ome> *written over*
141/461	**Jayle]** Ja<l>le *written over*
467	**Kay]** *sic*
473	**fayre,]** fayre. *in MS*
475	**ackowledged]** a<k>knowledged *written over*
142/499	**varietyes]** varietyes. *in MS*
512	**Light]** *inserted with a caret*
143/title	**The Tenth Section]** *From the beginning of this section until the end of the poem, JS separates his couplets with line breaks. In the interest of consistency, I have ignored this apparently unintended change and retained the line spacing of the first nine sections.*
144/584	**warders]** jaylors *below*
587	**crowne]** <p > crowne
596	**Fayling]** <Fainting> Fayling
597	**miserably lye]** miserabl<e>lye *written over*
599	**newly)]** *sic*
603	**most]** <right> *below*
145/616	**If att the least]** < > *below*
146/658	**without]** *inserted with a caret*
683	**Restlesse]** < > *below*
688	**Compassion]** Compassi<">on

147/698	**Savyour]** Sa< >your *written over*
699	**For]** for *in MS*
727	**waight's]** w<e>ight"s *written over*
727	**soules]** so<l>les *written over*
148/754	**doe]** <the> *below*
149/12	**him separate]** him <to> separate
14	**in that]** < > *below*
150/8	**Men]** <m>en *written over*
16	**speake of]** < > *below*
151/37	**fruites]** <works> *below*
153/40	**O]** < > *written over*
154/13	**we'ele]** w'eele *in MS;* <we will> *below*
155/36	**Lord]** <l>ord *written over*
156/17	**may]** <my> *written over*
3	**it was]** is was *in MS*
9	**they]** *inserted with a caret*
157/7	**fore-doomed]** fore-doom<ed> *written over*
7	**am to dye]** <to misery> *below*
158/34	**then]** <soe> *below*
160/8	**th']** th<e> *written over*
16	**refused]** refased *in MS*
161/33	**th']** th<e> *written over*
38	**As soone]** Assoone *in MS*
162/12	**a tyme]** a tyme <:>
163/17	**ffall]** < > *below*
27	**not . . . old]** < gives> *below*
28	**Tis . . . told]** < Lyves> *below*
32	**alter]** <answeare> *below*
36	**those destroy]** < > *below*
46	**Th']** Th<e> *written over*
54	**be]** <s>ee *written over*
55	**Hencefforth a stinking]** <Henceforth a > *below*
164/57	**shall headlong]** <shall downe> *below*
58	**Them downe]** <Headlong> them downe
63	**th'Accompts]** <they shall> th'Accompts
63	**they shall]** *inserted with a caret*
1	**for my]** < > *below*
2	**to me]** *inserted with a caret*
2	**in his]** < > *below*
165/6	**I noe more]** I < > noe more
6	**doe sin]** *inserted with a caret*

6	**doe]** soe *in MS*
1	**proclaym'de]** proclay<d>"de *written over*
2	**Nor]** < > *below*
13	**And I must]** *two lines above canceled* < >
14	**was never held]** < > *below*
166/2	**Divell]** <Divl> *below*
1	**All that thou . . . deare,]** *Directly above this poem are seven cancelled lines, all illegible except part of the final line:* <per JS >.
167/2	**And]** <Ev'ne> *written over*
8	**his next meale]** *inserted with a caret*
8	**shall Take]** shall <drinke> Take
10	**he is very]** <findes himselfe> *below*
168/9	**Shewing]** <And > *below*
29	**you love your]** <they their> *below*
170/26	**The same]** <It> *below*
7	**walkst on]** < > *below*
8	**shalt]** *inserted with a caret*
9	**fall, for]** fall, < then> for
171/title	*JS's running head for this poem reads* {Concerning Suretishippe & Almes} *on the first page and* {Concerning Almes & Suretishippe} *on the following two.*
9	**an]** <noe> *below*
11	**trouble]** *the r is inserted with a caret*
15	**deceave]** de<d>eave *written over*
34	**they'le]** they le, *in MS*
172/40	**povertie]** "povertie *in MS*
48	**Then]** The *in MS*
48	**or]** & *below*
70	**they]** < > *below*
173/79	**these]** th<o>se *written over*
82	**busenesse takes]** busenesse<ta?> takes
88	**fall]** <h > *below*
6	**wondrous light]** *Seven canceled lines follow this poem, all illegible except the last:* <per JS 17 Octobris 1646>.
10	**good]** *inserted with a caret*
174/3	**jest]** j< >st *written over*
19	**freindly]** < > *below*
33	**falye a]** fayle < > a
175/4	**harme]** *the r is* inserted with a caret
18–19	**Doe not . . . effect]** *Here the MS offers two uncanceled and one canceled version of each line, arranged side-by-side:*

               Then doe not cease <   > Doe not neglect
               To make a peace <a peace to buy> Peace to effect.

20	**somwhat]** < > *below*
176/1	**When]** < > *written over*
23	**our]** <thy?> *below*
25	**god]** *inserted with a caret*
27	**By which]** < y> *below*
177/12	**In Wales thou]** <In > *below*
178/4	**ours,]** ours < >,
4	**doe]** *inserted with a caret*
179/title	**Sacriligos]** Sacr<e>ligos
1	**to him, that shall]** <unto a man, to> *below*
2	**make]** Call *below*
180/19	**sith]** < > *written over*
181/17	**Thy]** Th<e> *written over*
23	**dishonor'd]** disho<n>nor"d
6	**flye]** < > *below*
182/title	**to Edward]** to <King> Edward
title	**King]** *inserted with a caret*
5	**was straight]** was <close> straight
10	**readily inclyne]** readily < > inclyne
13	**that sett]** th<e Tyme> *written over*
21	**Who humbly doth]** < > *below*
21	**remembrance bring]** remembrance < > bring
23	**Then]** <And> *below*
183/40	**at]** <the> *below*
43	**momentarie &]** < > *below*
43	**uncertayne gayne]** uncertayne < > gayne
50	**without]** *inserted with a caret*
50	**for]** *inserted with a caret above* < >
50	**cannot be]** < r> *below*
1	**Length]** <strength> *below*
185/12	**Loves to]** <will you> *below*
14	**his whore]** his <old> whore
14	**devotes]** de *inserted with a caret*
19	**A man]** < > *below*
20	**And never yett was]** < > *below*
35	**is He]** < > *below*
186/1	**Better]** *inserted with a caret*
1	**I beare]** I <better> beare
1	**who]** *written above the uncanceled* that

187/23	**formed]** fo< > *written over*
188/37	**(dear brother)]** (dear brother *in MS*
49	**Thy]** they *in MS*
64	**proud?]** *possibly* proud!
66	**uneven]** u<e>even *written over*
67	**That]** < > *below*
189/86	**than?]** *sic for* then?
91	**when]** <t>hen *written over*
94	**greene]** *inserted with a caret*
101	**usefull]** < >full *below*
115	**ffrom thence]** < > *below*
190/124	**we]** < > *written over*
132	**goes drying]** goes < > drying
145	**By seeing . . . Man]** *A canceled line above reads* <And if thou shalt here unto me say>.
191/166	**itt]** *inserted with a caret*
186	**Foolish]** Foolist *in MS*
193	**Bragg]** Br<g>gg *written over*
192/225	**thowsand Sinkes]** thousand < > Sinkes
193/244	**to]** <th> *written over*
260	**a greater]** agreater *in MS*
263	**how]** < > *below*
278	**The sight]** <Every?> *below*
194/293	**Ther]** <And > *below*
293	**noe]** *inserted with a caret*
295	**them name]** then < > name
297	**our neerest]** our <s > neerest
195/324	**falyd]** <quaild?> *below*
331	**Earth soe soone]** Earth < > soe soone
332	**such]** <soe> *below*
344	**should]** < > *below*
349	**Amayne]** <a > *written over*
350	**drive]** <Cast> *below*
356	**If on]** If <only> on
356	**onlie]** *inserted with a caret*
363	**thou]** *inserted with a caret*
196/373	**Broad]** <Lowe> *below*
374	**JStrangways]** <per> JStrangways
6	**god]** *sic*
7	**right]** <a>right
1	**Man]** <he> *below*

197/18	**Great]** <A>reat *written over*
34	**Nay]** <And?> *below*
40	**Wine]** Wine<s>
41	**clowde]** <cloud> *below*
43	**are therwith]** < > *below*
44	**Looke]** <See> *written over*
198/59	**toucheth]** < > *below*
73	**wither]** < > *below*
73	**art to]** < > *below*
78	**Nauseousnes]** N<e>useousnes *written over*
87	**Into . . . putt]** *an entire line* < > *is canceled below*
199/98	**Concider the]** Concider <well> the
200/140	**They]** < > They
140	**as]** *inserted with a caret*
144	**Th'Eccylpses . . . ryse]** *This line is offset left in the MS, but as this change seems not to signal a true section break, I have amended the margin accordingly.*
159	**what]** *inserted with a caret*
159	**things doe]** things < > doe
160	**doe]** *inserted with a caret*
173	**nought]** < > *below*
201/177	**from]** <&> *below*
196	**nothing]** <ther> *below*
196	**soe]** soe soe *in MS and written above* < >
202/231	**bitter]** < > *below*
203/259	**To love]** <And> to love
259	**in us should]** *inserted with a caret*
259	**Hatred move]** Hatred < > move
261	**To Desire]** <And> To desire
261	**great]** *inserted with a caret*
280	**Making]** <And> *written over*
283	**Doth]** <Does> *written over*
293	**should]** <did> *below*
296	**once]** < > *below*
204/302	**the]** < > *below*
304	**from]** < > *below*
205/341	**doe disallow]** doe <disallow> disallow
359	**his]** <our> *below*
363	**a day]** aday *in MS*
369	**seve'n]** < > *below*

206/393	**an]** < > *below*
399	**from]** < > *below*
207/10	**Breaking]** <And > Breaking
208/2	**doe not]** doe <me?> not
2	**me]** *inserted with a caret*
16	**uncleanenesse]** uncleanelesse *in MS*
35	**shipp' i' the]** shippe" < > I"the
209/40	**To]** with *written below, uncanceled*
210/24	**Is]** <But> *below*
211/57	**sow]** sow<e>
58	**to perceive]** to <find> perceive
63	**remembrance thy]** remembrance < > thy
63	**mind still]** mind <bee?> still
212/89	**man]** *inserted with a caret*
94	**with's hands]** with"s <his> hands
111	**us wyse]** u< > < >yse *written over*
213/132	**shall annoy]** shall <all> annoy
138	**Yet]** < > Yet
151	**good]** <such?> *below*
153	**subject in]** subject < > in
3	**ffirst]** < > *below*
3	**use]** < > *below*
7	**this]** <that> *written over*
214/20	**in's]** < > *below*
4	**To]** <ffor> To
4	**how]** *inserted with a caret*
9	**too]** to *in MS*
11	**then]** <ther?> *written over*
14	**whome we]** *inserted with a caret and written above* < >
14	**observe with]** < > *below*
17	**They]** < > They; *written over* The<y>
20	**we]** <you> *below*
215/22	**them]** < > *below*
31	**Graves]** < > *below*
32	**we]** < > *below*
34	**admonished]** < > *below*
42	**Theron doe]** <uppon itt> *below*
49	**us]** <me?> *written over*
51	**Th'increase]** Th"increase<s>
54	**his Death]** <mans> *below*
216/61	**he a]** he <then> a

70	**Till]** <And> Till
217/101	**I Beleeve]** < > *below*
4	**'twas]** <I>t"was *in MS*
5	**whom]** <wh ?> *written over*
218/24	**their]** *sic for* there
30	**be]** *inserted with a caret*
219/64	**have]** < > *below*
67	**pay]** <doe?> *below*
220/111	**whom]** < > *below*
113	**To]** < three?> *below*
114	**Isralites]** *sic*
123	**office]** *inserted with a caret*
221/150	**oft-tymes]** oft, tymes *in MS*
154	**Commands:]** Commands *in MS*
157	**voyce]** < i > *written over*
163	**dissembling]** dissembing *in MS*
222/174	**or]** <of> *written over*
183	**lawes]** lawes <doe teach>
184	**to'ascribe]** *sic*
203	**What was]** What < > was
223/214	**Rage]** < > *written over*
241	**Gods]** God *in MS*
224/268	**Impunitie,]** Impunitie, <to>
275	**But]** < > *written over*
225/title	**1685]** *sic*
21	**Cowardize]** <ff y> *below*
226/37	**Then]** <The same?> *below*
37	**Grace I'le]** Grace <then> I"le
13	**giveth to]** giveth <Liberally> to
14	**upbrayding]** upBrayding *in MS*
21	**he know]** *inserted with a caret and later canceled*: <doth not>
21	**not]** < > *below*
21	**right]** < > *below*
21	**holy]** *inserted with a caret*
227/29	**doth]** dot *in MS*
50	**And]** <A>nd *written over*
51	**not]** *inserted with a caret*
228/69	**you Carefull]** you < > Carefull
83	**will]** *inserted with a caret and written above* <must>
87	**yee]** <we> *written over*
92	**like t'a]** liketa *in MS*

229/101	**poor]** *inserted with a caret*
108	**to]** *inserted with a caret*
108	**adhere]** <Trewly ffeare> *below*
113	**unjust]** *inserted with a caret*
130	**breaking Gods]** breaking <of> Gods; *the cancelation was first inserted with a caret.*
130	**soe]** *inserted with a caret*
132	**soe comes next To]** soe comes <un> To, *which is written above* < >
134	**in peace]** *inserted with a caret*
134	**way]** way <in peace>
135	**not them]** not <unto> them; *cancelation inserted with a caret*
137	**He]** <Sure he> *below*
137	**a false hard]** <a hard> *below*
138	**And . . . Grave]** *This line is inserted in the right margin.*
139	**his]** *inserted with a caret above* <soe>
230/144	**shew]** shee *in MS*
146	**Divills beleeve]** Divills <doe?> beleeve
148	**Goe]** <Know> *written over*
162	**mountaynes]** < > *written over*
164	**them in]** then <in their> in
171	**us doe]** us <offend> doe
172	**not]** *inserted with a caret*
174	**Since . . . can]** *One line above is canceled:* <Since >.
175	**Commande]** <Commaunde> *written over*
231/178	**high windes]** high < > windes
180	**are]** <are?> *below*
180	**from dangers]** from <f > Dangers
199	**proceed]** <per > *written over*
207	**strife &]** <B > *below*
209	**not]** *inserted with a caret*
210	**Is Earthly]** Is <s > Earthly
210	**Dyvilish]** Dyv<e>lish *written over*
216	**sowe'n by]** sow"en < > by
232/218	**whence]** whenc<h> *written over*
223	**them]** *inserted with a caret, above* <it> *below*
228	**in vayne]** *inserted with a caret*
236	**perfectlie]** < > *below*
239	**sorrow]** <mourning> *below*
242	**selves in]** selves < > in
243	**withdraw]** <receave> *below*

<table>
<tr><td>244</td><td>Brethern speake] Brethern <doe not> speake</td></tr>
<tr><td>244</td><td>not] inserted with a caret</td></tr>
<tr><td>247</td><td>soe] <thus> below</td></tr>
<tr><td>248</td><td>a dooer] adooer in MS</td></tr>
<tr><td>252</td><td>then] inserted with a caret</td></tr>
<tr><td>233/257</td><td>One] <fo > written over</td></tr>
<tr><td>263</td><td>live we'le] live <and> we"le; the canceled <and> was inserted with a caret.</td></tr>
<tr><td>265</td><td>Though . . . choyse] <Although   ill> below</td></tr>
<tr><td>266</td><td>ffor surely he] <And   > below</td></tr>
<tr><td>267</td><td>ffor] <And> ffor</td></tr>
<tr><td>268</td><td>now] inserted with a caret</td></tr>
<tr><td>269</td><td>ffor] <ffor> below</td></tr>
<tr><td>273</td><td>And] <&> written over</td></tr>
<tr><td>290</td><td>patience waite] patience <   ght> waite</td></tr>
<tr><td>234/304</td><td>therin] in is written above <upon></td></tr>
<tr><td>315</td><td>him] inserted with a caret</td></tr>
<tr><td>318</td><td>he hath] he inserted with a caret above <he>; hath written over <have></td></tr>
<tr><td>235/334</td><td>In the] In < > The</td></tr>
<tr><td>2</td><td>Nor Lett itt be] written above <noe men>, which is written above <men may></td></tr>
<tr><td>2</td><td>know'n] <know> written over</td></tr>
<tr><td>2</td><td>how much] inserted with a caret and written above <th ></td></tr>
<tr><td>2</td><td>you give] you <doe> give</td></tr>
<tr><td>3</td><td>ffor soe] <If not,> below</td></tr>
<tr><td>25</td><td>privyde] sic</td></tr>
<tr><td>26</td><td>always wyll sure and] inserted with a caret and written above <might present></td></tr>
<tr><td>33</td><td>to] inserted with a caret</td></tr>
<tr><td>236/47</td><td>Superstition] Superstion in MS</td></tr>
<tr><td>48</td><td>much] <must> below</td></tr>
<tr><td>55</td><td>my] <they?> written over</td></tr>
<tr><td>55</td><td>preservation] <   y> preservation</td></tr>
<tr><td>59</td><td>which art in Heav'ne] <Give me the   > below</td></tr>
<tr><td>237/83</td><td>And] < > And</td></tr>
<tr><td>90–93</td><td>If . . . store] These four lines are inserted in the right margin.</td></tr>
<tr><td>90</td><td>If] <I> below</td></tr>
<tr><td>93</td><td>sake] inserted with a caret</td></tr>
<tr><td>108</td><td>Forgive . . . Remove] One line above is canceled:
<ffor   King   >.</td></tr>
</table>

108	**Remove]** <forgive> *below*
110	**Soe]** <&> *below*
238/118	**trew]** <always sure> *below*
124	**this]** <th > *written over*
128	**But . . . be]** *Two lines above are canceled:*
	<But if , >
	< nes >.
128	**But]** <And> *below*
129	**darknes]** *inserted with a caret*
130	**Two]** < > *written over*
133	**he]** < > *written over*
142	**Lay . . . meate:]** < de their > *below; inserted in the right margin:* || provyde their meate
144	**better]** *inserted with a caret*
144	**And are you not much better then are they?]** *sic*
239/155	**Much]** the u *is inserted with a caret* above <u?>
158	**Gentiles]** Gentliles *in MS*
9	**they]** *inserted with a caret*
14	**they injoy]** theyinjoy *in MS*
17	**mercifull]** < de> *below*
18	**Shall . . . day]** *A line written above is canceled:*
	< Ev"ry day>.
240/21	**persecuted]** The cu *is written above* <qu>.
22	**that's]** that"<s>s *in MS*
23	**us]** *inserted with a caret*
23	**wher surely]** wher <we finde> surely
26	**you]** *inserted with a caret*
26	**are]** *inserted with a caret*
36	**a Hill]** a <high> Hill; *the a is written above* < >.
36	**'Twilbe]** < > 'Twilbe
36	**seen &]** *inserted with a caret*
43	**Ev'ne]** *The n is written over* < >.
46	**destroy]** destry *in MS*
50	**one Jote or]** < >*below ;* on *in MS*
51	**all]** <all> *below*
51	**be]** be <all>
56	**sure]** <shall> *below*
58	**not exceed]** not <exceed?> exceed
241/64	**shall]** *inserted with a caret*
71	**meet with]** *inserted with a caret*
76	**But]** < > But

78	**then]** <soe> *below*	
85	**heard]** *inserted with a caret*	
242/106	**of]** *sic for* off	
112	**But pay]** <But performe> *below*	
119	**Hayre]** Hayre<s>	
122	**be]** *inserted with a caret*	
125	**to]** *inserted with a caret*	
140	**despight abuse]** despight < fe> abuse	
140	**way]** <D>ay *written over*	
243/148	**only you]** only <salute> you	
148	**you with the]** *inserted with a caret and written above* <the>	
149	**Doe . . . suite]** *This line is inserted below to replace a canceled line:* <Do you not with the Quakers therin sute?>.	
150	**be, in]** <in soe> *below*	
153	**aetatis suae]** aetatie suae *in MS*	
6	**in]** is *in MS*	
11	**thou]** *inserted with a caret*	
12	**thy]** <th> *written over*	
19	**right]** *inserted with a caret*	
19	**shall unto]** shal<be given> unto	
20	**What . . . Heav'ne]** *This line is inserted in the right margin.*	
20	**of]** < > *written over*	
21	**be sure then to find]** < > *below*	
244/28	**a serpent]** a <s f > serpent	
30	**well]** <hour> *below*	
39	**straight's]** *The* 's *is written above "* <s>.	
44	**the]** *inserted with a caret*	
50	**enter Heav'ne]** enter <into> Heav"ne	
50	**therin placed]** therin <shall> placed	
51	**keepes]** <walkes> *below*	
51	**all his]** *inserted with a caret above* <his>	
57	**have]** *inserted with a caret*	
58	**those]** these? *in MS*	
58	**these things to]** <soe > *below*	
61	**But]** <When> *below*	
67	**And]** < > *below*	
245/68–70	**Is . . . you]** *These lines are inserted in the right margin to replace three illegible lines.*	
245/75	**them]** *inserted with a caret*	
76	**Authoritie]** <a>uthoritie *written over*	
12	**Nights]** <n>ights *written over*	

14	**by]** *inserted with a caret*
246/25	**And . . . beleive]** *A line above is canceled:* <And I believe in God the Holy Goast>.
44	**I]** <then> *written over*
3	**can be]** can be < >
7	**the]** <thy> *written over*
247/12	**And . . . mercie]** *The line is inserted in the right margin.*
13	**pryson sett]** < > *below*
23–28	**Thy mercie . . . awry]** *This first refrain lacks the two lines which conclude all the other stanzas in the poem.*
33	**thou shalt]** thou < ly> shalt
248/57	**Bring]** <putt> *below*
73	**one]** on *in MS*
73	**Treade]** <step> Treade
250/143	**thee gon]** the gon *in MS*
166	**Anothers]** An<n?>thers *written over*
166	**occupyre]** occup<i>re *written over*
171–72	**To . . . see]** *These two lines are inserted in the right margin.*
251/177–78	**If . . . her]** *These two lines are inserted in the right margin.*
181	**And never]** And <lett > never
188	**doth]** <s?>oth *written over*
191	**hold]** *the h is written over* < >
252/227	**Lend]** <Lend?> Lend
253/265	**Not]** <beat> *written over*
265	**nor oppresse]** noropresse *in MS*
279	**thou shalt to him]** thou shalt shalt to him *in MS*
279	**give]** gives *in MS*
289	**false]** fase *in MS*
254/300–1	**Nay . . . Amisse]** *Two lines are inserted in the right margin; a line above is canceled, now illegible.*
303	**unwittingly]** *A canceled mark follows this line, indicating a half-line in the right margin that has been canceled.*
304	**itt]** <him> *below*
305	**doe]** <pray> *below*
312–19	**Thy mercies . . . fulfill]** *This refrain and the refrain of Section 10 do not align with those of previous sections; I have regularized them to conform to JS's apparent intentions.*
319	**fulfill]** f<i>lfill *written over*
320	**not]** *inserted with a caret*
255/339	**please]** *sic for* pleased
340	**holy]** <faithfull> *below*

347   **inheritt]** in < > in heritt *in MS*
5   **Pryviledge]** Pryv<e>ledge *written over*
7   **I wish . . . knowne]** *Five lines above are canceled:*

    <   >
    <Wherby they   >
    <But god so sent   >
    <This king   >
    <   >.

COMMENTARY

The following notes comment briefly on linguistic, cultural and historical obscurities. Where I was able to do so, I have also identified Strangways's sources. These notes, however, are not intended to be a comprehensive commentary on all aspects or on all particular details of the Commonplace Book.

I employ two methods of annotation. Where a specific word or phrase is the object of commentary, I have simply glossed that word or phrase. Where a note refers to an entire commonplace entry or poem, however, I have found it more efficient to refer to the entire entry with the abbreviation CP (for commonplace) and its number, or to the entire poem. I have also provided cross-references between entries in Section A and entries in Section B, or between items in the same section. For example:

Of Reproofe] See CP 173 (p. 84).
CP 173] See the poem "Of Reproofe & the right use therof" (pp. 164–65).
CP 105] See also the entries at A.24–28 (pp. 71–74).

Particularly in Section A, Strangways often provides his own citations, and where these are adequate and accurate (*e.g.*, vide Rom: 14:20), I have added nothing. Where they are inaccurate or incomplete in some significant way, however, I have corrected or amplified them when possible. Strangways refers repeatedly to several key texts, such as Foxe's *Acts and Monuments*, Sir Richard Baker's *Chronicle*, and Coke's *Institutes*, all works to which he apparently had access during his incarceration. In these cases, I have offered a descriptive note only for his first use and provided subsequent references in the most efficient way possible.

Though the logic of some of Strangways's biblical citations is not always clear, I have usually not tried to interpret or correct them, nor to comment on citations that do not encompass the entire section he intends (*e.g.*, Luke 1:32 for Luke 1:32–33 or 1 Corinthians 15:25 for 1 Corinthians 15:24–25). I have commented on his biblical references only where I thought commentary necessary or helpful. I reference the Authorized Version because it seems that this is the version he used, though it is clear that he also had with him, or knew, parts of the Vulgate, and probably earlier vernacular translations as well.

Strangways also references a variety of legal sources in the commonplace section, particularly the four volumes of Coke's *Institutes*, the body of statute law, and records of Parliament. Where his citations are clear and complete, as they usually are, I have added nothing. Where commentary is called for, however, I have offered brief amplifications or comments—and corrected errors—when I could, but I have not ordinarily tried to interpret his legal thinking. Because the body of statute law and parliamentary records has remained constant over the centuries, I have used readily available eighteenth-century editions of both, as noted in my list of Frequently Cited Works.

In the interest of conserving space, I have not glossed Strangways's many proverbial expressions in English and in Latin, nor a number of very broad moral subjects that exist in so many sources and analogues that they are impossible to comment upon meaningfully. Though I have identified many of his classical citations, I have translated or commented only when necessary. Unless otherwise noted, all citations for classical languages, including patristic writings, refer, in highly abbreviated forms, to the Loeb Classical Library editions (London: William Heinemann, and New York: Macmillan or Cambridge, Mass.: Harvard University Press, various dates).

Unless otherwise noted, the place of publication for all pre-1900 books is London.

Section A: Commonplaces

Numbering refers to running page and line numbers in the main text.

55/7	**Quid fugiam . . . habeo]** Cicero, *Atticus*, 8.7.
15	**Non semper . . . via]** Seneca, *Epistles*, 20.3.1, and see CP 43 (p. 60).
28–31	**50: Edw:3]** This entry aptly summarizes JS's political views. He probably refers to the Westminster Parliament of Edward III as good because it was able to force the king to reform his court before granting him the subsidies he desired. He probably refers to the Coventry Parliament of 6 Henry IV as ignorant (*Indoctum*) because in this so-called "laie mans parliament" no MPs knowledgeable in the law were permitted. See Holinshed, 2:703 and 3:30, and Coke, 4 *Institutes*, 2, 10.
30	**4 H:8: cap:8]** JS is here citing *The Statutes of the Realm* (abbreviated as *SR*, per my list of Frequently Cited Works), 4.H8.4, and see also CP 44 (p. 60).

29–30   **Auferat oblivio . . . Tegat]** Livy, *The History of Rome*, 28.29.4.3, and see note at 60/22. JS may also be citing William Camden, *Britannia* (1607) , "Northamptonshire" paragraph 14, http://www.philological.bham.ac.uk/cambrit/huntslat.html.

57/10–11   **Ut desunt . . . deos]** Ovid, *Ex Ponto*, 3.4.79–80.

31   **CP 11]** See the poem "Since Better, Holy'er, Wiser did encrease" (p. 149).

36   **CP 12]** See the poem "A Lady of suspected Chastitie" (pp. 151–52).

58/2   **Paulus Tertius]** Alessandro Farnese (1468–1549) was Pope Paul III from 1534 to 1549 during a period of intense reformist agitation, a movement which he combated vigorously. He approved of censorship and the Inquisition and was known for his worldliness and nepotism.

22   **Heylings Geogra]** Peter Heylyn, *Mikrokosmus: A Little Description of the Great World* (Oxford, 1621) was reprinted eight times by 1639. JS used the third (1627) or later edition.

24–25   **Lucus . . . bellum]** JS refers to perhaps the most famous examples of spurious etymology from the classical tradition. The original source is Maurus Servius Honoratus's commentary on Vergil, *Aeneid*, book 1, line 22: Georgius Thilo and Hermannus Hagen, eds., *Maurus Servius Honoratus: In Vergilii carmina comentarii* (Leipzig, 1881), http://www.perseus.tufts.edu.

31   **CP 18]** Actually Book 32, chapter 1 in the version JS used: Philomel Holland, trans., *The Historie of the World: Commonly called, The Naturall Histories of C. Plinius Secundus* (1635).

36   **CP 21]** Calculating biblical chronologies was common during the period, even from Saint Augustine onward (see *The City of God*, XII, xi–xii). Not long after JS began his incarceration, James Ussher (1581–1656), Archbishop of Armagh, became the most influential biblical chronologer, his system of dating eventually becoming part of marginal notes of the Authorized Version of the Bible beginning in 1701. See Ussher's *Annales Veteris et Novi Testamenti* (1650–54), as well as *The Annals of the World* (1658). JS concurs with Ussher's chronology concerning the date of the Flood, but not the giving of the law at Mount Sinai. JS may also be using some of the dates given in "A Perfite Supputation of the Yeres and

Times from Adam Unto Christ" appended to the Geneva Bible (sig. LLl.iii). See the discussion in F. F. Bruce, *History of the Bible in English*, 3rd ed. (New York: Oxford University Press, 1978), 109.

59/2   **Gen: 1:16]** Actually Gen. 1:26.

6   **10:12]** JS may intend Ex. 4:10–12.

7   **1 Sam: 11]** JS seems to intend 2 Sam. 11.

8   **Jeremy 20:14]** *I.e.*, Jeremiah 20:14.

9   **Noah . . . Drunkard]** Gen. 9:20–27.

16   **Theodoret]** *The Ecclesiasticall History of Theodoret Bishop of Cyprus. Devided into five Bookes* (1612), 55.

21   **4000-paces]** This figure was not universally accepted. For example, Peter Heylyn's *Cosmographie* (1652) gives the height as 5146 paces (Book III, 129).

36   **Gen 33:4]** JS may intend Gen. 33:3–11, but the relation between this passage and the topic of his entry is obscure.

39   **Psal: 101:6:7]** and see Ps. 101:8.

60/11   **CP 37]** Publius Cornelius Tacitus (55?–118? C.E.) was a Roman politician, orator, and historian. His works were much read in the English school curriculum of the period. See his *Agricola*, 12.2.1, 12.3.1.

14   **CP 38]** This reference is obscure.

20   **CP 39]** Rot: Par: refers to the collection known as the Rolls of Parliament, reprinted as *Rotuli Parliamentorum ut et Petitiones, et Placita in Parliamento* 6 vols. (1763). All subsequent references will be to this edition, abbreviated *RP*. Here JS seems to refer to *RP* 11.R2.35, but see also 11.R2.12 and Coke, 4 *Institutes*, 32–34.

22   **Auferat oblivio . . . tegat]** Livy, *The History of Rome*, 28.29.4.3, and see note at 55/29–30.

26   **CP 41]** JS refers to *The Statutes at Large*, abbreviated throughout these notes as *SL* (see the list of Frequently Cited Works): here, 5.H4.3 and 8.Eliz.13, respectively.

34   **CP 43]** Seneca, *Epistles*, 20.3.1, and see note at 55/15.

36   **CP 44]** See also note at 55/30.

61/1   **CP 46]** This etymology is not supported by the *OED*, s.v. "constable."

5   **CP 47]** Ussher, *Annals of the World* concurs with this dating; see also CP 4 (p. 57).

7   **CP 48]** Tubalcain was "an instructer of every artificer in brass and iron" (Gen. 4:22).

10   **Budæus]** Budæus, or Guillaume Budé, (1468–1540) was a
        French humanist. Scholar, diplomat, and librarian, he was
        instrumental in the establishment of the Collège de France
        under François I.

21   **Grace | hope |]** 1 Thess. 5:8; Heb. 6:19.

24   **Myrtilus]** Myrtilus was the chariot-keeper who arranged the
        death of his master Oenomaus during a race with Pelops by
        removing the lynchpins from Oenomaus's chariot. Rather
        than reward him, Pelops threw Myrtilus into the sea. The
        commonly accepted version of this story, however, depends
        upon Myrtilus's being drowned, not saved, so that Myr-
        tilus's father Hermes has a motive for issuing the famous
        curse upon the House of Pelops.

28   **Granatensis]** Luis de Granada (1504–88) was a popular spiri-
        tual writer, especially known for his manuals of prayer
        aimed at lay readers. Even in Protestant England, his works
        enjoyed wide popularity and influenced many imitators,
        who responded to his Christo-centric piety, as well as his
        emphasis upon cultivation of virtue and renunciation of
        worldly temptations. JS himself was much influenced by
        him. See the entry for Granada in *The New Catholic Ency-
        clopedia* and Louis L. Martz, *The Poetry of Meditation* (New
        Haven: Yale University Press, 1954), *passim.* Compare also
        the poem "Lewes de Granado doth relate" (p. 151).

31   **CP 53]** Manius Curius Dentatus was idealized for his spare,
        abstemious ways. Cf. Cato in Plutarch, *Lives*, 2:307–9, and
        also the note for the poem "In Decium Curium" (p. 156).

35   **CP 54]** This version of events seems derived more from legend
        than reality, and it exaggerates the More family's straitened
        financial circumstances. John More's will was proved 5
        December 1530, and in it he provided for his family, his
        servants, and even set aside funds for masses for his own
        soul. See the text of his will in Margaret Hastings, "The
        Ancestry of Sir Thomas More" in *Essential Articles for the
        Study of Thomas More*, ed. R. S. Sylvester and G. P. Marc'
        hadour (Hamden, Conn.: Archon Books, 1977), 92–103.

62/8   **CP 56]** Zeno of Cyprus (ca. 335–263 BCE) was a Stoic philo-
        sopher, influenced by, among others, the Academic philo-
        sopher Xenocrates (*OCD*). See also "A prodigall that Liv'de
        in huge Excesse" (p. 152), and note at 126/1–2.

63/4   **CP 62]** Pliny writes that Cato was past eighty, and he uses the

	name Massanissam, not Masanissa. The women who bore children at ages sixty and eighty are not mentioned anywhere in Book VII.
16	**Ell]** An obsolete measure of length, in England typically forty-five inches; also commonly used proverbially in contrast to an inch, as here (*OED*, s.v. "ell," 1.b).
21	**Gen: 24:5]** JS possibly intended Gen. 24:2–4..
22	**Gen: 32:53]** There is no such verse; JS possibly intended Gen. 31:53.
22	**Num: 5:25]** This citation is obscure.
63/39–64/1	**Paule to the Ephes:]** Eph. 4:26.
64/7	**Comminations]** Threats, used here with particular reference to divine railing or retribution, as in the Book of Common Prayer service "A Commination, or Denouncing of Gods Anger and Judgments against Sinners." And see *OED*, s.v. "commination," 1 and 2.
10	**CP 75]** Herodotus, *Histories*, 1.196.
24	**CP 77]** JS is not verbatim here, but he accurately paraphrases his source.
65/5	**submisse]** submissive (*OED*, s.v. "submiss," 1.a).
35	**CP 100]** Gen. 34:1–31, Gen. 20:3, Gen: 12:10–20, Gen. 38. See also the poem "In Adulterium et Adulteros" (p.167).
66/15	**CP 104]** See the poem "He Dares not far from Home goe" (p. 186).
17	**CP 105]** See also the entries at A.24–28 (pp.171–74).
32	**CP 112]** See the poem "Tanti valet, quanti vendi potest: Caveat Emptor" (pp. 169–70).
67/7	**besome]** A bundle of twigs, especially used as a broom (*OED*, s.v. "besom," 2).
68/24–25	**conciderans]** *sic* for *considerans*.
30	**CP 134]** Ovid, *Remedia Amoris*, 119.
38	**Jonathans arrowes]** 1 Sam. 20.
69/4–5	**Dividat haec . . . bibet]** JS's meaning here is obscure.
29	**CP 142]** Cf. Aulus Gellius, *Attic Nights*, 16.4.1.
37	**as they say]** JS refers to here the beliefs of various millenarian movements of the seventeenth century, such as Diggers, Fifth Monarchy Men, and Levellers, who posited a literal thousand-year terrestrial reign of Christ and the saints. Their authority was usually Rev. 20, in which such an occurrence is obliquely, even ambiguously, suggested. See Norman Cohn, *The Pursuit of the Millennium: Revolutionary*

> *Messianism in Medieval and Reformation Europe and Its Bearing on Modern Totalitarian Movements* (New York: Harper, 1961), and Katharine R. Firth, *The Apocalyptic Tradition in Reformation Britain: 1530–1645* (Oxford and New York: Oxford University Press, 1979). Cf. also Augustine, *The City of God*, XX.vii.

70/6   **Psal: 140:1]** JS may intend Ps. 110:1.

24   **Ephe: 4:11]** JS may intend Eph. 1:11.

71/2–3   **verse the 7]** JS may intend Rev. 20:7; 19:7 does not convey this sense.

72/4   **Eating . . . face]** Gen. 3:19.

31   **Ecclus 33:28]** Actually 33:27.

32   **Nos numerus . . . Nati]** Horace, *Epistles*, 1.2.27.

36–37   **Semper . . . occupatum]** St. Jerome, "Ad Rusticum" (*Select Letters*, 125.11).

73/23–24   **Isys . . . Image]** In Western thought the Egyptian goddess Isis, sister and wife of Osiris, was identified with the *magna mater* and sometimes the Virgin Mary. She is more typically associated with a cow, not an ass: Martha Ann and Dorothy Myers Imel, *Goddesses in World Mythology* (Santa Barbara, Ca: ABC-CLIO, 1993), 83. Here JS may be conflating two episodes from William Aldington's translation of Apuleius's *The Golden Ass* (1566). In Book VII.27–28, the protagonist Lucius, transformed into an ass, bears an unnamed goddess upon his back, and is revered by a group of villagers. In Book XI, Lucius is finally rescued by the goddess Isis, who appears to him in a divine vision.

28   **Plato . . . Commonwealth]** JS seems to have in mind either *Republic* 10 (521a) or *Laws* 11 (936c), though neither refers so specifically to "pylfering & whoring & all kind of base villanie."

33–34   **sed quid. . . retinebitur]** Horace, *Odes*, 3.24.35.

74/11   **Diana of Ephesus]** Acts 19:23–40.

24–25   **Hucksters, Engrossers Forestallers, Regraters]** JS refers to vendors, brokers, and middlemen, all terms commonly used pejoratively in contemporary analyses of social abuses to identify hoarders or profiteers (*OED*, s.vv. "huckster," 1.c and 2.a; forestaller, 1). See also Coke, *3 Institutes*, chapter 89.

76/21–22   **worm . . . quenched]** Mark 9:44, 48, and see Is. 66:24.

77/15   **Galen]** Galen (ca. 130–201 CE) was a Greek physician whose medical theories became the basis for centuries of European

	and Arabic medical science. By the seventeenth century, his nearly absolute authority had begun to weaken.
16–17	**valley . . . death]** Ps. 23:4.
24	**88.9]** Ps. 88:9 refers to affliction, not death.
24	**Esay 38:8:9]** actually Is. 38:18.
78/14	**Caesars]** Mark 12:17, and see Matt. 22:21, Luke 20:25.
17–18	**we . . . unto]** Matt. 22:21.
79/13	**Heb 12:18]** This citation is obscure, but JS might intend Heb. 12:28.
80/10	**Rom: 12:12]** This citation is obscure, but JS might intend Rom. 13:1–2.
11–12	**post of]** *I.e.*, post off, to put off, delay, or postpone (*OED*, s.v. "post," [*intr.*] IV.7.b).
81/23	**Luk: 8]** Actually Luke 21:19.
82/5	**Acts 11:15]** Actually Acts 18:26.
9	**Crœssus]** King Crœsus (c. 560–546 BCE) was the last Lydian king, whose kingdom fell to the Persians under Cyrus (*OCD*). His name became proverbial for wealth and splendor, but also for the moral precept that wealth cannot buy happiness or ultimate success. See the poem "A prodigall that Liv'de in huge Excesse" (p. 152).
83/25	**sett by]** Esteemed, regarded highly (*OED*, s.v. "set," VII.91.c).
84/1	**CP 173]** See the poem "Of Reproofe & Of the Right Use Therof" (pp. 164–65).
5	**perswadetur]** *sic* for *persuadetur*.
22	**Statutes at Large fol: 42]** The folio number is less relevant than the statute itself, which appears to be that of 30 Oct., of 7 Edward I: "every man shall come without all force and armour well and peaceably" to parliament. See the related idea at p. 87/29–31. "Statutes at Large" is used here as a generic term for any number of works comprising the large and often reprinted corpus of statute law, such as *The Statutes at Large* (London: Newton and Bill, 1618 and 1621), Fardinando [*sic*] Pulton's *A Kalendar or Table comprehending the effect of all the Statutes* (London: Stationers' Company, 1606 and later eds.), and *A Collection of Sundry Statutes Frequent in Use* (London: Fletcher et al. for the Stationers' Company, 1618 and later), to cite only a few of the many editions in circulation at this time.
32	**5ᵗᵒ H:4: num: 24: act not printed]** This record has since been incorporated into *RP* 5.H4.24.

32   **Commission of Array]** A method of raising troops employed in 1642 to defend the Royalist cause. Local gentry were commissioned to conscript all men between the ages of 15 and 60, from which group commissioners would select soldiers fit for military duty. The commissioners became the administrative basis of the Royalist initiative.

34   **Cokes Jurisdiction of Courtes]** *I.e.,* Sir Edward Coke, *The Fourth Part of the Institutes Of the Laws of England: Concerning the Jurisdiction of Courts* (1644).

34–36   **published since . . . howse of commons]** 2 *Institutes,* 746.

85/6   **pleas of the Crowne]** *I.e.,* Sir Edward Coke, *The Third Part of the Institutes of the Laws of England: Concerning High Treason, and other Pleas of the Crown, and Criminall Causes* (1628 and 1644).

8   **king de facto & an usurper]** presumably a slip of the pen; JS seems to intend "not an usurper."

86/22   **CP 181]** Giovanni de Medici (1485–1521), the second son of Lorenzo the Magnificent, was made Pope Leo X in 1513 and was responsible for concluding the Fifth Lateran Council in 1517 (see CP 207, p. 93). He is remembered as an enlightened patron of the arts and learning, but he also restored the sales of indulgences in order to fund his patronage. In calling him "that monster of men," JS may have in mind his censuring and later excommunication of Martin Luther and his contributions to the persecution of early Protestants.

87/17–18   **negative oath]** The Self-Denying Ordinance of 9 December 1644 forbade MPs from commanding armies. The result of this ordinance, which became law on 3 April of the following year, was principally that Oliver Cromwell was appointed as lieutenant general of the New Model cavalry, despite his also being a Member of Parliament. The measure was widely resisted by conservatives such as JS. See Ian Gentles, "Self-Denying Ordinance (1644)" in Ronald H. Fritze and William B. Robison, eds., *Historical Dictionary of Stuart England, 1603–1689* (Westport, Conn.: Greenwood, 1996) and the poem "Concerning The negative oath" (p. 207).

24   **Magna Charta]** See, for example, Coke, 2 *Institutes,* 2–3. JS's interest in the Magna Carta was typical of his age, during which the somewhat neglected document "was revived in a striking fashion," largely owing to Coke's influence. See Anne Pallister, *Magna Carta: The Heritage of Liberty* (Oxford:

Clarendon, 1971), 2–3, and see chapters 2–3, *passim*.

27   **5-acts of parliament**] See Francis Proctor, *A New History of The Book of Common Prayer*, "Revised and Rewritten" by Walter Howard Frere (London: Macmillan, 1920), chapters 3–4.

30–31   **7-Edw: 1**] *SL* 7.Edw.1.1, and see note at 84/22.

88/11–12   **Exilium Hugonis . . . tyme**] More properly, 15 Ed 3.2. See T. B. Howell, *A Complete Collection of State Trials*, 33 vols. (1811–26), sections 23–38. "Their oracle" is Sir Edward Coke: see notes at 88/26 and 88/31–32.

21   **2: H: 5**] Possibly an error: there seems to be no clear connection between this item and any of the statutes under Henry V.

26   **the Statute of -2: Edw: 2:**] There is only 1 statute of 2.Edw.2, and its connection to this item is obscure.

31–32   **their Oracle agrees with the same**] *I.e.*, Sir Edward Coke. Cf. *3 Institutes*, chapter 1.

37   **petition of right**] A petition against royal abuses drafted by Sir Edward Coke and presented to King Charles during the parliament of 1628/9. The petition called for the end to several perceived abuses by the king, particularly the forced billeting of soldiers. Though little came of the petition itself, it became the basis for some of the reforms of 1641–42. See Derek Hirst, *Authority and Conflict: England 1603–1658* (Cambridge, Mass.: Harvard University Press, 1986), 151–59.

89/4   **monopolyes, & shippe monie**] Monopolies granted exclusive rights to produce or trade a commodity; in the mid-seventeenth century, the term could also suggest the unethical or illegal buying up of large quantities of merchandise in order to secure control over that commodity, a practice sometimes called *engrossing* (*OED*, s.v. "engross," II.3, and see note at 74/24–25). Cf. Coke, *3 Institutes*, chapters 85 and 89. Ship money was a method of obtaining revenue that prior to 1635 had been used only as an emergency measure to finance the shipping trade. By 1637 it had been imposed across the entire country and became a rallying point for opponents of the king. The Long Parliament abolished the tax on 5 July 1641.

9–10   **third of November . . . January-1641**] This is the period following the affair of the "Five Members," when Charles I left London for Hampton Court. His action drew sharper lines between Royalist and Parliamentarian sympathizers, in

<table>
<tr><td></td><td>effect creating parties for each cause. See Conrad Russell, The Fall of the British Monarchies, 1637–1642 (Oxford: Clarendon, 1991), 451–53. In this statement, JS clearly identifies himself in this section as a "Constitutional Royalist" as described in Smith, Constitutional Royalism.</td></tr>
<tr><td>15</td><td>Monies Raysed . . . Kingdome] The syntax here is potentially misleading. JS seems to intend something like "never before used," and hence illegitimate. These were in fact means employed in the 1640s to raise revenue, which he clearly resisted. In his Authority and Conflict, Derek Hirst argues that the highly unpopular excises of the 1640s reopened the issues of the 1628 debates (in which JS was prominent), noting the "virulence of constitutionalist hostility to an excise, or sales tax, which was seen as a vehicle for arbitrary rule" (238).</td></tr>
<tr><td>16</td><td>part 20 & 5:] A system of assessing personal property for the purposes of levying fines.</td></tr>
<tr><td>17</td><td>meat monie] I.e., the excise levied on foods and drinks.</td></tr>
<tr><td>90/14</td><td>Collection of ordinances-727] This citation is too vague to be recovered.</td></tr>
<tr><td>26</td><td>cap 11 4ta pars institut˜] actually Coke, 3 Institutes, not his 4 Institutes.</td></tr>
<tr><td>30–31</td><td>3^{tiâ} pars institut˜] I.e., Coke, 3 Institutes.</td></tr>
<tr><td>36</td><td>Stamford] William Stanford (or Staunford), Les Plees del Coron (1583), fol. 158.</td></tr>
<tr><td>91/16</td><td>CP 188] See part of the poem "The Ten Commandements" (p. 250/145–50).</td></tr>
<tr><td>17</td><td>Angerona] Angerona was the Roman goddess of unhappiness, usually associated with silence and the winter solstice. She was often portrayed with her mouth bound or her finger to her lips. See Ann and Imel, Goddesses in World Mythology, 149, and see the entry in OCD.</td></tr>
<tr><td>92/6</td><td>CP 196] See the poem "Noli altum Sapere" (pp. 183–84), and cf. Luis de Granada, Granados Devotion: Teaching How a Man May Truly Dedicate Himselfe Unto God, trans. Francis Meres (1598), 326–330.</td></tr>
<tr><td>15</td><td>CP 198] Cf. Rhetoric 1.1.4 (1355a39–b2).</td></tr>
<tr><td>21</td><td>CP 199] Many variations of this famous story exist, giving several different reasons for Tiresias's blindness. JS is here following a version in which Tiresias is blinded as punishment for seeing Minerva naked. Another states that Hera</td></tr>
</table>

struck him blind when he judged that women derive more pleasure than men from sexual intercourse (*OCD*).

93/1   **queis**] An archaic form of *quibus*.

5   **CP 203**] JS is clearly in error here, as Boniface died 18 July 1270, some thirty-four years before this event was to have taken place. The subject, however, is very typical of JS's concern with the preservation of law (here, his cherished Magna Carta) and with the preservation of ecclesiastical privileges.

18   **CP 204**] JS in fact underestimates: this charter was, in one form or another, reconfirmed sixteen times in Edward III's reign alone and at least twelve other times during the reigns of Richard II and Henry IV.

28   **CP 206**] Ambrose (c. 339–397) was bishop of Milan and an important force in defining and promoting early Christian theology, especially in relation to secular power. He was created bishop in 374 and was particularly vigorous in combating paganism and resisting Arianism. This episode occurred with Valentinian II (372–92) and is discussed in Letter XXI, *Nicene and Post-Nicene Fathers*, 2nd Series (Grand Rapids, Mich.: Eerdmans, 1954), 10:427–29, and see also 10:206.

34   **CP 207**] The Lugdune and Lateran Councils were a series of ecumenical councils held, respectively, at Lyons and Rome between 1123 and 1517. JS appears to refer to the Fourth Lateran (1215) and possibly also the First Lugdune councils (1245), which took up the matters of tithing and the financing of a crusade (*ODCC*).

94/19   **Him only . . . serve**] Matt. 4:10; Luke 4:8.

24   **Give unto God . . . Gods**] Matt. 22:21; Mark 12:17; Luke 20:22.

29   **CP 212**] Foxe, 1.182.

95/1   **CP 213**] Stories of Alexander the Great's vulnerability to women were legion in the Middle Ages and Renaissance, and this tale was one of the most often repeated. See George Cary, *The Medieval Alexander*, ed. D. J. A. Ross (Cambridge: Cambridge University Press, 1967), 329–30, and W. W. Tarn, *Alexander the Great*, 2 vols. (Cambridge: Cambridge University Press, 1948), 2:335–38.

24   **Sheild patience**] Eph. 6:16 refers to the shield of faith, not patience.

36   **Ille sapit . . . heri**] Martial, *Epigrams*, 5.58.8.

38   **Quo justitor . . . armis**] Virgil, *Aeneid* I, 544–45.

96/1   **CP 220]** See "A Man, Lives forty yeares, before he knowes" (p. 186).

4   **CP 221]** See "A Man, Lives forty yeares, before he knowes" (p. 186).

21   **CP 224]** This is the standard characterization of Henry VI; see, for example, the description in one of JS's favorite sources: Sir Richard Baker, *A Chronicle of the Kings of England From the Time of the Romans Goverment unto the Raigne of our Soveraigne Lord King Charles* (1643), 90–91.

29   **CP 225]** Baker, *Chroncile*, 60.

38–39   **Avaro quid . . . vivat?]** An epigram of Publius Syrus: see J. Wight Duff and Arnold M. Duff, eds., *Minor Latin Poets*, Loeb Classical Library (Cambridge, Mass.: Harvard University Press and London: Heinemann, 1968), 16.

97/9   **Libertyes & priviledges]** These terms have specific contemporary resonance in the 1640s, as king and Parliament debated the rights, duties, and limits of royal power. JS shows his belief that liberties function as "immemorial possessions" and transcend even political authority.

9   **CP 229]** JS returns to the points made in this entry in the poem "A discourse betweene King Henry the third & the pryor of Saint Johns Hospitall" (pp. 179–80).

23–24   **Putt off . . . other]** *I.e.,* to show respect by doffing one's hat and bowing.

98/2–3   **Sir Richard Bakers Cronicle]** Sir Richard Baker, *A Chronicle of the Kings of England From the Time of the Romans Goverment unto the Raigne of our Soveraigne Lord King Charles* (1643). See notes for CP 224 and 225 (p. 96). This volume contains multiple paginations, which Strangways generally follows accurately. I have, therefore, made comments only where necessary.

33   **Pag: 79]** Actually p. 80.

37   **pag: 79]** Actually p. 80.

99/36   **pag: 27]** Actually pp. 26–27.

100/27   **the-33-yeare of his raigne]** Baker places this event in the thirty-seventh year (p. 66).

101/32   **her-14th-yeare]** Baker places this event and the one following in her seventeenth year, and on page 118, not 117.

102/23   **CP 241]** *SR* 6.Ed.6.16.

103/3   **CP 249]** "Newters" are those who remain neutral, taking no side in a conflict (*OED*, s.v. "neuter," II.4.a and b). Because they refused to side with one or other party, or temporized, neuters were the subject of significant social controversy in the period. See Mark Stoyle, "Neutralism" in Ronald H. Fritze and William B. Robison, eds., *Historical Dictionary of Stuart England, 1603–1689* (Westport, Conn.: Greenwood, 1996). Solon (?638–?559 CE) was an Athenian statesman remembered for reforming Athenian law. In Plutarch, *Lives*, 1: 457, he is reported to have disenfranchised (but not executed) neuters.

13   **Lyverie & Seizin]** Livery of seisin (or *livery de seisin*) is the legal transference of property into a person's possession (*OED*, s.v. "livery," 5.c).

16   **damage ffeasant]** A legal term describing damages to property, usually caused when a beast has trespassed into another's land (*OED*, s.v. "damage-feasant").

25   **CP 254]** This may have been a commonplace saying of Henry VIII, but the history of the Reformation under his reign certainly suggests that he did not follow this advice.

104/1   **CP 258]** There is a long rabbinical tradition of enumerating the various fatal diseases resulting from the Fall, ranging in number from 70 or 72 to 903, or JS's figure of 907. See the discussion in Louis Ginzberg, *The Legends of the Jews* (Philadelphia: The Jewish Publication Society of America, 1968), 5:123, n.129.

17   **wickett]** door or gate (*OED*, s.v. "wicket," 1.a); cf. Matt. 7:13–14.

24   **CP 260]** Though otherwise correct in this entry, JS erroneously designates Pope Sylvester II (c. 945–1003), who was not elevated to the papacy until 999. Cf. Foxe 1.16–17.

29   **CP 261]** Foxe, 1.223.

31   **CP 262]** Foxe, 1.236.

105/1   **CP 263]** Foxe, 1.236.

4   **CP 264]** Foxe, 1.238. JS mistakenly writes the year 1067, not 1076.

10   **CP 265]** Foxe, 1.248.

17   **Tully]** Marcus Tullius Cicero (106–43 BCE) was a Roman orator, essayist, and politician. His works were very popular in the English curriculum of this period, with the result that his moral and literary influence was very substantial. The phrase "no god a mercy" means something of no great value: see *OED*, s.v. "god-a-mercy," 2 (citing this sentence from Foxe, 1.149).

20	**CP 268]** Foxe, 1.153, 171.
23	**CP 269]** Horace, *Carmen*, 2.14.21
27	**CP 270]** Foxe, 1.165.
106/2	**CP 271]** Foxe, 1.168.
6	**CP 273]** Foxe, 1.193.
8	**CP 274]** Foxe, 1.192.
10	**CP 275]** Foxe, 1.200.
16	**CP 276]** Foxe, 1.201–2 and see also 1.184.
18	**CP 277]** Foxe, 1.203.
20	**Fox: pag: 206]** Actually 1.203.
21	**CP 278]** Foxe, 1.200.
29	**CP 279]** Foxe, 1.206
31	**CP 280]** Foxe, 1.206.
107/7	**CP 281]** Foxe, 1.206.
12	**CP 282]** Foxe, 1.207.
23	**writte of Ease]** A certificate of discharge from employment (*OED*, s.v. "ease," III.9).
29	**CP 287]** Foxe, 1.217. See also note at CP 207 (p. 93).
32	**CP 288]** Vergil, *Aeneid*, 1.148–53.
108/9	**Fox: Pag: 333]** Actually 1.331–33.
10	**CP 293]** Suetonius, *Lives of the Caesars* [The Deified Augustus], Book II, 43.3. See Philemon Holland, trans., *The Historie of the Twelve Caesars, Emperours of Rome* (1606), 51.
14	**CP 294]** Foxe, 1.349.
24	**CP 297]** Foxe, 1.352–5.
33	**CP 298]** Foxe, 1.353.
36	**CP 299]** Matt. 7:3–4 and Luke 6:41–42.
109/2	**participate]** To impart or share (*OED*, s.v. "participate," I.2).
20	**him which sayd . . . none]** Acts 3:6.
24	**Solomon sayth . . . instruction]** Prov. 9:9.
110/3	**CP 308]** Gen. 8:11.
35	**Counterscarffe]** *I.e.*, counterscarp, the outer defensive wall or ditch of a fortification (*OED*, s.v. "counterscarp," 1).
110/37–111/5	**Garden . . . vyneyard]** Song of Sol. 2:15.
111/24	**Avicen]** Avicenna (980–1037) was an Arab physician and philosopher whose medical writings, especially *The Canon*, gained great authority in the West from the twelfth century. He combined Aristotelian and Neo-Platonic ideas in his works.
32	**CP 323]** This story is retold in many sources, as in Holinshed, 1:443.

34   **Concerning the Covenant]** JS refers in this section to the so-
        called Scotch or National Covenant, a statement of Scottish
        political and religious unity which threatened the authority
        of Charles I. Like most Royalists, JS resisted the terms of the
        Covenant. See J.S. Morrill, "The National Covenant in Its
        British Context," in J. S. Morrill, ed., *The Scottish Covenant in
        Its British Context, 1638–51* (Edinburgh: Edinburgh Univer-
        sity Press, 1990), 1–30.

112/23 **fowre Generall Councells . . . Episcopacie]** Cf. *SR* 1.Eliz.1.

113/1   **The Plea of the L: Hunsdon]** This entry may be a version of a
        petition made by John Carey, Baron Hunsdon (c. 1608–
        1677), who was indicted for high treason on 12 July 1644.
        See *Journals of the House of Commons* (1803), 3.559.

114/20 **Petition of Right]** See note at 88/37.

30   **Symonides]** Simonides of Ceos (556?–468? BCE) was a Greek
        lyric poet of considerable generic range, principally remem-
        bered for his elegies and epigrams. See John Molyneux,
        Simonides: A Historical Study (Wauconda, Ill: Bolchazy-
        Carducci Publishers, 1992).

32   **CP 325]** Foxe, 1.404.

115/4   **CP 328]** Foxe, 1.420.

10   **CP 329]** Cf. Foxe 1.374–75, 377.

14   **CP 330]** Foxe, 1.443. The year is actually 1279; see also the
        statute of 15 Nov. of 7.Ed.1.

18   **CP 331]** Foxe, 1.443.

21   **CP 332]** Foxe, 1.444.

26   **CP 333]** Foxe, 1.445.

116/9   **CP 340]** JS probably refers to the *udjat*-eye of the Egyptian god
        Horus, which was typically understood to offer protection.
        See W. V. Davies, *Egyptian Hieroglyphs* (Berkeley and Los
        Angeles: University of California Press, and London: The
        British Museum, 1987), 20.

21   **CP 342]** Actually Pliny, *Natural History*, 7.21, and see 36.4–5.
        The reference to Cicero's *Academic Questions* follows the
        annotation of several contemporary Latin editions.

26   **CP 343]** Foxe, 1.135–36. Constantine's protection of his bishops
        is clearly seen here as confirming JS's own politics.

117/1   **22th of Proverbs]** Prov. 22:1.

5–7   **The Severall Mottoes . . . Second]** JS's interest in the mottoes of
        ancient and modern rulers is quite consistent with his
        general fascination with commonplaces, proverbs, and

<table>
<tr><td></td><td>adages. In the interest of space, I have not identified the many historical figures quoted here. His source, which I could not identify, may not even have been a published work.</td></tr>
<tr><td>34–35</td><td>my mind to me a kingdome is] Cf. the popular poem by Edward Dyer, "My Mind To Me a Kingdom Is," which is in turn based upon this piece of proverbial wisdom.</td></tr>
<tr><td>119/6</td><td>tergiversations] Evasions, equivocations, or desertions (OED, s.v. "tergiversation," 1 and 2) .</td></tr>
<tr><td>120/12</td><td>like Senacharib] 2 Kings 19:35.</td></tr>
<tr><td>122/1</td><td>miserecordia] sic for misericordia.</td></tr>
<tr><td>26</td><td>Lynceus] was an Argonaut famed for his sharp-sightedness. See Horace, I Epistles, 1.28.</td></tr>
<tr><td>28</td><td>CP 350] Crysippus (ca. 280–207 BCE) was a Stoic philosopher whose system built upon the doctrines of Zeno of Cyprus. He was the third head of the Stoa, succeeding Cleanthes (ca. 331–232 BCE). See 126/1–2. Crantor (ca. 335–275 BCE) was a philosopher of the Academy of Athens. He wrote a commentary on Plato's Timeas and was an important influence on Cicero. See Horace, Epistles, 1.2.4, and CP 351 (p. 122).</td></tr>
<tr><td>32</td><td>CP 351] Horace, Epistles, 1.2.4, see CP 350 (p. 122).</td></tr>
<tr><td>123/19–20</td><td>man liveth . . . God] Matt. 4:4; Luke 4:4.</td></tr>
<tr><td>22</td><td>say with Job] Job 31:17.</td></tr>
<tr><td>124/1</td><td>CP 364] Zoroaster is described thus in Pliny, Natural History, 7.16.</td></tr>
<tr><td>13</td><td>CP 369] Saint Jerome, Letter 123.10, in Nicene and Post-Nicene Fathers, 2nd Series (Grand Rapids, Mich.: Eerdmans, 1954), 6:233.</td></tr>
<tr><td>18</td><td>Of Anger] In this section JS follows a long classical and Christian tradition of examining the causes of anger and counseling the avoidance of it. See in particular Aristotle, Rhetoric 2.2; Plutarch, "On the Control of Anger," in his Moralia, 6.93–159; and Seneca, "Of Anger," in his Moral Essays, Book III (1.106–355). Important seventeenth-century works include Thomas Draxe, Bibliotheca Scholastica Instructissima (1616), 9–10; Francis Bacon, "Of Anger" in his The Essays, or Counsels, Civill and Morall (1639); and Jeremy Taylor, "Remedies against Anger" in his The Rule and</td></tr>
</table>

Exercises of Holy Dying (1651), section 4.8. See note at 125/32.

28-31   **Jewish Doctors . . . bread]** Gen. 40:1. Tradition blamed the baker for gross negligence in allowing a pebble to be baked into Pharaoh's bread and the butler for allowing a fly to fall into his cup. And in some versions they were even charged with trying to poison Pharaoh and harm his daughter. See the discussion in Louis Ginzberg, *The Legends of the Jews* (Philadelphia: The Jewish Publication Society of America, 1968– 69), 2:60, 5:342, nn.143, 152.

125/1   **The Apostle]** Eph. 4:26 and see note at 125/20.

3   **the serene]** A light fall of moisture or rain after sunset in hot climates, regarded as noxious or hurtful (*OED*, s.v. "serene" [n]).

13   **that of Solomon]** Eccles. 7:9.

20   **Ephes: 9–26]** Actually Eph. 4:26.

24   **Archytas]** (fl. ca. 400–350 BCE) was a Pythagorean philosopher and mathematician and a friend of Plato.

25   **A phylosopher]** JS probably refers to the story told by the philosopher Taurus about Plutarch. See Aulus Gellius, *Attic Nights*, 1.26.

25   **Xenocrates]** The successor of Plato, Xenocrates (339–314 BCE) was the head of the Academy in Athens.

32   **Pysystratus]** Pisistratus (d. 527 BCE) was a tyrant of Athens, responsible for developing the city as a panhellenic artistic and architectural center from about the 560s (*OCD*). The episode is recounted in Seneca, "Of Anger," 3.11.4, in *Moral Essays*, 1: 283. See note at 124/18.

35-37   **Cato . . . him]** The episode is mentioned in Seneca, "On Anger," 3.38.2, in *Moral Essays*, 1: 345. Neither of Cato's modern biographers mentions this episode, however: Nels W. Forde, *Cato the Censor* (Boston: Twayne, 1975), and Alan E. Astin, *Cato the Censor* (Oxford: Clarendon, 1978). See note at 156/1.

126/1-2   **Cleanthes . . . Budgett]** Cleanthes (ca. 331–c. 232 BCE) was a Stoic philosopher and the successor to Zeno of Cyprus (ca. 333–262 BCE). A "Budgett" is a sack, wallet or bag, or its contents (*OED*, s.v. "budget," 1.a).

14   **ownors]** A variant spelling of *honours* (*OED*, s.v. "honour").

20-21   **father . . . doe]** Luke 23:34, and see 136/275-76.

Section B: Poetry

128/3   **Md]** *I.e.,* memorandum?

15   **The Lord John Pawlett Marquesse of Winchester]** Paulet
           (1585–1675) was a Catholic supporter of the royal family.
           Captured at Basing House by Cromwell's forces on 16
           September 1645, he was committed to the Tower on charges
           of high treason on 18 October. On 14 March 1649 the
           commons resolved not to proceed against him for high
           treason, but he remained in prison nonetheless. During his
           incar-ceration, he translated Jacques Hugues Quarré, *Devout
           Entertainment of a Christian Soule* (1648). (*DNB*; Bayley, 54–5;
           Thomas Wright, *Political Ballads Published in England During
           the Commonwealth* (C. Richards for the Percy Society, 1841),
           89).

15–16   **Sir ffrancis Howard]** Howard was a Royalist colonel, of Corby
           Castle, Cumberland. He was committed to the Tower on 22
           January 1647 (Wright, *Political Ballads,* 92). Regarding How-
           ard and several other prisoners named in this list, see also
           *A True Relation of the Cruell and Unparalleled Oppression
           which Hath Been Illegally Imposed Upon the Gentlemen Pri-
           soners in the Tower of London* (1647), *passim.*

16   **Sir Edward Hales]** was a Baronet of Tunstall, Kent, and served
           as MP for Queensborough in the Isle of Sheppey (Wright,
           Political Ballads, 91; *DNB*).

16   **Sir Benjamin Ayloffe]** was probably son of William Ayloffe (d.
           1585). The contemporary ballad entitled "A Loyall Song"
           alludes to "Honest Sir Ben" (Wright, *Political Ballads,* 92).

16–17   **Sir ffrancis Wortley]** was a baronet and zealous Royalist. He
           was captured 3 June 1644 at Walton House and was not
           released until about 1649. He was apparently the author of
           the ballad "A Loyall Song," reprinted and annotated by
           Wright (*Political Ballads,* pp. 88, 90–91, 87–99, and *passim*).
           See also *DNB.*

17   **Sir Lewys Dyve]** (1599–1669) was Sir John Strangways's son-
           in-law, having married his daughter Howarda in 1624.
           Dyve was commander of the garrison at Sherborne Castle,
           and he was captured along with Strangways on 15 August
           1645. He escaped on 15 January 1649 (*DNB*; Bayley, 282
           and 286).

17–18   **Sir John Hewett]** (1614–58) was a Royalist divine and at

Oxford one of Charles I's chaplains. He probably is the J.H. who contributed verses to the Royalist apologia *Eikon Basilike* (1649). He is said to have taken up collections in his church for the exiled king. He was committed to the Tower on 28 January 1646 and was later beheaded by order of Cromwell's high court of justice on 8 June 1658 (*DNB*; Wright, *Political Ballads*, 93).

18   **Sir Thomas Lunsford]** (1610?–1653?) had been nominated for the position of Lieutenant of the Tower, but the Commons successfully petitioned the king to withdraw the nomination on the grounds that he was morally unfit for the office. He was captured at Hereford by Colonels Birch and Morgan in December 1645 and was committed to the Tower, where he remained until 1 October 1647. In August 1649 he left England for Virginia, where he died, probably in 1653 (*DNB*; Wright, *Political Ballads*, 93; Bayley, 50–51 and 56–58).

18–19   **Sir Winckfeild Bodenham]** was a native of Rutland. He was committed to the Tower on 31 July 1643. He was possibly related to the literary editor John Bodenham (Wright, *Political Ballads*, 96; *DNB*).

19   **Sir Henry Bedingfeild]** a Baronet of Norfolk, he was probably the father of Sir Henry (1633–87) and a bencher at Lincoln's Inn. He was committed to the Tower on 22 January 1647 (Wright, *Political Ballads*, 92; *DNB*).

19   **Sir Walter Blunt]** a Baronet of Worcestershire, Blount was committed to the Tower on 22 January 1647 (Wright, *Political Ballads*, 92).

19–20   **David Jenkings Esquire]** (1582–1663) Jenkins was taken prisoner at the siege of Hereford on 18 December 1645 and committed to the Tower on charges of high treason. He was the author of many pamphlets, some of which were collected as *The Works of that Grave and Learned Lawyer, Judge Jenkins* (1648) (Wright, *Political Ballads*, 90; *DNB*).

20   **Gyles Strangways esquire]** (1615–1675) the son of Sir John, he was captured at Sherborne along with his father and his brother-in-law Lewis Dyve on 15 August 1645. After his release in 1648 he had a gold medal struck which commemorated his incarceration. See Mary Freer Keeler, *The Long Parliament, 1640–41: A Biographical Study of Its Members* (Philadelphia: The American Philosophical Society, 1954),

353; Bayley, 291; John Hutchins, *The History and Antiquities of the County of Dorset* (Westminster: William Shipp and James Whitworth Hodson, 1863), 2:664.

20   **Sir John Marley]** Morley was committed to the Tower on 18 July 1645 but later was removed to the Fleet prison by order of the Commons on 1 October 1647. H. G. Tibbutt, ed., *The Tower of London Letter-Book of Sir Lewis Dyve, 1646–47* (Streatley, Bedfordshire: Befordshire Historical Record Society, 1958), 87; Wright, *Political Ballads*, 94.

20–21   **Sir Wyllyam Moreton]** a descendent of Cardinal Morton, Archbishop of Canterbury (d. 1500), Morton was imprisoned on 17 August 1644 and later was removed to Peter House on 1 October 1647. In 1645 his property was sequestered. (Tibbutt, *The Tower of London Letter-Book*, 87; Wright, *Political Ballads*, 95; *DNB*).

21   **Thomas Coningsbye Esquire]** was committed to the Tower in November 1642 for reading the King's Commission of Array in his native Hertfordshire (Wright, *Political Ballads*, 95).

21–22   **Michael Hudson]** (1605–1648) was a Royalist divine and for a time tutor to Prince Charles. Later he was made one of the king's royal chaplains. In January 1647 he was captured at Hull and imprisoned in the Tower. He escaped in early 1648 but was killed in the siege of Woodcroft House, Northamptonshire on 6 June 1648 (*DNB*).

22   **Sir Henry Vaughan]** (1587?–1659?) was captured at the Battle of Naseby on 14 June 1645 and committed to the Tower until his removal to the Fleet prison on 1 October 1647. He is described in a cavalier song recorded in John Webb and T. W. Webb, *Memorials of the Civil War Between King Charles I. and the Parliament of England as it affected Herefordshire and Adjacent Counties* (1879), 2.30 (*DNB*; Wright, *Political Ballads*, 96).

22   **Thomas Violett esquire]** (d. 1662) a goldsmith and London alderman, Violett was committed to the Tower on 6 January 1644, where he remained until his removal to the King's Bench Prison on 1 October 1647 (Tibutt, *The Tower of London Letter-Book*, 87; Wright, *Political Ballads*, 87; *DNB*).

23   **Thomas Slaughter esquire]** is possibly related to a John Slaughter who is listed among the eighteen signatories *A True Relation of the Cruell and Unparalleled Oppression* (1647). See note at 128/15–16.

24   **Doctor Wrenne Bishoppe of Elye]** (1585–1667) Matthew Wren was the protégé of Lancelot Andrewes and chaplain to Prince Charles. The object of articles of impeachment following the fall of Archbishop Laud, he was convicted on 5 July 1641. He was imprisoned on and off from 30 December 1641 through 15 March 1660 (*DNB*).

30–35   **The ffree Prysoner . . . Joseph Hall the Bishoppe of Norwich]** Joseph Hall (1574–1656) was bishop of Exeter and Norwich. He was one of thirteen bishops tried by Parliament in late 1641 for high treason and was committed to the Tower on 30 December 1641. By the 1640s Hall had already made a very considerable reputation as a satirist, polemical writer, and author of theological, political, and occasional works. This prose tract was published as *The Free Prisoner: Or, the Comfort of Restraint* in his *Three Tractates* (1646), and was according to Hall "written some while since in the tower" (Wynter, 6:539). See also A. Davenport, ed. *The Collected Poems of Joseph Hall, Bishop of Exeter and Norwich* (Liverpool: University Press, 1949), xiii–lx. Strangways's versification of this work generally follows Hall's text very closely. I have, therefore, noted only significant departures from the original.

130/32   **Expert Drake, or Candish]** Sir Francis Drake (1540?–1596) was the first Englishman to circumnavigate the globe. He died on a voyage to the West Indies. Thomas Cavendish (1560?–1592) was the third Englishman to make the same voyage; he, too, died at sea, on route to the Americas and the Pacific.

48   **Mynes]** This is JS's more concrete and personal rendering of Hall's "underworking of others" (Wynter, 6:539).

131/72   **Josephs]** Ps. 105:18, following Hall's phrasing, which in turn follows that of the Book of Common Prayer. The version of the Psalms in use during this period derives from the Coverdale Bible translation, not the Authorized Version.

93   **Anachorites]** *I.e.*, anchorites, or hermits.

132/113   **Tycho Brahe]** The Danish astronomer Brahe (1546–1601) sought to reconcile Ptolemaic and Copernican astronomical systems, positing a motionless earth around which revolves the sun, around which in turn revolve five planets.

114   **Trunke]** Perspective trunk, or telescope (*OED*, s.v. "trunk," III.14). Brahe was perhaps better remembered for the enormous quadrant, sextant, and globe he commissioned: John

Allynde Gade, *The Life and Times of Tycho Brahe* (Princeton: Princeton University Press for the American-Scandinavian Foundation, 1947), 36–38.

117   **Moonets**] Small moons or satellites (*OED*, s.v. "moonet," citing this passage from Hall).

123   **The Equinocti'all**] The terrestrial equator (*OED*, s.v. "equinoctial," B.1 and 2).

124   **Crosse**] The constellation The Southern Cross.

124   **Triangle**] The constellation Triangulum.

130   **Morning Starre & Sev'ne starrs**] *I.e.*, the planet Venus and the constellation The Pleiades, or Taurus.

131   **Char'les-wayne**] The constellation Ursa Major (*OED, s.v,* Charles's Wain).

143   **Mechanicks**] Workers or tradesmen, here used contemptuously (*OED*, s.v. "mechanic," B.1.b).

133/167   **subacted**] Subdued, subjected (*OED*, s.v. "subact" [pa. pple. and ppl. a]).

134/213–14   **Into the . . . Retyrednes**] Hos. 2:14.

135/228–29   **Abr'am. . . Angells?**] Gen. 18.

239–40   **Saint Paul's Bonds . . . And Peters**] Acts 12:3–7, 16. Lammas Day, August 1, is the celebration of Saint Peter in Chains.

136/274   **the Bishoppes now must downe**] This is JS's more concrete and topical version of Hall's "railing on our profession in the streets, and rejoicing in our supposed ruin" (Wynter, 6:543).

275–76   **Father . . . say**] Luke 23:34, and see 125/20–21.

286   **with th'Apostle . . . free**] 2 Tim. 2:9.

294–95   **Cornelius did Teach**] Cornelius was pope from 251 to 253. He was exiled and soon after died when Roman persecutions recommenced in 253.

137/318   **fees**] *I.e.*, those collected by jailors.

138/367   **Little Ease**] A dungeon in the Tower of London famous for its narrowness; more generally, any cell of especially strict or uncomfortable confinement (*OED*, s.v. "little-ease"). The phrase is JS's addition.

375–76   **that flight . . . call it**] Plato, *Phaedo*, 114.

139/379   **He . . . Lazarus**] John 11:1–46.

140/421   **As in a glasse . . . night**] 1 Cor. 13:12.

141/457–62   **Symeon . . . stock't**] Saint Simeon Stylites (c. 390–459), the first of the Stylites, or "pillar monks," Christian ascetics who lived atop pillars. He was influential in converting pagans and promoting early Christianity by his example (*OCD*). In this passage Strangways conflates the imprisonment of Peter and the stocking of Paul and Silas (see Acts 12 and 16). His reference to Peter stocked between two leopards is not biblical, and may be a conflation of Acts 12:6, where Peter is bound between two soldiers, and a well-known passage from Ignatius of Antioch in which he likens the soldiers who bind him to leopards: see "Letter to the Romans," 5:1, in *The Apostolic Fathers*, trans. Kirsopp Lake, 2 vols. section 21 (London: Heinemann, and New York: Macmillan, 1912), 1:231–33.

482	**With Isaacks . . . Rehoboth]** Gen. 26:20–22.
490–91	**as Varro . . . House]** Marcus Terentius Varro (116–27 BCE) was a Roman historian, linguist, and polymath, who was reputed to have written some six hundred volumes, treating nearly all fields of knowledge. Hall himself gives the citation "magna domus homuli" (Wynter, 6:546).
142/498	**Land-scipps]** Landscapes (*OED*, s.v. "landscape").
505	**with the Psalmist . . . Man]** Ps. 8:3–4, 144:3.
523	**Ther . . . joy]** Ps. 16:11.
143/535	**bread of Teares]** Ps. 80:5.
568	**Fayths Helmett]** Eph. 6:16–17.
144/572	**Crowne of Glory]** Proverbial for wisdom and patience or for the heavenly reward given to the faithful; see especially Prov. 4:9 and 16:31.
583	**Engins]** Devices, instruments (*OED*, s.v. "engin," 4, 6, and 7).
583	**Saucie Jacks . . . warders]** Jacks are low fellows, here used contemptuously (*OED*, s.v. "jack," 2.2). This section is added by JS.
588–89	**Saint Stephens . . . martyrdome]** Acts 6–7, especially 7:54–60.
590–92	**the storie . . . Machabees]** 2 Mac. 7:1–23.
593–97	**the forty bold Armen'ian men]** The Forty Martyrs of Sebaste were martyred in Sebaste, Lesser Armenia ca. 320. They were left naked upon the ice of a frozen pond, with baths of hot water around the pond's shore to tempt them to apostatize. Thirty-nine remained faithful, while one apostate, in Hall's words, died "uncomfortably in the bath." According to Hall, Gaudentius of Brescia (fl. 400), whose sermons were greatly admired for their style and their borrowings from classical authors such as Terence, Cicero, Vergil, and Ovid, related this story (Wynter, 6:548). See *ODCC*, s.v. "Sebaste".

145/612   **Mole]** John Mole (or Molle) was held prisoner for thirty years, hence a model of religious fortitude (Wynter, 6:307 and 6:548).

632   **Blessed be the god of Comfort]** 2 Cor. 1:3.

635   **A crowne of life & immortalitie]** Hippolytus of Rome, *Treatise on Christ and Antichrist*, 31.5, glossing 2 Tim. 4:8, http://www.earlychristianwritings.com/text/hippolytus-christ.html.

642   **Tyme-Professors]** Temporizers, time-servers.

146/656–58   **Incensers . . . Frankinsence]** Incensors are those who incite or instigate (*OED*, s.v. "incensor"). Saint Marcellinus, also Pope (d. 304), was reported to have apostatized during the persecutions of Christians under the Emperor Diocletian in 303.

660   **Lybellaticks]** Christians who, under threat of persecution, obtained false certificates that they had sacrificed to heathen gods (*OED*, s.v. "libellatic"). JS took the term directly from Hall (Wynter, 6:549), though the earliest citation recorded in the *OED* is from 1873.

667   **Solyman the Great]** Suleiman I (ca. 1494–1566), reigned as Sultan of Turkey during the height of Ottoman political and cultural greatness (1520–66). Curiously, Hall refers to "Solyman the Second," though the figure now known as Süleyman II was born in 1641 and reigned only from 1687 until his death in 1691.

147/713   **& me]** Is an addition, yet another way that JS personalizes Hall's original (Wynter, 6:550).

149/1–18   **Since BETTER, HOLY'ER . . . encrease]** See CP 11 (p. 57).

1–6   **The Papists cry up blind Obedience]** Cf. the poem "The Rules of Trew Obedience" (pp. 213–14).

3   **Schismatickes]** A usually contemptuous term for those who promoted or countenanced breaches in the church; for JS, Puritans or other religious radicals. See J. S. Morrill, *The Revolt of the Provinces: Conservatives and Radicals in the English Civil War, 1630–1650* (London: Allen & Unwin; New York: Barnes and Noble, 1976), 35.

150/7   **Right-Principles doth build]** Cf. Jer. 22:13.

13   **Granados]** *I.e.,* grenades.

18   **strong-works]** *I.e.,* fortifications.

151/33–34   **wher a Legion . . . Lodg'd]** Cf. Mark 5:1–14, especially verse 9.

37–38   **fruites . . . peace]** Cf. James 3:18 and see 231/215–16.

1   **Lewes de Granado doth relate]** See CP 52 (p. 61). Socrates (c.470–399 BCE) was, along with his pupil Plato, among the most influential of the ancient Greek philosophers, known especially for his theories of virtue and justice, and celebrated for his execution on charges of corrupting the Athenian youth. On Crœsus, see note at 82/9.

1–9   **A Lady of suspected Chastity]** See CP 12 (pp. 57–58).

152/1–12   **A prodigall . . . Excesse]** See CP 56 (p. 62).

9   **all in all to me]** The phrase "all in all," used as a refrain in this poem, occurs many times in the New Testament as an epithet for God or Christ. See 1 Cor. 12:6 and 15:28; Eph. 1:23; Col. 3:11.

153/32   **My fayth . . . Eye]** Cf. Rev. 7:17 and 21:4.

154/6   **Puisnè]** A junior or younger person, applied in the period to legal appointments (as in a puisné judge), but here used contemptuously in a more general sense. The word is a form of the modern English *puny* (*OED*, s.v. "puny").

10–18   **Jacob . . . despise]** Gen. 27:30–39; Num. 11:27–29; Num. 16; 1 Sam. 18:8.

22   **Concussations]** Violent shaking or agitations (*OED*, s.v. "concussation").

25–26   **And who . . . commaund]** Prov. 27:4.

156/1   **Great Curius]** Manius Curius Dentatus (d. 270 BCE) was a Roman general and consul, known for his defeat of the Samnites in 290, thus ending a fifty-year war. He became idealized for his simplicity, severity, and honesty, especially through the writings of Cato the Censor (see note at 125/35–37). The story recounted in this poem is one of the most famous of such edifying tales (*OCD*). See also CP 53 (p. 61).

157/2   **States Commaund]** JS's properties were sequestered after his arrest (Bayley, 312, 400, and see Introduction, pp. 11–13).

5–7   **eldest sonne . . . dye]** Sir Giles Strangways was captured at Sherborne Castle along with his father and brother Colonel James Strangways, mentioned in the next line. JS himself was imprisoned on charges of high treason (Bayley, 289–91 and see Introduction, pp. 10–12).

13   **Cast away his rod]** Cf. Job 9:34.

16   **thyne arrowes . . . hart]** Cf. Ps. 38:2.

158/30   **purchase from the parlament my peace]** JS unsuccessfully appealed to the Commons for release on 28 November 1645 (Bayley, 295 and see Introduction, 12–13).

164/1–19   **Comfort for an afflicted Soule]** This poem is characteristic of
JS's "affliction" poems. It combines many aspects of conventional Christian appeals for patience in the face of suffering,
but with particular echoes of Job 5:17 and Prov. 3:11–12. See
also the following poem, "Of Reproofe & of the right use
therof" (p. 164).

1–12   **Of Reproofe ... Therof:]** See the poem "Comfort for an afflicted
Soule" (p. 164), as well as CP entries 33, 35, 135, 173 (pp. 60,
68, 84).

165/12   **by Reprooffe ... not worse]** A conventional image, as in Prov.
10:17, 13:18, 15:32, 17:10.

2   **Ahabs Title ... vyne-yard]** Cf. 1 Kings 21.

15   **Formalitie]** In addition to the term's general meaning, JS
intends a more restricted sense of empty or meaningless
outward show in matters of religion (*OED*, s.v. "formality,"
6). See also Richard Hooker, *Of the Lawes of Ecclesiastical
Politie, Eight Bookes* (1639), book 5, section 39.

16   **wolfe ... on]** Cf. Matt. 7:15.

17   **your foundation]** Cf. Matt. 7:24–27, Luke 6:48–49.

167/4   **Dreames & visions of the night]** Cf. Isa. 29.7–8 and see also Job
4:13 and 33:15.

1–38   **In Adulterium et Adulteros]** Gen. 20:1–18; 34:1–31; 38:1–30.
See also CP 100 (pp. 65–66).

169/1–6   **Wealth . . . Renew:]** The sentiments of this poem are based
upon Prov. 19:4, 7.

169/title   **Caveat Emptor]** See CP 112, (p. 66).

170/title   **In Defence of Holy-Dayes]** Cf. Richard Hooker for a contemporary discussion of the matter of holy days: *Of the Lawes of
Ecclesiastical Politie*, book 5, sections 69–72.

11   **Clay ... potters hand]** Cf. Is. 64.8, Jer. 18:6, Rom. 9:21.

171/4   **stay]** a thing or person affording support (*OED*, s.v. "stay," 1.b).

37   **the Commaundments sake]** Cf. Matt. 22:38–40.

172/42   **Sheild & Sunne]** Ps. 84:11.

48   **Rust or be lost underground]** Cf. Matt. 6:19–20.

60   **strong Speare, & Mighty Sheild]** Cf. Ps. 91:4. See also note at
195/352.

173/92–93   **Howse-Rome ... Complayne]** Cf. 1 Tim. 6:8.

1–2   **we be made poore ... dore]** JS greatly exaggerates his poverty,
for despite losing some £35,000 during the Interregnum, he
and his son Giles remained extremely well-to-do. See *A True
Relation, passim*, and Introduction, pp. 14–16

7–10   **He will . . . before]** Cp. Job 42:10, 12.

174/19–22   **But he . . . bin]** Cf. the poem "Of Reproofe & of the right use therof" (pp. 164–65).

175/title   **Begin well: & End well]** Cf. Luke 14:28–30.

176/8   **Bryde]** *I.e.*, bridegroom, as supported by *OED*, s.v. "bride," [n¹], 2.

177/1   **wott]** To know, be aware of (*OED*, s.v. "wit" [v¹], B.I.1.e).

2   **trott]** *I.e.*, trot: to bustle, move quickly (*OED*, s.v. "trot," [v], 2), but there seems to be some kind of pun intended, since the word can also mean an old woman or beldame (s.v. "trot," [n²]).

12   **Wales]** A region proverbial for danger and lawlessness, as in this description by Sir Thomas More: "a countrey being far of from the law and recourse to iustice . . . robbers and riuers [*i.e.*, reavers, plunderers] walking at libertie vncorrected" in Richard S. Sylvester, ed., *The History of Richard III*, in *The Complete Works of St. Thomas More* (New Haven and London: Yale University Press, 1963), 2:14.

178/5–8   **A Good man . . . heare]** Cf. Prov. 17:4.

1–24   **Concerning the ending . . . Peace]** This poem appears to refer to peace negotiations between Charles I and the Parliament during the summer of 1646.

4   **intayle]** To leave as an inheritance that cannot be voided or altered (*OED*, s.v. "entail," [v²], 2).

179/4   **Third descent]** *I.e.*, the third generation (*OED*, s.v. "descent," 9).

title   **A discourse . . . Hospitall]** King Henry III contended often with the clergy over the matter of liberties and privileges, as shown in this episode. See CP 229 (p. 97).

4   **distrayne]** To levy a distress or force payment or action, usually to satisfy a debt (*OED*, s.v. "distrain," II.7.a and c; II.8).

180/6   **Charters, Lybertyes, and, Rightes]** See CP 229 (p. 97).

16   **non obstante]** *Notwithstanding*: license or permission to proceed in spite of established laws or practices to the contrary. Henry III introduced this practice, by which his granting of charters could contravene written law; it was revoked by the Bill of Rights (*OED*, s.v. "non-obstante," A.1.a, b, and c). See Foxe, 1.377 and Baker, *Chronicle*, 122.

181/title   **Of the Bishoppe of Herefords sermon . . . Isabell]** This sermon was preached before the Queen in 1326, by Adam of Orlton (d. 1345), who was successively Bishop of Hereford, Worcester, and Winchester. Orlton was in open

	conflict with Edward II and called for the king's removal on the grounds that the kingdom's well-being depended upon such extreme measures (*DNB*). See T. B. Howell, *A Complete Collection of State Trials*, 34 vols. (1816–28), sections 39–40.
3	**out of the booke of Kings**] 2 Kings 4:19, as noted by JS in his marginal gloss.
182/title	**Upon the Lord Seaton . . . England**] Sir Alexander Seton (fl. 1311–1340) was an advocate for Scottish independence. As keeper of Berwick, he defended the town from an English siege in 1333. His son Thomas was offered as a hostage and when the Scottish garrison eventually refused the terms of the treaty, Thomas was hanged at the town gate on King Edward III's order. The event is described in Holinshed, 1:337.
4	**hugh**] A variant form of *huge* (*OED*, s.v. "huge").
183/title	**Noli altum Sapere**] Rom. 11:20, using the wording of the Vulgate Bible. See also CP 196 (p. 92).
184/11–12	**A Rich man . . . buy**] See CP 111 (p. 66) and CP 226 (p. 96).
185/23–24	**ffull well . . . life**] See CP 231 (p. 97).
186/1–4	**What Better Thing . . . Deo Gratias**] This poem is based upon Luis de Granada, *An Excellent Treatise of Consideration and Prayer* (1634), 83: "For as Saint *Augustine* saith; What thing is there that we can better conceive in our hearts, better pronounce with our mouthes, and better write with our Pens, then this short sentence *Deo Gratias*, Thankes bee unto God?"
1–13	**A Man, Lives . . . ex Tempore**] See CP entries 220 and 221 (p. 96).
8	**Take . . . Day**] Cp. Heb. 3:12–13.
1–12	**He dares . . . Theeves**] See CP 230 (p. 97).
5–6	**Tis a wise feate . . . Retreate**] See CP 232 (p. 97).
187/title	**A Motive to Humilitie . . . per JS:**] Many of the ideas and images in this poem and one that follows (see p. 196) are commonplace. However, JS was probably inspired by Luis de Granada, *Of Prayer and Meditation* (1633), especially the Tuesday and Wednesday morning exercises on the miseries of life and certainty of death (see in particular pp. 69–138).
33	**Enosh**] The claim that the name Enosh signifies forgetfulness does not correspond to what modern scholars believe, namely that it is derived from the Hebrew root meaning "man" or "human being." George Arthur Buttrick et al.,

eds., *The Interpreter's Dictionary of the Bible* 4 vols. (New York and Nashville, Tenn.: Abingdon Press, 1962), s.v. "Enosh."

188/66   **uneven]** Ill-formed (*OED*, s.v. "uneven," 4).

76–83   **Abraham . . . Clay]** Cf. Gen. 18:27.

189/103   **Earth . . . Eyes]** John 9:6–15.

190/129   **Mans Body . . . clay]** Job 4:19.

141   **God wylls . . . goe]** Cp. Jer. 18:1–6.

191/161   **But Dust thou art]** Gen. 3:19.

169   **That Second Adam Chryst]** Cf. 1 Cor. 15:45–49.

192/211   **Lynx Eyes]** proverbially, keen-sighted (*OED*, s.v. "lynx," 4).

212   **Dung-hill . . . Snow]** Cf. Matt. 23:27 and Luis de Granada, *Of Prayer and Meditation* (1633), 75.

221–24   **Saint Austen . . . pertake]** Cf. Augustine, *Confessions*, Book II, chapter 2 .

225   **Sinkes]** *I.e.*, cesspools, sewers (*OED*, s.v. "sink," I.1.a and 6).

193/242   **Micah . . . thee]** Micah 6:14.

194/295–98   **Job . . . all]** Job 17:14.

304   **the wyse Syrach . . . proud]** Sirach 17.32 [RSV].

317   **English men . . . doe Call]** From Lat. *monumentum*, reminder, token. See note at 215/33.

321   **A Holy Father . . . Bones]** This image is so conventional that JS may be referring to any number of "holy fathers."

195/341–50   **Holy Job . . . agayne]** Job 10:9 and 33:6.

352   **thy Buckler & Defence]** A proverbial expression for divine protection, occurring many times in the Old Testament. See, for example, Ps. 91:4 and note at 172/60.

355   **King David sayth]** Ps. 103:13.

196/368–73   **Saint Austen . . . Deepe]** A commonplace idea in Augustine's *The City of God*: cf., for example, Book I, preface, and Book 16.4.

1–10   **The voyce said Cry!]** This poem is based upon Is. 40:6–8.

title   **Another Motive to Humilitie . . . vizt]** See note at 187/title.

197/18–21   **Aristotle . . . itt]** The sentiment is not specifically Aristotelian, but rather seems to merge Aristotle's authority with an Augustinian conception of human frailty and sinfulness.

198/60   **begotten are in filthy Lust]** Cf. Jam. 1:15.

86   **nutt]** Apparently the nipple, though this sense is not specifically supported by the *OED*, but see a possible analogue: s.v. "nut," III.9.a.

199/130–31   **Galen . . . Infirmityes]** Vaguely following Galen, early modern ophthalmologic treatises often quantified the diseases of the eye, as in M. Andreas Laurentius, *A discourse of the Preservation of the Sight*, trans. Richard Suphlet, Shakespeare Association Facsimiles 15 (London: Oxford University Press for The Shakespeare Association, 1938), and Richard Banister, *A Treatise of one hundred thirteene diseases of the eyes* (1622). See also the note at 77/15.

200/167   **Calenture]** fever (*OED*, s.v. "calenture," 1).

201/204–5   **Great . . . howre]** Cf. Is. 28:1, 4.

202/233   **The End . . . heavines]** Cf. Prov. 14:13.

249–51   **Eleven kyndes . . . togither]** Cf. St. Thomas Aquinas, *Summa Theologiae*, 60 vols. (New York: McGraw-Hill and London: Eyre & Spottiswoode, 1964), 19:26–31, *i.e.*, section 1a. 2ae. 23.4.

203/286–87   **Job to Cry . . . am I]** Job 7:20.

204/301   **Job . . . WARRE]** The sentiments of Job only generally, but see also Eccles. 8:8.

324–26   **Againe . . . leade]** Cf. Matt. 7:13–14.

329   **provene]** to originate, proceed, or arise from (*OED*, s.v. "provene").

205/338–39   **Suiting . . . should]** Rom. 7:15; Gal. 5:17.

362–63   **the just man . . . seven Tymes]** Prov. 24:16.

206/391   **Man . . . Blade]** Cf. Is. 40:6–8. The rest of this catalogue consists of conventional images of the transitory quality of human life.

207/title   **Concerning The negative oath]** See note at 87/17–18.

208/29   **Ravens of the Rocke]** "Ravens of the valley" in the original, Prov. 30:17.

209/title   **Of the Meditation of Death . . . Death]** Cf. Luis de Granada, *Of Prayer and Meditation* (1633): "for this cause the Philosophers said, *That the life of a wise man, was nothing else but onely a continuall cogitation and thinking of death*" (159).

210/11–12   **prophet David . . . Doe good]** Cf. Ps. 34:14, 37:27.

211/47–50   **Holy King Josias . . . plac'd]** 2 Kings 23:16–20.

54–55   **Cast the love . . . Style]** Cf. Phil. 3:19.

59–62   **Remember thy end . . . Sin]** Sirach 7:36.

85–88   **Our Savyour . . . stay]** John 9:4.

212/96   **Trench]** To touch upon, concern (*OED*, s.v. "trench," III.6 and 7.a–d).

105–6   **wyse man . . . might]** Eccles. 9:10.

115–16   **Great Saint Gregory]** Saint Gregory (c. 540–604) was elected as Pope Gregory I in 590. One of the most influential and widely read of the early church fathers, he was often cited by later writers on a range of theological topics. The passage cited here probably refers to his *Moralia on Job*, Book XIII.xxix.33, with reference to Job 17:1. See E. B. Pusey, J. H. Newman, J. Keble, and C. Mariott, eds., *Library of the Fathers of the Holy Catholic Church* (Oxford, 1845), 21:105–6.

213/title   **The Rules of Trew Obedience]** Cf. the poem "The Papists cry up blind Obedience" (p. 149).

214/1   **Wyse Seneca]** Lucius Annaeus Seneca, "The Younger" (c. 4 BCE–65 CE), was a Stoic moral philosopher, political advisor, dramatist, and orator. His works constituted an important part of the early modern educational curriculum and were much admired by Christian moralists of the early modern period.

15   **Cathedrall Men]** Theologians and scholars, here used derisively (*OED*, s.v. "cathedral," 3).

215/33   **men them Monuments doe Call]** See note at 194/317.

56   **we Earth shalbe]** Gen. 3:19.

216/93   **Joyncture]** A jointure is the holding of property jointly by husband and wife, here specifically an inheritance received by a wife at the death of her husband and held until her own death (*OED*, s.v. "jointure," 4.a and b).

217/1–2   **Mercyes . . . fare]** Prov. 12:10.

12   **Returne . . . Day]** Cf. Heb. 3:13.

title   **The Affliction of Israell]** This poem is paraphrased from Joseph Hall's prose meditation of the same name, a work based upon Exodus 1 and 5. Hall's meditation was published in 1640 and reprinted as part of a series of meditations on biblical stories, called *Contemplations*, in *The Works of Joseph Hall B. of Norwich* (1647), 825–27. And see Wynter, 1:70–74.

218/9   **change of Copyes]** an alteration in one's fortunes or store (*OED*, s.v. "copy," A.I.1.a).

27–28   **John . . . away]** John 3:30.

219/59   **smurt]** A variant form of *smart* (*OED*, s.v. "smart").

78–79   **seed of Jacob . . . Affliction]** Gen. 32:22–32.

220/101   **God . . . reynes]** Jer. 11:20; Ps. 7:9; Rev. 2:23.

222/207   **Quitting]** *i.e.*, requiting. The phrase suggests the *lex talionis*, or law of retribution.

225/title   **When I was Taken . . . life:]** This poem refers to JS's brief imprisonment in the wake of Penruddock's Revolt in March

	1655. The uprising was an attempt to restore Charles II, but it failed. JS's dating of the poem, 1685, is an obvious error.
8	**after-clapps**] Specifically, an unexpected stroke or blow after the recipient has ceased to be on guard (*OED*, s.v. "after-clap"). An after-clap is an especially apt image for JS's arrest seven years after his release from the Tower in 1648.
17	**Busking**] Perhaps a dialect form of *basking*, for *busking* means only "hasten, hurry, or hie." However, this supposition is not supported by the *OED*, s.v. "busk." It is also possible that JS intended *basking* and *busking* is merely a slip of the pen.
226/title	**The Epistle of Saint James . . . 1665**] This and the following biblical paraphrases very closely follow their sources, allowing for a certain general poetic latitude. I have, therefore, commented only when JS's departures or additions are particularly important.
227/48	**Intised**] A variant spelling of *enticed* (*OED*, s.v. "entice").
231/215–16	**For sure . . . peace**] See also 151/37–38.
232/229	**want's**] *I.e.*, lacks.
235/title	**The sixt Chapter of Saint Mathew**] Though JS follows the sequence of verses in Matthew 6, it is worth noting that he extrapolates and improvises a good deal more than is his usual practice in other biblical versifications.
241/69	RACHA] A much-debated word whose meaning has been variously understood to mean "fool," "vain fool," "dolt," "empty fellow," or "rebel." Buttrick et al. eds., *The Interpreter's Dictionay of the Bible*, s.v. "raca."
243/149	**Quakers**] In Matt. 5:47, *publicans*. *Quakers* is an amendment by JS, apparently singling out this Protestant sect for hypocritical religious exclusivity.
149	**suite**] Used intransitively: to aim at, seek to obtain, or pursue; to conform oneself to, fall in with; to be suitable for (*OED*, s.v. "suit," 7.a, 13.a, and 14.a).
245/title	**The Apostells Creede**] The following three statements of faith appear together in the Book of Common Prayer from 1549 onward, and they were often inscribed in the walls of English churches. JS's decision to versify these texts may reflect specifically the exhortation to godparents in the section devoted to the "Publick Baptism of Infants." In the 1662 version, they are enjoined: "and chiefly ye shall provide, that he may learn the Creed, The Lord's Prayer,

	and the Ten Commandments, in the vulgar tongue." See Proctor, *New History*, 584–85. I am grateful to George W. Williams and Rowan Greer for guidance on this note.
246/32	**Catholique]** This term was used by English Protestants to identify the English church, seen as "purified from the accumulated inventions and abuses of Rome," as well as to define the church universal. Douglas Bush, *English Literature in the Earlier Seventeenth Century*, 2nd ed. (Oxford: Clarendon, 1962), 336. Of course, JS's use of an initial capital here violates modern usage, which differentiates *catholic* (universal) from *Catholic* (Roman church).
248/86–87	**The words . . . thyne owne]** This addition to the Ten Commandments seems curiously at odds with Strangways's convictions. The insistence upon an unmediated commandment from God ("my words & not thyne owne") would seem to suggest a non-conformist position rather than the generally centrist, pro-episcopal, and pro-prayer book position that he maintained in his political life and which he defends throughout his commonplace book.
249/120	**Lippe Labour]** Empty or idle words (*OED*, s.v. "lip-labour").
250/138	**peculiar]** A private interest or concern (*OED*, s.v. "peculiar," B.I.2).
145	**Swift . . . speake]** Jam. 1:19.
149	**Anger a short Madnesse is]** see CP 188 (p. 91).
152–54	**And doe not Call . . . fyre]** Matt. 5:22.
166	**occupyre]** To possess or deal with sexually (*OED*, s.v. "occupy," 8). JS is perhaps punning on "occupy her" in this curious spelling.
251/195–96	**Yet God . . . hand]** Deut. 25:11–12.
252/245	**Runnes]** In this sense, scans over (*OED*, s.v. "run," 13.c), echoing Hab. 2:2.
253/292–93	**Nor . . . same]** Cf. Ps. 101:5.
255/1	**Upon the Oxford monie . . . ffirst]** This poem refers to an issue of Charles I, minted between 1642 and 1646 at Oxford and commemorating the king's September 1642 declaration to the Privy Council at Wellington, Shropshire, in which he promised to uphold the Protestant religion, the laws of England, and the liberty of parliament. See Stephen Mitchell and Brian Reed, eds., *Standard Catalogue of British Coins: Coins of England and the United Kingdom*, 27th ed. (London: Seaby, 1992), 185–90 and 201–4.

Title and First-line Index

All page numbers refer to the pagination in this edition.

Section A: Commonplaces

Only major divisions and titled sections of the Commonplace section are included in this Index.

A Note of Diverse Remarkable & Strange accidents Taken out
    of Sir Richard Bakers = Cronicle — 98
A Short prayer before our going to heare the word preached — 55
Certayne Notes & Rules to Direct us & Incite us to & in the
    service of God — 78
Concerning the Covenant — 111
Concerning the Necessitie: Choyce & use of particular Callings — 71
Delinquencie is perpetratio delicti, or derelictio Legis — 84
I may pleade a forreigne plea: otherwayes attainted &
    Convicted in a forraigne Countie: or his Majesties pardon — 87
It is But a fancie of Inconciderate Spyritts to dreame That the
    Soule sleepeth till the day of Resurrection — 74
Monies Raysed severall wayes never used in this Kingdome — 89
Of Anger — 124
Of the choyse of a Callinge — 74
Short Notes Concerning Church Goverment — 80
That the — 1000 — yeares of Chryst his visible Rayne upon
    Earth is against Scripture — 69
The Plea of the L: Hunsdon — 113
The Severall Mottoes of the Severall Emperors Ending with
    Ferdinand the Second — 117

Section B: Poems

Only those poems actually titled by Strangways are included here as titles, but all first lines are given.

Titles

1: Tanti valet, quanti vendi potest: 2: Caveat Emptor	169
A discourse betweene King Henry the third & the pryor of Saint Johns Hospitall	179
A Meditation of Death or a preparation to Death	214
A Motive to Humilitie	187
A Private Meditation	158
Against false & pretended = Freinds and ffreindshippe	173
Another Motive to Humilitie	196
Begin well: & End well	175
Comfort for an afflicted Soule	164
Concerning Almes & Suretishippe	171
Concerning the Ending of Our Unhappie differences by Peace	178
Concerning The negative oath	207
De Miserecordia Domini	217
Good Counsaile & Safe for these Tymes	170
In Adulterium et Adulteros	167
In Decium Curium	156
In Defence of Holy-Dayes	170
In Invidum	153
In Sacriligos	179
Noli altum Sapere	183
Of Freindshipps Break-Bonds	184
Of Reproofe & of the right use therof	164
Of the Bishoppe of Herefords sermon at Oxford preached before Queene Isabell	181
Of the Meditation of Death. Or a præparation to Death	209
The 5th Chapter [of The Epistle of Saint James in verse]	233
The 7th Chapter of Saint Matthew	243
The Affliction of Israell	217
The Apostells Creede	245
The Epistle of Saint James Cap: 2	228
The Epistle of Saint James Cap: 4	232
The Epistle of Saint James in verse by Sir John Strangways	226
The ffree Prysoner: or the Comfort of Restraint	128
The fifth Chapter of Saint Matthew	239
The fourth Chapter of the booke of Wisdome	162
The Misery of Warre	179

The Parable of the Ten Virgins: Matthew the 25th   176
The Rules of Trew Obedience   213
The sixt chapter of Job Translated into Verse   160
The sixt Chapter of Saint Mathew   235
 The Ten Commandements   246
The third Chapter of Saint James   230
The — 30 — Chapter of the Proverbes of Solomon Beginning
        at the — 7th — verse — to the end therof   208
The — 7th — chapter of Micah Translated into verse   180
Three Good: Three bad: Ten Happie things The Author in
        these verses sings   184
Upon the Lord Seaton refusing to deliver Barwicke to
        Edward the third King of England   182
Upon the Oxford monie Coyned King Charles the ffirst   255
Virtus ipsa, sibi præmium   177
When I was Taken up by the Souldyers & Kept At Dorchester
        & Weymouth by them   225
Wouldst thou in Quiett gladly Dwell? Then doe the Things
        I heare doe Tell   177

First Lines

A Lady of suspected Chastitie   151
A Man, Lives forty yeares, before he knowes   186
A prodigall that Liv'de in huge Excesse   152
A servant of god, & of Chryst the Lord   226
A Trayt'rous Bishoppe, hystoryes record   181
Adulterie & Ravishment   167
All that thou hast is not too deare,   166
Almightie God to whom all harts Alone   246
Armyes & pow'res know noe inferiour freinds   179
Birds fly away when stones are att them Cast   184
Brute Beastes, which of right Reason want the use   174
By Death my Ill's had ended long agoe   149
Egipt a long tyme had to Israells Men   217
Fayth & Respect are seldome found   168
Feare not (my sonne) if that we be made poore   173
Fowre sorts of men discourage me to Crave   185
From whence Come warres & Brawlings Amongst you   232
Goe too ye Rich men now sigh, Mourne & weepe   233

Great Curius that thrice Tryumph'de in Rome	156
He Dares not far from Home goe, who beleeves,	186
He that a good thing doth, to a bad end	166
He that for doing well, seekes recompence	177
He that intends a howse to build	175
He that shall seeke lost Creditt to regayne	225
I always shall him for my freind approve	164
I am Resolv'de I will not breake my Troth	207
I doe in publique here protest	173
I Rather would vertue then children have	162
If by my selfe, my selfe weare to be try'de	158
If thyne Obedience thou wouldst have to be	213
In God th'almightie father I beleive	245
In Tyme of need, thy neighbour Lend	171
In Tyme of yo're, when Barwicke was Scotch Land	182
It is a snare, to him, that shall, devoure what holy is	179
Judge not, & soe you shall not judged be	243
Keepe farre from him that hath the power to kill	170
Lett not Trew fayth in Chryst worke this effect	228
Lewes de Granado doth relate	151
Lord how are we from Snarling Come to byte	150
My Brethren be not Manie masters! Why?	230
My person's seiz'd, my howse, my goods, my Land	157
Noe Humane Reason can amend his sence	177
Nor Length of Tyme, nor multitude of men	165
O God / Thy Nature & thy propertie	152
Open myne eyes O Lord that I may see	187
Say what you will, Tis not safe for the State	178
Short is the sentence of the greatest Doome	155
Since BETTER, HOLY'ER, WISER did encrease	149
Sir I doe here present unto your veiw	196
Sir whiles you pittie my afflicted State	129
Strayne not at things that are beyond thy Length	183
Take heede you give not your Almes before Men	235
The Grand Commaunder of the Hospitall	179
The man that good is, hardly will	178
The Meditat'ion of Our Dying day	209
The Mercyes of the Wicked Crewell are	217
The Papists cry up blind Obedience	149
The Protestant Religion	255
The State wherin I stand is now soe bad	155

The voyce sayd Cry! He sayd, What shall I Cry?   196
The world is bad! I, tis god wott   177
Those that oppose themselves against the King   167
Three things ther are that doe delight my mind   184
Tis not a Fast proclaym'de can Countenance   165
To Eliphaz thus answear'd Job & sayd   160
Two Maximes make most men mis-treade   169
Two things have I requir'd before I Dye   208
Wealth maketh many freinds: but he that's poore   169
What Better Thing, in my hart Can I beare?   186
What I beleeve to be the Right   166
What ill soever is upon thee brought   164
When Jesus Chryst himselfe did preach   176
When Jesus saw the multitude, he went   239
When wickednes condemned is   167
Wher Envye raignes ther is noe roome for peace: 153
Why doth one day another soe excell   170
Woe is me, for, I am, ev'ne as when they   180
Wyse Seneca the quest'ion asketh why   214

SECOND SERIES

VOL. III. *The dyaloge called Funus*, A Translation of Erasmus's Colloquy (1534), and *A very pleasaunt & fruitful Diologe called The Epicure*, Gerrard's Translation of Erasmus's Colloquy (1545), edited by Robert R. Allen, 1969.

VOL. IV. *Leicester's Ghost* by Thomas Rogers, edited by Franklin B. Williams, Jr., 1972.

THIRD SERIES

VOLS. V–VI. *A Collection of Emblemes, Ancient and Moderne*, by George Wither, with an introduction by Rosemary Freeman and bibliographical notes by Charles S. Hensley, 1975. (o.p.)

FOURTH SERIES

VOLS. VII–VIII. *Tom a' Lincolne* by R. I., edited by Richard S. M. Hirsch, 1978.

FIFTH SERIES

VOL. IX. *Metrical Visions* by George Cavendish, edited by A. S. G. Edwards, 1980.

SIXTH SERIES

VOL. X. *Two Early Renaissance Bird Poems*, edited by Malcolm Andrew, 1984.

VOL. XI. *Argalus and Parthenia* by Francis Quarles, edited by David Freeman, 1986.

VOL. XII. Cicero's *De Officiis*, trans. Nicholas Grimald, edited by Gerald O'Gorman, 1987.

VOL. XIII. *The Silkewormes and their Flies* by Thomas Moffet (1599), edited with introduction and commentary by Victor Houliston, 1988.

SEVENTH SERIES

VOL. XIV. John Bale, *The Vocacyon of Johan Bale*, edited by Peter Happé and John N. King, 1989.

VOL. XV. *The Nondramatic Works of John Ford*, edited by L. E. Stock, Gilles D. Monsarrat, Judith M. Kennedy, and Dennis Danielson, with the assistance of Marta Straznicky, 1990.

SPECIAL PUBLICATION. *New Ways of Looking at Old Texts: Papers of the Renaissance English Text Society, 1985–1991*, edited by W. Speed Hill, 1993. (Sent gratis to all 1991 members.)

VOL. XVI. *George Herbert, The Temple: A Diplomatic Edition of the Bodleian Manuscript (Tanner 307)*, edited by Mario A. Di Cesare, 1991.

VOL. XVII. Lady Mary Wroth, *The First Part of the Countess of Montgomery's Urania*, edited by Josephine Roberts. 1992.

VOL. XVIII. Richard Beacon, *Solon His Follie*, edited by Clare Carroll and Vincent Carey. 1993.

VOL. XIX. An Collins, *Divine Songs and Meditacions*, edited by Sidney Gottlieb. 1994.

VOL. XX. *The Southwell-Sibthorpe Commonplace Book: Folger MS V.b.198*, edited by Sr. Jean Klene. 1995.

SPECIAL PUBLICATION. *New Ways of Looking at Old Texts II: Papers of the Renaissance English Text Society, 1992–1996*, edited by W. Speed Hill, 1998. (Sent gratis to all 1996 members.)

VOL. XXI. *The Collected Works of Anne Vaughan Lock*, edited by Susan M. Felch. 1996.

VOL. XXII. Thomas May, *The Reigne of King Henry the Second Written in Seauen Books*, edited by Götz Schmitz. 1997.

VOL. XXIII. *The Poems of Sir Walter Ralegh: A Historical Edition*, edited by Michael Rudick. 1998.

VOL. XXIV. Lady Mary Wroth, *The Second Part of the Countess of Montgomery's Urania*, edited by Josephine Roberts; completed by Suzanne Gossett and Janel Mueller. 1999.

VOL. XXV. *The Verse Miscellany of Constance Aston Fowler: A Diplomatic Edition*, by Deborah Aldrich-Watson. 2000.

VOL. XXVI. *An Edition of Luke Shepherd's Satires*, by Janice Devereux. 2001.

VOL. XXVII. *Philip Stubbes: The Anatomie of Abuses*, edited by Margaret Jane Kidnie. 2002.

VOL. XXVIII. *Cousins in Love: The Letters of Lydia DuGard, 1665–1672, with a new edition of* The Marriages of Cousin Germans *by Samuel DuGard*, edited by Nancy Taylor. 2003.

VOL. XXIX. *The Commonplace Book of Sir John Strangways (1645–1666)*, edited by Thomas G. Olsen. 2004.

MRTS